NON-BORING TEST PREP S

# Tutor Ted's Guide to the SAT*

Ted Dorsey, M.A.
Martha Marion
Mike Settele
Jacob Osborne

For more information, visit our website: **www.tutorted.com**

Book Design: Sherri Nielsen
Book Layout: Anita Johnson

ISBN: 978-0-9834471-5-3

## STAY CONNECTED!

**We love to connect with our students!**
Follow us on Twitter, add us on Facebook, or just send us an old-fashioned email!

 TWITTER @tutorted

 FACEBOOK /tutorted

 INSTAGRAM @tutorted

 YOUTUBE /tutorted

 EMAIL sayhello@tutorted.com

## Special Thanks!

Special Thanks to:
Matt Casper
Maryann Dorsey
Nathan Fox
Wes Carroll
Uma Incrocci

# Table of Contents

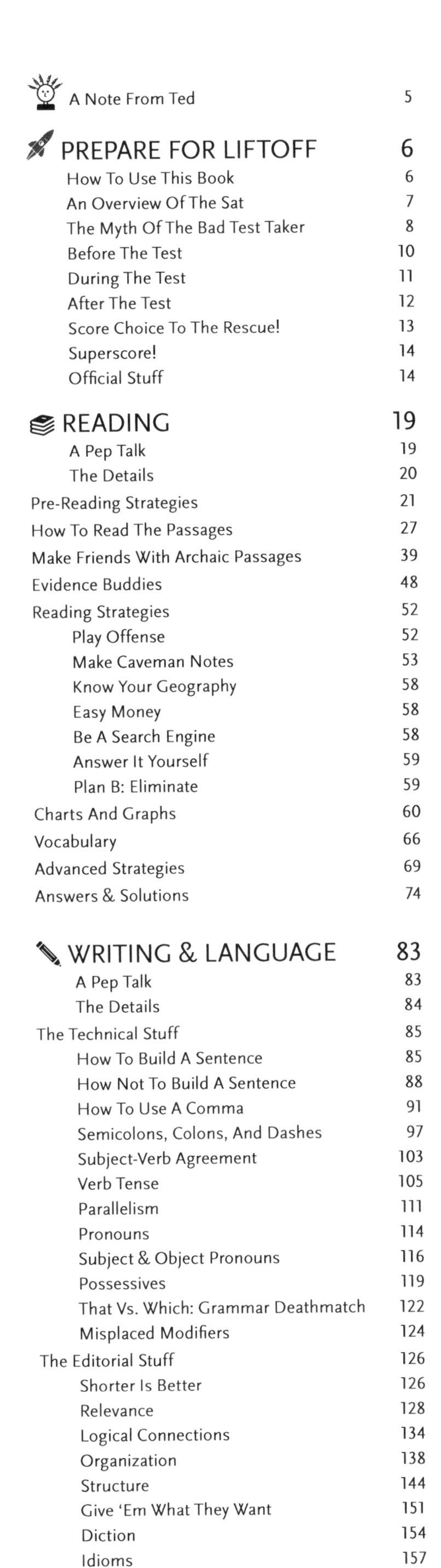

Tutor Ted®

# A Note from Ted

If you're reading this, you're in the midst of the college admissions process—one of the most exciting and anxiety-provoking journeys of your life.

**So much of that anxiety arises from the uncertainty of it all. You know you want to go to college—you probably even have some dream schools in mind—but you don't yet know if they are going to admit you. That is stressful!**

Allow us to alleviate some of that uncertainty. The SAT, a test that invokes dread in so many high school juniors and seniors, is *really not that bad.*

Is it fun? Nope.

Can you know literally everything on the test? You bet you can.

You want to get to the point where there are NO SURPRISES on the SAT. When you know what's coming, that's when you'll be able to put up a really big score. We're here to help you do that. That's our job!

Practice reading difficult passages, and learn to read for structure. Polish up your grammar knowledge, and know the SAT's tricks for writing more difficult questions. Refresh your algebra chops, and get comfortable with the advanced stuff, like Remainder Theorem.

**Do that, and guess what happens?**

You become more knowledgeable. As a result, you become more confident on the SAT. With confidence and knowledge on your side, you score higher on the SAT. And with a higher score on the SAT, you increase your chances of admission everywhere you apply.

Sound good? OK then, let's get started.

TED

# How to Use This Book

## READ THE CHAPTERS.

Use them to learn the stuff you don't know. Semicolons, for example. Be honest: do you really know how to use a semicolon? Are you sure?

If you are also using Tutor Ted's Complete SAT Course (and may we highly recommend that you do? Check it out at learn.tutorted.com. As a book owner, you can get 50% off the retail price with the coupon code BOOKHALFOFF), use the book and the course side-by-side. Watch a lesson with me, then complete the exercise questions in the book that follow.

## APPLY THE STRATEGIES.

Just as important as learning all of the content of the test is finding your own personal test-taking approach. We've got effective strategies for attacking all sections of the SAT. Read the strategies, try them out for yourself, and find the approach that works for you.

## PRACTICE UNDER TEST-REALISTIC CONDITIONS.

The College Board, beloved guardian of the SAT, has released eight practice tests that are dead in-line with what you'll see on the day of the test. Do those eight tests!

When you run out of those, use the four tests we wrote and included in both the online course at learn.tutorted.com and in our book, "Tutor Ted's SAT Practice Tests."

Why practice tests? They tell you which topics you've mastered and which ones you need to study more. Plus, they help you figure out how well your strategy is working. Are you working too slowly on the Reading, or maybe too quickly? Do you need to be more careful to avoid careless errors on the Math? What is the right amount of time to spend planning your essay?

**Does this plan sound more like common sense and less like magic? If so...good! SAT improvement is simple: know the stuff, have a strategy, and practice. We give you expert advice, you do the work, and your SAT score improves.**

That is the magic.

## Now let's get into some details.

Your job on the SAT is to answer 154 multiple-choice questions and write one essay.

Yes, the essay is technically optional, but like everything else in the college admissions process that's optional, it's mandatory.

## Are you ready for the world's shortest, simplest, most effective SAT advice?

You should always answer all of the questions. You do not get penalized for wrong answers, so even if you have to guess you should answer all of the questions.

***Hot Tip:*** You should even guess on free-response math questions if you have to. Read the question to see what it's asking you to find. If it's an angle measure in degrees, guess something reasonable, like 40, or 75. If it's a fraction, well, guess a fraction. Totally stuck? Guess 0.

Every correct answer is right for a reason. Read the questions carefully. Don't overcomplicate or overthink these questions. Always have a specific, justified reason for choosing what you did.

**The SAT really is a simple, straightforward test. It's boring, but it's predictable. Let's talk about that.**

## AN OVERVIEW OF THE SAT

The Reading Test asks 52 questions in 65 minutes. By the standards of standardized testing, that is a luxurious amount of time! It's also a clue that you actually *need* that amount of time to find the answers. Keep this in mind: the name of the section includes the adjective "Evidence-Based." They were not joking around when they did that. You want to find evidence in the passages to justify every answer you pick—literally, every single one.

The Writing and Language Test asks 44 questions in 35 minutes. This section is about two things: the technical aspects of grammar and the editorial expertise you need to make an essay better. With a little practice, you can know ***exactly*** what to expect on this section, and score significantly better here as a result. In other words: do not sleep on the Writing and Language Test.

The Math Test includes two sections: one on which you don't get to use your calculator, and one on which you do. The No Calculator section asks 20 questions in 25 minutes, and the Calculator Allowed section asks 38 questions in 55 minutes. Hot SAT math topics include algebra, more algebra, and yet a little bit more algebra. Just kidding. Well, kind of. The section focuses on linear and quadratic equations, algebraic simplification, chart and graph reading, and a few advanced topics. The limited focus of the SAT Math Test makes it an easier test to prep.

The (optional-but-not-really-optional) Essay is a 50-minute analytical task with the same question every time. You'll be given a persuasive essay or speech, and your job is to understand it and analyze its rhetorical techniques.

## THE MYTH OF THE BAD TEST TAKER

Before I go any further, I've got something important to say. Ready? OK. There is no such thing as a Bad Test Taker. There is no chromosome that predisposes you to perform poorly on tests. There is such a thing as an *unprepared* test taker, but that's different. Students get labeled as Bad Test Takers when they don't perform up to a certain level during a timed test. But the name does not fit the individual.

Some people point to anxiety as the explanation for poor test performance. Let's talk about anxiety for a minute. Take a look at this graph:

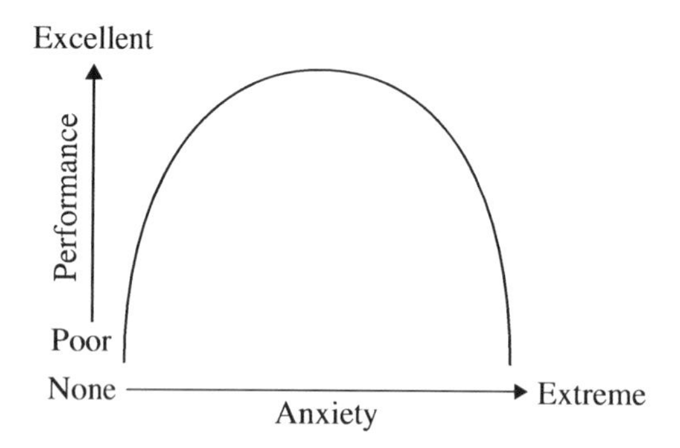


What this shows is a classic finding of psychology across every discipline from academics to athletics to music. The graph shows that at either extremely high or extremely low levels of anxiety, performance is poor. However, at moderate levels of anxiety, performance is at its peak!

In other words, anxiety is actually your friend. You WANT to be a little anxious and/or nervous. It is not a lot of fun to feel anxious or nervous...but it is actually beneficial to you if you are.

What I think students need to perform at their best is a reasonable amount of anxiety PLUS a healthy dose of confidence. When will you perform your best on the SAT, or on any other test you ever take? When you know the content of the test, right?

### Let's put it another way.

If you learn the material and concepts on the test, and familiarize yourself with the strategies and techniques necessary to do well, you will come out on the other side confident, with just the right amount of anxiety, ready to face the test. And when you're in that position, you'll score higher.

There is no such thing as a Bad Test Taker, just test takers who are unprepared. And you're not going to be one of those people.

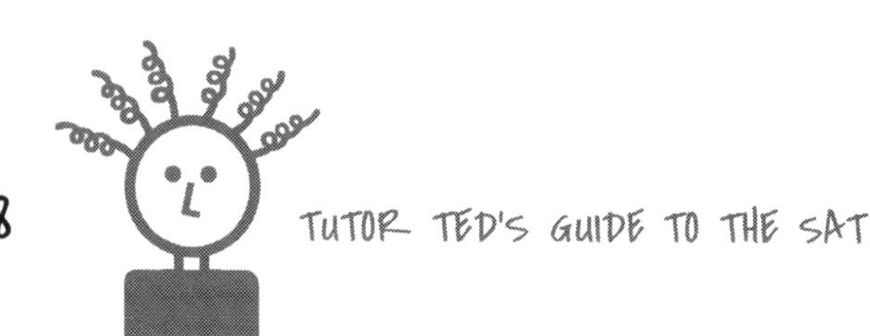

## PRACTICE, PRACTICE, PRACTICE... PRACTICE?

What's the right amount of time to devote to SAT prep? No one answer is right for everyone, but we've got some guidelines. We recommend that ALL students take a minimum of four practice tests before their actual exam. The College Board has released eight tests (so you're covered), all available at this link:

**collegereadiness.collegeboard.org/sat/practice/full-length-practice-tests**

Because many of our students take more than eight practice tests during their prep, we wrote four of our own. They are published in "Tutor Ted's SAT Practice Tests" and are available on our online course too.

**learn.tutorted.com**

When should you take those practice tests? Take one at the very beginning of your prep. That will help you establish a baseline score and show you where you need to focus your energy during prep. Take the other tests as you study. Our rule of thumb is that you shouldn't take another practice test until you think you'll do better on the next test than on the previous one.

Also, don't wait till just before your actual SAT to take all of your practice tests—you'll get a lot more benefit when you have some time between practice tests.

## DO I NEED A TUTOR?

The decision to work with a tutor is a personal one for each student. It is a matter of how you study and learn best. Some students are independent and can manage their time and practice diligently until they understand a concept or problem. Others can use guidance and encouragement along the way, and might better understand a problem by talking it through with a tutor. You can always start with self-study and work with a tutor later on.

If you decide you would like to work with someone, Tutor Ted is here to help. Our expert tutors are equipped with the best technology and will work with you face-to-face via the computer, just like they would in person. The difference? You can connect from anywhere, at any time, on any device, to get the support you need. Visit our website (www.tutorted.com) for additional information about our services.

## THE NEED FOR SPEED

With 154 multiple choice questions to complete in three hours, you don't want to waste any time trying to figure out how many minutes you have remaining in a section. The SAT proctors are instructed to warn you when each section is approximately halfway complete, and when five minutes remain.

That's helpful, but it's not as much info as you would like to have.

One really bad option is to rely on the clock in the classroom. Sure, you COULD use it to figure out that if it is 9:18 am now and the section ends at 9:55am, you have 37 minutes remaining. But when you're frazzled and anxious and racing against the clock do you really want to? Silent digital watches are a great option to help you keep an eye on the clock, and they are allowed in the test room.

Bring a watch with you into the test room, one with no beep. That'll help you keep a close eye on how much time you have left on any section of the test.

## BEFORE THE TEST

What should you do in the days leading up to the test? Hopefully you've completed at least four practice tests and feel confident that you know what to expect on the real exam. The heavy studying should be out of the way by now, but we do recommend you look back at your practice tests to review the problems you've learned how to solve. Remind yourself of the strategies that have worked for you. If you feel like you have to, you could do a timed section or two, but in those last couple of days, focus on reviewing—and sleeping!

## WALK IN YOUR OWN SHOES

A great way to ease your nerves before the test is to visualize what you will do on the actual test day. This might sound silly but it really does help!

Picture yourself arriving at the test center a little early. You are certain that you have your admission ticket, ID card, pencils, digital watch, and calculator because you packed them the night before. You sign in and find a seat. You take out your pencils and calculator, put your watch on your wrist, and put everything else under your seat. Everyone settles in and the proctor reads the long list of instructions. Later, he/she starts the timer or writes the end time for the first section. You are working at a good pace as you move through each section. You might have a moment of panic here and there, but overall you can feel that the work you put into preparing for the test is paying off now. Before you know it the test is over and you breathe a huge sigh of relief.

Give this visualization a try! It can help calm you during the week of the test and boost your performance on test day too.

## THE SAT DIET

What is the magical meal you can eat that will give you a 1600 on the test? Yeah... unfortunately, that meal does not exist. However, you can eat in a way that will put you in the best possible performance shape for the test. Here are the rules:

- ***Eat a well-balanced dinner the night before the test.***
- ***Eat a breakfast the morning of the test that includes protein. You need long-term fuel!***
- ***Don't eat a sugary breakfast that will make you crash.***
- ***Bring a snack or two with you to the test—something healthy and substantial, like a Clif bar.***

It's going to be a long morning: make sure you are fueled up!

## GET SOME SLEEP!

Is this the most obvious advice ever given? Well, maybe...but there is a twist. You want to get not just ONE good night of sleep before the test but TWO. If you're testing on a Saturday, that means getting good sleep on Thursday and Friday nights.

One more piece of sleep advice: don't try to go to bed at 6:30pm or anything crazy. Go to bed at a time that will let you get eight solid hours of sleep.

## DURING THE TEST

Remember that anxiety, though not fun at all to experience, is not your enemy. That said, you want to have a strategy to calm yourself down if you feel overly anxious. Feel free to use this tip or find another that works for you. Ready?

### Okay, here it is:

Put your pencil down. Go on. It's okay. Now close your eyes and visualize your favorite beach. Here are a few suggestions: Waikiki. Paradise Beach. Bora Bora. Can you picture it? Good. Now, with that image in mind, count to five. Take deep, slow breaths as you listen to sound of the waves crashing, smell the salty air, and dig your toes into the warm, grainy salt. Feels good, right? Now open your eyes, pick up your pencil, and keep plugging along.

Repeat as necessary.

## WHAT TO DO WHEN YOU'RE STUCK

Here are some great ways to get un-stuck:

***Read the question one more time, slowly and carefully.***

***Write down all of the given information in a Math problem.***

***Refer back to the passage on a Reading question***

***Underline all the big words in the answer choices, and evaluate based on those.***

If after a minute goes by you still can't solve it, follow the next step:

## KNOW WHEN TO FOLD 'EM

The SAT used to penalize you for guessing incorrectly. It does not do that anymore. Take advantage!

Do NOT spend 2-3 minutes on a hard question on your first pass—even if you get it right, it may cost you the time you need to answer several easier questions later in the section. When you feel like you-can't find the right answer, try to eliminate answer choices and make a good guess. Do not hesitate to skip and come back. Circle the question number in your test booklet and return to it if you have time at the end of the section.

## WHEREVER YOU GO, THERE YOU ARE

Keep this in mind: you can only answer one question at a time. That means that it is not beneficial to stress about a question that came before or one that will come next. Focus on the question that you're on and remember: you are allowed to make mistakes. Your job is to do your best, not to be perfect.

## TAKE A BREAK

The Gods of the SAT, in a rare act of kindness, have granted you a 10-minute break after the Reading Tests. How should you spend that time? Use it to refuel. Eat the snack bar or sandwich you brought with you. Walk around a bit. Get some water. Use the restroom. Get up and move around a bit—you want to get your blood flowing.

Oh, and stay away from the people who are obsessively discussing the test. You will have plenty of time to talk about the test later.

Clear your mind so you can come back to the test focused and calm.

## AFTER THE TEST

You'll get your SAT score about two weeks after you take the test. During the wait, it's your job to chill and not think about the SAT. You've already done your part.

## IF AT FIRST YOU DON'T SUCCEED...

...try, try again! One of the best things about this test is that you can take it multiple times. People typically do better on something when they've done it once before. The experience of taking the test the first time, spending time doing some additional practice work, focusing on your schoolwork to get even smarter than you were—these factors will most likely lead you to a higher score on your second attempt at the SAT.

If you didn't reach your target score by the spring of junior year, we highly recommend re-testing in the fall of your senior year. 90% of our students earn their highest score in the fall of senior year. Join that group by taking the SAT then.

How many times can you re-test? College admissions officers we have spoken to say that seeing three or fewer test dates on a student's record is totally normal, and that four or more test scores starts to look fishy. You don't really want to take the SAT more than three times, right? If you do the prep—you work through this book and take at least four practice tests from the College Board website and our companion book—you won't need more than three shots at the test.

## UNHAPPY WITH YOUR SCORE? SCORE CHOICE TO THE RESCUE!

Things get a little awkward when you ask this specific question:

Do I have to submit all of my SAT scores to the colleges on my list?

I'll explain.

First things first, I strongly recommend you wait until you have finished the testing process and have your list of schools finalized before you submit any scores at all. Sure, when you sign up for the test, you can submit your scores for free to four colleges. What if the scores you get does not represent you well?

Here's where Score Choice comes in. Score Choice is a College Board program that allows you to submit scores from whichever test dates you choose. Suppose you took the SAT twice, and on your second try you scored much higher than you did on your first. You would rather submit only that second, better test score, which would make you look better on paper.

Here's the trick, though: some schools say that you are required to submit ALL of your test scores. Some will even make you sign an affidavit stating that you did so.

Where it gets awkward is that they don't know whether you did or did not submit all of your test scores. Here's what College Board says:

> ***"Colleges cannot opt out of or reject Score Choice. Score Choice is a feature available to students. However, some colleges require students to submit all SAT scores. Be sure to check college websites to learn more about their score send policies.***
>
> ***"Colleges set their own policies and practices regarding the use of test scores. The College Board does not release SAT test scores without student consent. Colleges and scholarship programs receive only the scores applicants send them."***

You see what I mean? You're required by some schools to submit all your SAT scores, but because of Score Choice they don't know if you've taken the SAT once or fifteen times.

Trust your sense of ethics to help you make a decision on how to submit your scores.

Even with Score Choice available, by the way, we still recommend you take the test a maximum of three times. If you do thoughtful prep, you won't need more than three chances to take the SAT!

## MIXED RESULTS? SUPERSCORE!

Many colleges superscore the SAT. That means that they will cherry-pick your highest section scores from multiple test dates and consider your application based on those.

Here's an example:

| | Reading and Writing | Math | Total |
|---|---|---|---|
| March SAT | 680 | 710 | 1390 |
| October SAT | 740 | 650 | 1390 |
| Superscore | 740 | 710 | 1450 |

This student got a 1390 on both her first and second test...but her superscore is a 1450! Sweet!

To find out whether the schools you are applying to look at SAT superscores, search the web for "Which colleges superscore the SAT?"

## OFFICIAL STUFF

Sign up for the actual exam at collegeboard.org. That's also where you'll go to check your scores and send score reports to colleges.

To study with us for the SAT, visit learn.tutorted.com. If you're thinking about tutoring with us, reach out by calling 310-600-9595 or emailing contact@tutorted.com.

For printable answer sheets to use when you complete practice tests or sections, visit tutorted.com/resources.

# 5 PASSAGES

Fiction x 1
Political History x 1
Social Science x1
Science x 2

?

## HOW LONG?

**52 Questions**
*that's 1 minute, 15 seconds per question*

65 MINUTES

# READING The Breakdown

One set of paired passages

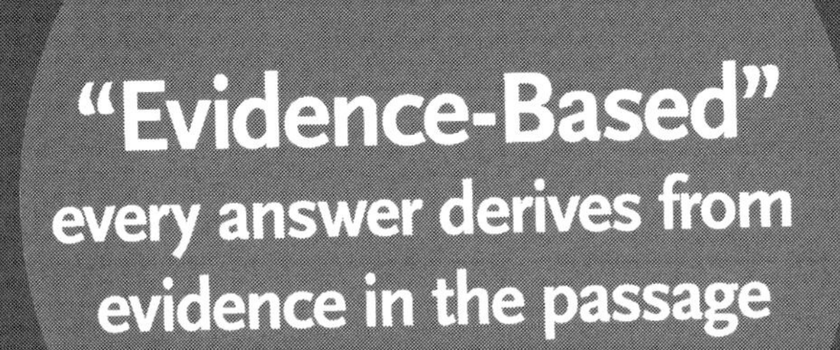


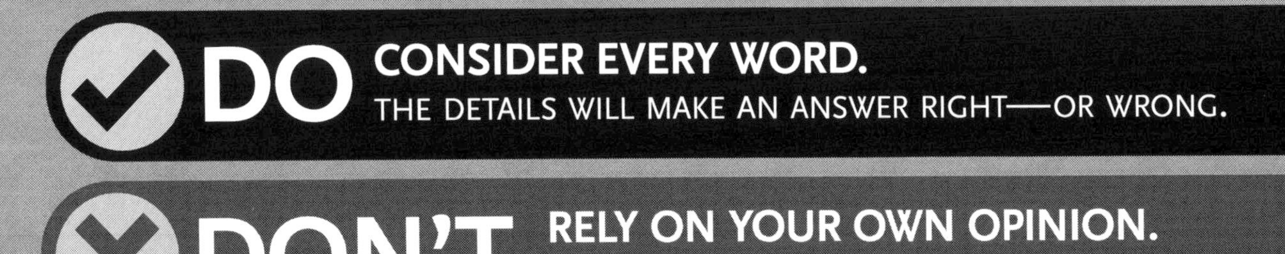

Tutor Ted®

# A Pep Talk

## Let's start by ripping the Band-Aid off: SAT Reading is tough.

To do it right, to do it *really well*, you've got to exert some sharp close-reading skill on passages that are, to put it generously, *not all that interesting*.

But there's good news, too. Let's enjoy some of that.

***The skills you'll develop on SAT Reading are actually useful in college.***

Reading closely is exactly what you'll be expected to do in a college English course. Answering questions carefully and precisely is what you'll do in ALL of your college courses. You'll be a step ahead in college when you learn to do that now.

***Reading is the first section of the test.***

You'll be energized and ready to take it on. And when you're done with it, you've got the hardest part of the test out of the way.

***Strategies make this section a lot more manageable.***

You'll go in with multiple techniques for solving evidence questions. You'll have a set of "pre-reading" strategies. You'll know what to expect on different types of questions, and even what to look for to find correct answers.

## In other words, when you have a game plan, you'll improve on this section.

## Simple as that.

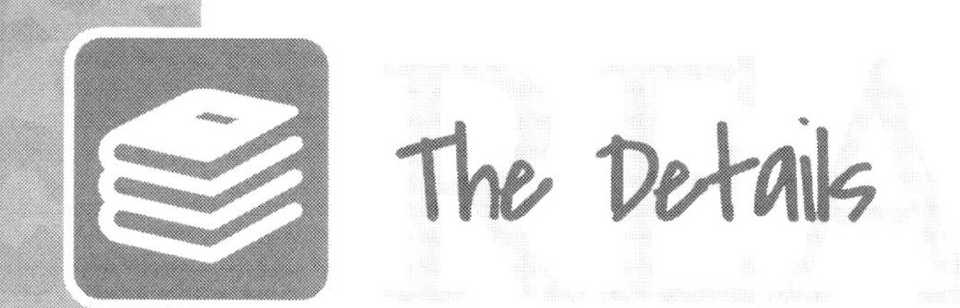


**What's on the SAT Reading Test? Here are the details.**

*SAT READING: 52 QUESTIONS IN 65 MINUTES*

Surprisingly generous on the timing...but a warning that these questions take a little more thinking to solve than typical reading comp questions.

**Five passages (six if you count the paired passages separately), within the following categories:**

## FICTION — ONE PASSAGE

These range from *really easy* to *really hard*, typically depending on how old the source material is.

## POLITICS, PAST AND PRESENT — ONE PASSAGE

SAT says these come from "either a U.S. founding document or a text in the Great Global Conversation they inspired." Not a bad description. Could be a little more concise.

## SOCIAL STUDIES — ONE PASSAGE

Something from psychology, sociology, or economics. Not that you care, but these passages are my second-favorite after fiction.

## SCIENCE — TWO PASSAGES

These can get a little technical—just remember you don't need to be a scientist to do well here. You just need to mind the details.

### *"EVIDENCE-BASED"*

Reading is part of your "Evidence-Based Reading and Writing" score. You think that adjective "Evidence-Based" was included by accident? Your #1 job on this section is to find evidence that justifies your answer. That's probably the most time—and energy—consuming aspect of the Reading section.

### *CHARTS AND GRAPHS!*

And you thought there was no Science section on the SAT! When a question tells you to reference the charts and graphs to solve it, that's a guarantee you'll need to use those sources.

# Pre-Reading Strategies

*THE STRATEGIES IN THIS SECTION ARE "PRE-READING" TECHNIQUES.*

Yep! Our SAT Reading strategy is going to kick in even before we start to read the passages.

**There are two pre-reading steps: Pre-Highlighting and Read the Fine Print. You ready?**

## PRE-HIGHLIGHTING

Here's a strategy that will make you a happier camper. It's called pre-highlighting, and it's going to:

- ***make the passages more readable by visually breaking them up.***
- ***save you time by identifying ahead of time the spots in the passage that will become important when you answer the questions.***
- ***show you what's important within the passage.***
- ***improve your performance on those questions because you'll already have thought about the questions before the test even asks them.***

Have I sold you on pre-highlighting yet? It *might* seem a little laborious and time-consuming at first, but believe me—once you get in the habit of doing this, you're going to love it. You're going to want to do it in your free time. Your friends will invite you out on Saturday and you'll say, "thanks, but I'm going to stay in and pre-highlight." Maybe not that. You're going to like it, though.

Let's get to the point. What is pre-highlighting? What you're going to do is mark all of the spots in the passage that you know are going to be important.

Here's what you do. As soon as you get to a new passage, flip straight to the questions. *Don't read the questions*—just scan them for line numbers. If a question mentions lines 22-24, go to the passage and put a neat bracket around the left side of those lines. If a question asks about one word in line 50, underline that word in line 50. Do that for all of the questions. Once you do, it will look something like this:

This passage is from "The Snowflake Man of Vermont" by Keith C. Heidorn. This article was originally published in "The Public Domain Review" under a Creative Commons Attribution-ShareAlike 3.0.

In 1885, at the age of 20, Wilson Alwyn Bentley, a farmer who would live all his life in the small town of Jericho in Vermont, gave the world its first ever photograph of a snowflake. Throughout the following winters, until his death in 1931, Bentley would go on to capture over 5000 snowflakes, or more correctly, snow crystals, on film. Our belief that "no two snowflakes are alike" stems from a line in a 1925 report in which he remarked: "Every crystal was a masterpiece of design and no one design was ever repeated. When a snowflake melted, that design was forever lost."

It started with a microscope his mother gave him at age 15 which opened the world of the small to young Wilson. A lover of winter, he made plans to use his microscope to view snowflakes. His initial investigations proved both fascinating and frustrating as he tried to observe the short-lived flakes. So that he could share his discoveries, he began by sketching what he saw, accumulating several hundred sketches by his seventeenth birthday. When his father purchased a camera for his son, Wilson combined it with his microscope, and went on to make his first successful photomicrograph of a snow crystal on 15 January 1885.

In addition to the development of the hardware, Bentley also had to devise a protocol to capture a snow crystal and transport it with minimal damage to the camera's field of vision. What he found worked best was to capture the crystals on a cool velvet-covered tray. Taking care not to melt the crystal with his breath, he identified a suitable subject and lifted it onto a pre-cooled slide with a thin wood splint from his mother's broom and nudged it into place with a turkey feather. The slide was then carried into his photographic shed and placed under the microscope. The back-lit image was focused using a system of strings and pulleys he devised to accommodate his mittened hands. Once focused, the sensitized glass plate—the "film"—was exposed and stored for further processing, development and printing.

Bentley also devised his own processing methods. In addition to developing the original image, he also created a post-development process to enhance it. Since each photograph was taken of a white snow crystal against a white background, Bentley was dissatisfied with the initial photograph. He felt he could improve the contrast and enhance the detail if he presented the crystal against a dark background. To do this, he painstakingly scraped away the dark emulsion surrounding the snow crystal image from a duplicate of the original negative using a sharp penknife and steady hand. The altered image was then carefully placed upon a clear glass plate and then printed, giving it a dark background. Even after years of practice, this post-production process often took as long as four hours for a complex snow crystal.

With 70-75 photographs per storm and notes on the conditions under which they were collected, Bentley accrued a considerable understanding of snow. In 1897, he became acquainted with Professor George Perkins, a professor of geology at the University of Vermont, and they prepared the first paper on snow crystals published in the May 1898 issue of Appleton's Popular Scientific entitled "A Study of Snow Crystals."

Unfortunately, Bentley was so far ahead of his time that he wasn't fully appreciated by contemporary scientists. They didn't take this self-educated farmer seriously. From his large data archive, Bentley's analysis convinced him that the form the ice crystal took (hexagonal plate, six-sided star, hexagonal column, needle, etc) was dependent on the air temperature in which the crystal formed and fell. Nearly three decades would pass before Ukichiro Nakaya in Japan would confirm this hypothesis.

Notice how some of those pre-highlights overlap? That's fine. It's useful, in fact—you now know that particular section of the passage is *really* important.

Does it feel like you're pre-highlighting *too much* stuff? Mark it all anyways—trust me. As you keep doing it, you'll get faster at it. And once you get to the questions, you'll see the advantage of drawing your attention to the parts of the passage that matter.

***Hot Tip:*** Be precise with your pre-highlighting. If the question asks about a specific word in a line, underline that word. If an evidence question includes lines 52-55 and 55-56, end the first bracket at the bottom of line 55 and start the second one at the top of it. Having clear starting and stopping points will be extremely helpful when you're answering evidence questions.

## EXERCISE #1: Don't sweat it.

The part that just tests you on whether you were paying attention or not.

1. When you first get to a Reading passage on the SAT, you should

   A) jump in and start reading.
   B) pre-highlight the passage based on line numbers in the questions.
   C) think again about whether college is really for you.

2. Pick all that apply. When you pre-highlight, you should

   A) highlight every single line reference in the passage.
   B) read the questions carefully as you go.
   C) work precisely but quickly.
   D) pray to the gods of severe weather that a freak storm will knock out the power and thus make it impossible for you to complete your SAT.

## EXERCISE #2: Sweat it.

Use the line references to pre-highlight this SAT-like reading passage.

This passage is adapted from the speech of President Roosevelt at laying of the cornerstones of gateway to Yellowstone National Park, Gardiner, Montana, April 24, 1903.

...The Yellowstone Park is something absolutely unique in the world, so far as I know. Nowhere else in any civilized country is there to be found such a tract of veritable wonderland made accessible to all visitors, where at the same time not only the scenery of the wilderness, but the wild creatures of the Park are scrupulously preserved; the only change being that these same wild creatures have been so carefully protected as to show a literally astounding tameness. The creation and preservation of such a great natural playground in the interest of our people as a whole is a credit to the nation; but above all a credit to Montana, Wyoming and Idaho. It has been preserved with wise foresight. The scheme of its preservation is noteworthy in its essential democracy. Private game preserves, though they may be handled in such a way as to be not only good things for themselves, but good things for the surrounding community, can yet never be more than poor substitutes, from the standpoint of the public, for great national playgrounds such as this Yellowstone Park.

This Park was created, and is now administered, for the benefit and enjoyment of the people. The government must continue to appropriate for it especially in the direction of completing and perfecting an excellent system of driveways. But already its beauties can be seen with great comfort in a short space of time and at an astoundingly small cost, and with the sense on the part of every visitor that it is in part his property, that it is the property of Uncle Sam and therefore of all of us. The only way that the people as a whole can secure to themselves and their children the enjoyment in perpetuity of what the Yellowstone Park has to give is by assuming the ownership in the name of the nation and by jealously safeguarding and preserving the scenery, the forests, and the wild creatures...

The preservation of the forests is of course the matter of prime importance in every public reserve of this character. In this region of the Rocky Mountains and the great plains the problem of the water supply is the most important which the home-maker has to face. Congress has not of recent years done anything wiser than in passing the irrigation bill; and nothing is more essential to the preservation of the water supply than the preservation of the forests. Montana has in its water power a source of development which has hardly yet been touched. This water power will be seriously impaired if ample protection is not given the forests. Therefore this Park, like the forest reserves generally, is of the utmost advantage to the country around from the merely utilitarian side. But of course this Park, also because of its peculiar features, is to be preserved as a beautiful natural playground. Here all the wild creatures of the old days are being preserved, and the love of adventure and the hardihood to take advantage of it, with small regard for what their fortune may be. I can not too often repeat that the essential feature in the present management of the Yellowstone Park, as in all similar places, is its essential democracy—it is the preservation of the scenery, of the forests, of the wilderness life and the wilderness game for the people as a whole, instead of leaving the enjoyment thereof to be confined to the very rich who can control private reserves.

Pre-highlights:
Lines 3-5 ("Nowhere . . . visitors")
Lines 8-10 ("the only . . . tameness")
Lines 14-15 ("It has . . . foresight")
Lines 15-17 ("The scheme . . . democracy")
Lines 24-26 ("This Park . . . people")
The word "preservation," line 42
Lines 48-49 ("Congress . . . bill")
Lines 52-54 ("Montana . . . touched")
Lines 65-68 ("I can . . . democracy")

## READ THE FINE PRINT

You've finished pre-highlighting. Next step: read the fine print.

All of the passages on the SAT include an introduction that's typed up in about 8-point font. Because no one wants to read anything in 8-point font, almost everybody skips that little chunk of text. Don't skip it, though—reading it can be an advantage!

At the very least, that tiny text will give you the title of the passage. Hey, that's kinda useful! In other cases, that fine print will tell you who the characters in the story are, or it'll give you background info on the issue discussed in the passage. Whoa, that's not just helpful—that's vital!

## EXERCISE #1: The "Duh" One.

Just answer the question.

1. Each reading passage includes a tiny little fine print introduction. When you see it you should

   A) ignore it because *ugh*.
   B) read it because it could be helpful.
   C) hope *harder* for that severe storm that will cancel the SAT.

## EXERCISE #2: Read the Fine Print.

Read the following passage introductions (aka the fine print) and ask yourself what you should expect to see in the passage. Choose **all** the answers that apply.

**1**

This passage is adapted from Mary Wollstonecraft, "A Vindication of the Rights of Woman," published 1792.

A) This passage is about political philosophy.
B) This is a prose fiction passage.
C) This passage may be more difficult to read because of its age.

**2**

This passage is adapted from Hock et al. (2017) Connectivity and Systemic Resilience of the Great Barrier Reef. PLOS Biology.

A) This is a science passage.
B) This one might be technical.
C) This is an archaic passage.

**3**

This passage is adapted from Damon Alexander, "It's not what you know it's who you know: Political connectedness and political engagement at the local level." © 2015 Journal of Sociology.

A) This is a science passage.
B) This is a social science passage.
C) The thesis of this passage is hinted at in the title.

**4**

This passage is adapted from Chris Baraniuk, "How we breathe between words can be used to identify us." © 2017 New Scientist

A) This is a science passage.
B) This is an archaic passage.
C) This one will probably include research.

**5**

This passage is from Theodore Dreiser, *Sister Carrie*. The setting is Wisconsin in 1920. Looking to find work, Carrie has entered a shoe factory.

A) This is a social science passage.
B) This is a fiction passage.
C) Carrie is the most important character.

**6**

This passage is adapted from Erdman Palmore and Clark Luikart, "Health and social factors related to life satisfaction." © 1972 Journal of Health and Social Behavior

A) This is a science passage.
B) This is a historical political passage.
C) This is likely research-based.

**7**

This passage is adapted from Laura Sanders, "Staring into a baby's eyes puts her brain waves and yours in sync." © 2017 Growth Curve

A) This is a science passage.
B) This is a fiction passage.
C) The title is a strong clue.

**8**

This passage is adapted from Mark Jannot, "Inside the Race to Save the Florida Grasshopper Sparrow, North America's Most Endangered Bird." © 2017 Audubon Magazine

A) This is a social science passage.
B) This is a science passage.
C) This might be a technical passage.

# How to Read the Passages

**You pre-highlighted. You read the fine print. Guess what comes after those two pre-reading strategies? Yep: reading the passages.**

## *HOW TO READ THE PASSAGES*

How do you read an SAT reading passage? That might initially strike you as a really, really stupid question. "You just, uh, read them?" Well, we are definitely going to read them, but *how* we read them will depend on what kind of passage we are reading.

### First, though, let me sell you on why you want to read the passages.

I've had students who, when they come to me, don't read the passages. They worry that they'll run out of time. They go straight to the questions and look back at the passage to try and solve them one at a time. Also, they don't really feel like reading the passages.

Can I tell you how well those students do on the questions? Not very well. Ironically, they also *run out of time*. They have to look back at the passage to answer the questions, right? That means they end up reading and re-reading so much that they essentially read the passage *two or three times*. It's a vicious, terrible cycle—one that you can avoid by simply reading the damn things to begin with.

**The moral of the story? Read the passages.**

So what kinds of passages are there on the SAT? We've got four main types:

## FICTION

The fiction passages always show up first on the section. They can be contemporary (written in the last sixty years or so), or they can be archaic (old enough that only your great-great-granddad could enjoy it).

What do all fiction passages have in common? Characters. You'll always be meeting characters. So get to know 'em. Watch what they do, what they say, *how* they say it. The characters are likely pretty interesting—otherwise, why would the author have bothered to write about them, right?

Here's another thing the passages will have in common: those characters will be confronted with some sort of challenge. Think about the character and watch how they handle that particular situation. When you do that—get into the mindset of the character, see how they handle a challenge—*you might just find yourself enjoying the SAT Reading test*. Imagine that!

No, wait, stop. Don't imagine that.

## EXERCISE #1: Warm Up with Some Fiction

Give this fiction passage a read. Make sure you read the fine print before you get started—it might give you some really helpful context. After the passage, I'll ask you some conversational follow-up questions.

This passage is from Willa Cather, "Paul's Case: A Study in Temperament," originally published in 1906.

It was Paul's afternoon to appear before the faculty of the Pittsburg High School to account for his various misdemeanors. He had been suspended a week ago, and his father had called at the principal's office and confessed his perplexity about his son. Paul entered the faculty room, suave and smiling. His clothes were a trifle outgrown, and the tan velvet on the collar of his open overcoat was frayed and worn; but, for all that, there was something of the dandy about him, and he wore an opal pin in his neatly knotted black four-in-hand, and a red carnation in his buttonhole. This latter adornment the faculty somehow felt was not properly significant of the contrite spirit befitting a boy under the ban of suspension.

When questioned by the principal as to why he was there, Paul stated, politely enough, that he wanted to come back to school. This was a lie, but Paul was quite accustomed to lying—found it, indeed, indispensible for overcoming friction. His teachers were asked to state their respective charges, which they did with such a rancour and aggrievedness as evinced that this was not a usual case. Disorder and impertinence were among the offences named, yet each of his instructors felt that it was scarcely possible to put into words the real cause of the trouble, which lay in a sort of hysterically defiant manner of the boy's; in the contempt which they all knew he felt for them, and which he seemingly made not the least effort to conceal. Once, when he had been making a synopsis of a paragraph at the blackboard, his English teacher had stepped to his side and attempted to guide his hand. Paul had started back with a shudder, and thrust his hands violently behind him. The astonished woman could scarcely have been more hurt and embarrassed had he struck at her. The insult was so involuntary and definitely personal as to be unforgettable. In one way and another he had made all his teachers, men and women alike, conscious of the same feeling of physical aversion.

His teachers felt, this afternoon, that his whole attitude was symbolized by his shrug and his flippantly red carnation flower, and they fell upon him without mercy. He stood through it, smiling, his pale lips parted over his white teeth. (His lips were continually twitching, and he had a habit of raising his eyebrows that was contemptuous and irritating to the last degree.) Older boys than Paul had broken down and shed tears under that baptism of fire, but his set smile did not once desert him, and his only sign of discomfort was the nervous trembling of the fingers that toyed with the buttons of his overcoat, and an occasional jerking of the other hand that held his hat. Paul was always smiling, always glancing about him, seeming to feel that people might be watching him and trying to detect something. This conscious expression, since it was as far as possible from boyish mirthfulness, was usually attributed to insolence or "smartness."

As the inquisition proceeded, one of his instructors repeated an impertinent remark of the boy's, and the principal asked him whether he thought that a courteous speech to have made to a woman. Paul shrugged his shoulders slightly and his eyebrows twitched.

"I don't know," he replied. "I didn't mean to be polite, or impolite, either. I guess it's a sort of way I have of saying things, regardless."

The principal, who was a sympathetic man, asked him whether he didn't think that a way it would be well to get rid of. Paul grinned and said he guessed so. When he was told that he could go, he bowed gracefully and went out. His bow was but a repetition of the scandalous red carnation.

His teachers were in despair, and his drawing-master voiced the feeling of them all when he declared there was something about the boy which none of them understood. As for Paul, he ran down the hill whistling the soldiers' chorus from "Faust," looking wildly behind him, now and then, to see whether some of his teachers were not there to writhe under his light-heartedness.

1. Why does Paul infuriate the staff of the school so much?

2. Would you be friends with Paul if he went to your school?

3. What specific moments, symbols, or sentences do you think would become SAT questions?

## POLITICS, PAST AND PRESENT

You'll always read a primary-source passage (or two of them, if they are paired passages) about politics. Are you taking AP US History? Do you remember the Federalist Papers? Or passages by Mary Wollstonecraft, or Alexis de Toqueville? It's that kind of stuff. All of these passages will dig into deep political/philosophical ideas, like liberties and responsibilities. These passages will *usually* be archaic since they're often taken from historical documents.

Here's what you want to keep an eye on when you read these. Most importantly, you want to understand the author's main idea. Start by keeping in mind the big ideas you've studied in US History thus far. US History includes some pretty hard-fought debates about states' rights, the right of women to vote, slavery, civil rights...

Can we pause for a second to reflect on how absolutely messed up it is that slavery was legal in America about 150 years ago? Think about that for a second.

Heavy sigh.

OK! One thing you want to do on these passages is to follow the author's logic. Many of these passages are trying to persuade the reader. That means they'll follow a logical progression. Find it and follow along. Look for the examples the author cites. Find the connections he/she makes. If you get a set of paired politics passages (and you frequently will), identify the key points of difference between them. When you do, you'll know exactly what the questions are going to be about.

## EXERCISE #2: Keep it Going with Politics

Give this historical/political passage a go. Look for the author's logical point of view and see if you can follow it throughout. Then enjoy some light discussion questions at the end.

This passage is adapted from a speech by Frederick Douglass, "What to a slave is the Fourth of July?," originally delivered July 5, 1852.

Fellow-citizens, above your national, tumultous joy, I hear the mournful wail of millions, whose chains, heavy and grievous yesterday, are today rendered more intolerable by the jubilant shouts that reach them. My subject, then, fellow-citizens, is American slavery. I shall see this day and its popular characteristics from the slave's point of view. Standing there, identified with the American bondman, making his wrongs mine, I do not hesitate to declare, with all my soul, that the character and conduct of this nation never looked blacker to me than on this Fourth of July. Whether we turn to the declarations of the past, or to the professions of the present, the conduct of the nation seems equally hideous and revolting. America is false to the past, false to the present, and solemnly binds herself to be false to the future. Standing with God and the crushed and bleeding slave on this occasion, I will, in the name of humanity which is outraged, in the name of liberty which is fettered, in the name of the Constitution and the Bible, which are disregarded and trampled upon, dare to call in question and to denounce, with all the emphasis I can command, everything that serves to perpetuate slavery—the great sin and shame of America! "I will not equivocate; I will not excuse;" I will use the severest language I can command; and yet not one word shall escape me that any man, whose judgment is not blinded by prejudice, or who is not at heart a slaveholder, shall not confess to be right and just.

But I fancy I hear some one of my audience say, it is just in this circumstance that you and your brother abolitionists fail to make a favorable impression on the public mind. Would you argue more, and denounce less, would you persuade more and rebuke less, your cause would be much more likely to succeed. But, I submit, where all is plain there is nothing to be argued. What point in the anti-slavery creed would you have me argue? On what branch of the subject do the people of this country need light? Must I undertake to prove that the slave is a man? That point is conceded already. Nobody doubts it. The slaveholders themselves acknowledge it in the enactment of laws for their government. They acknowledge it when they punish disobedience on the part of the slave. There are seventy-two crimes in the state of Virginia, which, if committed by a black man (no matter how ignorant he be), subject him to the punishment of death; while only two of these same crimes will subject a white man to the like punishment. What is this but the acknowledgement that the slave is a moral, intellectual, and responsible being? The manhood of the slave is conceded. It is admitted in the fact that southern statute books are covered with enactments forbidding, under severe fines and penalties, the teaching of the slave to read or write. When you can point to any such laws, in reference to the beasts of the field, then I may consent to argue the manhood of the slave. When the dogs in your streets, when the fowls of the air, when the cattle on your hills, when the fish of the sea, and the reptiles that crawl, shall be unable to distinguish the slave from a brute, then will I argue with you that the slave is a man!

At a time like this, scorching irony, not convincing argument, is needed. Oh! Had I the ability, and could I reach the nation's ear, I would today pour out a fiery stream of biting ridicule, blasting reproach, withering sarcasm, and stern rebuke. For it is not light that is needed, but fire; it is not the gentle shower, but thunder. We need the storm, the whirlwind, and the earthquake. The feeling of the nation must be quickened; the conscience of the nation must be roused; the propriety of the nation must be startled; the hypocrisy of the nation must be exposed; and its crimes against God and man must be proclaimed and denounced.

1. On what primary basis is Frederick Douglass arguing against slavery?

2. What specific technique is Douglass advocating for the abolitionist movement?

3. Why, specifically, did Douglass highlight the Fourth of July in this speech?

## SOCIAL STUDIES

Quick question—who agrees with me that Social Studies teachers are literally the *dullest people on the planet*? I'm not saying they are ugly or rude or mean. They're generally really nice, actually. They just happen to be the *most boring people* that walk the earth.

Now that I've shared that 100% true thought, let's talk about social studies. What is it, anyways? It's economics, sociology, linguistics, history, demographics... you know, boring stuff. I'm kidding! Some of that stuff is not totally boring all of the time.

To be honest, these passages can be pretty interesting. And, social studies passages have other pluses, too. One is that they tend to be well organized. That's big. When a passage is well organized, you can expect certain things in certain places. The thesis, or at least the central question, will show up in the first paragraph. The beginning of each paragraph will include a topic sentence that tells you clearly what to expect. Concrete evidence will follow.

Knowing *what* to expect *where* in a social studies passage will make you a much more efficient reader. Read for big ideas, and keep them in mind. When you're presented with detailed evidence, read it and *get* it, but don't memorize it—you can always look back at it for reference.

Let's do one of these.

## EXERCISE #3: Find Your Groove With Social Studies

Enjoy this contemporary Social Studies passage. Keep an eye on the organization of the passage—and keep it in mind as you answer the discussion questions that follow.

This passage is adapted from Patrick Lin, "The Ethics of Autonomous Cars," published in 2013 for The Center for Internet and Society of Stanford Law School.

If a small tree branch pokes out onto a highway and there's no incoming traffic, we'd simply drift a little into the opposite lane and drive around it. But an automated car might come to a full stop, as it dutifully observes traffic laws that prohibit crossing a double-yellow line. This unexpected move would avoid bumping the object in front, but then cause a crash with the human drivers behind it.

Should we trust robotic cars to share our road, just because they are programmed to obey the law and avoid crashes?

Because the legal framework for autonomous vehicles does not yet exist, we have the opportunity to build one that is informed by ethics. This will be the challenge in creating laws and policies that govern automated cars: We need to ensure they make moral sense. Programming a robot car to slavishly follow the law, for instance, might be foolish and dangerous. Better to proactively consider ethics now than defensively react after a public backlash in national news.

Philosophers have been thinking about ethics for thousands of years, and we can apply that experience to robot cars. One classical dilemma, proposed by philosophers Philippa Foot and Judith Jarvis Thomson, is called the Trolley Problem: Imagine a runaway trolley (train) is about to run over and kill five people standing on the tracks. Watching the scene from the outside, you stand next to a switch that can shunt the train to a sidetrack, on which only one person stands. Should you throw the switch, killing the one person on the sidetrack (who otherwise would live if you did nothing), in order to save five others in harm's way?

This dilemma isn't just a theoretical problem. Driverless trains today operate in many cities worldwide, including London, Paris, Tokyo, San Francisco, Chicago, New York City, and dozens more. As situational awareness improves with more advanced sensors, networking, and other technologies, a robot train might someday need to make such a decision. Human drivers may be forgiven for making an instinctive but nonetheless bad split-second decision, such as swerving into oncoming traffic rather than the other way into a field. But programmers and designers of automated cars don't have that luxury, since they do have the time to get it right and therefore bear more responsibility for bad outcomes.

If you complain here that robot cars would probably never be in the Trolley scenario—that the odds of having to make such a decision are minuscule and not worth discussing—then you're missing the point. Programmers still will need to instruct an automated car on how to act for the entire range of foreseeable scenarios, as well as lay down guiding principles for unforeseen scenarios. So programmers will need to confront this decision, even if we human drivers never have to in the real world. And it matters to the issue of responsibility and ethics whether an act was premeditated (as in the case of programming a robot car) or reflexively without any deliberation (as may be the case with human drivers in sudden crashes).

Cars are maybe the most iconic technology in America—forever changing cultural, economic, and political landscapes. They've made new forms of work possible and accelerated the pace of business, but they also waste our time in traffic. They rush countless patients to hospitals and deliver basic supplies to rural areas, but also continue to kill more than 30,000 people a year in the U.S. alone. They bring families closer together, but also farther away at the same time. They're the reason we have suburbs, shopping malls, and fast-food restaurants, but also new environmental and social problems. Automated cars, likewise, promise great benefits and unintended effects that are difficult to predict, and the technology is coming either way. Change is inescapable and not necessarily a bad thing in itself. But major disruptions and new harms should be anticipated and avoided where possible.

1. How is this passage organized? Was the structure effective, in your opinion?

______________________________________________

______________________________________________

______________________________________________

______________________________________________

______________________________________________

______________________________________________

2. What is the major assumption about automated cars that underlies this passage? (From the perspective of someone in 2018, that is.)

______________________________________________

______________________________________________

______________________________________________

______________________________________________

______________________________________________

______________________________________________

3. What gap does the author propose between cars piloted by robots versus cars driven by people?

______________________________________________

______________________________________________

______________________________________________

______________________________________________

______________________________________________

______________________________________________

## SCIENCE

Lucky for you, there are TWO science-related passages on the SAT. In terms of readability, some of these passages are accessible, but others are pretty technical. If you want an example of the latter, check out the passage about DNA on the official College Board SAT #1. Hoo boy, is that technical!

Here's what you want to keep in mind on SAT's science-based reading passages.

First, relationships—science passages are often about connections and causation—as in, if we understand this one phenomenon, it might help explain another phenomenon.

Second, new terms and ideas—you'll frequently run into something new and novel, something you haven't before studied. Keep in mind that *whatever* it is, it is being introduced to you. You weren't expected to know what it was when you sat down. Don't be overwhelmed by technical terms—just note what's new and remember that you can (and should) look back at the passage to recall those crazy names while you're answering the questions.

Let's see a sample science passage.

## EXERCISE #4: Bring it Home with Science

Let's learn some science. Look for connection and causation, and remember: you don't need to memorize what's in the passage. Just note any unfamiliar terms so you can reference them when the questions bring them up.

This passage is adapted from Carla Campbell, et al., "A Case Study of Environmental Injustice: The Failure in Flint," 2016 (CC BY 4.0). The city of Flint, MI changed its water supply from Lake Huron to the Flint River, water not treated with an anti-corrosion chemical meant to prevent the release of lead from the water pipes' interior. This failure resulted in a massive spike in its citizens' blood lead levels.

Most Americans have now heard of the avoidable and abject failure of government on the local, state and federal level, environmental authorities, and water company officials to prevent the mass poisoning of hundreds of children and adults in Flint, Michigan from April 2014 to December 2015. The poisoning of the population in Flint was an insidious one. People drinking the contaminated water would never have known they had elevated blood lead levels (BLLs) without specific medical testing for it. In fact, if the water contamination had not been made public, most exposed children and their families would have never suspected they were being exposed over a 20-month period of time, and it would be expected that the water contamination and lead exposure would have continued up until today.

Lead exposure in young children can lead to decrements in intelligence, development, behavior, attention, and other neurological functions. Dr. Philip Landrigan and Dr. David Bellinger summarize the adverse effects of lead succinctly: "Lead is a devastating poison. It damages children's brains, erodes intelligence, diminishes creativity and the ability to weigh consequences and make good decisions, impairs language skills, shortens attention span, and predisposes to hyperactive and aggressive behavior. Lead exposure in early childhood is linked to later increased risk for dyslexia and school failure." The costs from lead poisoning are considerable, as are the cost savings for prevention of childhood lead poisoning. Researchers stated that in the United States and Europe the lead-attributable economic costs have been estimated at $50.9 and $55 billion dollars, respectively. They estimate a total cost of $977 billion of international dollars in low- and middle-income countries, with economic losses equal to $134.7 billion in Africa, $142.3 billion in Latin American and the Caribbean, and $699.9 billion in Asia, giving a total economic loss for these countries in the range of $728.6–$1,162.5 billion. A previous analysis showed that each dollar invested in lead paint hazard control results in a return of $17–$221 or a net savings of $181–$269 billion.

Historically, scientists in the companies that put lead in gasoline and paint became aware of the dangers of lead exposures but took much time to finally remove lead from these products. Many countries banned the use of lead-based paint in residential housing before the U.S. did. Historian Laura Bliss states, "Flint's tragedy is shedding light on a health issue that's been lurking in U.S. households for what seems like forever. But that demands the question: Why has lead poisoning never really been treated like what it is—the longest-lasting childhood-health epidemic in U.S. history?" She describes how in the 1950s, when "millions of children had had been chronically or acutely exposed (to lead)" and this had been linked to health problems—polio, for example. In the 1950s, "Fewer than sixty thousand new cases of polio per year created a near-panic among American parents and a national mobilization that led to vaccination campaigns that virtually wiped out the disease within a decade", write Dr. David Rosner and Dr. Gerald Markowitz. "With lead poisoning, the industry and federal government could have mobilized together to systemically detoxify the nation's lead-infested housing stock, and end the epidemic right there." Bliss then goes on to describe how "the industry's powerful leaders diverted the attention of health officials away from their products, and toward class and race" by associating childhood lead poisoning with that of a child "with 'ignorant' parents living in 'slums.'" Bliss goes on to state that "lead poisoning in children can be eradicated...

Today the cost of detoxifying the entire nation hovers around $1 trillion. Any federal effort to systematically identify and remove lead from infested households would be complex, decades-long, and require ongoing policy reform." "But it's also saving a next generation of children," Rosner says. "You're actually going to stop these kids from being poisoned. And isn't that worth something?"

This crisis was the result of failures on every level. The facts presented demonstrate that environmental injustice is the major and underlying factor involved in the events in Flint. Having a state-appointed emergency manager in charge took away the normal communication the City of Flint might have had with its residents and constituents. It is imperative to rebuild relationships with Flint's community and respond to community needs in order to make real and lasting change. Perhaps putting the Flint situation under a microscopic analysis may prevent future episodes of such environmental injustice.

1. How would you categorize the authors' approach in this passage? Persuasive? Objective?

2. Identify one single sentence that encapsulates the authors' purpose for writing this article.

3. Find one subjective (opinion-based) and one objective (fact-based) argument within the passage.

# Make Friends with Archaic Passages

**Archaic** *adj.* **\ är-ˈkā-ik \ :** having the characteristics of the language of the past and surviving chiefly in specialized uses

On test day, you will almost certainly see at least one passage with at least a hundred years of age on it. I call these archaic passages. Those guys are going to be harder to read just due to the fact that preferences for vocabulary and sentence structure change a lot over time. You likely won't "get" those passages as quickly as you would a contemporary passage. That's fine—you can still become friends with them.

## Just keep these three fun facts in mind:

***#1: Everyone taking the SAT has to read the same passages.***

That means it's hard for everybody else too.

***#2: Look for the stuff you understand and let it help you understand what you don't.***

These passages will often have a strong central theme. Once you pick it up in one place, look for it elsewhere; it's probably there too.

***#3: The more you read these, the easier they will become.***

Have you read any Shakespeare plays in English class? Have you noticed that when you first start, it is *freaking impossible*, but by Act IV, you're starting to cruise along? It's the same with these passages: the more you read them, the easier they will get.

## EXERCISE #1: Let's Start Practicing Now

Let's dig into a few archaic passages. When you read, I want you to do two specific things: underline ideas that you think are important to the author's point of view, and circle sentences that are really challenging to read because of the vocabulary and/or sentence structure.

This passage is adapted from Alexis De Tocqueville, "Democracy in America." Originally published in 1835.

Whenever a law which the judge holds to be unconstitutional is argued in a tribunal of the United States he may refuse to admit it as a rule; this power is the only one which is peculiar to the American magistrate, but it gives rise to immense political influence. Few laws can escape the searching analysis of the judicial power for any length of time, for there are few which are not prejudicial to some private interest or other, and none which may not be brought before a court of justice by the choice of parties, or by the necessity of the case. But from the time that a judge has refused to apply any given law in a case, that law loses a portion of its moral cogency. The persons to whose interests it is prejudicial learn that means exist of evading its authority, and similar suits are multiplied, until it becomes powerless. One of two alternatives must then be resorted to: the people must alter the constitution, or the legislature must repeal the law.

The political power which the Americans have intrusted to their courts of justice is therefore immense, but the evils of this power are considerably diminished by the obligation which has been imposed of attacking the laws through the courts of justice alone. If the judge had been empowered to contest the laws on the ground of theoretical generalities, if he had been enabled to open an attack or to pass a censure on the legislator, he would have played a prominent part in the political sphere; and as the champion or the antagonist of a party, he would have arrayed the hostile passions of the nation in the conflict. But when a judge contests a law applied to some particular case in an obscure proceeding, the importance of his attack is concealed from the public gaze, his decision bears upon the interest of an individual, and if the law is slighted it is only collaterally. Moreover, although it is censured, it is not abolished; its moral force may be diminished, but its cogency is by no means suspended, and its final destruction can only be accomplished by the reiterated attacks of judicial functionaries.

I am inclined to believe this practice of the American courts to be at once the most favorable to liberty as well as to public order. If the judge could only attack the legislator openly and directly, he would sometimes be afraid to oppose any resistance to his will; and at other moments party spirit might encourage him to brave it at every turn. The laws would consequently be attacked when the power from which they emanate is weak, and obeyed when it is strong. That is to say, when it would be useful to respect them they would be contested, and when it would be easy to convert them into an instrument of oppression they would be respected. But the American judge is brought into the political arena independently of his own will. He only judges the law because he is obliged to judge a case. The political question which he is called upon to resolve is connected with the interest of the suitors, and he cannot refuse to decide it without abdicating the duties of his post. He performs his functions as a citizen by fulfilling the precise duties which belong to his profession as a magistrate. It is true that upon this system the judicial censorship which is exercised by the courts of justice over the legislation cannot extend to all laws indiscriminately, inasmuch as some of them can never give rise to that exact species of contestation which is termed a lawsuit; and even when such a contestation is possible, it may happen that no one cares to bring it before a court of justice. The Americans have often felt this disadvantage, but they have left the remedy incomplete, lest they should give it an efficacy which might in some cases prove dangerous. Within these limits the power vested in the American courts of justice of pronouncing a statute to be unconstitutional forms one of the most powerful barriers which has ever been devised against the tyranny of political assemblies.

1. What is De Tocqueville's primary point in this passage?

2. Were there any moments that were especially hard to read on the first pass? Did context help you understand them?

3. Can you find 2-3 moments in the passage that you think the SAT would definitely ask you a question about?

This passage is adapted from Charlotte Brontë, "Jane Eyre." Originally published in 1847. The narrator is the central character, Jane Eyre.

John Reed was a schoolboy of fourteen years old; four years older than I, for I was but ten: large and stout for his age, with a dingy and unwholesome skin; thick lineaments in a spacious visage, heavy limbs and large extremities. He gorged himself habitually at table, which made him bilious, and gave him a dim and bleared eye and flabby cheeks. He ought now to have been at school; but his mama had taken him home for a month or two, "on account of his delicate health."

John had not much affection for his mother and sisters, and an antipathy to me. He bullied and punished me; not two or three times in the week, nor once or twice in the day, but continually: every nerve I had feared him, and every morsel of flesh in my bones shrank when he came near. There were moments when I was bewildered by the terror he inspired, because I had no appeal whatever against either his menaces or his inflictions; the servants did not like to offend their young master by taking my part against him, and Mrs. Reed was blind and deaf on the subject: she never saw him strike or heard him abuse me, though he did both now and then in her very presence, more frequently, however, behind her back.

Habitually obedient to John, I came up to his chair: he spent some three minutes in thrusting out his tongue at me as far as he could without damaging the roots: I knew he would soon strike, and while dreading the blow, I mused on the disgusting and ugly appearance of him who would presently deal it. I wonder if he read that notion in my face; for, all at once, without speaking, he struck suddenly and strongly. I tottered, and on regaining my equilibrium retired back a step or two from his chair.

"That is for your impudence in answering mama awhile since," said he, "and for your sneaking way of getting behind curtains, and for the look you had in your eyes two minutes since, you rat!"

Accustomed to John Reed's abuse, I never had an idea of replying to it; my care was how to endure the blow which would certainly follow the insult.

"What were you doing behind the curtain?" he asked.

"I was reading."

"Show the book."

I returned to the window and fetched it thence.

"You have no business to take our books; you are a dependent, mama says; you have no money; your father left you none; you ought to beg, and not to live here with gentlemen's children like us, and eat the same meals we do, and wear clothes at our mama's expense. Now, I'll teach you to rummage my bookshelves: for they *are* mine; all the house belongs to me, or will do in a few years. Go and stand by the door, out of the way of the mirror and the windows."

I did so, not at first aware what was his intention; but when I saw him lift and poise the book and stand in act to hurl it, I instinctively started aside with a cry of alarm: not soon enough, however; the volume was flung, it hit me, and I fell, striking my head against the door and cutting it. The cut bled, the pain was sharp: my terror had passed its climax; other feelings succeeded.

"Wicked and cruel boy!" I said. "You are like a murderer—you are like a slave-driver—you are like the Roman emperors!"

I had read Goldsmith's History of Rome, and had formed my opinion of Nero, Caligula, etc. Also I had drawn parallels in silence, which I never thought thus to have declared aloud.

"What! what!" he cried. "Did she say that to me? Did you hear her, Eliza and Georgiana? Won't I tell mama? But first—"

He ran headlong at me: I felt him grasp my hair and my shoulder: he had closed with a desperate thing. I really saw in him a tyrant, a murderer. I don't very well know what I did with my hands, but he called me "Rat! Rat!" and bellowed out aloud. Aid was near him: Eliza and Georgiana had run for Mrs. Reed, who was gone upstairs: she now came upon the scene, followed by Bessie and her maid Abbot. We were parted: I heard the words—

"Take her away to the red-room, and lock her in there." Four hands were immediately laid upon me, and I was borne upstairs.

1. Opinion time: is it easier to read archaic fiction than archaic political essays?

2. Were there any moments that were especially hard to read on the first pass? Did context help you understand them?

3. Can you find 2-3 moments in the passage that you think the SAT would definitely ask you a question about?

This passage is from F. Scott Fitzgerald, "This Side of Paradise." Originally published 1920.

The silence of the theatre behind Amory ended with a curious snapping sound, followed by the heavy roaring of a rising crowd and the interlaced clatter of many voices. The matinee was over.

He stood aside, edged a little into the rain to let the throng pass. A small boy rushed out, sniffed in the damp, fresh air and turned up the collar of his coat; came three or four couples in a great hurry; came a further scattering of people whose eyes as they emerged glanced invariably, first at the wet street, then at the rain-filled air, finally at the dismal sky; last a dense, strolling mass that depressed him with its heavy odor compounded of the tobacco smell of the men and the fetid sensuousness of stale powder on women. After the thick crowd came another scattering; a stray half-dozen; a man on crutches; finally the rattling bang of folding seats inside announced that the ushers were at work.

New York seemed not so much awakening as turning over in its bed. Pallid men rushed by, pinching together their coat-collars; a great swarm of tired, magpie girls from a department-store crowded along with shrieks of strident laughter, three to an umbrella; a squad of marching policemen passed, already miraculously protected by oilskin capes.

The rain gave Amory a feeling of detachment, and the numerous unpleasant aspects of city life without money occurred to him in threatening procession. There was the ghastly, stinking crush of the subway—the car cards thrusting themselves at one, leering out like dull bores who grab your arm with another story; the querulous worry as to whether someone isn't leaning on you; a man deciding not to give his seat to a woman, hating her for it; the woman hating him for not doing it; at worst a squalid phantasmagoria of breath, and old cloth on human bodies and the smells of the food men ate—at best just people—too hot or too cold, tired, worried.

He pictured the rooms where these people lived—where the patterns of the blistered wall-papers were heavy reiterated sunflowers on green and yellow backgrounds, where there were tin bathtubs and gloomy hallways and verdureless, unnamable spaces in back of the buildings; where even love dressed as seduction—a sordid murder around the corner, illicit motherhood in the flat above. And always there was the economical stuffiness of indoor winter, and the long summers, nightmares of perspiration between sticky enveloping walls... dirty restaurants where careless, tired people helped themselves to sugar with their own used coffee-spoons, leaving hard brown deposits in the bowl.

It was not so bad where there were only men or else only women; it was when they were vilely herded that it all seemed so rotten. It was some shame that women gave off at having men see them tired and poor—it was some disgust that men had for women who were tired and poor. It was dirtier than any battle-field he had seen, harder to contemplate than any actual hardship moulded of mire and sweat and danger, it was an atmosphere wherein birth and marriage and death were loathsome, secret things.

He remembered one day in the subway when a delivery boy had brought in a great funeral wreath of fresh flowers, how the smell of it had suddenly cleared the air and given everyone in the car a momentary glow.

1. What would you say this fiction passage is about?

2. Were there any moments that were especially hard to read on the first pass? Did context help you understand them?

3. Can you find 2-3 moments in the passage that you think the SAT would definitely ask you a question about?

This passage is adapted from Susan B. Anthony's speech, "On Women's Right to Vote." This was Anthony's stump speech; it was delivered in various locations in 1873.

Friends and fellow citizens, I stand before you tonight under indictment for the alleged crime of having voted at the last presidential election, without having a lawful right to vote. It shall be my work this evening to prove to you that in thus voting, I not only committed no crime, but, instead, simply exercised my citizen's rights, guaranteed to me and all United States citizens by the National Constitution, beyond the power of any state to deny.

The preamble of the Federal Constitution says:

"We, the people of the United States, in order to form a more perfect union, establish justice, insure domestic tranquility, provide for the common defense, promote the general welfare, and secure the blessings of liberty to ourselves and our posterity, do ordain and establish this Constitution for the United States of America."

It was we, the people; not we, the white male citizens; nor yet we, the male citizens; but we, the whole people, who formed the Union.

And we formed it, not to give the blessings of liberty, but to secure them; not to the half of ourselves and the half of our posterity, but to the whole people--women as well as men. And it is a downright mockery to talk to women of their enjoyment of the blessings of liberty while they are denied the use of the only means of securing them provided by this democratic-republican government--the ballot.

For any state to make sex a qualification that must ever result in the disfranchisement of one entire half of the people, is to pass a bill of attainder, or, an ex post facto law, and is therefore a violation of the supreme law of the land. By it the blessings of liberty are forever withheld from women and their female posterity. To them this government has no just powers derived from the consent of the governed. To them this government is not a democracy. It is not a republic. It is an odious aristocracy; a hateful oligarchy of sex; the most hateful aristocracy ever established on the face of the globe; an oligarchy of wealth, where the rich govern the poor. An oligarchy of learning, where the educated govern the ignorant, or even an oligarchy of race, where the Saxon rules the African, might be endured; but this oligarchy of sex, which makes father, brothers, husband, sons, the oligarchs over the mother and sisters, the wife and daughters, of every household--which ordains all men sovereigns, all women subjects, carries dissension, discord, and rebellion into every home of the nation.

Webster, Worcester, and Bouvier all define a citizen to be a person in the United States, entitled to vote and hold office.

The only question left to be settled now is: Are women persons? And I hardly believe any of our opponents will have the hardihood to say they are not. Being persons, then, women are citizens; and no state has a right to make any law, or to enforce any old law, that shall abridge their privileges or immunities. Hence, every discrimination against women in the constitutions and laws of the several states is today null and void, precisely as is every one against Negroes.

1. Can you identify 1-2 interesting rhetorical devices that Anthony included, and why those devices were effective?

2. Were there any moments that were especially hard to read on the first pass? Did context help you understand them?

3. Can you find 2-3 moments in the passage that you think the SAT would definitely ask you a question about?

# Evidence Buddies

**What's the secret to the Reading section of the SAT?**
It's in the name: "evidence-based," as in the Evidence-Based Reading and Writing section of the SAT.

Now, would I personally have included an adjective in the title like that? No, I would not have. Look, I don't write the tests—I just help students ace them.

The SAT's goal is to test you on the reading skills you'll use in college. In this case, that skill is *carefully extracting concrete evidence from a text.*

## I've got good news and bad news.

The bad news first: doing so is not a lot of fun. The good news is that it's not that hard. And finding evidence really is a skill you'll use in college, so when you get better at it, you'll be doing your future-self a solid. "Thanks, past-self!" your future-self will say to your present-self.

**Your #1 strategy on this test is to do the research.**
Now, is doing research my definition of fun? It is not. Again, good news and bad news: the bad news is that doing research can be tedious. The good news is that you have enough time to do it.

The SAT gives you 65 minutes to answer 52 questions. By the standards of standardized testing, that is luxurious! You've got loads of time to dig into those passages, and you want to use it to find the answers buried in the text.

You see, all of the right answers on the SAT have to derive directly from evidence in the passages. Some are even more explicit—they'll ask you to point out exactly which evidence you used to answer another question.

Questions that ask you to "find the evidence" travel in pairs—first you'll answer a typical reading question, then you'll identify the evidence in the next question.

**I'll call these guys Evidence Buddies.**
When you get one of these right, you'll often get the other one too. It's two for the price of one! Let's talk about the different ways you can approach these bad boys.

## THE FRONTAL ASSAULT

The most reliable way to solve these guys is to already know what evidence proves your answer before you even get to the evidence question. That's easier to do than it might sound. While you're answering the first question in a pair of Evidence Buddies, ask yourself: "How do I know this is right?" Then go look for it!

When you then move to the second question and you find an answer choice that features the same evidence you just found, you'll be nearly certain you got both questions right.

Now, does it always work to solve those guys that way? Not every time, no. (It's great when it does, though!) In case you couldn't find the evidence yourself on the first pass, here is the second-best way to tackle these questions:

## USE THE CLUES

You may know the answer to the first question but not the evidence that proves it. Well, it's right there in the next question! Dig into the four line references that the question cites. Conveniently, they are already marked up for you... courtesy of your pre-highlighting!

***Hot Tip:*** You want to be careful to avoid a really common trap on the SAT: evidence that proves half of your answer correct. This Reading test requires you to be a very technical, detail-oriented reader. Avoid falling for answers that feel like they're "good enough." Read the question stem carefully. Read the answer to the first question carefully. Then make sure that your evidence proves that statement in its entirety.

Less talk, more rock. Let me show you an example.

## EXERCISE #1: Harry Potter and the Half-Right Evidence

Read this mini-passage, then tackle the Evidence Buddies at the end.

If a small tree branch pokes out onto a highway and there's no incoming traffic, we'd simply drift a little into the opposite lane and drive around it. But an automated car might come to a full stop, as it dutifully observes traffic laws that prohibit crossing a double-yellow line. This unexpected move would avoid bumping the object in front, but then cause a crash with the human drivers behind it.

Should we trust robotic cars to share our road, just because they are programmed to obey the law and avoid crashes?

Because the legal framework for autonomous vehicles does not yet exist, we have the opportunity to build one that is informed by ethics. This will be the challenge in creating laws and policies that govern automated cars: We need to ensure they make moral sense. Programming a robot car to slavishly follow the law, for instance, might be foolish and dangerous. Better to proactively consider ethics now than defensively react after a public backlash in national news.

1. The author recommends that, in advance of the introduction of automated cars, we should
   - A) create new ways of avoiding hazardous objects.
   - B) use moral principles to govern a new legal model.
   - C) increase our level of trust in automated drivers.
   - D) rewrite laws to better accommodate autonomous vehicles.

2. Which choice provides the best evidence for the answer to the previous question?
   - A) "But an automated car might come to a full stop, as it dutifully observes traffic laws that prohibit crossing a double-yellow line."
   - B) "Should we trust robotic cars to share our road, just because they are programmed to obey the law and avoid crashes?"
   - C) "Because the legal framework for autonomous vehicles does not yet exist, we have the opportunity to build one that is informed by ethics."
   - D) "Better to proactively consider ethics now than defensively react after a public backlash in national news."

Let's discuss. First off, the right answers are 1) B and 2) C. The first question is meant to be hard—let's hit that one quickly before we get to the "half-right" evidence. Answer A is too literal; the problem to solve is not specifically about hazardous objects but about automated cars in general. Answer C would be a good thing, but it's not something specifically proposed by the author in the text. Answer D sounds pretty good, except for the verb "accommodate," which means "to fit in with the needs of." The idea is that we need to make automated cars work within our world—not the other way around.

So if the right answer to #1 is to "use moral principles to govern a new legal model," what evidence is most alluring? I would argue that both C and D get into the discussion about the idea of using ethics to establish rules for automated cars.

Why is D wrong? Because, while it mentions "ethics," it leaves out the "legal model" aspect. That's exactly what makes it half-right. You'll see answer choices like that all over the SAT—answers that tread the right turf but don't say *everything* you need them to say.

The point here: half-right answers are all-wrong.

Now, what if you get to a pair of these guys and you're not sure you know the answer to the FIRST question? Try this approach:

## THE BACK DOOR

Read the first question so you know really well what you're trying to find. Next, jump to the evidence question. Read the four line references carefully. See if you can use one to justify an answer to the first question. You find it? Great! That's two correct answers.

Now, the Back Door method can work. A lot of students even use it as their default approach. I want to give you a couple of reasons why you should only use it as a fallback option.

First, it's time and energy consuming. I'm a believer that, to get through the entire test at the highest level, you want to work as efficiently as you can throughout. You don't want to blow out the whole gas tank on the first section, in other words. Having to read and consider four pieces of evidence on every question (there are 10 of them per Reading test!) will take both a lot of time and a lot of energy. Knowing what you're trying to find will save you that time and energy.

Second, the evidence choices in the second question frequently pair up well with a wrong answer to the first question. If you find a pair of answers like that, guess what? You'll leave a set of Evidence Buddies thinking that you got two questions right when you actually got two questions wrong. And you don't want that.

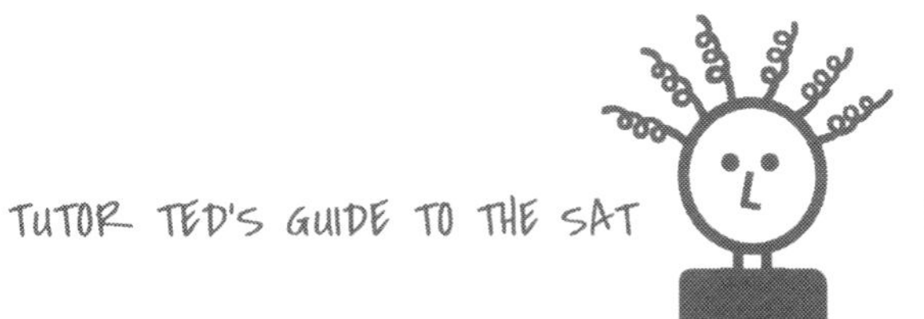

# Reading Strategies

This section is all about the fundamental things you want to be doing while you're reading to turn yourself into an SAT reading pro. Read on and step up your game a bit.

## PLAY OFFENSE

Many students treat the Reading section as a passive experience. They sit on their hands and stare at the passages while trying to absorb enough information to answer the questions. They are doing it wrong.

When I tell you to Play Offense, I am reminding you to read actively while you attack this section. Here are some techniques I strongly recommend you adopt. When you Play Offense, you'll arrive at the questions better informed and more equipped to find the right answers. Here are some specific ways you can Play Offense.

***Use your pencil.***

Underline key ideas, or transitions within the passage. Draw a box around important or unfamiliar terms. Circle the names of characters as they appear. Draw a star next to anything you find especially important or interesting.

***Ask yourself questions.***

What is the author trying to say? What is the style of this passage? Do you agree or disagree with the author's point of view? What are the most interesting and/or important aspects of the characters in the story? On a double passage, how do the two passages connect to one another?

***Ponder the Purpose of Paragraphs***

The most important thing you can do while you're reading is to pay attention to what is happening in each paragraph. What is its purpose? What jumps out at you? Is there any notable action, character development, or discovery? After you finish reading each paragraph, make a very brief note based on your interpretation. I call these "caveman notes." More on those in a minute.

When you Play Offense while you read, you will be more engaged and less prone to getting sidetracked by the occasional momentary daydream.

## MAKE CAVEMAN NOTES

How would a caveman summarize the purpose of a paragraph in 4 words or fewer?

PETA angry! Make law.

Short notes like these are what I call "caveman notes." Writing caveman notes after each paragraph will increase your comprehension AND save you significant time on most of the questions.

After you finish reading the passage, quickly review your caveman notes and think of them as a whole. What was that passage about? How does the author feel? Who had conflicting opinions? What was the *point*?

Try Playing Offense and taking Caveman Notes on the passage on the next page. You don't have to answer any questions yet—I just want you to get a sense of what you can do when you attack a passage.

On the page that follows, you'll see a version of the same passage with my caveman notes for your reference.

## EXERCISE #1

**INSTRUCTIONS:** While you read this passage, **underline key ideas or terms. Put a box around unfamiliar terms. Draw a star if you find an idea you think is really important.** Make caveman notes—**2-4 words that summarize the big ideas** within a section. I did this with the same passage, so after you're done you can look over to see how our version compares to yours.

This passage is from Noa Dzuba, The Science of Coffee. © 2008 by Noah Dzuba.

Legend has it that coffee was first discovered in Ethiopia when a goat herder ate some berries that seemed to make his goats surprisingly energetic. Sometime around 1000 AD, people in Arabia began to use the coffee bean to brew a drink. One thousand years later, coffee is not just a beverage—it is a worldwide cultural and economic institution. Picture the more than 21,000 Starbucks locations worldwide as evidence. Or consider the fact that coffee is the lead export of 12 different countries. Or simply consider this staggering fact: humans consume four hundred billion cups of coffee annually, making it the second most popular beverage in the world behind water.

The popularity of coffee has much to do with an alkaloid crystalline compound commonly known as caffeine. During the millennia that humans have consumed coffee and tea, the caffeine found in these plant-based beverages has been utilized to increase alertness in the morning or enhance productivity throughout the day. The eye-opening power of coffee is so well known that it's a cliché—mugs with cute sayings like "I don't start working until my coffee does," and television characters who seem to spend at least half their lives inside of coffee shops attest to that. It's almost enough to make you think that coffee's appeal is limited to its caffeine content. The question arises: are coffee and caffeine inseparable?

The question can be answered on two levels: the hypothetical (do people really want coffee that does not deliver caffeine?) and the practical (is it possible to effectively remove caffeine from coffee?). It makes sense to answer the questions in order: if people don't want coffee without caffeine, why should we bother to try?

Is caffeine the sole reason for coffee's appeal? Some say that they crave coffee for the smell or the taste. Others would say that those aspects are simply reminders of the caffeine content, a signal to the human brain to "get excited" about the energy boost to come. One factor to consider is that caffeine consumption has negative side effects such as anxiety and sleeplessness; these symptoms are so acute in some people that they cannot consume any caffeine at all. Other people simply do not desire the physical effects of caffeine. Anecdotally, some members of both of these groups still enjoy the ritual and taste of coffee. Though it's not a scientific result, we know that there are people who enjoy coffee but actively avoid caffeine.

The existence of this group who say "yes" to coffee but "no" to caffeine has led coffee producers to believe in the significant commercial potential of coffee without caffeine, which in turn has led to the science of decaffeination. Practically, decaffeinating a coffee bean is about as easy as unscrambling an egg. Caffeine molecules permeate the bean and are dispersed over the entirety of its contents. Not only that, but the flavor of coffee comes from more than 400 separate chemical compounds in the coffee bean. Taking the caffeine out of the bean without disturbing that delicate balance is nearly impossible. Yet, despite these logistical difficulties, modern science has managed to create a product: the "decaffeinated" coffee bean.

The most popular method of removing caffeine from the coffee bean relies on the use of a chemical solvent. Unroasted green coffee beans are steamed to force the caffeine in the beans to surface; then the caffeine is removed by washing the bean in the solvent. Methylene chloride is the chemical solvent most used in decaffeination and, even though it has been found to be toxic in high doses, the amount found in an average cup of coffee is well within the limits that the US Food and Drug Administration deems acceptable.

NOTES:

Recently, however, science has come up with a less toxic method. Known as the Swiss Water Process (despite the fact that the only factory that uses this process is located in Canada), it involves soaking coffee beans in water saturated with the flavor compounds in coffee. When a batch of new beans is soaked in this compound, the caffeine is free to leave the beans, but the saturation of flavor in the water prevents the beans from also giving off their delectable, non-caffeinated compounds.

Hope for an easier way to brew "decaf" arose in 2004 when scientists discovered a strain of coffee plant in Ethiopia that produces caffeine-free beans. The strain is not hardy enough to stand up to the rigors of commercial production, so it will have to be crossbred with a commercial variety before it is ready for market. The energy dedicated to taking the caffeine out of coffee attests to the popularity of the ritual born so many years ago, when some goats enjoyed the first ever "coffee buzz."

## EXERCISE #1

**INSTRUCTIONS:** Now compare your caveman notes and underlining to what I did on the same passage. Don't worry; there's no right or wrong way to mark up a passage! It just makes for an interesting comparison.

This passage is from Noa Dzuba, The Science of Coffee. © 2008 by Noah Dzuba.

Legend has it that coffee was first discovered in Ethiopia when a goat herder ate some berries that seemed to make his goats surprisingly energetic. Sometime around 1000 AD, people in Arabia began to use the coffee bean to brew a drink. One thousand years later, coffee is not just a beverage—it is a worldwide cultural and economic institution. Picture the more than 21,000 Starbucks locations worldwide as evidence. Or consider the fact that coffee is the lead export of 12 different countries. Or simply consider this staggering fact: humans consume four hundred billion cups of coffee annually, making it the second most popular beverage in the world behind water.

coffee is big

The popularity of coffee has much to do with an alkaloid crystalline compound commonly known as caffeine. During the millennia that humans have consumed coffee and tea, the caffeine found in these plant-based beverages has been utilized to increase alertness in the morning or enhance productivity throughout the day. The eye-opening power of coffee is so well known that it's a cliché—mugs with cute sayings like "I don't start working until my coffee does," and television characters who seem to spend at least half their lives inside of coffee shops attest to that. It's almost enough to make you think that coffee's appeal is limited to its caffeine content. The question arises: are coffee and caffeine inseparable?

coffee = caffeine

The question can be answered on two levels: the hypothetical (do people really want coffee that does not deliver caffeine?) and the practical (is it possible to effectively remove caffeine from coffee?). It makes sense to answer the questions in order: if people don't want coffee without caffeine, why should we bother to try?

Is caffeine the sole reason for coffee's appeal? Some say that they crave coffee for the smell or the taste. Others would say that those aspects are simply reminders of the caffeine content, a signal to the human brain to "get excited" about the energy boost to come. One factor to consider is that caffeine consumption has negative side effects such as anxiety and sleeplessness; these symptoms are so acute in some people that they cannot consume any caffeine at all. Other people simply do not desire the physical effects of caffeine. Anecdotally, some members of both of these groups still enjoy the ritual and taste of coffee. Though it's not a scientific result, we know that there are people who enjoy coffee but actively avoid caffeine.

why people like it

The existence of this group who say "yes" to coffee but "no" to caffeine has led coffee producers to believe in the significant commercial potential of coffee without caffeine, which in turn has led to the science of decaffeination. Practically, decaffeinating a coffee bean is about as easy as unscrambling an egg. Caffeine molecules permeate the bean and are dispersed over the entirety of its contents. Not only that, but the flavor of coffee comes from more than 400 separate chemical compounds in the coffee bean. Taking the caffeine out of the bean without disturbing that delicate balance is nearly impossible. Yet, despite these logistical difficulties, modern science has managed to create a product: the "decaffeinated" coffee bean.

decaf hard to make

The most popular method of removing caffeine from the coffee bean relies on the use of a chemical solvent. Unroasted green coffee beans are steamed to force the caffeine in the beans to surface; then the caffeine is removed by washing the bean in the solvent. Methylene chloride is the chemical solvent most used in decaffeination and, even though it has been found to be toxic in high doses, the amount found in an average cup of coffee is well within the limits that the US Food and Drug Administration deems acceptable.

chemical decaf

NOTES:

Recently, however, science has come up with a less toxic method. Known as the Swiss Water Process (despite the fact that the only factory that uses this process is located in Canada), it involves soaking coffee beans in water saturated with the flavor compounds in coffee. When a batch of new beans is soaked in this compound, the caffeine is free to leave the beans, but the saturation of flavor in the water prevents the beans from also giving off their delectable, non-caffeinated compounds.

water decaf

Hope for an easier way to brew "decaf" arose in 2004 when scientists discovered a strain of coffee plant in Ethiopia that produces caffeine-free beans. The strain is not hardy enough to stand up to the rigors of commercial production, so it will have to be crossbred with a commercial variety before it is ready for market. The energy dedicated to taking the caffeine out of coffee attests to the popularity of the ritual born so many years ago, when some goats enjoyed the first ever "coffee buzz."

NEW way?

## KNOW YOUR GEOGRAPHY

One more strategy to apply before attacking the questions: use your caveman notes and your understanding of the passage to create a mental map. A mental map is a sense of the organization of the passage. The test makers do not give you enough time to read the passage to the extent that you can absorb all of the details within it. That's how we read in the normal world, but this is not the normal world! Instead, you want to read and remember what happens where. Your brain should say to itself, "This is the part where they talked about how bees make honey. Over here is where they talked about the stages of bee maturation." Don't memorize the details; just know where the details will be when you need them.

Your caveman notes will be essential in helping you create your mental map. This step should not be a time-consuming process; rather, it's a technique you want to use while you are reading. Don't drown in the details—ride the wave of the bigger ideas. When you need to find the details, those ideas will help you know where to look.

**Now some strategies on how to step yo game up as you answer the questions.**

## EASY MONEY

SAT Reading questions are not arranged in order of difficulty, so feel free to bounce around. Identify the simplest questions and answer those first. I call these the "easy money" questions. As you read about the different question types, think about which questions look like they might be easier to answer. Find your favorite type of question. Jumping around within the questions can make the test less monotonous. More importantly, it can also help you figure out what the SAT thinks about the big ideas in the passage.

## BE A SEARCH ENGINE

Wouldn't it be great if you had a "find" command on the SAT? That would make the Reading test so easy it wouldn't even be funny. Since we don't have that luxury, we have to be our own search engine.

What does that mean? There are key words on every reading question, words that point towards the right answer. If you could type the key words into a search command, where would you look? Since you already have our mental map, you can use that to remember where in the passage the author used those key words. Now you have a vital head start on answering the questions—you know where to look.

## ANSWER IT YOURSELF

Which is faster: finding one right answer or finding three incorrect ones? Finding the correct one, right? Challenge yourself to answer the question on your own. When you do that, you can pounce on the right answer.

Here's a metaphor to convince you why it's valuable to Answer It Yourself *and a piece of life advice all-in-one*: don't go to the grocery store hungry.

Why? When you do, you end up buying a LOT more than you actually need, because your hungry stomach takes priority over your brain. On the SAT, don't rely on the answers to solve the question for you. You'll start to get creative, figuring out ways that wrong answers *could* be right answers.

Know what you're looking for, and go get it. You didn't really need those Oreo cookies, bag of Doritos, and donuts, anyway, did you?

## PLAN B: ELIMINATE

You weren't able to Answer It Yourself? Don't sweat it. It's a multiple choice test. The worst case scenario is that you have a one-in-four chance of getting the right answer. That ain't bad!

Start by finding any CLEARLY wrong answer choices. There are some terrible ones. Have a laugh at them, then cross them out and move on. Make an educated guess and, when in doubt, double-check your answer!

***Hot Tip:*** When you're carefully eliminating answer choices, you want to employ Advanced Strategy #1: Consider Every Word. You can jump ahead to the advanced strategies chapter now if you like. For now, I would give this advice: when you're down to just a couple of answer choices, a great strategy is to pick the answer that's most in-line with the main idea of the passage.

# Charts and Graphs

SAT Reading includes charts and figures within the Reading section and asks a half-dozen questions about them.

Aww! And you thought there was no science section on the SAT! Adorable.

:) :) :)

While we do have to deal with some pie charts and bar graphs, there is some good news:

***Questions about the charts and graphs are always in the same spot: at the end of the set of questions.***

***Any question that asks you to reference charts and graphs will warn you explicitly that you need to use them.***

***Your job on these questions is to report simple, clear facts from the data.***
***In other words, they're easy.***

***Hot Tip:*** On SAT chart/graph questions, the number one challenge is not to think too hard. The test makers think that you interpret too much and draw conclusions that are not justified by the graphs themselves. That's what the wrong answers tell us, anyway: the right answers are always justified by the graphs in a clear and obvious way. The wrong answers are seemingly logical conclusions that are not explicitly justified by the graph. You can avoid that trap by looking for the most easily provable answer.

Other than that, you want to follow the basic protocol that you always have for interpreting graphs: look at the axes carefully. Pay attention to units. If there's a key, make sure to use it. And again, draw the most literal information you can. There's no such thing as an answer that's too stupid if you can justify it based on the data.

OK, ready to put your data hat on? Wait...what? *You don't have a data hat?*

That's all right—we can live without one for now.

## EXERCISE #1: Meet the Graphs

Let's look at some graphs and charts typical of the ones you'll see on the SAT, then ask you questions based on them. Just remember when you answer these to *keep it literal*.

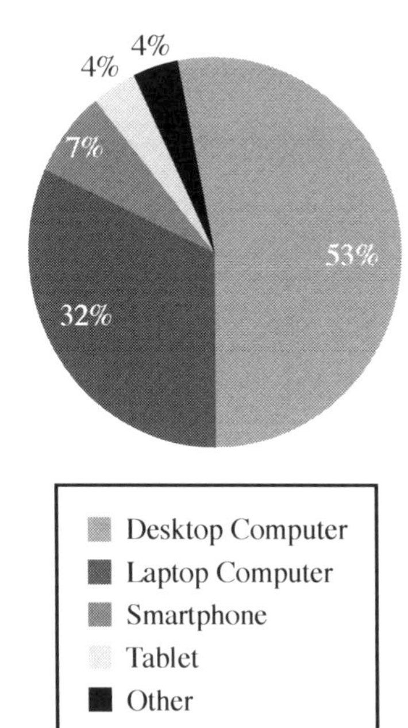


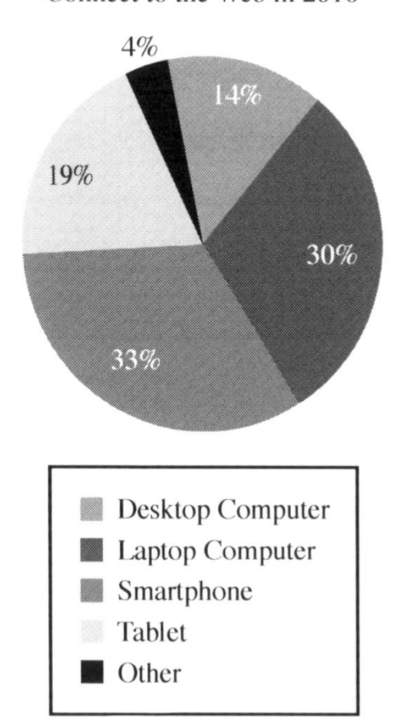


**1**

According to Chart 1, internet users in 2008 were likely to

A) use a laptop and a phone but prefer the laptop for internet use.
B) own both a laptop and a desktop computer
C) prefer desktop computers to laptop computers
D) use a computer to access the internet

**2**

Taken together, the two charts reflect a change between 2008 and 2016 in the

A) total number of internet users
B) number of users who prefer laptop computing
C) choice of device used to access the internet
D) popularity of internet usage

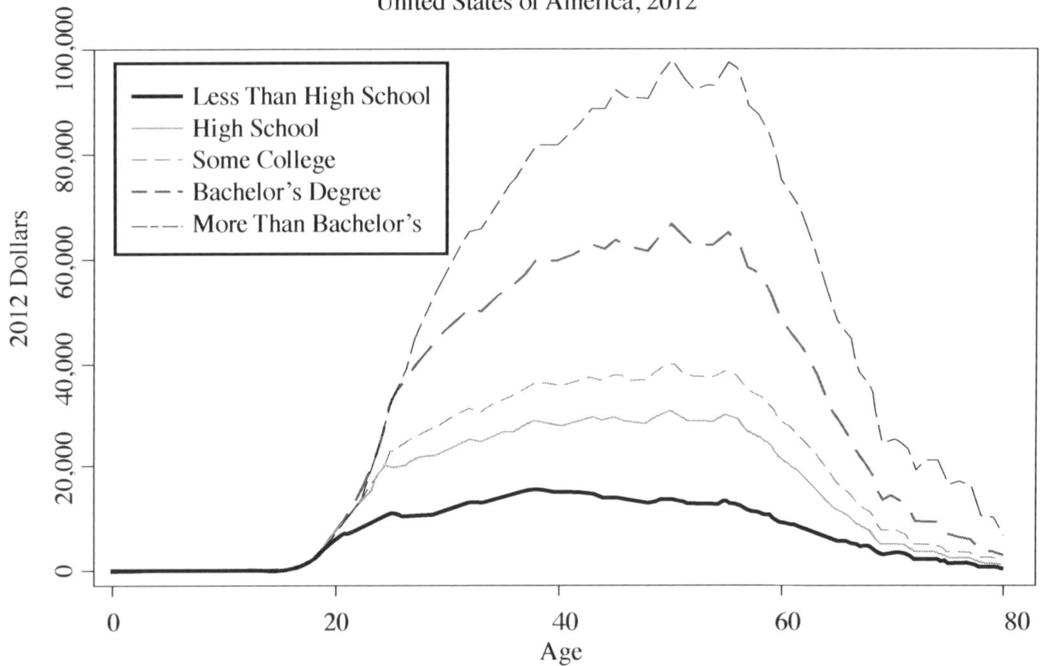


**3**

Which statement is best supported by the data in the figure?

A) Any student who receives more education will earn a higher income.

B) Age 60 is the year when people make the highest level of income.

C) Students who attend college make a higher income on average than those who don't.

D) Students with doctorate degrees make a higher income on average than those with masters degrees.

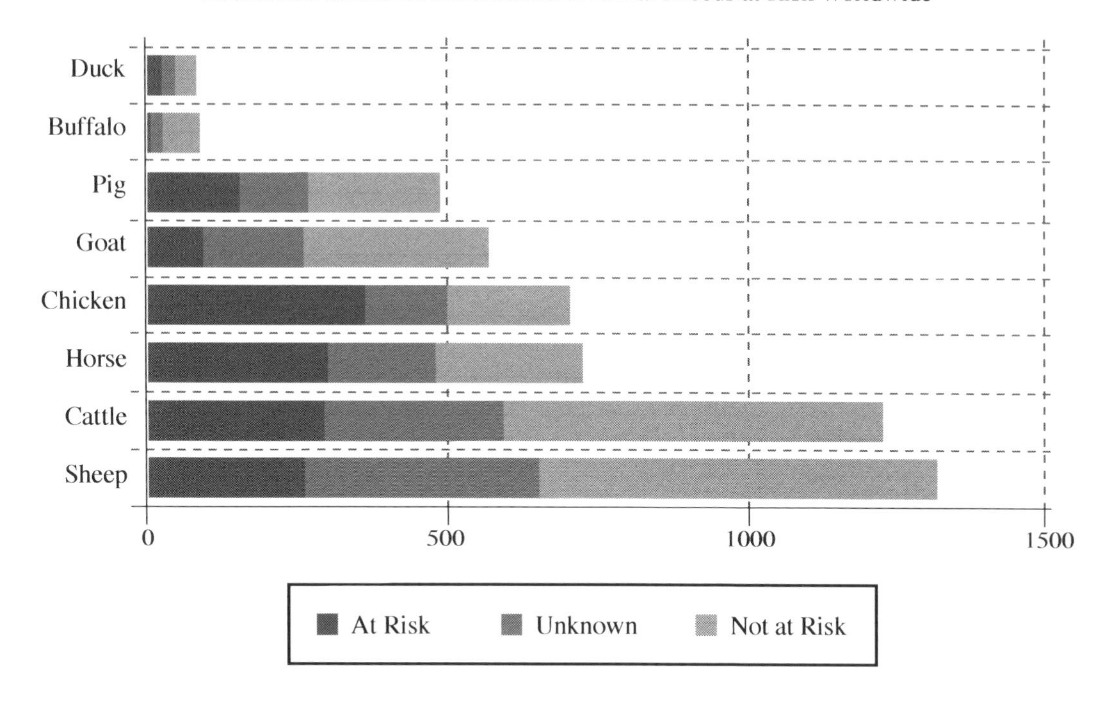


**4**

Which choice is best supported by the data in the figure?

A) There are twice as many breeds of domesticated cattle as there are of horses.

B) More goat species are at risk than pig species.

C) Of the animals in the figure, chickens have the greatest number of domesticated breeds that are at risk.

D) Sheep are the species most immediately threatened with extinction.

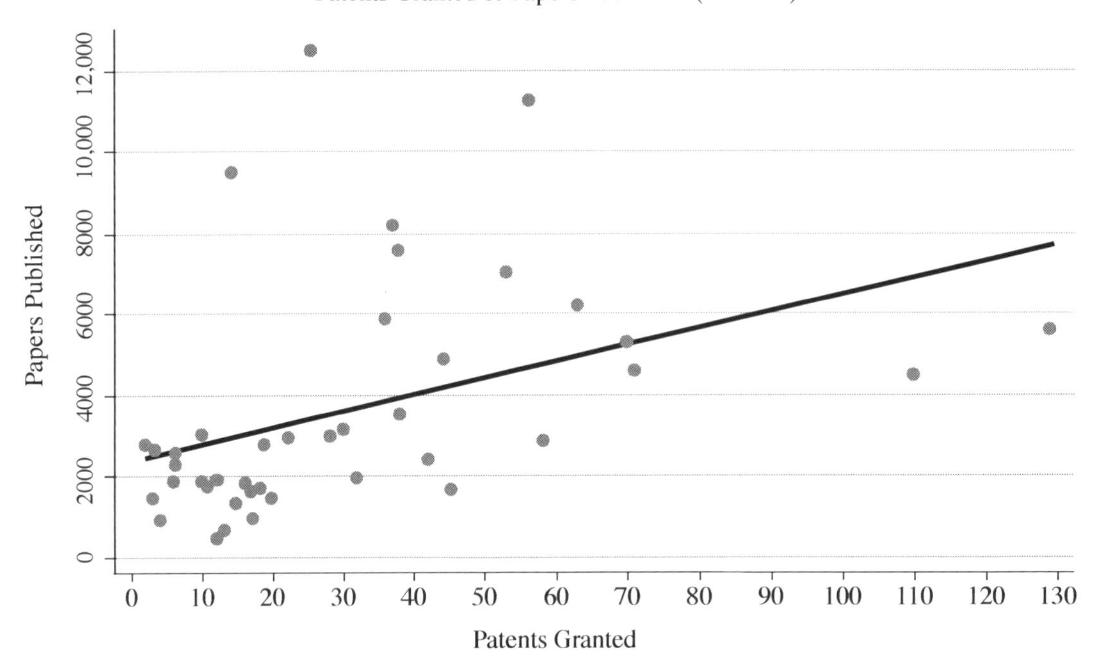


5

Which statement is best supported by the data in the figure?

A) There is a weak positive correlation between the number of papers published and the number of patents granted between 2006 and 2010.

B) There is a strong positive correlation between the number of papers published and the number of patents granted between 2006 and 2010.

C) There is a weak negative correlation between the number of papers published and the number of patents granted between 2006 and 2010.

D) There is a strong negative correlation between the number of papers published and the number of patents granted between 2006 and 2010.

Geographic Distribution of Henapavirus Outbreaks and Fruit Bats of Pteropodidae Family

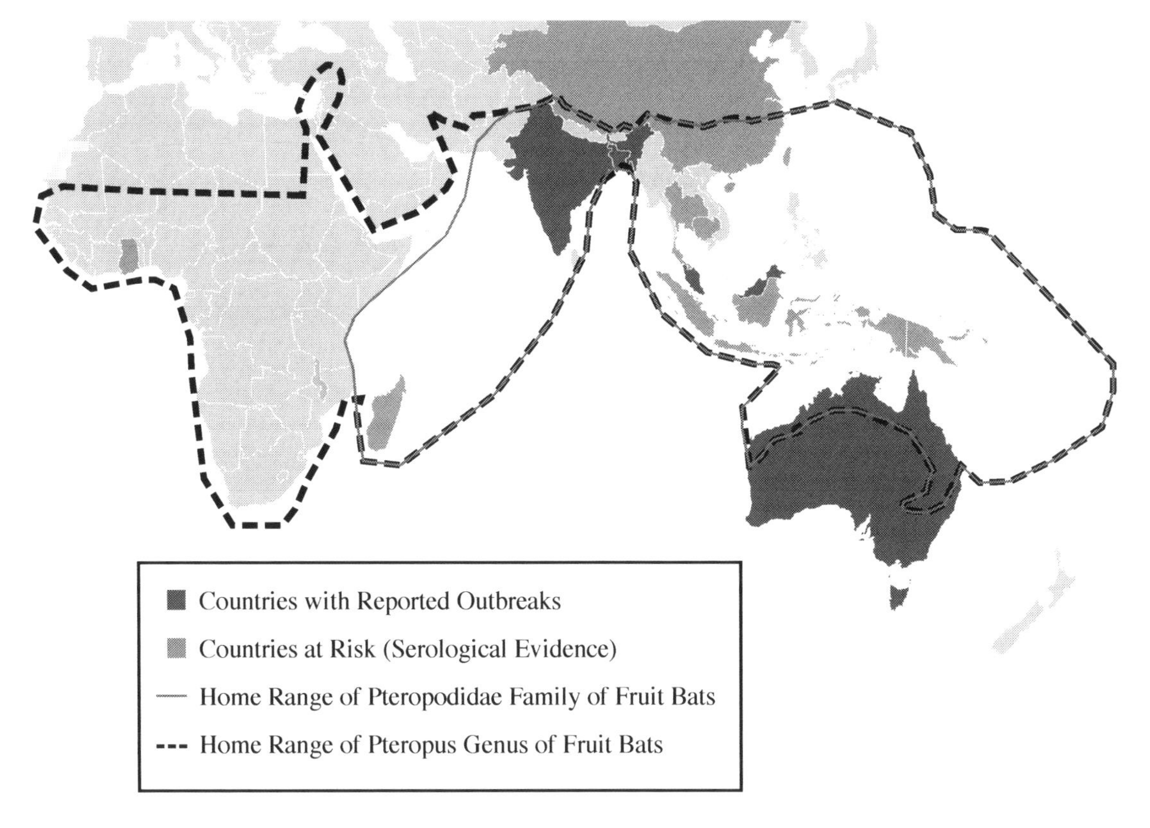


*In 2009, RNA sequences of three novel viruses related to known henipaviruses were detected in African straw-colored fruit bats in Ghana. The finding of these novel henipaviruses outside Australia and Asia indicates that the region of potential spread of henipaviruses may not be limited.*

**6**

Do the data in the map provide support for the claim in the passage that the henipaviruses have the potential to spread outside Australia and Asia?

A) Yes, because the map indicates that two countries in Africa are considered at risk.

B) Yes, because the habitat of one bat species already includes Africa, and the other species habitat is likely to expand.

C) No, because the primary areas of outbreak are located in Australia and Asia.

D) No, because the two bat species habitats only overlap in Australia and Asia.

# Vocabulary

SAT prep used to mean learning words like "calumnious" and "bureaucratization."

You think I'm kidding? Ask your older sister how she spent her spare time in high school. Chances are she says, "expending a plethora of frivolous hours perusing an esoteric lexicon."

### At that point, you should back out of the room as quietly as possible.

So you won't get the chance during your SAT studying to learn obscure vocabulary. I'm guessing you are OK with that. You will still have to answer vocabulary questions of another sort though—the SAT now asks you to identify the specific meaning of a commonly used word in context.

### Look at this sentence, for example:

> In 2012, research at the Large Hadron Collider provided concrete *support* for the existence of the theoretical Higgs Boson.

You know what the word *support* means; you've known that word since 3rd grade, in fact. That word happens to have many shades of meaning, however, and the SAT is going to make sure you know which one is being used here.

I've got a process for you to follow to solve these guys. It consists of three simple steps. Ready?

> ***Step #1: Read the sentence from the passage, leaving out the word in question.***
> ***Step #2: Come up with your own word (or words) to replace it.***
> ***Step #3: Look for an answer choice that means*** *precisely* ***the same thing as your replacement.***

Here's that same sentence, now featuring a question:

> In 2012, research at the Large Hadron Collider provided concrete *support* for the existence of the theoretical Higgs Boson.

1. As used in the sentence above, "support" most nearly means

   A) relief
   B) collaboration
   C) affirmation
   D) authorization

Let's walk through this one together. The first thing to do is read it without the word "support."

> In 2012, research at the Large Hadron Collider provided concrete ____________ for the existence of the theoretical Higgs Boson.

Now, come up with your own word to fit in that spot. My first instinct is a word like "evidence," or maybe "proof."

Finally, look for a synonym among the answer choices. Neither of our words was an option. What's the best match, though? Does "evidence" mean "relief?" Nope. How about "collaboration?" Definitely not.

What about the last two, "affirmation" and "authorization?" The nearest fit to our words, "evidence" and "proof," is definitely "affirmation."

And that's the right answer.

We were able to solve that one pretty cleanly on the first pass. When you follow that procedure—find your own replacement for the word in question, then match it to an answer choice—you can be pretty sure you got the question right.

***Hot tip:*** You want to act like you are a human dictionary on these guys. That's exactly what the test makers want you to do—think like a dictionary. Know what you're trying to find. Answer choices do not kinda work—the right answer should match the word in question ***precisely*** and ***perfectly***.

Let's try a couple more:

> Michael Friedman's belief was that songwriting could do more than entertain—it could document reality and explore our humanity.

2. As used in the sentence above, "belief" most nearly means

   A) position
   B) acceptance
   C) faith
   D) tradition

Let's dig in. First off, what would *you* say the word-in-question means? I would say something like "idea" or "conviction." Let's look for a match among the answer choices. I can pretty easily get rid of "faith" and "tradition." They are synonyms of "belief" but don't fit this context. "Acceptance" might be tempting, but when you plug it into the sentence, it doesn't fit the situation. We're talking about something that Michael believed, something that was important to him. It was a core belief of his—or a "position" he held. The answer is A!

One more, taken from archaic fiction this time.

> We go astray and do wrong, and bring ourselves into trouble with our fellow-men; there is no man or woman born into this world to whom some of these trials do not fall, and so I feel that some of them must happen to you.

3. As used in the sentence above, "trials" most nearly means

   A) attempts
   B) adversities
   C) citations
   D) examinations

To solve this guy, we ought to keep in mind our strategies for tackling archaic passages. One of the best ones we have is to rely on the context we understand to help us "get" anything we don't. What are some content clues in that sentence—words that help point out what the author is explaining? I'm looking at "wrong" and "trouble." So the context is pointing out the challenges that people face. That's probably a strong clue as to how the word "trials" is being used.

If we replaced "trials" with a word like "challenges," we'd look for that among the answers. If you know the word "adversities," you'd jump right for it. If not, you'd assess all the answer choices and get rid of the ones that don't mean *exactly* what you want them to mean. Are we talking about "attempts?" Attempts at what? That doesn't make sense here, does it? What about "citations," which can mean either "awards" or "speeding tickets." In either case, it makes no sense. "Examinations?" There are no clues to justify that we're talking about "trials" like they are experiments or tests, so no to that one too. Even if you did not know the meaning of "adversities," you could still get to the right answer so long as you look really carefully for the word(s) you're trying to find.

## Man, this SAT!

So far we've learned that even though there is no science section, you still have to analyze charts and graphs, and that even though they got rid of vocabulary, you still have to answer vocabulary questions! Next thing you know we're going to tell you that the optional essay isn't really optional!

## uh-oh...

# Advanced Strategies

You know the basics. Now it's time to ramp it up. Let's get hardcore. Let's take it to the next level. Let's give it 110%. *Let's insert another cliché here.*

## Ready?

**The theme of the advanced strategies is to use a scalpel—not a hatchet—when you're taking the SAT.**

First off, let's talk about what those two things are. A scalpel is what a surgeon uses in the operating room. A hatchet is what you use when you're fighting a grizzly bear in the woods.

On the SAT, you need to read with extreme precision. So: would you rather have a scalpel or a hatchet? And how does this extended metaphor play out on the SAT? Through the following advanced strategies.

### *ADVANCED STRATEGY #1: CONSIDER EVERY WORD*

You always want to read closely and carefully through the answer choices, considering the meaning of every word within them. The mistake you want to avoid is picking an answer that seems "good enough." You've got a generous amount of time, 65 minutes. You should use it to work hard—by reading carefully and analytically.

Huh, I feel like the tone of my advice made a general turn from "warm and encouraging" to "serious and strict" there. I guess this piece of advice is *just that important*. I've seen a bunch of students who, on their first SAT practice test, fall into the trap of picking the first answer that sounds reasonably appealing. Here's what you want to keep in mind: if SAT Reading feels like it's easy, you're doing it wrong.

Now, you don't need to treat every question like you're climbing Mount Kilimanjaro. If you read the question, you know exactly what you're looking for, and you find it—great! There are questions that will be as easy as that.

When it isn't that easy—when it gets more hardcore—here's what you want to do. On any question where the right answer does not jump off the page, you want to do the following:

***Start by eliminating all answer choices that are obviously, verifiably wrong.***

***In the answer choices that remain, underline every important word—every noun, verb, and adjective. Every word.***

***Make a comparison between the answer choices that are left. Use extreme prejudice. This is a test that asked you to differentiate between "offer an explanation" (the right answer) and "support a conclusion" (the wrong answer). Boy, is that difference subtle.***

***When in doubt, pick the answer choice more in keeping with the main idea of the passage. When all else fails, keep your answer on theme with what you got out of the passage.***

## ADVANCED STRATEGY #2: DON'T FALL IN LOVE WITH ONE WORD (AND DISREGARD THE REST)

This one is really a corollary to the last strategy. Some tempting answer choices on really difficult questions will include a word that you are going to *love*. Like, the perfect word, the ideal word you would use to describe the situation, your soulmate if your soulmate were a word. Don't fall in love with that answer choice based on just that one word. Make sure you read the rest of them too, yeah? Answer choices can start perfectly and then go off the rails. So don't be swayed by just one word.

## ADVANCED STRATEGY #3: READ THE QUESTION STEMS CAREFULLY.

Did you know that the beginning part of the question is called a "question stem"? Now you do, and you're welcome!

This strategy applies to the ENTIRE SAT. You want to read this test so damn carefully, the question stems in particular. Make sure you know what the point of the question is before you start to answer it.

I've seen questions that look like an evidence buddy to the question before, but are actually an unrelated, evidence-based question. How would you sniff out such a devious trick? By reading the question stem carefully.

## ADVANCED STRATEGY #4: USE YOUR PENCIL LIKE CRAZY.

Your biggest challenge during the Reading section is staying engaged. Unless you have the focused patience of a starfish stuck to the glass of a fish tank, you will not be able to remain totally focused throughout this section. That's a fact, but it's OK, too: we have tools to help us stay engaged.

The best one is your pencil. You want to use that thing like crazy. You should have pre-highlighted before you started reading, so you've already gotten started with this one. I would recommend you highlight with it while you read, too. Circle new vocabulary terms. Underline interesting, important ideas. Box words and phrases that you think might be important later. Take notes. When you answer questions, underline words in the answer choices.

The benefit here is two-fold: all the notes and highlights you're making will probably help you solve some questions, but more importantly, maybe, using your pencil will help you stay engaged. So don't sit on your hands during this section. Get in there and use that pencil like crazy.

## ADVANCED STRATEGY #5: KNOW YOUR OPERATIONAL VOCABULARY

Some of the most valuable vocabulary to know shows up in the questions. The meaning of these words is fundamental to understanding what an answer choice means.

Take "underscore" and "undermine" for example. "To underscore" means "to emphasize," while "to undermine" means "to weaken." Obviously that is an important difference to keep in mind!

Here are the operational vocabulary words that are the most important ones to know on the SAT.

| Useful Word | What It Means | Why It's A Good Word To Know |
|---|---|---|
| bolster | to support or strengthen | Because the SAT loves to use it; because most high school students don't know it; because if you guessed at what it means, you'd probably guess wrong. |
| underscore | to emphasize | Because it sounds so much like its buddy, "undermine"... |
| undermine | to weaken | ...which means pretty much the exact opposite of "underscore." |
| analyze | to examine methodically | I know you know this word, but I bring it up because I want to make sure your standards for "analyze" and "analysis" are high enough. "To analyze" means "to examine methodically," so make sure that, if you choose an answer with that word in it, that the author did indeed examine the subject *in depth*. |
| refute | to prove a statement false | Fairly easy word...I just want you to know it because it is the antonym of "support"—which is SAT's very favorite word—so I think you should know this one too. |
| illustrate | to explain by using examples | The examples are key here...just know that if illustrate is right, there has to be some sort of demonstration of the idea through an example or a story. |
| irony | a situation that seems to directly contradict expectations | Maybe my favorite word? In the Top 5, at least. When you're looking for irony, make sure that the result is in clear, direct opposition to what the reader, the scientist, or the character expects. In order to be ironic, it should point out a surprising incongruity. |
| assumption | something that is accepted to be true without proof | When you're asked about an assumption, think at the most basic level about the passage. Often assumptions will be fundamental, common-sense ideas that we all probably agree are true...but that the author never specifically proved to be true. |
| imply | to strongly suggest but not directly state | Many SAT questions ask you to recall what was stated in the passage. Questions about what was implied do not. In fact, these questions ask you to read between the lines. You can (and should) still find evidence to justify your answer to these questions. Just know that the right answer will be hinted at, not directly stated. |

| Useful Word | What It Means | Why It's A Good Word To Know |
|---|---|---|
| infer | to conclude indirectly from evidence | The idea behind "infer" is essentially the same as behind "imply"—you want to read between the lines to get these right. The difference between the use of these two words is that authors *imply* meaning and readers *infer* it. |
| explicit | clearly stated in detail | This one is the exact opposite of "infer" and "imply." If a question uses the word "explicit," make sure that your answer can be justified based on specific and clear textual references! |

## *ADVANCED STRATEGY #6: KEEP IT LITERAL*

Another way to say this one is this: don't get creative. This is advice I recommend ON THE SAT ONLY. In real life, creativity is what makes us human. The SAT is not a test that rewards creativity.

Hmm, did I just imply that the SAT is dehumanizing?

I'll let you answer that one.

Here's how this advice plays out on the SAT. Answers can be right simply by not being wrong. You don't want to extrapolate too much from the passage—remember, this test is "Evidence-Based." Draw simple, clear, some-would-say-boring conclusions from what you read in the passage and see in the graphs. Look for answers that are literal and uncreative. Let the Middle Manager/Accounting Professional inside you shine. On the SAT, only, though.

# READING: ANSWERS

# Answers

## PRE-READING STRATEGIES:

### PRE-HIGHLIGHTING

**EXERCISE #1**

1) B
2) A, C

### READ THE FINE PRINT

**EXERCISE #1**

1) B

**EXERCISE #2**

1) A, C
2) A, B
3) B, C
4) A, C
5) B, C
6) A, C
7) A, C
8) B, C

## HOW TO READ THE PASSAGES

### WARM-UP PASSAGE QUESTIONS

Look in the "Solutions" section that follows for sample answers to these guys.

## MAKE FRIENDS WITH ARCHAIC PASSAGES

### WARM-UP PASSAGE QUESTIONS

Look in the "Solutions" section that follows for sample answers to these guys.

## EVIDENCE BUDDIES

### HARRY POTTER AND THE HALF-RIGHT EVIDENCE

1) B
2) C

## CHARTS AND GRAPHS

### MEET THE GRAPHS

1) D
2) C
3) C
4) C
5) A
6) A

## VOCABULARY

1) C
2) A
3) B

# READING: SOLUTIONS

# Solutions

## PRE-READING STRATEGIES:

### PRE-HIGHLIGHTING

1) **B**

Jokes aside, you should really go to college. There are soft-serve ice cream machines there.

2) **A, C**

Choice B is tempting to pick, but the key with pre-highlighting is that you just want to show yourself what is going to be important within the passage. You'll have time to read (and think through) the questions carefully once you start to answer them. Also, Choice D would be kind of sweet actually, but then you'd just have to take the SAT next month.

### READ THE FINE PRINT

#### EXERCISE #1

1) **B**

This one is v important. It's part of the passage—read it!

#### EXERCISE #2

1) **A, C**

It's not choice B, but this woman's daughter *did* write one of the best novels ever (*Frankenstein*). Talk about a power family.

2) **A, B**

Science passages are not always technical, but they definitely can be!

3) **B, C**

Gotta love when they give the big idea away at the top!

4) **A, C**

"*New* Scientist" and *2017* might've been hints that it's not choice B.

5) **B, C**

If choice C were wrong, that would be an epic red herring.

6) **A, C**

It can't be choice B. They don't even mention the Constitution *once*.

7) **A, C**

This also might be the plot of a truly terrifying sci-fi movie.

8) **B, C**

When you started reading that title, you really didn't see "Grasshopper Sparrow" coming, did ya?

## HOW TO READ THE PASSAGES

### FICTION WARM-UP: "PAUL'S CASE"

1) Aside from the very real possibility that this kid is Lucifer reborn, it sounds from the passage that Paul's mockingly upbeat nature and general "light-heartedness" are what's really getting the teachers' goat(s?). There's nothing that pisses off a high school teacher more than a misbehaving student who isn't scared of or sorry about nothin'.
2) Come on, be honest... he'd be hilarious at prom.
3) There are a ton of juicy moments and symbols in this passage, but here are a few that stand out: that "scandalous" red carnation that the author keeps mentioning, and Paul's outfit in general; that whole cringe-y scene at the blackboard where we see Paul's "physical aversion" for his teachers; Paul's unnerving physical mannerisms; the phrase "baptism of fire"; Paul's one and only line of dialogue; and his grand and devilish exit. These all tell us a lot about the character and story we're dealing with.

### POLITICS WARM-UP: "WHAT TO A SLAVE IS THE FOURTH OF JULY?"

1) Douglass reminds his audience that slaves are *humans*, like anyone else, making slavery "the great sin and shame of America!" In fact, he says that he's not even going to engage in an argument on this point, because everyone *knows* that slaves are humans—the laws in slaveholding states prove it! (Again, I can't overstate how crazy it is that this all happened in this country only two lifetimes ago.)
2) He wants them to bring the heat, so to speak. Enough civil arguments. Enough gentle persuasions. This s**t is messed up, and he wants abolitionists to speak with "fire" and "thunder," and melt their opponents' faces off with "biting ridicule, blasting reproach, withering sarcasm, and stern rebuke." Look out, defenders of slavery—Freddy D is about to spit hot fire.
3) He's kind of like the friend who starts trashing you and your fiancée in front of your whole family when you're at the altar, except that he's very much in the right and not an unstable, lifelong moocher who almost ruined your marriage (looking at you, KAREN). The Fourth of July is 'Merica's "special day," and Douglass thinks that it's as good a time as any to forcefully remind everyone that there is a lot to NOT celebrate about the country. Also, we can't ignore the fact that Douglass used the day honoring the U.S.'s "freedom" from Britain to talk about all the people in the nation who still aren't free. Pretty smart guy, huh?

### SOCIAL STUDIES WARM-UP: "THE ETHICS OF AUTONOMOUS CARS"

1) This passage bounces back and forth between a couple of thought experiments and their real-world relevance to the debate over autonomous cars, ending with a slightly more zoomed-out conclusion. I'm a big fan of philosophy and hypotheticals, but can't speak for anyone else.
2) Automated cars are coming! Whether we like it or not. Just hope it goes better than *I, Robot* did.
3) In emergency scenarios, cars driven by people will be responding to the split-second, adrenaline-fueled decision-making of fallible humans; however, in those same scenarios, cars driven by robots will be responding to a set of preprogrammed decisions made by clear-headed human designers way before the accident ever happened. So, the author asks, what decisions should those designers make, and shouldn't the public have a say?

### SCIENCE WARM-UP: "A CASE STUDY OF ENVIRONMENTAL INJUSTICE"

1) Definitely persuasive, right? Any time you see the phrase "It is imperative..." in the final paragraph of a passage, and it's not in a quote, you know this author is trying to convince you of *something*.
2) How about that last one? "Perhaps putting the Flint situation under a microscopic analysis may prevent future episodes of such environmental injustice." It's got everything—a meta-reference to the very thing that this passage begins to do (putting the Flint situation under a microscope), as well as a call to action that seems like the author's ultimate, driving motivation.
3) An example of a subjective argument (though a convincing one) would be that environmental injustice is the "major and underlying factor involved...." An objective argument would be that "the costs from lead poisoning are considerable," since they cite some damn good public health research and specific figures to back it up.

## MAKE FRIENDS WITH ARCHAIC PASSAGES

### WARM-UP #1: "DEMOCRACY IN AMERICA"

1) Basically, the dude is saying that it's really good (and kind of ingenious) that American judges can only rule on specific cases and how specific laws apply to those specific cases. If they were allowed to openly challenge and strike down any law at any time, he thinks that judges would become corrupt political instruments used for oppression and tyranny. Woah, heavy stuff.
2) Whew, what *wasn't* hard to read on the first pass, right? That word "prejudicial" is a doozy, and how about this sentence: "Amer-

icans have felt this disadvantage, but they have left the remedy incomplete, lest they should give it an efficacy which might in some cases prove dangerous." Seriously, who even uses "lest" anymore? But hopefully on a second pass through, the central concept—the benefits of judges' limited powers in the American legal system—should have started to become clearer. If not, don't lose sleep over it; this passage is about as dense as they come.

3) Definitely be ready for questions about lines 27 – 35 ("If the judge... in the conflict") and lines 60 – 63 ("But the American... judge a case").

### WARM-UP #2: "JANE EYRE"

1) I'm gonna say heck yeah, because even in archaic fiction there's a story to follow. But maybe you're a political essay junkie, and you *like* reading paragraph after paragraph of the same twenty un-definable words written in different orders. To each her own.
2) Some of the early, non-dialogue stuff is a little hard to hang in there for, like the opening description of John, and the slightly confusing sentences at the end of the second paragraph. But hopefully it picked up for you when some of the talking and (pretty intense) violence started in the second half, and hopefully you were able to use the clear antagonism between the John and the main character as context for some of that tricky early stuff on your next pass through.
3) I'd definitely take a good look at the difficult section in lines 18 – 27 about how trapped and unsupported Jane is in her current situation. Also, John's nasty speech starting on line 55 seems like something the SAT test-makers would throw at you (seems like they might relate to the feeling of an unjust power trip...).

### WARM-UP #3: "THIS SIDE OF PARADISE"

1) An apt summary might be, "ugh New York is the worst amiright?" This is a vivid, cynical portrait of a place—in this case, the Big Apple—with a focus on the hordes of sad, poor, tired people who live there, and just how hard it is to get through a New York day.
2) That longggg sentence from line 32 to 43 is definitely not a cinch. Phantasma-what-was-that? Also, "moulded of mire." Sometimes you just have to tip your hat to the author and keep plowing on for clues about what in tarnation you just read.
3) That personification of New York in lines 21-22 is a testmaker's dream, and *definitely* ponder what that change of pace at the end is all about. Suddenly these wretched New Yorkers have a "glow" about them? I'd bet my Warby Parkers that they're going to ask you what's up with that.

### WARM-UP #4: "ON WOMEN'S RIGHT TO VOTE"

1) Anthony lays down the law, literally, when she quotes from the Constitution. She evokes the highest legal authority in the land right up top, and then goes on to show how that most powerful of documents unequivocally supports her position. She also uses some all-star parallelism in lines 40-49 when she daisy chains a couple "To them" sentences, a couple "It is" sentences, and a sequence of powerhouse lines beginning with "an oligarchy."
2) Wait, what? You mean you didn't know what a "bill of attainder" was? Or an "ex post facto law?" Just kidding, that's some first-class legal gobbledygook right there. But hopefully the sentences and paragraphs around that helped to clarify that Anthony thinks depriving women the right to vote is against the Constitution, and therefore illegal.
3) I could imagine a tricky little question about lines 27 – 32 ("And it is... the ballot), and what it says about Anthony's governing ethos. Also, what's she arguing at the very end there? The SAT is probably going to want to know that you know (Hint: She's taking a page from ol' Freddy D's book from earlier in the section).

## EVIDENCE BUDDIES

### HARRY POTTER AND THE HALF-RIGHT EVIDENCE

1) **B**

You might've been lured in by choice D, but

do you see now how only the first half feels right? Don't stop reading partway through! The author definitely isn't saying anything about "accommodating" autonomous vehicles—he's actually urging the public to be extremely thoughtful/skeptical about them.

**2) C**

See how this piece of evidence directly supports the idea of using morals to dictate a "new legal model" about automated cars? Again, choice D is half-right. That word "proactively" is realllly tempting, but that whole second half about a "public backlash" is codswallop.

## CHARTS AND GRAPHS

### MEET THE GRAPHS

**1) D**

These questions are all about *what the charts are actually saying.* Choice C isn't correct because it doesn't say anything about connecting to the internet, and the charts aren't about user *preference,* though it's very easy to make that incorrect logical leap.

**2) C**

Choice B references "computing," not internet connection, and also there's that word "preference" again.

**3) C**

Choice A is too absolute—the graph doesn't support sweeping claims about "any student," only the "average" one. Choice D looks good if you're doing this problem at near light-speed, but a closer look shows us that the graph doesn't distinguish between different kinds of graduate degrees.

**4) C**

If you answered choice B, oops! You looked at the full bar didn't you? Make sure to pay close attention to different colors and shades on SAT charts and graphs, because those test-makers *love* tripping up students on tedious little details like that. They love it, like, a weird amount.

**5) A**

Definitely brush up on the term "correlation" before your test. Lucky for you, we're going review it in the Math section in a couple chapters! (Seriously, stop thanking me—I don't do it for the praise. Well, I don't do it *entirely* for the praise.) By the way, if you answered choice B on this question, you were right that the trend is upward, or "positive," but the points aren't *that* close to the trend line, so the first part of the answer choice is off the mark.

**6) A**

Jeez, what an aggressively confusing map-passage-question combo. You might be better off answering this if it were written in Latin (especially if you took four years of Latin because you didn't get the memo that Vocab isn't an SAT section anymore). Basically, despite all of the other intentionally distracting information being thrown at you, the only part of this graphic that matters is that two African countries are shaded in as being "Countries at Risk" (yup, Madagascar's technically a part of Africa, kids). Choice B is wrong mostly because the data in the map say absolutely nothing about habitats being "likely" to do anything—that's another one of those dangerous logical leaps. Choice C and D are both irrelevant to the specific question being asked.

## VOCABULARY

**1) C**
**2) A**
**3) B**

See the explanations within the chapter for these three questions, friends!

4 PASSAGES

# 11 questions for each one

? HOW LONG?

35 MINUTES

*that's ~47 seconds per question*

# WRITING & LANGUAGE
## The Breakdown

**DID YOU KNOW**
Writing and Language counts for half of your SAT Reading score

**THE EDITORIAL STUFF**
logic and organization

**THE TECHNICAL STUFF**
sentence structure and punctuation

**DO** **KNOW THE RULES OF GRAMMAR.** THEY ARE ON EVERY TEST, AND THEY NEVER CHANGE.

**DON'T** **FORGET TO READ.** THE EDITORIAL QUESTIONS FREQUENTLY RELY ON WHAT IS IN THE PASSAGE.

Tutor Ted®

# A Pep Talk

**Writing & Language is the part of the SAT—the *only one*—that lets you know the SAT does not want to make you suffer.**

By comparison to the rest of the SAT, this section is the equivalent of a warm hug from your Grandma Judy. Of course, by comparison to rest of your life, it's like getting waterboarded in a detention camp, but let's take what we can get, right? Small victories?

Here's why I like this section so much: it's the easiest, quickest place to improve your score. Why? It tests the same stuff over and over again.

I'm going to teach you stuff like the difference between **"it's"** and **"its,"** the proper use of a semicolon, and how to find the answers to questions about the content of the passage. Once you know that stuff, guess what? You can't be fooled! You'll know everything there is to know. That includes the technical rules and the sneaky ways the College Board has of trying to make a question more difficult.

Plus, there's an added benefit to learning what's on the Writing & Language test. Since the rules of grammar are constant and universal, you're actually learning something that is useful to you in your life. You are actually becoming a better writer.

**What do you say? Let's build your Writing & Language score and make you a better writer, huh?**

## It's a win-win!

# The Details

Quick note before we get started: I break Writing and Language into two separate sections, the Technical Stuff and the Editorial Stuff. Here's an overview:

### The Technical Stuff

These questions test your grammar know-how—stuff like punctuation and sentence structure. Because these questions are based on fixed rules, you can learn all of this. Once you do, you'll lower your chance of making an error to nearly zero.

### The Editorial Stuff

Editorial questions ask you to think about how well an essay said what it was trying to say. These guys tackle how the essay should be organized, whether you should include an additional sentence, and even what the main idea of a passage is. Each question type has its own way that you can attack it, and you bet we're going to learn what those are.

Let's start with the Technical Stuff.

# THE TECHNICAL STUFF

You think you know how to use a comma, right? But do you *really* know? Most people take on grammar questions based on what "feels right" or "sounds right" to them. That instinctive knowledge is valuable! Now, let's pair it with the technical side of grammar—the reasons *why* what feels right is right. When you pair your good instincts with the knowledge that's on the test, you will become unstoppable. There won't be a question you can't handle.

Ready to pair that knowledge with your instincts? OK, let's go.

## HOW TO BUILD A SENTENCE

### Let's start with a simple question: how do you make a sentence?

To make a sentence, you need a subject and a verb. You also need to express a complete thought. The phrase, **"I grilled a giant piece of tofu,"** is a sentence because it's got a subject *("I")*, a verb *("grilled")*, and it expresses a complete thought.

On the other hand, the phrase, **"because my girlfriend is a vegetarian,"** is not a sentence, because it doesn't express a complete thought. Why not? It comes down to that word "because." That word at the beginning of the sentence turns it into an incomplete thought.

You are probably thinking, "hey, I could put those two phrases together to make a sentence." Or maybe you're thinking, "hey, I wonder what funny memes will come out of the PSAT this year?" Either way, **let's talk about how you can put those phrases together to make a sentence.**

## INDEPENDENT AND DEPENDENT CLAUSES

**An independent clause** is a clause *(a group of words with a subject and verb)* that can stand alone as a sentence. Basically, independent clause is a fancy name for a sentence.

### Here are some examples of independent clauses:

I never learned to read.

Smoking kills.

Sarah went to the market to stock up on Vitamin C.

Don't open it under any circumstances

I have to tell you about the hilarious thing I found in my bed this morning.

**A dependent clause** is a clause that expresses an incomplete thought. It has a subject and a verb, but it cannot stand alone as a sentence.

**Check out the examples of dependent clauses below:**

Although I have opened a book before

Whether you're riding in a car or talking on the phone

If you find a letter in the mailbox today

Because George felt bad about hurting Malia's feelings

Before we start today's lesson

Just because those dependent clauses can't stand on their own doesn't mean they can't be part of a sentence, though. Here are some of the ways you can combine clauses to create what's called **a complex sentence.**

## INDEPENDENT CLAUSE + DEPENDENT CLAUSE

Here's a common way people combine clauses—the most commonly used sentence construction in all of English, probably. Examples:

I grilled a giant piece of tofu because my girlfriend is a vegetarian.

I never learned to read although I have opened a book before.

I'd like to tell you a joke before we get started today.

We're going to get into comma rules in a few pages, but notice that we didn't use a comma when we put the independent clause first and follow it with the dependent clause. Look...you're learning grammar! And it's not totally terrible!

## DEPENDENT CLAUSE + COMMA + INDEPENDENT CLAUSE

This is the slightly racier version of the previous structure. It's like the PG-13 of sentence structures. Sadly there is no R-rated sentence structure. Don't even ask me about NC-17.

**When you start a sentence with a dependent clause, you have to put a comma after it before you get to the independent clause. Just like I just did!** That was accidental...but let's pretend it was a really, really good teaching moment instead.

Examples:

Before we start today's lesson, I have to tell you about the hilarious thing I found in my bed this morning.

If you find a letter in the mailbox today, don't open it under any circumstances.

Because he desperately needed supplies to build his diorama, Tony ran to the store.

That last sentence blows wide open a widespread grammar conspiracy... a grand conspiracy that goes all the way to the White House. You can start a sentence with the word "because." Wow. This might be heavy, so take a minute if you need it, OK? Yeah, you can start a sentence with because—you just need to follow that dependent clause with a comma and an independent clause.

## INDEPENDENT CLAUSE + SEMICOLON + INDEPENDENT CLAUSE

Why should two independent clauses not be able to join together and become one complete sentence? This is 21st century America!

You can put two independent clauses together; you just need to do so with a semicolon. Your next question might be about the usage of the semicolon—as in, when is the right time to use one? The most common use of a semicolon is when you have two closely related ideas, ideas so closely related that they need to be in the same sentence.

Why not just use a period? That's a good question. The author **Kurt Vonnegut** (he's crazy and great, check him out) said that the only thing semicolons do is prove that you went to college. It's a burning controversy in the hellish, fiery pit of grammar debate. My recommendation is that you learn how to use one so you can ace these questions on the SAT then decide for yourself whether you want to use them in your own writing.

> Please excuse the mess; we're just not into cleaning.
>
> Some people find the pop song catchy; others say that it's mushy and annoying.
>
> Never tell a lie to prove a point; you're more likely to embarrass yourself than change somebody's mind.

## INDEPENDENT CLAUSE + COMMA + COORDINATING CONJUNCTION + INDEPENDENT CLAUSE

One more piece of technical grammar training: the coordinating conjunctions are these seven little words:

***For***
***And***
***Nor***
***But***
***Or***
***Yet***
***So***

They are widely known by the acronym "FANBOYS." They also hang out at comic book stores whenever they aren't playing Halo on XBox.

"Wait, 'coordinating conjunction'?... aren't you getting a little TOO technical, Ted?" Look, I don't like it either. Believe me when I say that we try to keep our grammar prep as non-technical as possible. If I ever do introduce a technical term, it's because it's actually really helpful to know it. This one is such a key building block of sentences, that, yes, you actually want to learn what a coordinating conjunction is.

**Examples:**

Smoking kills, but clowns do too.

You can fit 20 clowns in a car, so clown transportation is really quite efficient.

I did not order a clown, nor did anyone else in this office.

## HOW NOT TO BUILD A SENTENCE

**Here is a red flag SAT error, a way you absolutely can't build a sentence.** You want to learn this because I can promise you the SAT will include this on every single test. OK, you ready?

My dad says that this rash is not contagious, he's a dermatologist.

See if you can break down the sentence. It's an independent clause ("My dad says this rash is not contagious"), then a comma, then another independent clause ("he's a dermatologist"). **That grammar mistake is so common it has its own name. It's called a comma splice**—aka two independent clauses separated by just a comma.

Train yourself to look for those, OK? You'll turn into a grammar ace once you can spot them.

## OK! Let's see what you know.

## EXERCISE #1: How Closely Were You Paying Attention

**1**

Identify the independent clause among the choices below:

A) While my grandmother is a martial arts master.

B) Because my grandmother is a martial arts master.

C) My grandmother is a martial arts master.

D) That my grandmother is a martial arts master.

**2**

Identify the dependent clause in the complex sentence below:

Those are the splintered boards that she broke with her pinkie.

A) Those are the splintered boards

B) that she broke with her pinkie.

**3**

Identify the independent clause in the complex sentence below:

When she goes grocery shopping in town, people move out of her way.

A) When she goes grocery shopping in town,

B) people move out of her way.

**4**

Identify the FANBOYS conjunction in the sentence below:

My grandmother is actually a sweet lady, but my friends are too scared to come over.

A) My

B) a

C) but

D) to

**5**

Consider the sentence below and select ALL that apply:

I couldn't open the pickle jar, so I asked my grandmother to do it.

A) This sentence has two dependent clauses.

B) This sentence has a FANBOYS conjunction.

C) This entire sentence is an independent clause.

D) This sentence has two independent clauses.

## EXERCISE #2: Let's do some SAT questions

Let's look at a few questions about clauses that you might see on the SAT. Read each sentence and choose the option that you think best replaces the underlined portion.

**1**

Since the word got out about my grandmother. The bullies at school never mess with me.

A) NO CHANGE
B) my grandmother: The bullies
C) my grandmother, the bullies
D) my grandmother and the bullies

**2**

She has been known to carry seven concrete blocks on her forehead. Before smashing the blocks into smithereens with that very same forehead.

A) NO CHANGE
B) forehead before
C) forehead, before,
D) forehead; before

**3**

People joke about how tough the actor Chuck Norris is, they would cry tears of blood if they saw my grandma in action.

A) NO CHANGE
B) is. And they
C) is they
D) is, but they

## EXERCISE #3: Let's fix some sentences because why not?

Insert commas, semicolons, and/or conjunctions to fix the following sentences. ***Warning:*** some sentences may be correct as written.

1. The game was over the crowd refused to leave.
2. While I was making dinner my dog started barking outside.
3. The band played for three hours and never took a set break.
4. If you are sick you shouldn't ride the subway.
5. He followed the team for fifty years it hardly mattered whether the team won or lost.
6. It isn't easy being tall but it's even harder to be short.
7. Maria is my only sister she is dutiful and decent.
8. Because Lana was so difficult to work with the studio decided to hire another actress.
9. This Twitter feed doesn't make any sense it reads like it is written by a computer.
10. The city could no longer call on Batman when local criminals began to cause problems.
11. To get a ticket you'd better buy online.
12. The famous designer decided that the town needed something really grand at its center he proposed a rose garden flanked by cascading waterfalls.

## HOW TO USE A COMMA

Guess how many ways there are to use a comma? Four. There are only four ways to use a comma. Can you learn four ways to use a comma? Yeah you can.

(OK, fine, there are a couple of other places we use commas, like before a quotation or between the thousands and hundreds place of a number...but there are only four ways to use a comma that you need to worry about on the SAT.)

**So here they are!** The four ways you need to think about when it comes to commas on the SAT. Here's a piece of good news too: you've learned two of these already.

***Hot Tip:*** These are the four ways when you want to use a comma on the SAT. If you are not in one of these four situations, you want to get rid of any commas. If you don't need one, don't include one. On the SAT, you should get rid of as many commas as possible!

### *WAY #1: USE A COMMA WHEN A SENTENCE STARTS WITH A DEPENDENT CLAUSE FOLLOWED BY AN INDEPENDENT CLAUSE.*

Boring, well-adjusted people start their sentences with an independent clause and follow it with a dependent clause. Like this:

> I jogged to work because my car had broken down.

Creative, eccentric, and/or unstable people reverse the order and put the dependent clause first. When they do that, they have to include a comma after the dependent clause.

> Because my car had broken down, I jogged to work.
>
> Although I am a pretty fast runner, I was still 10 minutes late to the morning meeting.

## EXERCISE #1: Just, add, commas,

Insert commas where needed in the following sentences.

1. While the Senator made his speech on Capitol Hill the activists organized outside.
2. After succumbing to pressure from animal rights activists the amusement park agreed not to keep Orca whales in captivity.
3. If the chef finds even the smallest objection to the dish he will send it back to the kitchen in anger.

### *WAY #2: USE A COMMA AND A COORDINATING CONJUNCTION **(FANBOYS)** WHEN LINKING TWO INDEPENDENT CLAUSES.*

Remember this? You just insert a comma and a coordinating conjunction (For, And, Nor, But, Or, Yet, So) to link two independent clauses.

**Samples:**

I'm pretty quick, but it's not like I'm Usain Bolt or anything.

I ran track in high school, so I know a thing or two about running.

To be honest, I was on the JV team, and we basically just stood and kicked the shot put around.

## EXERCISE #2: Where my FANBOYS at?

Fix these sentences with a comma and a FANBOYS conjunction.

1. Maria went to the market to buy groceries she forgot to bring her shopping list.
2. Professor Thompson loved the idea of teaching English full time he begged the president of the university to give him a chance to prove himself.
3. Naomi Foner wrote the screenplay to *Losing Isaiah* and *Running on Empty* her son, Jake Gyllenhaal, is far more well known.

### *WAY #3: USE COMMAS TO SEPARATE ITEMS IN A LIST OR MULTIPLE ADJECTIVES THAT DESCRIBE THE SAME NOUN.*

As I am sure you know, commas are handy for separating items in a list. Like so:

The doctor recommended plenty of rest some crackers and soda and a warm bath.

**That sentence is in desperate need of some commas, right?** One after rest, and one after soda? That's pretty basic, but let me share one more thing that's SAT-relevant. The SAT always includes what's called the Oxford Comma—the last comma before the "and" in a list. Example:

People have said my running style reminds them of a cross between an ostrich, a lemur, and a drunken Scotsman wearing a hat that's on fire.

The Oxford Comma is the one right before the "and." Just want to point that out to you because the SAT always includes it.

You also use commas to separate multiple adjectives that describe the same noun. For example:

a dusty heavy book

should be

a dusty, heavy book

because the two adjectives (dusty and heavy) each describe the book.

There is a trick here too, a situation when you do NOT use a comma to separate multiple adjectives: when one of the adjectives is so connected to the noun that together they become a unit.
**An example of that:**

the local organic grocery store

should NOT be written out as

the local, organic, grocery store

What's the difference? It has to do with the fact that the adjectives belong closely to the noun. Here's a trick that ALWAYS works to help you decide whether you need to include a comma between adjectives: ask yourself if you would include the word "and" between them. If the answer is yes ("a dusty and heavy book"), then include the comma; if the answer is no ***("the local and organic and grocery store")***, then you don't need a comma.

## EXERCISE #3: Comma, comma, and comma

Insert commas where needed in the following sentences.

1. I picked up grapefruit juice salt and soda from the local grocery store.
2. I never had a mom a dad a dog a friend or a good night's sleep.
3. When I looked into her eyes, I saw a wild angry animal.
4. To think clearly to feel deeply to love constantly: these are the objectives of an evolved human being.
5. My silent happy sister simply nodded her head in amazement.

### *WAY #4: USE COMMAS TO BRACKET OFF* ***"INESSENTIAL INFORMATION."***

By **"inessential information,"** I mean clauses (or words) that could be removed from the sentence without destroying the main idea of the sentence. **Take a look at this sentence:**

The Statue of Liberty, which sits in New York Harbor, is a cherished symbol of freedom.

The phrase **"which sits in New York Harbor"** is inessential in that sentence because it could be taken out without disrupting the functional parts of the sentence: **"The Statue of Liberty is a cherished symbol of freedom."**

I KNOW I promised not to get too technical... but I can't help myself here. **Inessential phrases like these are called "appositive phrases." Now you know.**

***Hot Tip***: Sometimes inessential phrases show up at the beginning or at the end of a sentence. In that case, you only need ONE comma to separate it from the rest of the sentence. Example of that:

Wearing a pair of bargain store high heels, I was not exactly in peak running performance condition.

## EXERCISE #4: Revenge of the Comma

Use a pair of commas (or just one comma) to bracket off inessential clauses or words.

1. My cousin Jared who I had never met until I was an adult plays soccer for the L.A. Galaxy.
2. I took a trip to New Orleans the birthplace of jazz to celebrate my graduation from music school.
3. A bona fide recess expert my nephew expounded on the value of playing tag with his friends.
4. Irving's novel which took him twelve years to write suffers from its long, poetic passages.

Those are the four major ways that commas are used. Remember: If one of these four situations does not apply to a sentence on the SAT, get rid of those commas!

## EXERCISE #5: Were you listening to the Dude's story?

**1**

*Comma Situation #1:*
Use a comma when a sentence starts with a dependent clause followed by

A) another dependent clause.
B) an independent clause.
C) any type of clause.
D) a really, really needy clause.

**2**

*Comma Situation #2:*
Use a comma and a FANBOYS conjunction to

A) link two dependent clauses.
B) link two independent clauses.
C) get backstage at a Bieber concert.

**3**

Can you begin a sentence with "Because"?

A) Always.
B) In some cases.
C) Never.
D) Because I said so.

**4**

*Comma Situation #3:*
Use commas to separate

A) the subject and the verb.
B) adjectives and nouns.
C) the items in a list.
D) my two Siamese fighting fish, Hamilton and Jefferson.

**5**

If you see multiple adjectives describing the same noun, use a comma whenever

A) you could substitute the word "and" for the comma.
B) there are more than two adjectives in a row.
C) the adjectives have different suffixes.
D) you feed the Gremlins after midnight.

**6**

*Comma Situation #4:*
Use commas to bracket off

A) names and dates only.
B) indirect objects.
C) inessential information.
D) your neighbor's unbearably yippy dog.

**7**

If a phrase of inessential information shows up at the beginning or end of the sentence, set it off from the sentence with

A) a semicolon.
B) two commas.
C) one comma.
D) the fortress at Helm's Deep.

## EXERCISE #6: Let's do some SAT questions

Now let's look at a few questions involving commas that you might see on the SAT.

**1**

That experience convinced me of the value, of pre-screening all performers for my children's birthday parties.

A) NO CHANGE
B) me, of the value
C) me of the value
D) me, of the value,

**2**

However, my son still remembers that strange, inexplicable, afternoon with Igor the Clown as being one of the most amusing of his life.

A) NO CHANGE
B) strange, inexplicable afternoon,
C) strange, inexplicable afternoon
D) strange inexplicable afternoon

**3**

Igor, who was an English major in college and originally started working as a clown as a way to support himself while he wrote his first novel.

A) NO CHANGE
B) college, originally starting
C) college, originally started
D) college and

**4**

Identify the version of the sentence that correctly uses a comma and a FANBOYS conjunction to link two independent clauses:

A) The business card for the birthday party clown was riddled with misspellings, he was the cheapest in the entire city.
B) The business card for the birthday party clown was riddled with misspellings, but he was the cheapest in the entire city.
C) The business card for the birthday party clown was riddled with misspellings and he was the cheapest in the entire city.
D) The business card for the birthday party clown was riddled with misspellings; but he was the cheapest in the entire city.

**5**

Identify the version of the sentence that correctly uses a comma to connect a dependent clause with an independent clause that follows:

A) He forgot his balloons, because he had to make balloon animals out of some latex gloves we kept under the sink.
B) Because he forgot, his balloons he had to make balloon animals out of some latex gloves we kept under the sink.
C) He forgot his balloons, he had to make balloon animals out of some latex gloves we kept under the sink.
D) Because he forgot his balloons, he had to make balloon animals out of some latex gloves we kept under the sink.

**6**

Select the option below that grammatically finishes the start of this sentence:

The only supplies he brought with him were

A) a set of rusty juggling knives a Darth Vader mask and a stuffed canary in a cage.
B) a set of, rusty juggling knives, a Darth Vader mask and, a stuffed canary in a cage.
C) a set of rusty juggling knives, a Darth Vader mask, and a stuffed canary in a cage.
D) a set of rusty juggling knives, a Darth Vader mask, a stuffed canary in a cage.

**7**

Identify the version of the sentence that correctly uses commas to set off inessential information.

A) The clown, whose real name we later learned was Jeff, told all of the kids at the party that he was from the planet Zithnu.
B) The clown whose real name we later learned was Jeff, told all of the kids at the party, that he was from the planet Zithnu.
C) The clown, whose real name, we later learned was Jeff told all of the kids at the party that he was from the planet Zithnu.
D) The clown, whose real name we later learned was Jeff told all of the kids at the party, that he was from the planet Zithnu.

## HOW TO USE SEMICOLONS, COLONS, AND DASHES

### *THE SEMICOLON*

;

Look, it's winking! Adorable!

As mentioned way back in the first section, **the semicolon (;) functions pretty much just like a period:** you have to have an independent clause **(aka a complete sentence)** on either side.

Here are some examples of semicolons at work:

> Sarah lost a lot of money in Las Vegas this weekend; it's an easy thing to do.
>
> The first time I fell into the pool it was funny; the second time it was embarrassing.
>
> Carl Pumphrey was an honorable man; nevertheless, he occasionally told a white lie if it happened to suit his purposes.

### EXERCISE #1: The basics of semicolons

Use a semicolon where appropriate in the following sentences.

1. Invest early when saving for retirement your money will grow exponentially as a result.
2. My brother specializes in vintage organs and keyboards when he hears a recording, he can easily identify both the instrument and the amplifier it was played through.
3. Jethro really wanted a double chili cheeseburger however, he ordered a sensible salad.

On that last one, a lot of people are tempted to use a comma before the word "however," like so:

> Jethro really wanted a double chili cheeseburger, however, he ordered a sensible salad.

That's a problem, though, because that would create that "comma splice" thing: two separate sentences separated with just a comma.

You see, the word "however" (and similar words, like "thus" and "therefore") looks and sounds like a conjunction; however, since it's not one of the FANBOYS, we can't use it to join two independent clauses with just a comma. That's top-shelf SAT grammar stuff right there. Keep working to learn that and you'll be on your way to being a better writer (and a candidate for an 800 on this section).

Here's one way we DO use the word "however" and its cousins, like "thus" and "therefore."

First, look at this sample sentence:

> Mr. Neilson, who is my college counselor, has advised me to look at Engineering programs.

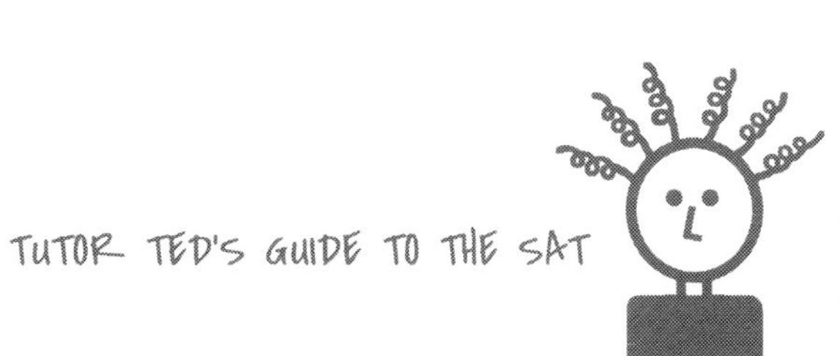

Just as "who is my college counselor" is simply an appositive clause within an independent clause, words like "however" can also be used between commas when they are unnecessary and removable within a sentence.

The reality, however, was much different.

The election results, therefore, were deemed invalid.

When you use words like "however" and "therefore" as removable, appositive-like phrases in the sentence, you can do so—you just need a comma on both sides.

## *THE COLON*

The colon is an essential part of your digestive system. It is also a piece of punctuation. Here's what a colon looks like.

:

And here are the rules for how to use them:

- It always has to follow an independent clause—that's a complete sentence, for those of you who have not picked that up yet.
- Don't use a colon after a word or phrase that's already setting up a list. In other words, don't use a colon after the words "for example" or "including."

**We use these guys in two different ways.**

To introduce a list. Examples:

The students were asked to bring only three things on the camping trip: a flashlight, a change of clothes, and a pocketknife.

Here's what you need to do in order to impress your boss: show up early, dress nicely, and speak your mind.

To extend, illustrate, or amplify an idea from the beginning of a sentence. Like so:

Samantha knew there was only one way to defeat the beast: punch it in its eye.

The magazine followed one simple rule: mock all people and cultures equally and relentlessly.

Keep in mind that the phrase that comes after the colon here can be an **independent clause or a dependent one.** Either way is fine—the rules for using the colon aren't as strict as those of the semicolon.

## *THE DASH*

—

The em-dash—also known as my favorite piece of punctuation—is easy to use and extremely versatile in a piece of writing.

**The dash can be used in a number of ways,** but on the SAT, dashes **are usually used to set off "inessential" information** in a sentence *(just like commas!)*. For example:

> Jared spent time on Oahu—the most populous of the Hawaiian Islands—before deciding to move back to Montana.

We call the information between the two dashes "inessential" because if we removed it, the sentence would still express a complete thought.

Dashes can also be used to express a sudden change in tone or thought within a sentence.

> I hope we can stay in Philadelphia for a little longer—or never leave at all!

## EXERCISE #2: The Easy Part

Answer the following questions based on what you just learned about semicolons, colons, and dashes.

**1**

You use a semicolon in the same situations where you would

A) use a dash
B) use a period
C) use a comma
D) use it or lose it

**2**

What do you ALWAYS need before a colon?

A) an independent clause
B) a list
C) a dependent clause
D) a small intestine

**3**

Select ALL of the options that can follow a colon.

A) a list
B) a dependent clause
C) an independent clause
D) a weird smell (jk don't choose this one)

**4**

Don't use a colon after a word or phrase that

A) finishes a thought
B) is a proper noun
C) is already setting up a list that follows
D) is about cologne

**5**

Use a pair of dashes to

A) set off inessential information
B) emphasize the subject and verb of the sentence
C) connect two independent clauses
D) run to two places very quickly

**6**

You can also use dashes to

A) create a dramatic pause
B) create a sudden change of tone
C) warm your SAT Essay grader's cold, iron heart
D) all of the above

**7**

Consider the following short passage and then choose the alternate version below that correctly integrates a semicolon:

Even though he was deathly afraid of heights, he applied for the job. Ever since he was was a boy, he had wanted to scrub skyscrapers.

A) Even though he was deathly afraid of heights; he applied for the job. Ever since he was was a boy, he had wanted to scrub skyscrapers.
B) Even though he was deathly afraid of heights, he applied for the job: Ever since he was was a boy, he had wanted to scrub skyscrapers.
C) Even though he was deathly afraid of heights, he applied for the job; ever since he was was a boy, he had wanted to scrub skyscrapers.
D) Even though he was deathly afraid of heights, he applied for the job, ever since he was was a boy; he had wanted to scrub skyscrapers.

**8**

Identify the grammatically correct version of the sentence:

A) During his first day on the job, the new window washer accidentally dropped a whole range of objects from his perch; car keys, wallet, loose change, inhaler, and several loads of vomit.
B) During his first day on the job, the new window washer accidentally dropped a whole range of objects from his perch: car keys, wallet, loose change, inhaler, and several loads of vomit.
C) During his first day on the job, the new window washer accidentally dropped a whole range of objects from his perch, car keys, wallet, loose change, inhaler, and several loads of vomit.
D) During his first day on the job, the new window washer accidentally dropped a whole range of objects from his perch. Car keys, wallet, loose change, inhaler, and several loads of vomit.

**9**

Identify the grammatically correct version of the sentence:

A) When one of the most senior window washers told him the secret trick for getting over his fear of heights: singing on the job.
B) Because one of the most senior window washers told him the secret trick for getting over his fear of heights: singing on the job.
C) Although one of the most senior window washers told him the secret trick for getting over his fear of heights: singing on the job.
D) One of the most senior window washers told him the secret trick for getting over his fear of heights: singing on the job.

**10**

Identify the version of the sentence that best sets off inessential information with dashes:

A) They promptly formed The Window Washers–a group that would go on to become Pennsylvania's most famous pop ensemble–and recorded their first single that very afternoon.
B) They promptly formed The Window Washers–a group that would go on to become Pennsylvania's most famous pop ensemble, and recorded their first single that very afternoon.
C) They promptly formed The Window Washers: a group that would go on to become Pennsylvania's most famous pop ensemble–and recorded their first single that very afternoon
D) They promptly formed–The Window Washers—a group that would go on to become Pennsylvania's most famous pop ensemble and recorded their first single that very afternoon.

## EXERCISE #3: The SAT-like Part

Now let's look at some semicolon, colon, and dash questions like the ones you'll see on the SAT.

**1**

All fans of workplace pop will appreciate The Window Washers' fear-fueled songwriting on their simple, but groundbreaking record, "Just Trying Not to Fall."

Choose the best answer.

A) NO CHANGE
B) simple
C) simple—
D) simple;

**2**

Despite the group's storied history of infighting, The Window Washers produced an impressive body of work, including: over 300 songs, 25 albums, and a feature-length, animated, sing-along film about Sam the Squeegee.

Choose the best answer.

A) NO CHANGE
B) work, including over,
C) work, it's over
D) work: over

**3**

The Window Washers were avid travelers—they still are: and they made a point of playing mid-air shows on the sides of skyscrapers all around the world.

Choose the best answer.

A) NO CHANGE
B) travelers, they still are—
C) travelers—they still are—
D) travelers and they still are

## SUBJECT-VERB AGREEMENT

We've been talking a lot about independent clauses and complete sentences. Meanwhile, we've skipped over the most basic building block of English: every sentence needs a subject and a verb, and the verb has to match its subject. **For example:**

"We is hungry" is wrong

and

"We are hungry" is correct.

Now here's the harder version: which of these is correct?

"Research into cosmic rays use the surface of the moon as a detector."

"Research into cosmic rays uses the surface of the moon as a detector."

**This is the classic subject-verb agreement trick. What is the subject of that sentence?** It's the first word of the sentence, **"research."** All that stuff that comes after **research**—"into cosmic rays"—serves as an adjective—that is, it describes **"research."** But it doesn't change the fact that **"research"** is the subject. The subject of the sentence is "research" and the verb should be **"uses."**

***Hot Tip:*** Look out for collective nouns when it comes to subject-verb agreement: Certain sneaky words ***(called collective nouns)*** represent groups but function as singular nouns. Words like team, family, gang, swarm, and bunch fit this category.

Here's a sample:

A family of raccoons lives in my backyard.

What is the subject, and what is the verb? That's the question you want to ask yourself on every one of these questions. Here, the subject is "family," (not "raccoons"). If "family" is the subject, then "lives" should be the verb because those two words match up: "A family lives."

***Hot Tip Part II:*** Certain pronouns are always singular. "Each," "every," and "any" are pronouns that always refer to ONE item within a group. Whenever you see one of those words, that subject is singular.

For example:

Each of the men was too terrified to enter the dance circle.

This sentence might sound strange because the plural "men" is right next to the singular verb "was." Since we're talking about "each" of the men, the singular verb is actually correct.

Keep in mind that some subjects are compound subjects. When two or more singular subjects are added together using the word "and," they become a plural subject. Like so:

Evan and Meg

As in...

Evan and Meg are two of our dearest friends.

Or...

Form and function

As in...

Form and function are the two factors we use to evaluate a new design.

Notice how in both of those cases, a singular subject plus another singular subject became a plural subject? It's literally the same as 1 + 1 = 2. When that happens—when we create a plural subject like that—we use a plural verb, like "are."

***Hot Tip:*** Suppose your sentence has an "either...or..." or "neither...nor..." around the subject. Now, suppose those two subjects are singular, as in "neither fame nor money." In that specific situation, the two subjects do NOT add up to become a plural, compound subject.

Sample:

Neither fame nor money motivates her to pursue professional success.

If you can believe it, that sentence is correct—"motivates" is the right conjugation of the verb in that spot. So beware "either...or..." and "neither...nor..."

## EXERCISE #1: Pick a Verb

Underline the subject and circle the form of the verb that agrees with it.

1. Anne and her family (**live**, **lives**) in that house.
2. The siding on the houses (**has**, **have**) been painted purple.
3. The basketball team (**hope**, **hopes**) to earn a trip to the playoffs this year.
4. Each of the songs on his record (**is**, **are**) an instant party-starter.
5. Economics (**was**, **were**) his declared major when he entered college.
6. The committee investigating differences in economic equality between racial and ethnic groups (**was**, **were**) organized by the state university.
7. Few of the houses (**is, are**) available for rent.
8. Either kale or arugula (**is, are**) my favorite vegetable.
9. Each of the teachers (**wear, wears**) a pin on her lapel.
10. Triton and Psamathe (**is, are**) two of the moons of Neptune.

## VERB TENSE

**Now you know that verbs have to match their subjects.** The other thing we need verbs to do is express a sense of timing. That's verb tense.

**For example, we might say:**

> "Yesterday, I ATE a sandwich."

or

> "I currently AM EATING another, even more delicious sandwich."

or

> "Tomorrow, I WILL EAT the greatest sandwich ever made by human hands."

**Whenever the SAT wants to test you on verb tense, it will give you some sort of sense of timing.** That could be a date, a timing word like "later," or another verb in the sentence that's in a certain tense. You have to have clues to determine what verb tense you need.

***Hot Tip:*** Keep verb tense in mind when it comes to inserting/moving a sentence around within a passage. It can give you the clue you need to put that sentence in the right place. We'll see that when we get to that chapter.

***Hot Tip Part II:*** Just like in the foreign language you study, we've got irregular verbs in English. Here's a list of the most commonly misused irregular past tense verbs in English. You don't need to memorize these, but I recommend reading through them 2-3 times and making sure you're comfortable with the weird ones (like "swum," which really is a word...)

**IRREGULAR VERB CHART**

| Infinitive | Simple Past | Past Participle |
|---|---|---|
| break | broke | broken |
| speak | spoke | spoken |
| awake | awoke | awoken |
| freeze | froze | frozen |
| forget | forgot | forgotten |
| get | got | gotten |
| ride | rode | ridden |
| rise | arose | risen |
| drive | drove | driven |
| write | wrote | written |
| eat | ate | eaten |
| fall | fell | fallen |
| give | gave | given |
| take | took | taken |
| shake | shook | shaken |
| put | put | put |
| quit | quit | quit |
| read | read | read |
| see | saw | seen |
| ring | rang | rung |
| sing | sang | sung |
| sink | sank | sunk |
| drink | drank | drunk |
| begin | began | begun |
| swim | swam | swum |
| come | came | come |
| run | ran | run |
| become | became | become |
| do | did | done |
| go | went | gone |
| grow | grew | grown |
| know | knew | known |
| throw | threw | thrown |
| fly | flew | flown |
| draw | drew | drawn |

How do you use that past participle tense? Simple: either with a helping verb, like has/have/had:

> I have swum in the pool twice this week.

Or as part of an adjective phrase, like so:

> Ridden down the steepest street in the neighborhood, the skateboard was hot to the touch due to the friction.

They're a little bit weird, aren't they? One of the reasons they sound weird to us is that people don't know how to use those words, so they avoid them. Since we don't hear them that often, they start to sound even weirder and more unfamiliar. It's a vicious cycle.

## EXERCISE #2: Pick a Tense

Pick the right verb tense based on the clues in the sentence.

**1**

Since 1965, the percentage of non-European immigrants to the United States grows steadily.

A) NO CHANGE
B) has grown
C) will grow
D) growing

**2**

By the time Marcel arrived, we waited for over three hours.

A) NO CHANGE
B) wait
C) were waiting
D) had been waiting

**3**

By the deadline next Tuesday, I wrote the entire essay.

A) NO CHANGE
B) have written
C) will have written
D) had written

**4**

Protozoa are single cell microorganisms.

A) NO CHANGE
B) were
C) have been
D) will have been

**5**

Candy bars have been enjoyed by millions ever since Joseph Fry introduced the first 'bar chocolate' to the world in 1847.

A) NO CHANGE
B) enjoyed
C) are enjoyed
D) were enjoyed

**6**

I toured Romania for six years after I become a pop star there.

A) NO CHANGE
B) have become
C) will have become
D) became

**7**

The musicians rehearsed long into the night and only realized that they had been playing for three straight hours when they looked at a clock.

A) NO CHANGE
B) play
C) has played
D) will play

**8**

Although Martin once has been a staunch advocate of the death penalty, years of experience as a public defender have made him reconsider its efficacy and fairness.

A) NO CHANGE
B) is
C) would have been
D) was

**9**

The idea of a flying car has been an unrealized dream for over a century, but when we do finally get flying cars, it will be pretty cool.

A) NO CHANGE
B) is
C) was
D) would be

**10**

She probably said yes if we had just asked her in the first place.

A) NO CHANGE
B) had said
C) would say
D) would have said

**11**

I had taken a bath when the doorbell rang.

A) NO CHANGE
B) was taking
C) took
D) had took

**12**

As a lifelong beach volleyball player, I generally spend a lot of time at the beach.

A) NO CHANGE
B) had spent
C) have spent
D) will have spent

## EXERCISE #3: Were You Paying Attention?

Answer the following questions about subject-verb agreement and verb tense.

**1**

What **two** things do verbs do for us in sentences?

A) match to the subject (tell us **who's** doing what)
B) describe the nouns
C) establish the tense of the sentence (tell us WHEN the action is happening)
D) become self-aware and plot against the human race

**2**

The part of the sentence connected to the verb – the thing **doing** the action–is called the

A) predicate
B) object
C) subject
D) sphincter

**3**

What tense should the verb(s) be in if a sentence begins with "A long time ago in a galaxy far, far away..."

A) past
B) future
C) present
D) any tense as long as Jar Jar Binks isn't there

**4**

Consider the following sentence and select the subject from the list below:

That GIF of the drunken cats was more sad than funny.

A) That
B) GIF
C) drunken cats
D) PETA

**5**

Consider the following sentence and select the subject from the list below:

The students taking the difficult chemistry test with their eyes closed, pencils broken, and papers upside-down are not really thinking this through.

A) students
B) test
C) eyes
D) pencils
E) papers
F) John Bender

## EXERCISE #4: SAT Time

Now let's look at a few questions about verbs that you might see on the SAT.

**1**

This lava spilled out, then hardened, forming the igneous bedrock that makes up the desolate islands.

A) NO CHANGE
B) is spilling
C) will spill
D) spills

**2**

My sister would drink from the stream by kneeling down on the slippery rocks and she submerged her head directly in the current.

A) NO CHANGE
B) which she would submerge
C) and submerging
D) that submerge

**3**

Once he was breaking open the piggy bank, he started to count the change that was inside: all $1.51 of it.

A) NO CHANGE
B) breaks
C) had break
D) had broken

**4**

Dedication to practice, mental toughness, and innate physical ability is one of the factors that determine whether or not a young athlete might be successful as a professional.

A) NO CHANGE
B) were one of the factors
C) are being some of the factors
D) are some of the factors

**5**

Evidence of seasonal deposits that may be linked with aqueous springs have been found by NASA's Mars Global Surveyor spacecraft.

A) NO CHANGE
B) having been found by
C) has found
D) has been found by

## PARALLELISM

The concept is pretty simple: whenever you have a list within a sentence—even a list with just two items—the format of the list has to be consistent.

Take a look at these two sentences. See if you can figure out which one has parallel structure.

> The First Amendment guarantees freedom of speech, freedom of the press, and freedom of assembly.
>
> The First Amendment guarantees freedom of speech, freedom of the press, and the people can assemble.

OK, that one's pretty easy. The first sentence has parallel structure. All of the items in the list are consistent because they all start with "freedom of..."

These can get harder, though. What about this one?

> Readers of the book's sequel have commented that it is at once familiar because of its similarity to the original but is trite and lacks creativity.
>
> Readers of the book's sequel have commented that it is at once familiar because of its similarity to the original and trite because of its lack of creativity.

Not as obvious, right? Here, the second sentence has parallel structure and the first one doesn't. Read the two comments about the book in the second sentence and keep an eye on the structure. The book is "familiar because of its similarity to the original" and "trite because of its lack of creativity." Notice how the format of those two comments is the same? They both have an adjective, then "because of," then a noun. That's parallel structure.

## EXERCISE #1: The Basics

First, let's make sure we know what parallel structure is.

1. Whenever you make a list within a sentence, all of the items need to:
   A) be the names of my two cats, TK and Max.
   B) keep a consistent grammatical format
   C) include the Oxford Comma
   D) listen to the Vampire Weekend song "Oxford Comma" right now

2. Select ALL of the following phrases that are parallel to each other.
   A) "...the steady rhythm of the beat..."
   B) "...the subtle melody of the string section..."
   C) "...the straight, soft tonality of the singer..."
   D) "...former UN Secretary General Boutros Boutros Ghali..."

## EXERCISE #2: Parallelism on the SAT

On these SAT-like questions, pick the version of the sentence with good parallel construction.

**1**

After she finished her philosophy doctorate, Marion found work as a consultant, a market analyst, and in the field of psychotherapy.

A) NO CHANGE
B) in consulting, analyzing markets, and later became a psychotherapist
C) as a consultant, a market analyst, and a psychotherapist
D) in consulting; later, in market analysis then as a psychotherapist

**2**

The film begins with human-like primates discovering primitive technology and when it ends humans have used technology to travel far out into space.

A) NO CHANGE
B) but by the ending humans have used
C) and ends with humans using
D) with the end when humans use

**3**

The school board member behaved like an ill-mannered child, pouting when her motion was defeated then refusing to consider any compromise.

A) NO CHANGE
B) and then would not consider
C) but would not consider
D) and not to consider

**4**

Before you can become a licensed therapist, you must earn an advanced degree, complete a certain number of clinical hours, and be passing a licensing exam.

A) NO CHANGE
B) a license exam must be passed by you
C) you need to pass a licensing exam
D) pass a licensing exam

**5**

Some people choose to drink tap water because it is environmentally friendly, others drink it because it is less expensive than bottled water.

A) NO CHANGE
B) Some people choose to drink tap water because it is environmentally friendly, but the others, they drink it because it is less expensive than bottled water.
C) Some people choose to drink tap water because it is environmentally friendly; others drink it because it is less expensive than bottled water.
D) With some people preferring tap water for its lesser expense, some others drink it because it is environmentally friendly.

**6**

Few popular musicians have courted as much controversy as Taylor Swift's career.

A) NO CHANGE
B) Taylor Swift
C) that of Taylor Swift
D) has the career of Taylor Swift

**7**

The fitness instructor Dove Rose tells her students to maintain proper form, completing each set, and taking breaks only when necessary.

A) NO CHANGE
B) complete each set and taking breaks only when necessary
C) with completion of each set and only taking breaks when necessary
D) complete each set, and take breaks only when necessary

**8**

Some say former President Jimmy Carter will be remembered as much for his humanitarian work after leaving the presidency than his time in office.

A) NO CHANGE
B) than he will be remembered for his time in office
C) as for his time in office
D) any more than his time in office

**9**

The noted critic wrote that the film was at once captivating because of its colorful characterizations but its pacing was ponderous.

A) NO CHANGE
B) although its pacing was ponderous
C) and it is ponderous in its pacing too
D) and ponderous because of its pacing

**10**

No journalist can claim absolute objectivity in recording the opinions of subjects; this journalist of the LA Times is no exception.

A) NO CHANGE
B) subjects, with this journalist of the LA Times being no exception
C) subjects; there is no exception for such a journalist as this one of the LA Times
D) subjects, while no exception can be made for this journalist of the LA Times

## PRONOUNS

Pronouns are stand-ins for nouns: he, she, it, they, etc. That way, instead of always having to say, **"that handsome devil, Tutor Ted,"** we can just say, **"him."**

Here's what you need to worry about when it comes to pronouns.

### *THE NOUN A PRONOUN REFERS TO HAS TO BE TOTALLY CLEAR.*

Pronouns always have an antecedent—the noun that they represent. If it's not clear which noun a pronoun represents, you've got a problem. **Here's an example:**

> The debt crisis created controversy in both Greece and Germany because
> it had not anticipated a downturn in economic growth.

**What does "it" refer to in that sentence?** We don't know! See, that's a problem. In that sentence, we need to restate the country that "had not anticipated a downturn" so the reader knows what the heck we're talking about.

### *PRONOUNS HAVE TO AGREE IN NUMBER TO THE NOUN THEY REPRESENT.*

If you've got a singular subject, you need a singular pronoun **(like "it")**, and if you have a plural subject, you need a plural pronoun **(like "they")**.

## EXERCISE #1: Literally the Easiest Quiz Ever

It might even be the easiest quiz in the history of the world. Are the following nouns plural or singular?

1. Zebras
2. Greek mythology
3. My cat TK
4. The Crab Nebula
5. The planets within our solar system
6. The universe, including all of spacetime, galaxies, stars, and planets

**Hot Tip:** Pronoun agreement gets tricky when it comes to collective nouns. You may remember from the Subject-Verb Agreement chapter that collective nouns are words that represent a group but operate as a singular noun—words like like "team," "tribe," or "family." You have to be careful with these guys—they seem plural but function grammatically like they are singular.

Here's an example:

The company insisted that they had no knowledge of the purported price fixing.

The pronoun "they" is incorrect there. It wants to refer to the "company," which is made up of a bunch of people but functions like a singular thing. Here's a corrected version:

The company insisted that it had no knowledge of the purported price fixing.

That still sounds strange, doesn't it? There's a good chance that whoever wrote that sentence would rewrite it to avoid the collective noun altogether. Since we're stuck with whatever sentences the SAT chooses to give us, we may not be able to avoid that awkwardness—so we might as well learn how to handle it, huh?

## EXERCISE #2: Pick a pronoun

Underline the antecedent for each pronoun and circle the pronoun that agrees with it.

1. Fans of the winning team showed (**its/their**) pride in a ticker tape parade down Main Street.
2. Some social conservatives argue that the traditional family model, and (**it/they**) alone, provides children with the best chance for future success.
3. While the debut album from the band was largely panned, (**its/their**) sophomore album has been touted as one of the best punk records in decades.
4. The Bonnaroo Music Festival features musicians and comedians that entertain the sizeable audience with (**its/their**) performances.
5. The city had a reputation for exceptional hospitality that was put to the test when (**it/they**) hosted football's Super Bowl in 2013.
6. Colin's collection of meteorites was sought after by astronomers who thought (**it/they**) could be put to better use in a laboratory.

## SUBJECT & OBJECT PRONOUNS

We've got one more pronoun situation: choosing between subject and object pronouns. Answering these questions is as easy as this question:

**Which of these is correct?**

Me am happy.

or...

I am happy.

You chose the second one, right? OK good, you know the difference between subject and object pronouns.

Here is a list of both:

***Subject: I, he/she, we, they, who***
***Object: me, him/her, us, them, whom***

We pick whether to use a subject or object pronoun depending on whether the pronoun is the subject of the verb *(the thing that's doing something)* or is the object of the verb (the thing that's receiving the action). For Example:

*I* do things, but things happen to *me*.

**These can get tricky when pronouns are compounded.** When you were young, your mom and dad might correct you for saying "Brian and me." Here's the thing: "Brian and me" is not always wrong—it depends on whether you're in the subject or object case. For instance, here's a situation where "Brian and me" is perfectly correct.

The sudden increase in business for our lemonade stand came as a surprise to Brian and me.

**Why is "me" correct here?** The reason is that "Brian and me" are indirect objects in this sentence.

Grammar terms aside, here's a great way to decide between using "I" and "me" when it comes to compound subjects: take Brian out of the sentence, then ask yourself whether you'd use "I" or "me" on its own. Did it come as a surprise to me, or did it come as a surprise to I? **"Me"** sounds a lot better in that version, right? That's because **"me"** is the right pronoun.

When you're in doubt about a subject or object pronoun, make your decision based on **how the sentence sounds** when you remove the other noun.

**Hot Tip:** The difference between "who" and "whom" is the exact same thing as the difference between "I" and "me." An easy way to choose between them is to ask yourself whether you'd answer a who/whom question with "I" or "me." If the answer is "I," you want "who," and if the answer is "me," you want "whom."

## EXERCISE #3: I versus me, etc.

**Instructions:** Pick which pronoun is the correct one to use in the following sentences.

1. They told the children that **(he/him)** is on a long vacation rather than in prison.
2. To Jeff and **(I/me)**, the news came as a surprise.
3. The committee finally agreed that the prize should be awarded to both **(we/us)** and **(they/them)**.
4. They gave the new blueprints to the development office and **(we/us)**.
5. Written by **(he/him)** and **(I/me)**, the new pamphlet is sure to revolutionize the world of 21st century pamphlets.
6. In the event of an evacuation, **(who/whom)** should I contact first?
7. For **(us/we)** teachers, the new world of education technology is both exciting and overwhelming.
8. With **(who/whom)** are you planning to meet?
9. **(Who/whom)** wrote the screenplay for that cult-favorite television show?
10. You have to choose between Susie and **(I/me)**.

## EXERCISE #4: Did you read this chapter?

**1**

Pronouns are

A) words used to connect clauses
B) stand-ins for nouns
C) articles
D) marine crustaceans that resemble large shrimp

**2**

Which of the following is NOT a pronoun?

A) I
B) you
C) she
D) the
E) we

**3**

Which of the following is a subject pronoun (it DOES something)?

A) him
B) me
C) I
D) her
E) Oh never mind, prawns is the word I was thinking of.

**4**

Which of the following is an object pronoun (it has something DONE TO it)?

A) we
B) them
C) he
D) they
E) Did you know people eat crawfish?

**5**

Select ALL that apply to using pronouns:

A) It has to be clear to what the pronoun is referring.
B) A pronoun can only be used in an independent clause.
C) A pronoun has to match in number to the noun it represents.
D) Seriously, there's a thing called a crawfish boil.

**6**

Which of the following pronouns is NOT strictly a plural pronoun?

A) they
B) them
C) you
D) their

**7**

Which is the correct pronoun for collective nouns like "family" and "company"?

A) it
B) they
C) their
D) They're basically like underwater insects, but apparently they're delicious.

**8**

What's the best technique for deciding whether to use "I" or "me" after another person ("Brian and I/me") in a sentence?

A) Always use "I".
B) Always use "me".
C) Don't ever use "I" or "me".
D) Remove the other person from the sentence and see which pronoun makes sense.
E) Invite your friends and family over and hash it out over a steaming pot of boiled crawfish.

## EXERCISE #5: Some SAT pronoun questions

Now let's look at a few questions about pronouns that you might see on the SAT.

**1**

The raging wildfire that tore through the preserve for most of July scorched all trees, grasses, and topsoil in its path.

A) NO CHANGE
B) on their
C) in their
D) on its

**2**

There is a new, divisive opinion among some modern art critics that they can better understand pieces by looking to their one side rather than directly at them.

A) NO CHANGE
B) one side of them
C) they're side
D) one's side

**3**

On September 26, the first army battalion marched through the streets of the capital, displaying their awesome might and striking fear into the hearts of the civilians who remained.

A) NO CHANGE
B) they're
C) that they
D) its

## POSSESSIVES

You know that apostrophes form contractions like "don't," or "can't." Right? Great.

You may also know that we use apostrophes to show possession.

If Charlie owns a hat, **you can say that it's Charlie's hat.**

If Lisa owns a scarf, then **that's Lisa's scarf.**

If Lisa thinks that she's the rightful owner of Charlie's hat, then Charlie might say that **that's Lisa's problem.**

And people aren't the only ones that can possess other things. **For instance, you can say**

the painting's brilliant colors

or the fire's warm glow

or the day's end

So to show possession, you just add a quick "apostrophe s." But what if you have a subject that's already plural? What if two boys own hats? In that situation, you start with the plural noun (boys), and simply add an apostrophe at the end of the word (boys'). You don't need to bother adding another "s." You just write **"boys' hats."**

### *IT'S A SPECIAL OCCASION: IT'S VS. ITS*

Here's the old "exception to the rule." Don't you love those? "Its" and "it's" trip some folks up because they seem to break the rules. Here's what you've got to do: memorize this simple rule:

it's = "it is," or "it has"

its = possessive form of "it"

**Got it?** So if you want to say,

"It is a good idea to invest in the stock market,"

you would say

"it's a good idea."

If, on the other hand, you wanted to say how much you loved a painting's beautiful colors, you would say

"I sure do love its beautiful colors."

One thing that's NOT a thing is this word:

its'

That thing is not a word. Just... no. If you see it on the SAT, it is wrong, 100% of the time.

## EXERCISE #1: it's versus its

Choose between "it's" and "its" in the following sentences.

1. **It's/Its** time to go home.
2. This house has **it's/its** own power plant.
3. **It's/Its** a good idea to wear a shirt if you go to the opera.
4. Do you think **it's/its** ready?
5. I saw the play during **it's/its** initial run.
6. **It's/Its** been a long, hot summer.

## POSSESSIVE WORDS AND THEIR SOUND-A-LIKE FRIENDS

### Their, There, and They're; You're and Your; Who's, and Whose

Here's the next set of guys you want to memorize. Trust me, you'll be a much better writer when you know how you're supposed to use these!

**they're** = **"they are"** (like "it's," it's a conjunction)

**their** = the possessive form of **"they"**

**there** = a place or position *(over there)*

**you're** = **"you are"** (another conjunction)

**your** = the possessive form of **"you"**

**who's** = **"who is"**–or– **"who has"** (yep…a conjunction!)

**whose** = the possessive form of **"who"**

## EXERCISE #2: Let the right one in

Pick a word to correctly complete these sentences.

1. I wonder what **they're/their/there** discussing.
2. **Who's/Whose** sweatshirt is that?
3. **They're/Their/There** cat is pregnant again.
4. **You're/Your** going to need stitches on **you're/your** forehead.
5. We are going to **they're/their/there** house next time.
6. **Whose/Who's** coming over for lunch?
7. Have you seen **they're/their/there** new Buick?
8. **You're/Your** invited to the party.

## EXERCISE #3: Easy does it

First, the basics.

**1**

Select the TWO uses of an apostrophe from the list below:

A) creating a contraction
B) matching a pronoun with its subject
C) showing possession
D) freaking out all of its punctuation mark friends by creepily levitating

**2**

People are the only subjects that can possess other things.

A) true
B) false
C) Do evil spirits count?

**3**

Consider the sentence below and select the best answer:

I admired the building's intricate design.

A) The building belongs to me.
B) The intricate design belongs to the building.
C) The building belongs to the intricate design.
D) It had those crazy Airblade hand dryers in all the bathrooms.

**4**

When multiple girls bake multiple pies, you refer to these desserts as

A) the girls pies
B) the girl's pies
C) the girls' pies
D) What kind of pie? It's important to know.

**5**

"It's" represents

A) "it is" or "it has"
B) "it is" or "it was"
C) the possessive form of "it"
D) Stephen King's crowning achievement, hands down

**6**

Which of the following is just really not a thing?

A) its
B) it's
C) its'
D) January 21st: National Squirrel Appreciation Day

**7**

"Their" is

A) a place
B) the plural possessive form of "they"
C) a contraction of "they are"
D) a fake word because i before e, amiright?

**8**

"Who's" is

A) a contraction of "who is" or "who has"
B) the possessive form of who
C) another spelling of whose
D) the sound of an owl and a snake arguing

## EXERCISE #4: Now, some SAT questions

Now let's look at a few questions about apostrophes that you might see on the SAT.

**1**

Though dysentery halted the groups progress for a month, they were back on the Oregon Trail soon enough.

A) NO CHANGE
B) group's progress for a month,
C) groups' progress for a month,
D) group's progress for a month

**2**

The legendary writer and naturalist began his observations during childhood, in the forests around his familys' home in western Massachusetts.

A) NO CHANGE
B) family's
C) families'
D) Families

**3**

A long period of "salutary neglect" from the British crown ensued, and its' effect on the development of state and national identity in the colonies was immeasurable.

A) NO CHANGE
B) it's
C) among historians, it's
D) its

## THAT VS. WHICH: GRAMMAR DEATHMATCH

That vs. which—there can only be one! You'll have to know the difference between how these guys are used when you take the SAT.

When learning that difference, I am going to do you a huge solid and NOT teach you about restrictive and non-restrictive clauses. You don't even know how nice I am being to you right now, but you're welcome.

Instead, I'm going to show you the difference. Think about the difference between these two phrases and how you'd use them in a sentence.

The play that premiered in New Jersey

The play, which premiered in New Jersey,

In the first phrase—the one that uses "that"—notice how the descriptive phrase is more closely tied to the play than the "which" phrase in the second. The phrase "the play that premiered in New Jersey" is referring to one thing, and it's important that we know it premiered in New Jersey.

In the "which" version, you could lift the "which" phrase out of the sentence if you like. It's inessential, like those appositive phrases we learned about earlier. In fact, that phrase IS an appositive phrase.

Here's how you might finish up the sentences that start with those phrases:

> The play that premiered in New Jersey was much the same as the regional production in Pasadena.
>
> The play, which premiered in New Jersey, was lauded by critics and would go on to win the Pulitzer Prize for Drama.

When we use the "that" version, we're more closely tied to that description of the play. When we use the "which" version, we can pretty much take the sentence in any direction we want.

***Hot Tip:*** Whether you have a comma or not will determine whether to use "which" or "that." We ALWAYS use a comma with a "which" phrase, and we NEVER use one with a "that" phrase. Look for the comma (or the absence of a comma) and you'll know right away which choice is correct.

## EXERCISE #1: The one that just involves basic reading

Warm-up.

1. Descriptive phrases are more essential and closely tied to what they're describing when they start with
   A) that.
   B) which.
2. We always use a comma before a descriptive phrase beginning with
   A) that.
   B) which.

## EXERCISE #2: It it that, or is it which?

Is it which or is it that?

1. Nassau Hall **that/, which** is the oldest building on campus, was constructed in 1756.
2. The Red Car is the name of the old public transit system **that/, which** operated in Los Angeles in the early 20th century.
3. I'm sorry to say, but the cat **that/which** I saw in our yard exploded yesterday.
4. Curling **that/, which** is the second most popular sport in Canada, has become surprisingly popular worldwide.
5. The regional accent **that/, which** you have depends both on where you were born and how long your family has lived there.

## MISPLACED MODIFIERS

Last but *certainly* not least, my favorite grammar topic: misplaced modifiers. This one is great. Once you know this rule, the questions become so easy it almost feels like you're cheating.

Here's the deal: whenever a sentence starts with a phrase like these two...

> Hoping to see her friends,
>
> Driven to the brink of extinction,

...the very next thing in the sentence has to be whatever those modifying clauses are describing.

For instance, in the first example you could follow the modifying clause with something like:

> Hoping to see her friends, Mary went to the coffee shop.

You could NOT write...

> Hoping to see her friends, the coffee shop was Mary's destination.

...because the coffee shop was not hoping to see her friends. Coffee shops don't have friends.

In the second example, you could write:

> Driven to the brink of extinction, the Leopard Lizard has been declared an endangered species by a conservation group.

You could NOT write:

> Driven to the brink of extinction, a conservation group has declared the Leopard Lizard an endangered species.

Why? Because the conservation group, as far as we can logically determine, has not been driven to the brink of extinction.

## EXERCISE #1: Your favorite ones

This is the easy part.

**1**

Phrases that describe (or modify) a noun in the sentence have to be

A) right next to the noun they are describing (or modifying).

B) pretty much anywhere.

C) in a special place where they can feel like they belong.

D) kidding me right now.

**2**

After a phrase like "A book series that has captivated millions of readers," you probably want to immediately include

A) a book series—probably "Harry Potter."

B) a complete description of the rules of Quidditch.

C) I hear it's fun, but I have a really hard time believing Quidditch is fun in the "real" world. I mean, you can't fly… you just carry a broom between your legs. Is that fun?

## EXERCISE #2: Not your favorite ones

On these SAT-like questions, look for the misplaced modifier and use it to help find the correct answer.

**1**

Surprised to have emerged from the accident without a scratch, the scooter that Noah was riding was almost completely destroyed.

A) NO CHANGE

B) the scooter that Noah had been riding was almost completely destroyed

C) having ridden the scooter, it was almost destroyed

D) Noah saw that his scooter was almost completely destroyed

**2**

Though poorly manufactured and prone to frequent breakdowns, the new car was so aesthetically pleasing that many consumers paid a premium to buy one.

A) NO CHANGE

B) many consumers paid a premium to buy one of the new cars

C) a premium was paid by many consumers to buy one of the new cars

D) the new car's aesthetics were so pleasing that many consumers paid a premium to buy one

**3**

Swollen by heavy rainfall, Matt and Michael were overwhelmed by the waterfall's majesty.

A) Matt and Michael were overwhelmed by the waterfall's majesty

B) Matt and Michael overwhelmed the waterfall and its majesty

C) the waterfall's majesty overwhelmed Matt and Michael

D) the majestic waterfall overwhelmed Matt and Michael

**4**

The team of writers set out to write a musical satirizing the landscape of "self-help," a movement that swelled in popularity in the late 20th century.

A) NO CHANGE

B) about "self-help" through a musical satire,

C) a satire of "self-help" staged as a musical,

D) a "self-help" satirical musical,

# The Editorial Stuff

## THE EDITORIAL STUFF

It's fair to say that, compared to the Technical Stuff on this Writing and Language section, the Editorial Stuff questions are just *a little bit worse*. Not *terrible* or anything, but questions that make us do some work that we would otherwise be happy not to do. Like read the passage. *Man*, are they dull, these passages. And they're written in a tone that could generously be described as somewhere between neutral and uninspired. Want an example? The first passage in the official SAT book is titled "Whey To Go," and it's about whey, a byproduct of yogurt. I rest my case.

Here's the good news (and we're always looking for good news): you can solve Editorial Stuff questions in reliable, predictable ways. And we're about to learn those.

So let's go!

## SHORTER IS BETTER

First rule, and maybe the most fun one too: whenever you can, you want to make the essay as concise as possible. That means cutting out unnecessary or redundant words. In other words, shorter is better! When you're choosing between three longer answer choices and one that consists of only a word or two, you can bet the short one is going to be right.

Take a look at this, for example:

1. The Kennedy Center works all over the globe to eradicate poverty.

   A) NO CHANGE
   B) poverty around the world.
   C) poverty both at home and abroad.
   D) poverty at an international level.

Notice that all of the answer choices are grammatically fine. That means that the grammar is not the problem. The right answer here is (A). Here's the long explanation: the sentence says that the Kennedy Center works "all over the globe." If you say that, you sure don't need to say "around the world," or any of the other choices. In other words, the shortest version is the correct one.

Is there an easier strategy to use than "shorter is better"?

No.

***Hot Tip:*** Now, is the shortest answer always right? Sadly, no. The essay has to be grammatical, not just short. Bias yourself in favor of picking shorter answers, but for heaven's sake, make sure the sentence makes sense before you just pick the shortest one!

## EXERCISE #1: Why can the SAT be like this?

How basic can we get?

1. On the SAT, shorter
   A) is longer.
   B) is cooler.
   C) is better.

## EXERCISE #2: Why must the SAT be like this?

On these SAT-like questions, pick the best way to fix the underlined part of the sentence.

**1**

Monique's take on neo-retro art was unique and could not be replicated.

A) unique
B) unique without replication.
C) not replicated by her.
D) unique to the point of not being replicated.

**2**

Puerto Rico became an "unincorporated territory" of the United States at the end of the Spanish-American War as part of the Treaty of Paris, which was a document ending the War under agreed terms.

A) Treaty of Paris, which was a document ending the war.
B) Treaty of Paris.
C) Treaty of Paris. It was a document ending the war under agreed terms.
D) Treaty of Paris; this document ended the war.

**3**

As I looked at all the unfamiliar maps and graphs, I felt very confused.

A) NO CHANGE
B) confused and uncertain.
C) confused without clear understanding.
D) confused like my mind couldn't make sense of anything.

**4**

I cannot explain the mysteries of the Ouija board.

A) NO CHANGE
B) cannot explain or fully articulate
C) cannot explain or describe in any detail
D) cannot explain and also cannot describe

**5**

That summer proved to be very memorable.

A) NO CHANGE
B) memorable and difficult to forget.
C) memorable as some things can be.
D) memorable and unforgettable.

**6**

When I went to Chicago after graduating high school, I didn't consider myself a skilled rider of underground trains.

A) NO CHANGE
B) person who knew everything there was to know about underground trains.
C) master of the art of traveling by public transportation.
D) veteran subway rider.

**7**

Though the car is energy-efficient, it can only travel the very shortest distances.

A) NO CHANGE
B) distances that are shortest in length.
C) shortest and least long distances.
D) smallest distances in length.

**8**

The committee deemed the idea to cover all of the county's farmland with asphalt both fiscally prohibitive and extremely short-sighted.

A) NO CHANGE
B) fiscally prohibitive.
C) extremely short-sighted.
D) both that it would cost too much money on top of the fact that it was dumb in the long-run.

If you went through those questions and just picked the shortest one by sight, I respect that... except that there is a sneaky devil in there, one where the shortest answer is NOT right. If you didn't spot it the first time, see if you can find it now.

## *RELEVANCE*

Information within a piece of writing can be completely true yet have no important connection to the topic at hand. The oldest known bowhead whale lived until it was at least 211 years old.

See what just happened there? We're talking about rhetorical strategies and then BAM! Out of nowhere, a bowhead whale shows up. Not cool, bowhead whale... not cool.

The SAT will say, "At this point, the writer is considering adding the following sentence." Whether you want to add that sentence or not depends on its relevance.

This can be tricky! A sentence can be on-topic but not appropriate at that moment in the passage. To figure these out, you want to know a few things:

The intent of the passage. Try to summarize the passage as a whole in one concise sentence. Ask yourself: Does this sentence help to support that idea?

The focus of the current paragraph. Separate from the main idea of the passage, think about what the current paragraph is trying to say. Look back at the topic sentence. Is the new sentence relevant to the paragraph?

***Hot Tip:*** A great place to look for a passage's topic and main idea is the title—whatever the author named the passage will always give you a strong idea what the passage is about.

***Hot Tip II:*** Just because an answer choice is loaded with detail doesn't make it too long and/or wrong. The SAT likes to include details if they help explain a concept or an unfamiliar term. In the case of additional detail, shorter is not always better.

## EXERCISE #1:

In this exercise, underline KEEP if the bold portion of each mini-essay is relevant to the essay and should remain or DELETE if it is irrelevant and should go bye-bye.

1. By June of 1907, when Mark Twain sailed from New York to London to receive the honorary degree of Literary Doctor from Oxford University, he was already one of the most famous authors in the world. **While many writers die in obscurity only to have the world discover their genius posthumously, Twain cultivated then fastidiously maintained his celebrity while he was alive.** The one thing he hadn't achieved, up to this point, was official acknowledgment from the world of academia. Despite his public statements to the contrary, he really did care what others thought—especially those in ivory towers.

   A) KEEP
   B) DELETE

2. Did you know that you can make your own massive soap bubbles at home? You can! All you need is dishwater detergent, water, and glycerin**, which you can find at your local drugstore.** Mix ½ cup of detergent, 4 cups of water, and 4 tablespoons of glycerin in a container. Then dip a bubble wand into the mixture and make some bubbles!

   A) KEEP
   B) DELETE

## EXERCISE #2:

Read the paragraph, think about what the main idea is, then cross out the part of the passage that is irrelevant.

1. The first Women's World Cup was held in 1991 in China, and it included 12 teams. Since then, the competition has grown in popularity and skill level. The 2011 Women's World Cup Final, between the U.S. and Japan, was widely seen to have demonstrated the highest level of play in WWC history, and Homare Sawa of Japan became the oldest player to score a goal.

2. How many people are on Facebook? The number grows every day. What started as a way for college students to keep track of their friends online has turned into something that everybody and her mother (and even her grandmother) is using. Mark Zuckerberg recently settled a lawsuit with the Winklevoss twins regarding the founding of Facebook. Whether or not it was Mark Zuckerberg's original intention, Facebook is now a way for young and old alike to communicate online.

3. "One man's trash is another man's treasure." There is no better example of this aphorism than that of the makers of "found object" art. One time I found a fifty-dollar bill on the street and used it to buy a new pair of skinny jeans. The found objects art scene, of course, is not uniform or exclusive; it includes anyone who takes lost or discarded items—from bicycle chains to old tires to faded photographs of complete strangers—and turns them into things of beauty.

4. When the Super Bowl is the most watched event in American Broadcasting, can we really still say that baseball is "America's Pastime"? Baseball was invented before the Civil War, and was based on a British game called Rounders. Even basketball is now more popular than baseball. The question is: did baseball change? Or did we?

5. Some people don't pay their taxes, and these people are called scofflaws. The American tax code does not pretend to be simple. There are different tax rates for different income brackets, as well as a host of tax breaks and deductions that a taxpayer can itemize. Some say that this complexity reflects the natural complexity of society; others argue that it is unfair and basically amounts to a government subsidy to the tax accounting industry.

6. Behind the barn, which was built in 1873 by a Danish farmer by the name Viktor Schmeichel, flowed a creek that changed personas with the seasons. In winter it was a stoic, old man who kept his secrets, but in the spring it became a giddy child, skipping about in wonder at every twist of light. In the summer the creek became a loudmouth drunk, holding court in the middle of a party. But the one you waited for was the autumn creek, the mother, who would hold you to her bosom, calm and strong, just as she caught and cradled the most magnificent of leaves.

7. The term "prom" comes from the word "promenade," a dance step practiced in classic English and American social dances. Movies about high school tell you that prom is supposed to be the greatest night of your life, but where they got that I'll never know. It seems to me that if you go into anything thinking it's got to be the "best ever," you're only setting yourself up for disappointment. Luckily, if you go into it just trying to live in the moment and have a good time, it's likely that you will.

8. In his Drivers' Ed class, Ryan had seen the videos of the horrible wrecks and mangled bodies, cautionary tales meant to scare kids into good driving habits. But he had never seen anything like this. The entire highway was paved with broken glass; the smell of burning gasoline invaded his nostrils. Drivers' Ed is a mandatory class in some school districts, but others treat it as an extracurricular or private activity.

9. By now most people know that reality TV is somewhat scripted, but I never understood how much until a friend of mine was on a reality show. It was a show on which a group of supposed friends allow the viewing public into their social scene. But the "reality" in my friend's case was that none of the people even knew one another before they were cast as friends, and casting is the process by which producers find people to be on their shows. The producers told these "friends" what to talk about, and writers edited scenes to manufacture the juiciest narratives.

## EXERCISE #3: Let's add a layer of complexity.

In this exercise, if the underlined portion of each mini-essay is relevant and should stay where it is, circle "KEEP." If it is irrelevant and should be deleted, circle "DELETE." If it is relevant but doesn't make sense where it is, circle "MOVE."

1. The Salton Sea is not technically a "sea," but it certainly is as salty as one. Geographically speaking, it is a saline, endorheic rift lake. It is the largest lake in California, and its salt concentration makes it saltier than the Pacific Ocean (though less salty than the Great Salt Lake in Utah). <u>Did you know that there is a sea in the middle of the desert in California?</u> Throughout the Spanish period of California history, the Salton Sea was used as a salt mine, but since the 1920s it has primarily served as a tourist attraction and recreation area.

   A) KEEP
   B) DELETE
   C) MOVE

2. As both a former diver and volleyball player, I believe it is important for kids to engage in both individual and group activities. From diving I learned that sometimes responsibility rests on me alone. When I succeeded, it was because I was at my best; when I failed, I was the only one to blame. Volleyball, on the other hand, taught me how to check my ego. <u>Being a member of a team taught me communication skills, and it taught me to appreciate the skills of others that I may not possess myself.</u> At 5 feet, 2 inches, I could serve and defend, but no one in her right mind would ask me to jump above an eight foot net to block a spike.

   A) KEEP
   B) DELETE
   C) MOVE

3. The crowd moved like a tidal wave, pushing relentlessly forward like a single entity. Who would have thought that the release of a mere video game could cause such a crush of humanity outside a Best Buy at six in the morning? <u>Most Best Buy stores are open from 10am until 9 or 10pm.</u> You could see fevered anticipation in the eyes of those first few customers, many of whom had camped out in the parking lot the night before, as they exited cradling the thin, rectangular video game box like a newborn child.

   A) KEEP
   B) DELETE
   C) MOVE

## EXERCISE #4: Let's Do Some SAT Questions

Now let's look at a few questions about Relevance that you might see on the SAT. Read the following mini-essays and answer the corresponding questions.

In "Harry Potter" lore, J.K. Rowling, then a struggling, single mom, first started writing the Harry Potter series on cocktail napkins in a bar. She may still be a single mom whose children's names are David, Mackenzie, and Jessica, but she is no longer struggling. Between book sales, merchandise, and film revenue, Harry Potter is one of the most successful franchises in history, having generated revenues of over 20 billion dollars.

**1**

The writer is considering deleting the underlined portion. Should it be kept or deleted?

A) Kept, because it further supports why Rowling's life story is so remarkable.
B) Kept, because it provides crucial details in an otherwise vague sentence.
C) Deleted, because it is unnecessary and ends up distracting from the paragraph's primary focus.
D) Deleted, because including only the first names of Rowling's children is too informal.

Originating in South America, the tomato has become one of the world's staple fruits. The tomato began to spread to almost every part of the world following the colonization of the Americas by the Spanish. [6] The earliest known European reference to the tomato can be found in a description of plants written in 1554 which names the tomato the "pomo d'oro," or "golden apple." Today, whether it's being used in Italian sauces or in the classic BLT, modern world cuisine, it seems, would be lost without the tomato.

**2**

At the "[6]" in the passage, the writer is considering adding the following accurate information:

The fruit contains large amounts of lycopene, which is now known to have health benefits.

Should the writer make this addition here?

A) Yes, because it builds upon a claim made about the tomato in the preceding sentence.
B) Yes, because it provides a logical link to the information that follows in the paragraph.
C) No, because it unnecessarily states information that's implied later in the paragraph.
D) No, because it doesn't fit logically in this paragraph about the history of the tomato.

The room seemed to have been frozen in time. Everything, from his well-worn little league cap to the signed photo of Kobe Bryant telling him to "Stay in School," was exactly as it had been when he'd last inhabited the space between these four walls. <u>Only the view from the window had changed.</u> The large willow, which used to mesmerize him during the day with its hypnotic swaying then frighten him at night with branches that turned into long, reaching fingers, was no longer there. "The roots were starting to tear up the sidewalk, so the city cut it down," his mother informed him casually as she unloaded the dishwasher.

**3**

The writer is considering deleting the underlined sentence. Should the sentence be kept or deleted?

A) Kept, because it provides a critical link to the following sentences about the missing willow.
B) Kept, because it gives a key insight into the relationship between the protagonist and his mother.
C) Deleted, because it contradicts the focus of the paragraph, which is that his room has not changed at all.
D) Deleted, because its formal tone is out of place compared with the rest of the paragraph.

## LOGICAL CONNECTIONS

Sneaky questions, these guys look like you just have to worry about one word to solve them...and then they turn into full-on reading comprehension questions!

How does that happen? Well, when it comes to picking a logical connecting word (like "thus," "still," "ultimately," or any other similar word), you need to know how the idea you're introducing relates to the other ideas in the passage. To get that, you likely have to read that whole paragraph, or even (gulp) the entire passage.

Whatever level of research is required, you want to figure out the logical relationship between the ideas in the passage. For instance:

1. Kenneth is academically unqualified for the job at the university; ________, he has exhibited a terrible attitude towards the other professors and staff.

   A) moreover
   B) however
   C) therefore
   D) even so

Let's think about this one. In the first part, we learn that Kenneth is unqualified. In the second, we learn that he also has a bad attitude. These two things do not reflect terribly well on Kenneth. In fact, those two thoughts are related to each other—they both make the point that Kenneth should probably be fired.

The word "moreover" *(which means the same as "furthermore," or "in addition")* is the right choice to link those two ideas together. The two ideas in the sentence both say something negative about Kenneth, but they are positively related to each other—since they both agree that Kenneth is pretty much a dickhead.

***Hot Tip:*** The most important thing to know to get these questions right is the definition of the words and phrases they're going to give you as answer choices. Let's learn those! The good news is that a lot of these words mean basically the same thing, so we can learn them within groups of related words.

Here is a selection of the most common words, linked by common meaning:

**These all have to do with addition or continuation.**

*Moreover*

*Furthermore*

*Additionally*

*Likewise*

> Kenneth is academically unqualified for the job at the university; moreover, he has exhibited a terrible attitude towards the other professors on staff

**Use these when the clause or sentence that follows provides specific evidence to justify the claim that came just before it.**

*For example*

*For instance*

*In fact*

Turtles have long lifespans; in fact, they can live longer than one hundred and ninety years.

**Other words show a negative relationship between the ideas of a sentence—in other words, the ideas in the sentence work in different or surprising ways from each other.**

*Nevertheless*

*Even so*

*In spite of*

*Nonetheless*

*However*

*Though*

*Otherwise*

His visit was unexpected; nevertheless, I was pleased to see him.

I could see that the professor was doing his best to explain the theory to me; however, I continued to find the idea utterly baffling.

My grandfather's comment angered me; even so, I decided to respond calmly.

**Some sentences have a cause and effect relationship—as in, the second thing happened because of the first thing. These are the words you would use to suggest that relationship.**

*Therefore*

*Consequently*

*Because of*

*Thus*

*As a result*

The American public loves a lowbrow summer comedy; thus, American Pie 8 has done big business at the box-office.

I think, therefore I am.

There has been a great deal of rain this season; as a result, the reservoirs are full.

**Other words connect two ideas or events that happen before or after one another. These words signify a temporal relationship ("temporal" means "related to time").**

*Subsequently*

*Ultimately*

*Finally*

*Eventually*

The monkeys were the first to climb aboard the ark, then the lions and tigers, and, finally, the goats; eventually, all the animals found their way onto Noah's ship.

***Hot Tip:*** If you see two words among the answer choices that both signify the same type of relationship between the two clauses (for example "furthermore" and "moreover"), you can get rid of them because they are both wrong. If they mean the exact same thing, then neither one of them can be the one right answer.

## EXERCISE #1: The Basics

1. When it comes to picking a logical connecting word like "however" or "therefore," you need to focus on
   A) just the word itself.
   B) just the sentence it's in.
   C) the whole paragraph, and potentially the whole passage.

## EXERCISE #2: The Advanceds

On these SAT-like questions, you want to pick the best word(s) to link the ideas of the sentence(s).

**1**

Every day thereafter, I would spend the morning with my three comrades; __________, we'd go our separate ways for the rest of the day.

A) since
B) so
C) then
D) therefore

**2**

__________ our dogs are dependent on us, traveling is not an option.

A) Because
B) In spite of the fact that
C) So
D) Moreover

**3**

Many construction projects across the city are in need of laborers; ______, there's a shortage of workers throughout the entire county.

A) instead,
B) in fact,
C) consequently,
D) however,

**4**

It is important to mix the batter thoroughly; ________ the muffins will come out lumpy and bitter.

A) whereas
B) otherwise
C) in fact
D) then

**5**

It can be difficult to travel to distant reaches of the globe; __________, it was far more difficult for people of the 19th century.

A) again
B) however
C) in that case
D) unfortunately

**6**

There is nothing quite like driving a convertible on a quiet ocean road _______ cruising through the city on a summer night with the top down.

A) while
B) whereas
C) or
D) because

**7**

Traditional basket-weaving is based on the same idea ______________ it requires a good deal more time and energy.

A) although
B) while
C) therefore
D) because

**8**

The organizers of the festival feel that each film must meet the high standards of quality typical of high-profile film festivals. ___________ , they want the filmmakers to directly participate in promoting the festival.

A) For example
B) In addition
C) However
D) For instance

**9**

Self-appreciation and self-discipline are the central principles of the technique, _________Barrani claims has a success rate of over ninety percent.

A) which
B) considering
C) through
D) despite

**10**

I've always considered cats to be lazy animals. On a recent trip to Africa, ___________, I encountered some cats that made me reconsider my point of view.

A) nevertheless
B) thus
C) moreover
D) however

**11**

Positive reinforcement of good behavior can lead to serious improvement in the behavior of prison inmates; __________, negative reinforcement can cause frustration, isolation, and eventually violence.

A) consequently
B) conversely
C) therefore
D) as a result

**12**

School counselors requested that all students submit a full inventory of career interests but ___________ loosened that requirement when it proved to generate more paperwork than the office could handle.

A) therefore
B) ultimately
C) furthermore
D) even so

## ORGANIZATION

One thing SAT clearly cares a LOT about on this section is organization. We've got to put their ideas in the right order and make sure that sentences do the job they are supposed to do. Here is what you want to think about when it comes to moving/inserting a sentence in a new location.

Look for specific clues. Keep in mind that this is a standardized test. That means that right answers have to be justifiably correct. The test makers (and what a lively bunch that must be!) have to include clues to justify the right location for every sentence.

What kind of clues should you look out for? Here are a few.

### *PRONOUNS*

Even words as seemingly simple as "this" can be dead giveaways. Imagine you are relocating a sentence that starts with the phrase, "This idea..." What do you need to have right before that sentence? Whatever "this idea" is!

## EXERCISE #1: Use a pronoun clue.

Use a clue from a pronoun to help figure out the correct sequence of the sentences in this paragraph.

[1] In an era before the Internet, their efforts spread the word about—and empowered—a social movement. [2] Over the course of a decade, the bilingual newspaper *La Raza* created a voice and a platform for the Chicano Rights movement. [3] *La Raza* empowered a generation of photographers not only as journalists but also as activists to document the progress and the vitality of Chicano activism. [4] The *La Raza* archive of over 20,000 photos reveals the role these images played in articulating the social and political concerns of the Chicano Movement.

1. To make this paragraph most logical, sentence 1 should be placed
   A) where it is now
   B) after sentence 2
   C) after sentence 3
   D) after sentence 4

### *TRANSITION WORDS*

If a sentence you're trying to place includes a word like "however" or "for example," you've got to make sure that sentence ties in to whatever came right before that spot.

## EXERCISE #2: Now Try a Transition Word

Use a transition word to help determine the logical sequence of the paragraph.

[1] When Barack Obama visited Cuba in March of 2016, Havana was alive with anticipation. [2] The entire country, it seemed, felt optimistic that relations between the US and Cuba would resume a sense of normalcy. [3] Now, the Trump administration has released new, restrictive travel rules for Cuba. [4] The question at this point, with two years of new regulations in place, is this: is it even possible for relations to go back to the way they were before?

1. To make this paragraph most logical, sentence 3 should be placed
   A) where it is now
   B) before sentence 1
   C) after sentence 1
   D) after sentence 4

## VERB TENSE

This is a powerful tool for answering some of the hardest Sequence and Structure questions. Certain verb tenses do certain kinds of work. For example, when we're recounting stories, we almost always use the simple past tense. When we're relating a fact, we use present tense. Look at the verb tense(s) in the sentence you are placing. Is it a storytelling sentence? A statement of fact? What about a projection into the future? Use that sense of timing to put the sentence in the right spot.

## EXERCISE #3: Verb Tense!

Use a verb tense clue to determine the logical sequence of this paragraph

[1] The Renaissance, a period of cultural rebirth, is conventionally regarded as the end of the Middle Ages. [2] Though the Renaissance represents new modes of thinking in domains as far ranging as science and politics, it is most acutely represented in art. [3] Painters and sculptors have drawn on the inspiration of the Renaissance throughout the centuries that followed. [4] Art began to reveal a strong sense of humanism, an elevation of man's place in the universe.

1. To make this paragraph most logical, sentence 3 should be placed
   A) where it is now
   B) before sentence 1
   C) after sentence 1
   D) after sentence 4

## PURPOSE

Some sentences are meant to be topic sentences. Others are clearly meant to be concrete details. If you were a sentence, what type would you be? Ignore that question...that's not important. Anyway, read the sentence you're placing and assess what kind of sentence it sounds like, then put it in the right spot (topic sentences at the beginning of a paragraph, detail sentences supporting claims from previous sentences) in the passage.

## EXERCISE #4: What is the Purpose?

Think about the purpose of the sentence in question and use that to determine the logical sequence of this paragraph.

[1] What appears to be a simple process actually involves multiple transmission platforms. [2] Have you ever looked at your cell phone, tablet, or laptop and wondered how on earth that small device knows, well, *everything*? [3] Cellular data networks transmit and receive data to and from your connected device over a range of radio frequencies. [4] So valuable are radio frequencies that cell phone companies spend billions to secure the rights to a certain bandwidth.

1. To make this paragraph most logical, sentence 2 should be placed
   A) where it is now
   B) before sentence 1
   C) after sentence 3
   D) after sentence 4

## RELEVANCE AND REDUNDANCY

Now...do you need to include the sentence at all? Some questions will give you the option of leaving the sentence out of the passage entirely. Whether you want to keep or kill a sentence depends on two things: relevance and redundancy.

### *RELEVANCE*

Make sure that the sentence you're placing isn't just "on topic." Lots of sentences that should be deleted will somehow connect to the topic of the passage—they just won't be strictly necessary. Make sure that the new sentence is working to help make the author's point—if it does, it'll be relevant.

## EXERCISE #5: Keep it Relevant.

Think about the relevance of the new sentence and use it to determine whether or not you should add that sentence to this paragraph.

**1** Today when someone points a camera at us, we smile. This is the cultural and social reflex of our time, and such are our expectations of a picture portrait. But in the long history of portraiture the open smile has been largely, as it were, frowned upon.

1. At this point, the author is considering adding the following sentence.

   Historically, portraiture has captured the images of the rich and powerful.

   Should the writer make this addition here?

   A) Yes, because it provides an important historical background detail about portraiture.
   B) Yes, because it establishes why portraits have been useful to historical scholars.
   C) No, because it distracts from the paragraph's focus on one element within portraits.
   D) No, because it contradicts the claim made elsewhere in the paragraph.

### *REDUNDANCY*

A really simple reason not to include a sentence is because what's in the sentence has already been stated elsewhere in the passage. These can be a little tricky because they'll require you to read around a little bit to see if the new sentence is redundant. This "Writing and Language" test is definitely also a reading test, so don't be afraid to dig in and do some reading!

## EXERCISE #6: Redundancy. Redundancy.

Read the paragraph and use your reading comp skill to determine whether or not you need to add the new sentence to this paragraph.

The publishing revolution of the sixteenth and seventeenth centuries witnessed an explosion of printed material, democratizing information and pushing it into the hands and sight of more people than ever before. A large single sheet of cheap paper could be printed with a proclamation, adorned with a woodcut, and sent out among the masses. These broadsides were sold for a penny on street corners, pasted on ale-house walls, and stuck up on market posts. <u>With affordable paper available, sharing a printed message to a mass number of people was now a possibility.</u> **1**

1. The writer is considering deleting the underlined sentence. Should the sentence be kept or deleted?
   A) Kept, because it reveals the elements which made the printing revolution possible.
   B) Kept, because it details the reasons why people printed at that time.
   C) Deleted, because it blurs the paragraph's focus on free speech.
   D) Deleted, because it repeats information that has been provided earlier in the paragraph.

## STRUCTURE

Next up: structure. I talked about a sentence's "purpose" in the last section. Thinking about the job of a particular sentence is a great clue to use when re-ordering a passage. Let's break down the various purposes a sentence might have.

### *INTRODUCTIONS*

Introductions should introduce. Take a minute to fully absorb that brain-melter. Your life will forever be split into two parts: life before you read that sentence, and life after.

**OK, so an introduction only has one job, but it can accomplish that job in a few different ways.** An introductory sentence could provide the thesis of the essay, but it doesn't have to do that. It could ask an interesting question, or it could introduce an interesting detail that will be explained later. Whatever the specific nature of introductory sentence is, it needs to kick start the essay and be relevant to the central idea.

**Introductions also set the tone.** Tone is the label we use to describe *how* something is written. Tone can be formal, informal, analytical, personal, earnest, humorous, or anything in between. On the SAT, the tone is typically academic and dry. If you think I am being either funny or hyperbolic, you have not read enough SAT passages.

After you read the first sentence, you should be able to answer the question, **"what kind of essay am I expecting to read?"**

Let's take a look at some sample introductory sentences. What can you tell about these essays just based on their first sentences?

> Many people associate the idea of school integration as a struggle limited to 1960s America, but there are still many places, especially in the American South, where school districts use "busing" to ensure school racial balance.

**I can tell that this essay:**

- is informative.
- will strike a pretty neutral tone.
- is relatively formal.

> For many high school students, community service is just another thing they have to add to their already heavy loads of schoolwork, extracurricular activities, sports, and for some, part-time jobs.

**I can tell that this essay:**

- is persuasive.
- will likely present a negative opinion about required community service
- is relatively opinionated

> When the sky turned green, we knew it was going to be a mean one.

**I can tell that this essay:**

- is a piece of either personal memoir or fiction.
- will be informal and lyrical in tone.
- intends to create a feeling of mystery and suspense.

## EXERCISE #1: Make an Introduction

Pick the sentence that best introduces each essay.

1. No. But did its scientists believe so thoroughly in the drug's possible benefits that they only saw what they wanted to see? Perhaps. However, allegations of a company-wide cover-up go too far. Investigators have uncovered a total of zero communications which link the mistakes made in the Cronifrin trials to a concerted effort on the part of Well Bridge to defraud the public in the name of financial gain.

   A) Did Well Bridge Inc. purposefully shred documents related to the possible dangers of the drug Cronifrin?
   B) Did Well Bridge Inc. purposefully bury results of the experimental drug trials that contradicted its desired results?
   C) Did Well Bridge Inc. purposefully expose wrong doing on the part of the pharmaceutical company involved in the Cronifrin scandal?
   D) Did Well Bridge Inc. gain financially because it released only positive results from the Cronifrin drug trials?

2. I went on my first cruise recently, and believe me, when they say "all inclusive," they mean it. Breakfast and lunch are basically all-day buffets. Dinner, while a more formal affair, is no less extravagant. One night I couldn't decide between the duck and the lobster tail, so the waiter asked me if he should just bring both. The kitchen threw in an extra lobster tail just for giggles! Afterward, I was surprised that I didn't have to be rolled out of the dining room like a giant medicine ball! The craziest thing is that every dinner is a three-course affair. I simply can't imagine eating a three-course dinner in my own home...every night!

   A) If the thought of gaining 8 lbs. in a week seems impossible, try going on a cruise!
   B) When I travel, I generally like to be in control of my own travel and itinerary, but I have to say there's something refreshingly simple about a cruise.
   C) "All-inclusive" is a term the travel industry uses to indicated that all of one's meals are included in the price of the trip.
   D) I detest travel by boat; it seems that any time I choose to set foot on a boat, I get seasick.

3. Italian "prosecco," a slightly sweet sparkling wine, was the first to challenge the dominance of champagne, but recently Spanish "cavas" have also entered the fray. Now restaurants as well as grocery stores are starting to classify the whole lot as simply, "bubbly," without any reference to an old-school hierarchy that always favored champagne.

   A) Sparkling wine cannot truly be called "champagne" unless it hails from the Champagne region of France.
   B) Champagne has long been the drink of success and celebration, seen as both a symbol of wealth and privilege and a way to mark special occasions even for the non-millionaires among us.
   C) While "champagne" remains the worldwide standard for sparkling wine, other varietals have been gaining in popularity in recent years.
   D) Sparkling wines provide a refreshing and exciting alternative to regular wine.

## TRANSITIONS

Metaphorically, transitions are bridges. They help you get from one "idea island" to another smoothly and comfortably. The key to a transition is to acknowledge the previous idea while simultaneously introducing the next; if you don't include both a reference to what came before and what's coming up, something will be missing

***Hot Tip:*** Transition sentences are frequently wrong because they create "half a bridge" between what came before and what comes next. Try walking over half a bridge sometime—it's not pleasant.

Here's an example of a "half bridge" transition:

**Part I:**

> Politicians running for office will all tell you that "Washington is broken," but it seems that many of them fall into the same dysfunctional traps as their predecessors.

**"Half Bridge" Transition:**

> These traps include being preoccupied with fundraising for re-election immediately upon taking office.

**Part II:**

> Congress members only serve for two years.

Notice how the transition sentence does a good job of continuing the previous thought from Part I because it starts with the phrase, **"These traps include."** The problem is that it does nothing to introduce the idea in Part II about the length of a congressional term, which makes that next sentence seem like it's coming out of nowhere.

### Let's try it again with a transition that bridges both ideas.

**Part I:**

> Politicians running for office will all tell you that "Washington is broken," but it seems that so many of them fall into the same dysfunctional traps as their predecessors.

**Full Transition:**

> These traps include being preoccupied with fundraising for re-election immediately upon taking office, a reasonable concern given their short terms in office.

**Part II:**

> Congress members only serve for two years.

Transitions don't always have to create a perfectly logical flow. In fact, sometimes a writer will use a purposefully abrupt transition in order to create drama or surprise. For example:

> It seemed that nothing could go wrong. The day was perfect, quiet except for the sound of the birds in the trees. Quiet, that is, until an alien space ship ripped through the earth, drilling a massive hole from New York to the Philippines.

**Obviously, there is an abrupt transition there, when the alien space ship lands and starts wrecking stuff.** However, even the simple addition of the phrase **"that is"** helps to smooth that transition so that the sudden change of ideas still makes sense to the reader.

Also, any time you ever see the phrase, "it seemed that nothing could go wrong," you can be pretty sure that something is about to go terribly, terribly wrong.

***Hot Tip:*** When the SAT asks you to make a transition, it will almost always ask you to create a transition between paragraphs. To solve these questions, read the paragraphs before and after the transition sentence. Yes, the whole paragraph! (Sorry about that—remember, I don't make the test.) Knowing what happened in the preceding paragraph and what's about to happen in the next is exactly what you need to know to solve these.

## Here's an example:

> Anthropologists estimate that the first evidence of the human domestication of animals occurred over 15,000 years ago with the appearance of the first domesticated dogs. Reasons for domestication vary. Some animals, like goats, sheep, and pigs, were domesticated primarily for the commodities they provide, like milk, meat, and wool. Animals like horses, oxen, and dogs were domesticated to provide help with various kinds of work like hauling, hunting, and protection.
>
> **However, only one animal seems to have been tamed uniquely for the purpose of human companionship: the domestic cat.** Even though dogs have always been great human companions, only the domesticated cat originally dwelled indoors with humans.

Let's talk about why this transition is working. The phrase **"tamed uniquely for the purpose of human companionship"** draws its relevance from the idea in the first paragraph that other animals were domesticated for reasons other than companionship. The use of the word **"however"** sets up the contrast between the cat and other animals. It connects the ideas and therefore creates a seamless transition between the two paragraphs.

## EXERCISE #2: Transitions!

Read each partial essay and choose the answer that provides the most logical transition between Part I and Part II.

**Part I:**

Historically, when America goes to war, a host of wartime songs follow, from the homefront-focused "Tie a Yellow Ribbon" during WWII to the anti-war anthem "Fortunate Son" during the Vietnam War. So why is it that in the first decade of the 21st century, with the United States simultaneously fighting wars in Iraq and Afghanistan, was there a surprising dearth of war-related popular music to be heard on our radios and iPods?

**Part II:**

[1] There have been multiple films made about America's most recent wars. So why the silence in popular music? Perhaps the lack of a military draft made the war seem less relevant to the majority not in the military.

1. Which choice should be inserted at [1] in order to create a smooth transition between the paragraphs?
   - A) Other art forms have not been so absent from the conversation.
   - B) Doesn't it seem like every time you purchase a new technological gadget like an iPod, a better version comes out within a week?
   - C) Films like "American Sniper" and "The Hurt Locker," for example, dealt with multiple aspects of the war in the Middle East.
   - D) Artists like Lady Gaga sing about serious subjects like sexuality and religion, but what about war?

## CONCLUSIONS

Like transitions (see how I just transitioned right there?), conclusions also do several jobs at the same time. A good conclusion should flow logically and smoothly from the previous sentence, and complete the thoughts in the passage. There are a TON of ways to write a concluding sentence (the least favorite of which, to me, is to restate the thesis sentence), but every GOOD concluding sentence should:

- remain relevant to the main idea.
- never undermine the main idea of the passage.

***Hot Tip:*** Even though both we and the SAT pretty much hate the ol' "thesis restatement as concluding sentence," a good conclusion WILL often refer to something mentioned in the introduction—like a metaphor or a "hook"—thereby "book-ending" the essay. When you're picking a concluding sentence, looking back at the intro is therefore a pretty darn good idea.

## EXERCISE #3: Conclude It!

Select the sentence that best concludes each partial essay.

1. Many people associate the idea of school integration as a struggle limited to 1960s America, but there are still many places, especially in the American South, where school districts use "busing" to ensure school racial balance. In the '80s, when I was in elementary school in Arkansas, my parents got a letter each July informing them what school I would be attending the next year. I would take a bus to whatever school the letter said. Far from being burdensome and disruptive, busing made me who I am today.

   A) I still think about busing to this day.
   B) Kids these days would hardly tolerate busing the way we did.
   C) Busing was more common then because neighborhoods and cities were more racially segregated.
   D) I know I benefited from the experience, even if the government's policies for school integration have never been perfect.

2. For many high school students, community service is just another thing to add to their already-heavy load of schoolwork, extracurricular activities, sports, and part-time jobs. Today's kids are already so over-scheduled, so overburdened, that adding a community service requirement into the mix is basically telling kids to kiss any time they thought they might still have to themselves goodbye. At the same time, setting up community service as a requirement implies that if students had the option, they would choose not to do any.

   A) In conclusion, it is a bad idea to require students to complete a community service requirement to graduate because it will do more harm than good.
   B) With everything else high school students have to do nowadays, why force them into an activity that carries a mixed message about service?
   C) Students are simply too busy to do community service.
   D) If helping people is the point of the whole thing, schools should look at other ways that students can help besides community service.

# SEQUENCE AND STRUCTURE ROUND-UP!

## EXERCISE #1: World's Easiest Questions.

1. When deciding where to place a sentence within a passage, you should focus on which of the following (select all that apply)?
   A) pronouns
   B) transition words
   C) whether you enjoy reading the passage
   D) whether reading the passage makes you wish you'd been born a peasant factory worker in Bangladesh because then at least you wouldn't have to take the SAT
   E) verb tense
   F) the "purpose" of the sentence

2. The two reasons NOT to include a sentence in a passage are (select two, duh)
   A) boring-ness
   B) redundancy
   C) personal preference
   D) irrelevance

## EXERCISE #2: Re-order!

Read—then reorder—the sentences so they are in the correct order.

**1** Matt and Caroline, born within three months of one another, had never known a world without dual-family barbecues, summer vacations, and holiday parties.

**2** By the time they were 17, though, something was clearly changing, and neither of them knew what to do about it.

**3** Thus, Matt and Caroline had been best friends since before they could walk.

**4** After establishing their careers, both couples even had kids at the same time.

**5** Their parents had gone to college together, then all moved to another college town to pursue lives in academia.

A) Correct Order: ___, ___, ___, ___, ___

**1** I have long-term back problems from the strenuous impact put onto my body while I was still growing.

**2** Female Olympic gymnasts reach the ideal physicality for the sport by the age of 16.

**3** Competitive women's gymnastics is one of the few sports in which many of the world's top competitors are legally children.

**4** I can point to more serious injuries as well: one of my teammates actually broke her neck, ending her athletic career, at the age of 15.

**5** I was never an Olympic gymnast, but as I did compete for ten years, I can attest to the physical demands of and potential for injury in the sport.

A) Correct Order: ___, ___, ___, ___, ___

## GIVE 'EM WHAT THEY WANT

The alternate title for this chapter is "Read the Question Stems Carefully," and hopefully you know why I chose what I did. *That said...* if I could give everybody who is taking the SAT one single piece of good advice, it would probably be, across the entire SAT from Reading to Math to the Essay, to *read the question stems carefully*.

By the way, you may have figured this out already, but the question stems are the first part of the question—the part that leads into the answers. You probably refer to these guys as "the questions." I got a little technical there. Sorry—spend too much time with these tests and you can get a little carried away.

That is especially true on the Writing & Language section. Many questions—more than one-quarter of all of them, actually—will tell you exactly what they want you to provide in your answer.

**Your strategy? Give 'em what they want.**

Read these questions carefully, underline what it is they want you to deliver (is it a transition? A concrete detail?) and make *sure* you deliver precisely that.

### Let's look at one of these together.

1. Which choice clearly and effectively cites a possible benefit of meditation?

   A) the deep-breathing techniques required as part of meditation.
   B) the relaxed and contented feeling that often results from meditation.
   C) the dedication required to begin a meditation practice.
   D) the challenges of maintaining the calmness of meditation in everyday life.

Chances are you've already gotten this question right, but let's back up for one second to think through why the right answer (B, for the record) is right. What is the question asking you to deliver? I recommend underlining that part of the question. Here, it's pretty much one word: benefit.

Answer choice B has a really clearly stated benefit: "the relaxed and contented feeling." You might be ready to claim that a deep-breathing technique COULD be another benefit. That *may* be true, but on the SAT, as soon as you hear yourself saying an answer *may* be right, you probably just found a wrong answer.

***Hot Tip:*** If an answer choice feels like it's about 70% right, then it's wrong. The SAT wants to write tempting wrong answers. Right answers are 100% right. Wrong answers can be tempting but still wrong. Don't settle for answers—when you settle, you're likely settling for a wrong answer.

## EXERCISE #1: These are the easy ones.

**1**

Select ALL that apply. When the SAT gives you a question with a clear indication of what they want you to deliver within the answer, you should

A) pick your answer based on what sounds best.
B) read the question stem carefully and underline what they want.
C) give 'em what they want.
D) consult a clairvoyant animal—preferably a squid.

## EXERCISE #2: Now with Realistic SAT Questions

Read the question stem and any introductory text carefully. In the question, underline what they want. Then give 'em what they want.

Oak trees, like all living organisms, have a life cycle. Oak trees begin as seeds, or acorns. If an acorn finds favorable conditions—good soil, sun, and water—it will sprout. In its infancy, an oak tree is a seedling. It then proceeds into its juvenile phase as a sapling. When it matures, it will be what we know and recognize as an oak tree, capable of creating new acorns to create the next generation of trees. <u>An oak tree can live up to 1,000 years and endure many hardships throughout its long life.</u>

**1**

Which choice best completes the description of the oak tree's life cycle?

A) NO CHANGE
B) When an oak tree declines and dies, its rotting leaves and wood provide the soil with fertilizer.
C) In the fall, the tree's chlorophyll production slows, and it prepares anthocyanin, which produces its trademark red color.
D) Just like the "chicken and the egg" conundrum, scientists are challenged to explain which came first, the tree or the acorn.

More than 8,000 volunteers walk every quadrant of the city trying to count every member of the local homeless population. An accurate count will <u>allow the city to apply for and effectively deploy federal and local funding</u> to support a continuum of programs ranging from access centers, emergency shelters, safe havens, and transitional and permanent housing, as well as access to services designed to develop the skills required to attain stable housing.

**2**

Which choice most effectively sets up the examples given at the end of the sentence?

A) NO CHANGE
B) provide city officials with more accurate census data
C) increase the reported population of the city by tens of thousands
D) represent the homeless community as citizens, just like you and me

The word "robot" made its first appearance in a 1920 play by the Czech writer Karel Čapek entitled *R.U.R.*, for Rossum's Universal Robots. Deriving his neologism from the Czech word "robota," meaning "drudgery" or "servitude," Čapek used "robot" to refer to a race of artificial humans who replace human workers in a futurist dystopia.

There was, however, an earlier word for artificial humans and animals, "automaton," stemming from Greek roots meaning "self-moving." <u>The engineer Hero of Alexandria described automata involving elaborate networks of siphons that activated various actions as water passed through them.</u>

**3**

Which choice provides a concrete example that continues to prove the central claim of the paragraph?

A) NO CHANGE
B) Centuries later, the French King Henri IV hired the Italian engineer Tomaso Francini to build him some waterworks for the royal palace at Saint Germain en Laye.
C) Although no ancient automata survive, the ideas behind the devices live on.
D) Many people trace the origins of robots to the work of Alan Turing, who wrote about the possibility of machine intelligence in the '40s and '50s.

## DICTION

Diction is a fancy term for **"word choice."** While the SAT has gotten rid of those old school SAT words like "salubrious" and "chimerical," they still ask vocabulary questions—they just do it a different way. On diction questions, you'll see four answer choices that, out of context, mean exactly the same thing. The goal is to pick the one that's right *in that context*.

To do that, you want to think about small differences between words and the situations in which we use them. My recommendation on a diction question is to follow this simple process:

- ***Go back to the sentence in the passage.***
- ***Read the sentence without the word in question.***
- ***Ask yourself what word (or set of words) you would use in that spot. Find a synonym of what you came up with among the answer choices.***

***Hot Tip:*** Whenever you get an answer on these questions, it has to fit the sentence in the passage perfectly. Read your choice back into sentence and make sure that you're happy with how it works in that situation. If it's not perfect, it's not right.

In addition to thinking about the specific meanings of individual words, you want to think about the situations when you might (or might not) use a particular word.

Here's an example:

The words "beautiful" and "handsome" both describe a person who is good looking, right? Charlize Theron and Jon Hamm, for example. You can disagree with everything else in this book, but it is a fact that Theron and Hamm are both really good-looking individuals.

### Now, do we use those words interchangeably? Oh hell no.

We use the word **"beautiful"** to describe a wide range of things, from people to paintings to sunsets to Instagrammed photos of someone's lunch—well, maybe not that last one.

**"Handsome,"** however, is only used in certain contexts. A handsome man, a handsome town square, maybe. It would be strange to call a painting or a sunset "handsome"—that's just not how we use that word.

To solve diction questions, you've got to be thinking about the specific meanings of words we use and the situation in which we use them. The good news is that we think that way pretty much all of the time. Our language brains are programmed to notice small shades of meaning, even if we don't consciously think about them very often.

## EXERCISE #1: Connotate.

Each of the following word pairs means roughly the same thing, though one has a positive connotation and the other a negative one. Write a plus sign next to the positive word, and a minus sign next to the negative one.

1. Inexpensive ___ Cheap ___
2. Childish ___ Youthful ___
3. Stubborn ___ Determined ___
4. Talkative ___ Long-winded ___
5. Lackadaisical ___ Relaxed ___
6. Elite ___ Snobbish ___
7. Pushy ___ Assertive ___
8. Inquisitive ___ Nosy ___

***Hot Tip:*** Want to enact a microaggression on someone? Just describe them using the version of any of these words with a negative connotation. It works like magic!

## EXERCISE #2: Spot the Difference.

Each of the following pairs of words means roughly the same thing... but there is an important difference between them. See if you can state that difference.

1. Know / Suppose

_______________

2. Halt / Conclude

_______________

3. Surrender / Forfeit

_______________

4. Approve / Accept

_______________

5. Dislike / Loathe

_______________

6. Thrifty / Miserly

_______________

## EXERCISE #3: SAT Time.

Now let's try out some SAT-type questions. Read the sentence and pick the word that fits the context.

**1**

While they generally have poor eyesight, bats possess a sense of hearing that is particularly intense.

A) NO CHANGE
B) knowing.
C) acute.
D) clear.

**2**

Upon gazing for the first time at the hideous monster, the damsel receded in horror.

A) NO CHANGE
B) returned
C) ebbed
D) recoiled

**3**

Miranda was granted Employee of the Year because of both her innovative ideas and her consummate professionalism.

A) NO CHANGE
B) entitled
C) named
D) presented

**4**

To the astonishment of the university faculty, the 10-year old math prodigy completed the seemingly impossible problem in record time.

A) NO CHANGE
B) finalized
C) ended
D) finished off

**5**

One of the goals of The United States Department of Energy is to reduce the amount of oil we import from foreign countries.

Which of the following alternatives to the underlined portion would NOT be acceptable?

A) lower
B) decrease
C) minimize
D) contract

**6**

My sister and I were Irish, after all, and we had longed for years to hike among the verdant hills of our mother country.

Which of the following alternatives to the underlined portion would NOT be acceptable?

A) NO CHANGE
B) inside
C) through
D) across

## IDIOMS

Next up, the ones that don't make any sense.

An idiom is a standard phrase, like "to come to terms with." The words "to" and "with" have almost no meaning in that phrase, but we know that "to come to terms with" sounds good and "to come by terms on" does not.

In real life, idioms often refer to common phrases, like "to bend over backwards" or "to let the cat out of the bag." (I have a question about that last one: who says that phrase, and why? And can they stop, please?) On the SAT, we don't have to correct phrases like those. Instead, we're looking for non-standard phrasings, like the example, "to come by terms on." We just don't use that phrase in English, which makes that an idiom error.

***Hot Tip:*** Most SAT idiom questions just ask if a phrase uses the correct prepositions, the little words that typically describe position, like "on," "by," etc.

There is no logic behind idioms. You just have to ask yourself, "do we say it this way?"

## EXERCISE #1: Did you learn what an idiom is?

1. An idiom is

   A) a subtle difference in meaning between two words.
   B) a standard phrasing in a language.
   C) What did you just call your brother?

2. To solve idiom questions, you should

   A) ask yourself how you would say that particular phrase.
   B) consult with a trusted religious authority figure.
   C) I heard what you said. Go to your room.

## EXERCISE #2: Some SAT idiom questions.

**1**

Despite numerous failures in the early stages of testing, I had confidence with our initial design.

A) NO CHANGE
B) confidence in
C) confided with
D) confided in

**2**

Warren would not accept either a financial reward nor a gift for locating the family's golden retriever.

A) NO CHANGE
B) or
C) but
D) besides

**3**

The doctor is extremely concerned in the appallingly high rate of childhood obesity in his community.

A) NO CHANGE
B) concerning in
C) concerned about
D) concerning about

**4**

Sandra Graham, an academic whose expertise ranges from motivation to cognitive development, made the point that even a seemingly simple intervention can have a lasting effect on a child's academic success.

A) NO CHANGE
B) affect on
C) effect in
D) affect in

**5**

The motivational speaker argued that anyone, regardless of circumstance, is capable to achieve greatness.

A) NO CHANGE
B) in achieving
C) of achieve
D) of achieving

**6**

Although stories of spectacular "overnight" success proliferate in the media, many of these successes were actually proceeded by years of hard work, setbacks, and failure.

A) NO CHANGE
B) proceeded in
C) preceded by
D) preceded in

**7**

To truly excel at debate, one must not only be able to be argumentative for one's own position but also to anticipate and rebut possible counterarguments.

A) NO CHANGE
B) effectively argue
C) argue the effects of
D) project for

## STYLE (OR KEEPIN' IT ACADEMIC)

Style. The SAT doesn't have much. That's a sad fact, but it's true. When it comes to picking an answer on Writing & Language, you want to do what the chapter title says—you want to *keep it academic.*

Here's what I mean. Suppose you had to choose between the adjectives "crazy massive" and "substantial" on the SAT. Every single time, "substantial" would be right. Why? Because that word is academic.

**You might ask, "by academic, Ted, do you mean dry and tedious?"**
**I would reply, "yes."**

Here's another example. One of these will be right on the SAT, and one will not. See if you can figure out which one's which:

Light pollution *poses a significant challenge* to local astronomers

Light pollution *is a huge problem* for local astronomers.

Both of those phrases ("poses a significant challenge" and "is a huge problem") are trying to say the same thing. One of them is phrased in the academic style so clearly preferred by the SAT. Do you know which one? It's the first one: "poses a significant challenge."

***Hot Tip:*** What you're reading right now is not, for the most part, written in an academic tone. If you want to read some stuff written in that tone, you can find it in familiar spots, like the news section of your local newspaper or your history, government, and economics textbooks. Pick up one of those, flip to a random page, and start reading—you'll get a sense of what an academic tone sounds like right away.

Let's see if I can get you tuned into how the SAT keeps it academic.

## EXERCISE #1: The easy part.

1. When it comes to tone, the SAT likes to
   A) keep it academic.
   B) keep it fun, fresh, and readable.
   C) you're joking with B), right?
2. "Keeping it academic" roughly means
   A) to use language that is vividly descriptive
   B) to use language that is overly complex and wordy
   C) to use dry, concise language that possibly could put you to sleep

## EXERCISE #2: Tone agreement.

This one is about tone consistency. Each example contains two sentences. Figure out whether the two sentences agree or disagree in tone and circle the corresponding answer.

1. Curiosity, which is NASA's most advanced robotic rover to explore Mars, was deployed inside the Gale Crater in order to find evidence that the crater once held a massive lake. Wouldn't that be something?
   A) Yes, those sentences are perfect together
   B) Uh...not so much.

2. If I had a nickel for every time someone nearly ran me over with a shopping cart at Whole Foods, I might have enough money to shop at Whole Foods. Some grocery stores have significantly higher prices than others.
   A) Two peas in a pod!
   B) I can't even read those two sentences in the same sitting.

3. Although Thomas Edison is the first inventor to come to mind for many Americans, he is not the only prolific inventor in our history. Jerome Lemelson, for instance, held over 600 patents on devices from magnetic tape recorders to bar code scanners.
   A) These sentences belong together like two lovebirds.
   B) These sentences should break up.

4. Quick: who is the best football player in history? The answer might not be as clear as you thought.
   A) Yup, that's a keeper.
   B) Horrible. Horrible.

5. Philip Glass and Terry Riley are both composers of contemporary classical music that has been labeled as "minimal." Characteristics of this style include a steady rhythmic pulse, repetition, and gradual transformation.
   A) Crank up the minimal music and let's have a party because those two sentences are great together!
   B) This simply won't do.

6. According to an NPPGA report, farmers in North Dakota grow over 2.7 billion pounds of potatoes annually. Jumpin' Jack Flash... that's a lot of 'taters!
   A) I see nothing wrong with pairing those two sentences.
   B) Really? 'Taters?

## EXERCISE #3: SAT.

On these SAT-like questions, pick the version of the phrase that "keeps it academic."

**1**

The air quality regulations aim to <u>reduce</u> odors from processing plants in the neighborhood.

A) NO CHANGE
B) say adios to
C) dwindle
D) deflate

**2**

The annual event <u>plays up</u> food, traditional music and dance, and a collection of arts and crafts.

A) NO CHANGE
B) features
C) brings a ton of attention to
D) puts a spotlight on

**3**

The police captain claimed that department officials are downplaying crime statistics and thus giving a <u>misleading portrait</u> of violence in the city.

A) NO CHANGE
B) not-too-pretty picture
C) tricky puzzle
D) fake, unreal depiction

Tutor Ted®

# WRITING & LANGUAGE: ANSWERS

# Answers

## CHAPTER 1: THE TECHNICAL STUFF

### HOW TO BUILD A SENTENCE

#### EXERCISE #1

1) C
2) B
3) B
4) C
5) B and D

#### EXERCISE #2

1) C
2) B
3) D

#### EXERCISE #3

1) The game was over, but the crowd refused to leave.
2) While I was making dinner, my dog started barking outside.
3) The band played for three hours and never took a set break. (NO CHANGE)
4) If you are sick, you shouldn't ride the subway.
5) He followed the team for fifty years; it hardly mattered whether the team won or lost. Or: He followed the team for fifty years, and it hardly mattered whether the team won or lost.
6) It isn't easy being tall, but it's even harder to be short.
7) Maria is my only sister; she is dutiful and decent. Or: Maria is my only sister: she is dutiful and decent. Or: Maria is my only sister—she is dutiful and decent.
8) Because Lana was so difficult to work with, the studio decided to hire another actress.
9) This Twitter feed doesn't make any sense—it reads like it was written by a computer. Or: This Twitter feed doesn't make any sense; it reads like it was written by a computer.
10) The city could no longer call on Batman when local criminals began to cause problems. (NO CHANGE)
11) To get a ticket, you'd better buy online.
12) The famous designer decided that the town needed something really grand at its center, so he proposed a rose garden flanked by cascading waterfalls. Or: The famous designer decided that the town needed something really grand at its center: he proposed a rose garden flanked by cascading waterfalls.

### COMMAS

#### EXERCISE #1

1) While the Senator made his speech on Capitol Hill, the activists organized outside.
2) After succumbing to pressure from animal rights activists, the amusement park agreed not to keep Orca whales in captivity.
3) If the chef finds even the smallest objection to the dish, he will send it back to the kitchen in anger.

#### EXERCISE #2

1) Maria went to the market to buy groceries, but she forgot to bring her shopping list.
2) Professor Thompson loved the idea of teaching English full time, so he begged the president of the university to give him a chance to prove himself.
3) Naomi Foner wrote the screenplay to *Losing Isaiah* and *Running on Empty*, but her son, Jake Gyllenhaal, is far more well known. Or: Naomi Fomer wrote the screenplay to *Losing Isaiah* and *Running on Empty*, yet her son, Jake Gyllenhaal, is far more well known.

#### EXERCISE #3

1) I picked up grapefruit juice, salt, and soda from the local grocery store.
2) I never had a mom, a dad, a dog, a friend, or a good night's sleep.
3) When I looked into her eyes, I saw a wild, angry animal.

4) To think clearly, to feel deeply, to love constantly: these are the objectives of an evolved human being.
5) My silent, happy sister simply nodded her head in amazement.

### EXERCISE #4

1) My cousin Jared, whom I had never met until I was an adult, plays soccer for the L.A. Galaxy.
2) I took a trip to New Orleans, the birthplace of jazz, to celebrate my graduation from music school.
3) A bona fide recess expert, my nephew expounded on the value of playing tag with his friends.
4) Irving's novel, which took him twelve years to write, suffers from its long, poetic passages.

### EXERCISE #5

1) B
2) B
3) B
4) C
5) A
6) C
7) C

### EXERCISE #6

1) C
2) C
3) C
4) B
5) D
6) C
7) A

## SEMICOLONS, COLONS, AND DASHES

### EXERCISE #1

1) Invest early when saving for retirement; your money will grow exponentially as a result.
2) My brother specializes in vintage organs and keyboards; when he hears a recording, he can easily identify both the instrument and the amplifier it was played through.
3) Jethro really wanted a double chili cheeseburger; however, he ordered a sensible salad.

### EXERCISE #2

1) B
2) A
3) A, B, and C
4) C
5) A
6) D
7) C
8) B
9) D
10) A

### EXERCISE #3

1) B
2) D
3) C

## SUBJECT-VERB AGREEMENT AND VERB TENSE

### EXERCISE #1

1) live
2) has
3) hopes
4) is
5) was
6) was
7) are
8) is
9) wears
10) are

### EXERCISE #2

1) B
2) D
3) C
4) A
5) A
6) D
7) A
8) D
9) A
10) D
11) B
12) A

### EXERCISE #3

1) A and C
2) C
3) A

4) B
5) A

## EXERCISE #4

1) A
2) C
3) D
4) D
5) D

# PARALLELISM

## EXERCISE #1

1) B
2) A, B, and C

## EXERCISE #2

1) C
2) C
3) A
4) D
5) C
6) B
7) D
8) C
9) D
10) A

# PRONOUNS

## EXERCISE #1

1) plural
2) singular
3) singular
4) singular
5) plural
6) singular

## EXERCISE #2

1) their
2) it
3) its
4) their
5) it
6) it

## EXERCISE #3

1) he
2) me
3) us, them
4) us
5) him, me
6) who
7) us
8) whom
9) Who
10) me

## EXERCISE #4

1) B
2) D
3) C
4) B
5) A and C
6) C
7) A
8) D

## EXERCISE #5

1) A
2) B
3) D

# POSSESSION

## EXERCISE #1

1) It's
2) its
3) It's
4) it's
5) its
6) It's

## EXERCISE #2

1) they're
2) Whose
3) Their
4) You're, your
5) their
6) Who's
7) their
8) You're

### EXERCISE #3

1) A and C
2) B
3) B
4) C
5) A
6) C
7) B
8) A

### EXERCISE #4

1) C
2) B
3) D

## THAT V. WHICH

### EXERCISE #1

1) A
2) B

### EXERCISE #2

1) which
2) that
3) that
4) which
5) that

## MISPLACED MODIFIERS

### EXERCISE #1

1) A
2) A

### EXERCISE #2

1) D
2) A
3) D
4) A

# CHAPTER 2: THE EDITORIAL STUFF

## SHORTER IS BETTER

### EXERCISE #1

1) C

### EXERCISE #2

1) A
2) B
3) A
4) A
5) A
6) D
7) A
8) A

## RELEVANCE

### EXERCISE #1

1) DELETE
2) KEEP

### EXERCISE #2

1) and Homare Sawa of Japan became the oldest player to score a goal.
2) Mark Zuckerberg recently settled a lawsuit with the Winklevoss twins regarding the founding of Facebook.
3) One time I found a fifty-dollar bill on the street and used it to buy a new pair of skinny jeans.
4) Many Major League Baseball players come from Latin America and the Caribbean.
5) Some people don't pay their taxes, and these people are called scofflaws.
6) which was built in 1873 by a Danish farmer by the name Viktor Schmeichel
7) The term "prom" comes from the word "promenade," a dance step practiced in classic English and American social dances.
8) Drivers' Ed is a mandatory class in some school districts, but others treat it as an extracurricular or private activity.
9) and casting is the process by which producers find people to be on their shows.

### EXERCISE #3

1) MOVE
2) KEEP
3) DELETE

### EXERCISE #4

1) C
2) D
3) A

---

## LOGICAL CONNECTIONS

### EXERCISE #1

1) C

### EXERCISE #2

1) C
2) A
3) B
4) B
5) B
6) C
7) A
8) B
9) A
10) D
11) B
12) B

---

## SEQUENCE

### EXERCISE #1

1) C

### EXERCISE #2

1) A

### EXERCISE #3

1) D

### EXERCISE #4

1) B

### EXERCISE #5

1) C

### EXERCISE #6

1) D

---

## STRUCTURE

### EXERCISE #1

1) B
2) A
3) C

### EXERCISE #2

1) A

### EXERCISE #3

1) D
2) B

---

## SEQUENCE AND STRUCTURE ROUND-UP!

### EXERCISE #1

1) A, B, E, and F
2) B and D

### EXERCISE #2

1) 1, 5, 4, 3, 2
2) 3, 2, 5, 1, 4

---

## GIVE 'EM WHAT THEY WANT

### EXERCISE #1

1) B and C

### EXERCISE #2

1) B
2) A
3) A

---

## DICTION

### EXERCISE #1

1) + –
2) – +
3) – +
4) + –
5) – +
6) + –

7) – +
8) + –

### EXERCISE #2

1) To "know" suggests greater certainty than to "suppose."
2) "Halt" suggests an abrupt and usually temporary stop, while "conclude" simply indicates an ending.
3) "Forfeit" suggests giving up before one has begun, while "surrender" usually happens after some sort of battle. We also use "forfeit" more for things like sports and "surrender" to describe more serious conflicts like war.
4) "Accept" has a less positive/less willing connotation than "approve."
5) "Loathe" is a more extreme version of "dislike."
6) "Thrifty" has a positive connotation, while "miserly" is negative.

### EXERCISE #3

1) C
2) D
3) C
4) A
5) D
6) B

## IDIOMS

### EXERCISE #1

1) B
2) A

### EXERCISE #2

1) B
2) B
3) C
4) A
5) D
6) C
7) B

## STYLE

### EXERCISE #1

1) A
2) C

### EXERCISE #2

1) B
2) B
3) A
4) A
5) A
6) B

### EXERCISE #3

1) A
2) B
3) A

Tutor Ted®

# WRITING & LANGUAGE: SOLUTIONS

# The Solutions

## CHAPTER 1: THE TECHNICAL STUFF

### HOW TO BUILD A SENTENCE

#### EXERCISE #1

**1) C**

This is pretty basic—the independent clause is the one that can stand alone as a sentence. Keep in mind that you don't necessarily need to memorize the grammar vocabulary. You just want to know it so you know how to use it.

**2) B**
**3) B**
**4) C**
**5) B and D**

#### EXERCISE #2

**1) C**
**2) B**

Don't be afraid to choose the answer choice without punctuation! Just as the College Board doesn't like extraneous words and information, it *really* doesn't like extraneous punctuation. If both your ear and the rules indicate that the sentence is complete without punctuation, leave it out!

**3) D**

#### EXERCISE #3

**1)** The game was over, but the crowd refused to leave.
**2)** While I was making dinner, my dog started barking outside.
**3)** The band played for three hours and never took a set break. (NO CHANGE)
**4)** If you are sick, you shouldn't ride the subway.
**5)** He followed the team for fifty years; it hardly mattered whether the team won or lost. Or: He followed the team for fifty years, and it hardly mattered whether the team won or lost.
**6)** It isn't easy being tall, but it's even harder to be short.
**7)** Maria is my only sister; she is dutiful and decent. Or: Maria is my only sister: she is dutiful and decent. Or: Maria is my only sister—she is dutiful and decent.
**8)** Because Lana was so difficult to work with, the studio decided to hire another actress.
**9)** This Twitter feed doesn't make any sense—it reads like it was written by a computer. Or: This Twitter feed doesn't make any sense; it reads like it was written by a computer.
**10)** The city could no longer call on Batman when local criminals began to cause problems. (NO CHANGE)
**11)** To get a ticket, you'd better buy online.
**12)** The famous designer decided that the town needed something really grand at its center, so he proposed a rose garden flanked by cascading waterfalls. Or: The famous designer decided that the town needed something really grand at its center: he proposed a rose garden flanked by cascading waterfalls.

### COMMAS

#### EXERCISE #1

**1)** While the Senator made his speech on Capitol Hill, the activists organized outside.
**2)** After succumbing to pressure from animal rights activists, the amusement park agreed not to keep Orca whales in captivity.
**3)** If the chef finds even the smallest objection to the dish, he will send it back to the kitchen in anger.

#### EXERCISE #2

**1)** Maria went to the market to buy groceries, but she forgot to bring her shopping list.
**2)** Professor Thompson loved the idea of teaching English full time, so he begged the president of the university to give him a chance to prove himself.
**3)** Naomi Foner wrote the screenplay to *Losing Isaiah* and *Running on Empty*, but her son,

Jake Gyllenhaal, is far more well known. Or: Naomi Foner wrote the screenplay to *Losing Isaiah* and *Running on Empty*, yet her son, Jake Gyllenhaal, is far more well known. ***Note:*** Grammatically speaking, the words "but" and "yet" are essentially interchangeable; "but" is simply more commonly used.

## EXERCISE #3

1) I picked up grapefruit juice, salt, and soda from the local grocery store.
2) I never had a mom, a dad, a dog, a friend, or a good night's sleep.
3) When I looked into her eyes, I saw a wild, angry animal.
4) To think clearly, to feel deeply, to love constantly: these are the objectives of an evolved human being.
5) My silent, happy sister simply nodded her head in amazement.

## EXERCISE #4

1) My cousin Jared, who I had never met until I was an adult, plays soccer for the L.A. Galaxy.
2) I took a trip to New Orleans, the birthplace of jazz, to celebrate my graduation from music school.
3) A bona fide recess expert, my nephew expounded on the value of playing tag with his friends.

   Not all appositives require two commas because not all appositives come in the middle of a sentence. For a sentence like this one, where the appositive clause introduces the sentence, you only need one.
4) Irving's novel, which took him twelve years to write, suffers from its long, poetic passages.

## EXERCISE #5

1) **B**
2) **B**
3) **B**
4) **C**
5) **A**
6) **C**
7) **C**

## EXERCISE #6

1) **C**

   Another reminder that the SAT wants you to remove as many commas as possible!
2) **C**
3) **C**

   This question requires you to fight a battle on two fronts (commas and verb conjugation), but if you remember that appositive clauses set off "inessential information" and thus could be removed from the sentence entirely, you can fight both at once. We need the comma after the word "college" to complete the appositive phrase, which eliminates choices A and D. If we then remove the appositive clause, only C is a complete sentence.
4) **B**

   Answer choice A is a comma splice, C neglects to put a comma before the conjunction (and the conjunction itself indicates the wrong kind of relationship between clauses), and D is incorrect because a semicolon can only be used to combine two independent clauses.
5) **D**
6) **C**
7) **A**

---

## SEMICOLONS, COLONS, AND DASHES

## EXERCISE #1

1) Invest early when saving for retirement; your money will grow exponentially as a result.
2) My brother specializes in vintage organs and keyboards; when he hears a recording, he can easily identify both the instrument and the amplifier it was played through.
3) Jethro really wanted a double chili cheeseburger; however, he ordered a sensible salad.

## EXERCISE #2

1) **B**
2) **A**
3) **A, B, and C**
4) **C**
5) **A**
6) **D**

**7) C**

Remember that a semicolon and a period are grammatically interchangeable. If you replace the semicolons in the answer choices with periods, you should see pretty clearly that C is the only choice where the semicolon separates what could be two complete sentences.

**8) B**

First of all, ew! Where is all this vomit coming from?! Ok, now let's get to the construction of this sentence: a classic example of an independent clause followed by a colon followed by a list. Even though we use commas to connect items in a list, the colon makes clear that the word "perch" completes the previous thought and is not itself part of the list.

**9) D**

Remember how a colon must follow an independent clause? Answer choice D is the only option where the first clause could be a standalone sentence (the definition of an independent clause), and thus it is the only possible correct answer.

**10) A**

If you remember that dashes—as in the clause containing the grammatically inessential information I'm writing right now—come as a pair, you can eliminate any answer choices where the initial dash doesn't have a partner. That leaves us with A and D. Here it gets a little bit tricky, so ask yourself- what is more essential to a sentence? The subject of the sentence or an adjective phrase further describing that subject? The subject, of course! It's nice to get a little detail on what The Window Washers are all about, but the name of the band itself is more important structurally.

## EXERCISE #3

**1) B**

Another question where the best punctuation is no punctuation. Surprising? Hardly.

**2) D**

The list at the end of this sentence is practically begging us to include a colon, which eliminates answer choices B and C. But remember, a colon replaces, not follows, words like "including." Thus, D is the only remaining option.

**3) C**

The em-dash is all about the buddy system. Don't let your em-dash travel without its buddy!

---

## SUBJECT-VERB AGREEMENT AND VERB TENSE

## EXERCISE #1

**1) live**

**2) has**

"Siding," which is singular, is the subject of this sentence. "On the houses" is just an adjective phrase further describing the siding.

**3) hopes**

Is a "team" comprised of more than one person? Yes. However, how many teams are we talking about? One.

**4) is**

"Each" is the subject here, with the prepositional phrase "of the songs on his record" simply further describing each what. Since the word "each" implies "each individual thing by itself," it is always singular.

**5) was**

Don't let the "s" on the end of the word fool you. If you were majoring in Economics, how many majors would you have? Uno.

**6) was**

**7) are**

**8) is**

Much like "each," there's an unspoken *one* after the word "either." Here, that would mean that either one or the other (kale or arugula, not both) is the preferred vegetable. Though the author of the sentence is overlooking the obvious fact that asparagus beats the pants off of either of these leafy greens, he/she has only one favorite, and thus the verb should be singular.

**9) wears**

**10) are**

### EXERCISE #2

**1) B**

"Has grown" is the only choice that correctly indicates that the time frame of the growth begins in 1965 and continues to the present.

**2) D**

"Had been waiting" correctly indicates that the waiting spanned more than three hours from a certain point in the past to a later point, still in the past, when Marcel arrived.

**3) C**

"Will have written" is the only choice to correctly acknowledge that next Tuesday is in the future.

**4) A**
**5) A**
**6) D**
**7) A**
**8) D**

If this sentence were differently constructed, one could perhaps make an argument for answer choice A. However, the word "once" clearly indicates that Martin no longer holds his former position on the death penalty, so we must choose D.

**9) A**
**10) D**

The key word here is "if." "Would have" indicates a hypothetical situation that might have happened but did not. In other words, it might have or "would have" happened if not for some event that prohibited it from happening—in this case, the failure to ask.

**11) B**

Though I do like to imagine an absurd reality where someone's been hypnotized to take a bath every time they hear a doorbell, this one's gotta be B.

**12) A**

C is a tempting runner-up, but we generally use the perfect tense (has/has/have) when there's a clearer indication of the timeline. Refer back to questions 11-13 for examples.

### EXERCISE #3

**1) A and C**
**2) C**
**3) A**
**4) B**
**5) A**

### EXERCISE #4

**1) A**
**2) C**

When the subject of a sentence is doing more than one thing, we generally want the tenses of those verbs to match. Here, our subject's drinking process is comprised of two steps: kneel-ing and submerg-ing.

**3) D**
**4) D**
**5) D**

Another example of the ol' "singular subject followed by prepositional phrase containing a plural noun" trick! Oh SAT, you are so predictable! What is the subject here? Evidence. Would you say "evidence has" or "evidence have"? That's right, which leaves us choosing between C and D. Did the evidence find NASA's spacecraft? That seems unlikely. No, NASA's spacecraft found the evidence or, rearranged, the evidence "has been found by" NASA's spacecraft.

---

## PARALLELISM

### EXERCISE #1

**1) B**
**2) A, B, and C**

### EXERCISE #2

**1) C**
**2) C**

If you cut out some of the fat, "begins with discovering" and "ends with using" are the most grammatically parallel phrases.

**3) A**

The school board member behaved badly in two ways: pout-ing then refus-ing.

**4) D**
**5) C**

Yes, this question is about parallelism, but it's also about punctuation. The rules of parallelism should help you eliminate answer choices B and D (heck, you don't need much more than a good ear to hear that these choices are awkwardly worded). To win the battle of A versus C, you must go back to comma/semicolon rules. Because this sentence features two independent clauses without a coordinating conjunction, these clauses must be combined with a semicolon rather than a comma.

**6) B**

Parallelism in comparisons means comparing "apples to apples." Here, we are comparing musicians to a musician. You could also compare the careers of other musicians to that of (the career of) Taylor Swift, but you can't compare careers to people or vice versa.

**7) D**
**8) C**
**9) D**

Let's think of these parallel phrases more as parts of speech than anything else. The sentence sets up that the critic found the film captivating (adj.) because of its colorful characterizations (n.). Thus, when we structure the parallel clause, we have to put those parts of speech in the same order: ponderous (adj.) because of its pacing (n.). It also doesn't hurt that the phrase "because of its" in answer choice D is a perfect match!

**10) A**

---

## PRONOUNS

### EXERCISE #1

**1) plural**
**2) singular**
**3) singular**
**4) singular**
**5) plural**
**6) singular**

### EXERCISE #2

**1) their**
**2) it**
**3) its**

It's those pesky collective nouns again! Remember, it's only one band, so the pronoun must be singular.

**4) their**
**5) it**
**6) it**

Are you starting to recognize the SAT's favorite tricks? The subject here is "collection," not "meteorites," so the pronoun "it" is correct.

### EXERCISE #3

**1) he**
**2) me**

If you remove "Jeff and," the correct answer should be pretty clear.

**3) us, them**

Remember that object pronouns always follow prepositions (to/for/by/with/from/ etc). Which sounds better—"it was awarded to we" or "it was awarded to us"?

**4) us**
**5) him, me**
**6) who**
**7) us**
**8) whom**
**9) Who**
**10) me**

Just like to/for/by/with/from, "between" is a preposition. Which pronouns follow prepositions? Object pronouns!

### EXERCISE #4

**1) B**
**2) D**
**3) C**
**4) B**
**5) A and C**
**6) C**
**7) A**
**8) D**

### EXERCISE #5

**1) A**

The pronoun decision is the easy part of this question. Since "wildfire" is the subject, we need to use the singular pronoun "it." The battle between A and D relies on your nuanced understanding of the language, and your only real option is to ask yourself "how do we usually say that?" The words "in" and "on" here have basically no meaning, but generally speaking we say "in its path" rather than "on its path" when discussing natural forces like fires, hurricanes, tornadoes, etc.

2) **B**

This is a tricky one, and one probably best answered by process of elimination. C is incorrect because "they're" is a contraction for "they are." A is out because the pronoun "their" is unclear as to which plural noun it is referring: critics or pieces. That leaves us deciding between B and D, and the SAT's preference for parallel structure should make B the more attractive candidate.

3) **D**

---

## POSSESSION

### EXERCISE #1

1) **It's**
2) **its**
3) **It's**
4) **it's**
5) **its**
6) **It's**

### EXERCISE #2

1) **they're**
2) **Whose**
3) **Their**
4) **You're, your**
5) **their**
6) **Who's**
7) **their**
8) **You're**

### EXERCISE #3

1) **A and C**
2) **B**
3) **B**
4) **C**
5) **A**
6) **C**
7) **B**
8) **A**

### EXERCISE #4

1) **C**

Ooh, this one is sneaky! How many groups are we talking about? The word "group" is a collective noun, so if it's only one group, regardless of the number of people in it, it would be singular and therefore the possessive "group's" would be correct. However, the pronoun "they" after the comma indicates that we are talking about more than one group, so the plural possessive "groups' progress" in answer choice C is the only valid option.

2) **B**
3) **D**

---

## THAT V. WHICH

### EXERCISE #1

1) **A**
2) **B**

### EXERCISE #2

1) **which**
2) **that**
3) **that**
4) **which**
5) **that**

---

## MISPLACED MODIFIERS

### EXERCISE #1

1) **A**
2) **A**

### EXERCISE #2

1) **D**

While both Noah and the motorcycle could have emerged from the accident without a scratch, only Noah is capable of being surprised.

2) **A**

What is poorly manufactured and prone to breakdowns? The new car. If you selected D, remember that it's possessive. The subject of "new car's aesthetics" is actually "aesthetics," just as in the phrase "Jose's dog," the subject would be the dog and not Jose.

3) **D**
4) **A**

This question flips the script by asking us about the first clause instead of the second. Since the second clause is set, we see that "movement" must be the subject of the sentence. Which choice most directly introduces something that could be described as a movement? "Self-help" is the only choice that fits the bill, but you could also work it backwards by realizing that "musical satire," "musical," and "satirical musical" are all basically the same thing.

# CHAPTER 2: THE EDITORIAL STUFF

## SHORTER IS BETTER

### EXERCISE #1

1) **C**

### EXERCISE #2

1) **A**
2) **B**
3) **A**
4) **A**
5) **A**
6) **D**
7) **A**
8) **A**

If you got this one right, congratulations! You found the exception to the rule "shorter is better." We want to eliminate redundant words and phrases, but "fiscally prohibitive" and "extremely short-sighted" tell us two *different* things, both relevant to the sentence.

## RELEVANCE

### EXERCISE #1

1) **DELETE**

While this piece of information isn't completely irrelevant, the first clause is way too broad. In addition, if you read the paragraph without the sentence in question, you should be able to recognize that the ideas flow better without it.

2) **KEEP**

Again, the paragraph is not terrible without this piece of information, but ask yourself: does it provide relevant information not found anywhere else in the paragraph? Yes. That's a good reason to keep it.

### EXERCISE #2

1) and Homare Sawa of Japan became the oldest player to score a goal.

Good for Homare Sawa, but the focus of the paragraph is about the sport's growing popularity, not the age of its players.

2) Mark Zuckerberg recently settled a lawsuit with the Winklevoss twins regarding the founding of Facebook.

The Winklevoss twins apparently invested that lawsuit money into bitcoin! Wow, that fact is just as irrelevant as the sentence you should delete from this paragraph!

3) One time I found a fifty-dollar bill on the street and used it to buy a new pair of skinny jeans.

Any time a paragraph changes POV (from 3rd person to 1st person, as is the case here), that's a big hint that the odd-man-out sentence should be deleted.

4) Many Major League Baseball players come from Latin America and the Caribbean.

This passage's question as to whether baseball is "America's pastime" focuses on its waning popularity rather than the nationalities of its players.

5) Some people don't pay their taxes, and these people are called scofflaws.

It can be tricky when the irrelevant part is the first thing you read because you have not yet developed an understanding of the main idea. However, once you get a couple more sentences into this one, it should be clear that the first sentence does not introduce the idea that the tax code is complex.

6) which was built in 1873 by a Danish farmer by the name Viktor Schmeichel

Pay attention to style here. This passage is lyrical, using figurative language to create

a moody, almost meditative tone. The background information about the barn interrupts this flow of thought with information that seems too dry and informative to fit the rest of the passage.

**7)** The term "prom" comes from the word "promenade," a dance step practiced in classic English and American social dances.
This is another one where the tone of the irrelevant sentence is a mismatch for the rest of the passage.

**8)** Drivers' Ed is a mandatory class in some school districts, but others treat it as an extracurricular or private activity.
Another tone issue AND this information is too broad in scope.

**9)** and casting is the process by which producers find people to be on their shows.
Thanks but no thanks for the info.

## EXERCISE #3

**1) MOVE**
While this sentence technically could be deleted, the passage is most improved by moving it to the beginning. This way it acts as a hook that both draws us into the passage and tees up the clarification in the second sentence: the Salton Sea is not actually a "sea."

**2) KEEP**
This sentence provides a needed transition from a discussion about the benefits of participating in individual sports to those of participating in team sports.

**3) DELETE**
This sentence is irrelevant and should be deleted.

## EXERCISE #4

**1) C**
**2) D**
**3) A**

# LOGICAL CONNECTIONS

## EXERCISE #1

**1) C**

## EXERCISE #2

**1) C**
This sentence is about chronology, and "then" is the only option that indicates time.

**2) A**
"Because" and "so" both indicate the correct relationship between clauses (cause and effect), but "because" is the only choice that can begin a sentence.

**3) B**
This one's tricky and might best be solved by working backward. C is out because the city's need for laborers did not cause the national shortage. A and D are both words that indicate contrast, and if two answers are correct for the same reason—guess what?! They're both wrong! B works because the phrase "in fact" indicates a broadening of scope. (Ex: The people were angry; in fact, they were so angry that they took to rioting in the streets!) In this sentence, not only is there a need for workers in the city; the problem is even bigger in scope—there's a shortage countrywide!

**4) B**
We are looking for contrast, and "otherwise" serves it up on a muffin-laden platter.

**5) B**
D is probably the tempting wrong answer here, but we need to convey contrast. Yes, it's contrast between something hard and something really hard, but those ideas are still in opposition. (Ex: Sure, I've got a split lip and a black eye, but you should see the other guy!)

**6) C**
Here are two delightful ways to experience life from inside a convertible—choose one or the other!

**7) A**
Classic contrast.

**8) B**

You may have chosen B pretty easily, but you can also work this one backwards. A and D mean the same thing, so they must both be wrong. Then we can ask, do these thoughts agree or contrast? They agree.

**9) A**

We're just continuing the thought.

**10) D**

Okay, I hear you. Aren't A and D both contrast words? Yes. And isn't it true that if two words work for the same reason they both have to be wrong? Righto. So what gives? Basically, this one comes down to using your ears. Based on how we use these two words, "however" definitely works better in the sentence.

**11) B**

If you're less familiar with the word "conversely," it helps to notice that all three of the remaining choices indicate a cause and effect relationship between clauses. Does positive reinforcement leading to good things actually cause negative reinforcement leading to bad? No. They're simply two sides of the same coin.

**12) B**

Once again, we're looking at a timeline. School officials loosened the requirements after they realized what a pain in the butt it was to do the paperwork.

---

## SEQUENCE

### EXERCISE #1

**1) C**

This question can be tricky until you realize that sentence 1 contains the pronoun "their." Well, who are they? The sentence before should tell us. Sentences 2 and 4 talk about La Raza, but as a collective noun La Raza is an "it" not a "they." The only possible "they" is sentence 3's "photographers," whose efforts are surely the ones being referred to in sentence 1.

### EXERCISE #2

**1) A**

Finding the correct answer to this question is all about the transition word "now" at the beginning of sentence. Sentences 1 and 2 both deal with the past, and sentence 4 poses a question based on the information in sentence 3. Therefore, our transition from the past to the present is correct as written.

### EXERCISE #3

**1) D**

This one is tough because some of these sentences talk about the past in the present tense (for example, the Renaissance happened in the past but is currently regarded as the end of the Middle Ages). However, if you realize that sentence 4's past tense "began" needs to precede sentence 3's time traveling "have drawn," you'll find that placing the sentence after sentence 4 is your only option.

### EXERCISE #4

**1) B**

What is the purpose of sentence 2? It certainly seems like a hook designed to draw the reader into the passage. Where does a hook go? At the beginning!

### EXERCISE #5

**1) C**

Definitely not relevant. This passage is about smiling for pictures, not about the historical subjects of portraiture.

### EXERCISE #6

**1) D**

The only possible reason to keep this is that it somewhat resembles a conclusion. However, a quick glance at the answer choices tells you that's not an option. Phrases like "pushing it into the hands and sight of more people than ever before" and "sold for a penny" provide us with this same information, so the sentence is redundant and should be deleted.

## STRUCTURE

### EXERCISE #1

**1) B**

The follow-up question suggests the issue at hand may have stemmed from an unconscious bias that, while problematic, was not intentional. The first question should introduce the opposite point of view, and B is the choice that most strongly suggests the scientists buried the negative results on purpose.

**2) A**

This passage is about the insane amount of food you end up eating on a cruise. Answer choice A both introduces this idea and maintains a consistent tone with the rest of the passage.

**3) C**

C is the only option that introduces the "other varietals" the passage discusses in the following sentences.

### EXERCISE #2

**1) A**

If you work this one backwards, B is just very stupid, and C and D are both "half bridge" answer choices. C refers to films (paragraph 2) but doesn't walk us back to paragraph 1. D refers to music (paragraph 1) but doesn't leave us on the dry land of paragraph 2. Answer choice A spans both: "have not been so absent" reminds us of the aforementioned absent songs, and "other art forms" refer to the films in the first sentence of paragraph 2.

### EXERCISE #3

**1) D**

The first clause of this conclusion refers directly back to the previous sentence, and the second refers back to the "struggle" described in the first sentence.

**2) B**

Here, it's the second clause that refers directly back to the previous sentence with the phrase "mixed messages about service," while the first clause gives a shout out to the opening sentence of the passage. ***Hot tip:*** The SAT wants you to know that conclusion sentences do not have to begin with "in conclusion," so if you come across an answer choice that begins this way, it's almost certainly wrong.

## SEQUENCE AND STRUCTURE ROUND-UP!

### EXERCISE #1

**1) A, B, E, and F**
**2) B and D**

### EXERCISE #2

**1) 1, 5, 4, 3, 2**

1: Here's the deal with Matt and Caroline.
5: Backstory of how their parents met.
6: Here's how their parents got even closer.
3: Now you understand why sentence 1 is true.
2: Aaaaaand...Matt and Caroline are now definitely thinking about kissing. Good luck, guys!

**2) 3, 2, 5, 1, 4**

3: Here's a claim about competitive gymnastics.
2: Here's a specific detail supporting that claim.
5: Here's personal testimony supporting that claim and introducing the claim that this situation can be bad.
1: Here's a specific detail supporting this second claim.
4: Here's another specific detail that provides even greater support because it is a more extreme example.

## GIVE 'EM WHAT THEY WANT

### EXERCISE #1

**1) B and C**

### EXERCISE #2

**1) B**

The key word in this question stem is "completes." The passage already describes the oak tree as a seedling, juvenile, and mature tree. What completes this

cycle? Why irreversible, inescapable death, of course!

2) A

If we're looking to "set up the examples," we need to ask ourselves—what are the examples? The end of the sentence describes a bunch of programs and services for homeless people the city is trying to support. What most directly sets up those examples? The idea that an accurate census helps get the money, honey!

3) A

The key phrases in this question stem are "concrete examples" and "prove the central claim." First all, let's get rid of any answer choices that don't provide "concrete examples" of anything. That eliminates C and D. Between A and B, only A relates to the paragraph's central claim that "automaton" comes from ancient Greece.

## DICTION

### EXERCISE #1

1) + –
2) – +
3) – +
4) + –
5) – +
6) + –
7) – +
8) + –

### EXERCISE #2

1) To "know" suggests greater certainty than to "suppose."
2) "Halt" suggests an abrupt and usually temporary stop, while "conclude" simply indicates an ending.
3) "Forfeit" suggests giving up before one has begun, while "surrender" usually happens after some sort of battle. We also use "forfeit" more for things like sports and "surrender" to describe more serious conflicts like war.
4) "Accept" has a less positive/less willing connotation than "approve."
5) "Loathe" is a more extreme version of "dislike."
6) "Thrifty" has a positive connotation, while "miserly" is negative.

### EXERCISE #3

1) C
2) D
3) C
4) A
5) D
6) B

## IDIOMS

### EXERCISE #1

1) B
2) A

### EXERCISE #2

1) B
2) B

Did you notice the word "either" in the sentence? If so, you probably remembered that "either" always goes with "or" and "neither" with "nor." Why? Some English guy hundreds of years ago said so.

3) C
4) A

Yeah I know, these words drive everyone crazy. If you can find a trick to memorizing them, please let me know! Otherwise, you've just to remember that "affect" is the verb and "effect" is the noun. (Ex: The effects of climate change are affecting our community in many ways.)

5) D
6) C
7) B

Remember parallelism? To "truly excel at debate," one must do two things: to "argue" and to "anticipate/rebut." While D also gets the verb tense right, it's just an incredibly awkwardly-worded way to say what we're trying to say.

## STYLE

### EXERCISE #1

1) A
2) C

## EXERCISE #2

**1) B**
**2) B**
**3) A**
**4) A**
**5) A**
**6) B**

## EXERCISE #3

**1) A**

If this question were held on the red carpet, B would be voted worst dressed. Style-wise, it's just a total fail. C and D are wrong more for reasons of diction than style. They just don't mean what we need them to mean.

**2) B**

If you think about everything the SAT cares about- diction, style, conciseness, and keeping it academic- B should be a no-brainer.

**3) A**

If you take the rationale for the previous question and add the SAT's hatred of redundancy (see answer choice D), A should likewise be the obvious choice.

## NO CALCULATOR

*25 minutes. 20 questions.*

*(1 minute, 15 seconds per question)*

## WITH A CALCULATOR

*55 minutes. 38 questions.*

*(1 minute, 27 seconds per question)*

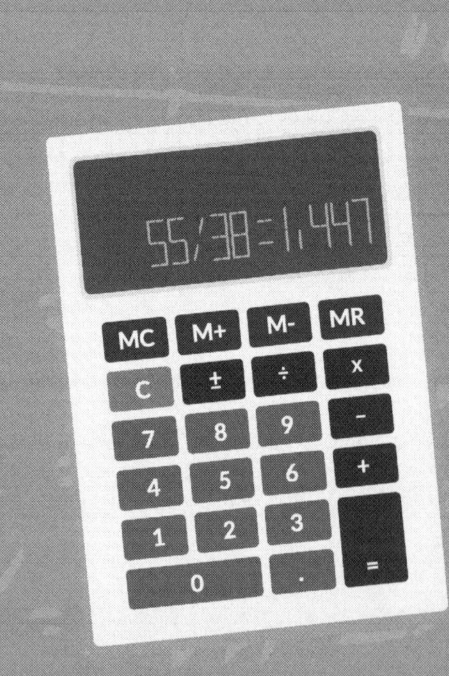

# MATH The Breakdown

## 3 MAJOR TOPICS

- Algebraic Simplification
- Linear Equations
- Quadratic Equatitons

BEST THING YOU CAN DO?

**know your algebra!**

Tutor Ted®

# Pep Talk

**SAT Math, your last multiple choice task on test day, is really pretty manageable.**

Wait whaaaaaat?

I'm so used to sharing bad news with you that even I'm surprised that I said that. It's true, though.

That's not the only good news, either: the math content on the SAT is really focused on a handful of topics. The three most important ones are algebraic simplification, linear equations, and quadratic equations. Those topics make up about 75% of the content of the test.

We'll start with those three topics. As you can imagine, you want to get really comfortable with all three of those. When you are, you'll have a bulk of the math test under your belt.

After that, we'll dip into the other topics that show up on the SAT. We'll close out with some strategies that will make your life easier on the SAT Math test.

And then you'll be an SAT Math wiz-ard! And then we'll throw a party to celebrate how smart you are!

I like this plan!

# The Details

**SAT Math! Here's what to expect.**

## TWO SECTIONS:

### *MATH, NO CALCULATOR—20 QUESTIONS IN 25 MINUTES*

15 Multiple Choice questions, 5 Free Response questions

### *MATH, CALCULATOR PERMITTED—38 QUESTIONS IN 55 MINUTES*

30 Multiple Choice questions, 8 Free Response questions

Each set of questions is arranged in order of increasing difficulty—for example, on the Calculator section, the multiple choice questions from 1-30 ascend from easy to hard, and free response questions 31-38 also ascend from easy to hard.

## What's on the test?

**Algebra for DAYS.**
Everything you can do in Algebra is on this test. Linear and quadratic equations in particular. Yes, there's some Geometry, but there is literally 10x more Algebra.

**An Assortment of Some Pretty Miscellaneous Topics**
Ranging from statistics to polynomial division.

**Charts and Graphs.**
This is the SAT, after all.

**Plenty of Word Problems**
Because who doesn't love word problems?

## High-five.

As on the rest of the SAT, there is no guessing penalty, which means you should answer ALL of the questions, even if you have to guess.

***Hot Tip:*** Ready for the best value to guess on a free response question? It's 0.

# Your Algebra Toolbox

**If your teachers have done a good job, then this section should read like a review chapter.**
If this content is new to you, then your teachers haven't done a good job.

(Side note that will not help you with your SAT prep at all: I had an idea one time for a reality show starring teachers and tutors. Sort of like Top Chef, but for education instead of food. The idea crashed and burned with my TV producer friends. Why? Because no one wants to watch a TV show about education. We would have an easier time getting a show made that just involves people getting hit in the face by projectiles. Which makes me think...what about a show in which teachers get hit in the face by projectiles? We might really have something there.)

OK, back to the reality of education, which will not be televised. You've got a set of skills you want to employ on this test, and on Algebra in general, and we're going to walk through them now. They are critical to your survival, so pay attention.

## ORDER OF OPERATIONS

**Otherwise known as PEMDAS (or GEMDAS, with the 'P' for 'parentheses' replaced with a 'G' for 'grouping), and here's what it means:**
When you simplify an Algebraic expression or equation, you want to do it in the sequence of that word PEMDAS. So:

> ***'P' means you should simplify anything within parentheses or brackets first.***
> ***'E' means you should handle exponents next.***
> ***'M' and 'D' mean you should do any multiplication or division after you handle the exponents.***
> ***'A' and 'S' mean you should do any addition or subtraction as your last step.***

### Let's do an order of operations problem together.

$$4 + [1 - 2(2 + x)]^2$$
$$= 4 + (1 - 4 - 2x)^2$$
$$= 4 + (-2x - 3)^2$$
$$= 4 + (-2x - 3)(-2x - 3)$$
$$= 4 + (4x^2 + 6x + 6x + 9)$$
$$= \boxed{4x^2 + 12x + 13}$$

Notice how that problem took five solid steps to get from the initial expression to the simplified version? Yeah, it should take about that long. Go step-by-step, show your work, and you'll avoid pitfalls along the way.

## Let's do some practice.

## Order of Operations

**1**

If $2x + 10 = 18$, what is the value of $x + 15$?

A) 4
B) 9
C) 19
D) 24

**2**

If $m = 6$, how much greater is $4m$ than $-2m$?

A) 6
B) 12
C) 24
D) 36

**3**

If $6y + 18$ is 16 less than 40, what is the value of $y + 2$?

A) 4
B) 3
C) 1
D) -5

**4**

$$\frac{10}{d} = 400$$

In the equation above, what is the value of $d$?

A) 4,000
B) 250
C) 40
D) 0.025

**5**

$$3x - 6.9 = 2.4(x - 2)$$

What value of x is the solution of the equation above?

**6**

If $t = 4\sqrt{3n}$, what is $3n$ in terms of $t$?

A) $\frac{t}{2}$
B) $\frac{t}{4}$
C) $\frac{t^2}{4}$
D) $\frac{t^2}{16}$

**7**

When $4x$ is decreased by 8, the result is less than 40. If $x$ is an integer, what is the greatest possible value of $x$?

**8**

$$\frac{x + y}{4} = 8$$

$$\frac{y}{4} = 5$$

If $(x, y)$ is a solution to the system of equations above, what is the value of $x$?

A) 20
B) 12
C) 3
D) $\frac{3}{4}$

## COMBINE LIKE TERMS

I abbreviate Combine Like Terms as 'CLT.' That always makes me think of a 'BLT,' aka a Bacon, Lettuce, and Tomato Sandwich, even though the two things have absolutely nothing in common. Maybe I just like having a reason to think about a BLT. Anyway, you want to combine like terms, or CLT, a lot on this test.

### What are like terms?

Any term that has the same variables raised to the same powers.

For example, $x^2$ and $3x^2$ are like terms, because they both have an $x$ squared as their variable term.

$4xy$ and $3y$ are not like terms because they have different variables, $xy$ and $y$.

$2y^3$ and $4y^2$ are not like terms because they have different exponent values.

5 and 3 are like terms. We call these guys constants (because unlike variables, which are always changing, these guys always remain the same), and they are *always* like terms.

### Let me show you an example of how this works.

$$3xy^2 + 2xy - 3y^2x + 4y - 2xy$$

The key here is to see that $3xy^2$ and $3y^2x$ are like terms...the variables are just written in different orders. Once we rearrange the expression so the like terms are next to each other, it's clear how nicely this one will reduce to just one term.

$$3xy^2 + 2xy - 3y^2x + 4y - 2xy$$

$$= 3xy^2 - 3y^2x + 2xy - 2xy + 4y$$

$$= \cancel{3xy^2} - \cancel{3xy^2} + \cancel{2xy} - \cancel{2xy} + 4y$$

$$= \boxed{4y}$$

## Practice? Sure, why not.

## Combine Like Terms

**1**

$$t + 3t - 1 + 4 = 10 - t - t - t$$

In the equation above, what is the value of $t$?

A) 1
B) 2
C) 7
D) 13

**2**

$$2x^2 - 3x - 8$$
$$4x^2 - x + 7$$

Which of the following expressions represents the sum of the two polynomials shown above?

A) $6x^2 - 4x - 1$
B) $6x^2 + 4x - 1$
C) $6x^4 - 4x^2 - 1$
D) $6x^4 + 4x^2 - 1$

**3**

Nikita and Desmond work at the same restaurant. Last week, Nikita worked $b$ hours each day for 6 days, and Desmond worked $c$ hours each day for 4 days. Which of the following represents the total number of hours worked by Nikita and Desmond last week?

A) $4b + 6c$
B) $6b + 4c$
C) $10bc$
D) $24bc$

**4**

$$w^2 + z$$
$$w - 2z$$

Which of the following is equivalent to the sum of the two expressions shown above for all values of $w$ and $z$?

A) $w^3 - z^2$
B) $w^3 - 2z^2$
C) $2w^2 - z$
D) $w^2 + w - z$

**5**

Which of the following is equivalent to $5(y^2 + y) - 2(y^2 + y)$?

A) $9y$
B) $3y^2 - 3y$
C) $3y^2 + 3y$
D) $3y^3$

**6**

$$\sqrt{(3x + 7)} + 5 = x + 6$$

What is the solution set of the equation above?

A) {-2}
B) {3}
C) {-2, 3}
D) { -2, 0, 3}

**7**

The sum of $4x^2 - 8x + 17$ and $-x^2 + 9x + 29$ can be written in the form $ax^2 + bx + c$, where $a$, $b$, and $c$ are constants. What is the value of $a + b + c$?

**8**

The formula below is used to calculate $R$, the total revenue from a movie showing, where $p$ is the price of one adult ticket, $A$ is the number of adult tickets sold, $q$ is the price of one child ticket, and $C$ is the number of child tickets sold.

$$R = pA + qC$$

Which of the following correctly gives $C$ in terms of $R$, $p$, $A$, and $q$?

A) $C = R - pA - q$

B) $C = \frac{R}{q} - pA$

C) $C = \frac{R - pA}{q}$

D) $C = \frac{R - q}{pA}$

## DISTRIBUTION AND FACTORING

Again, this hopefully feels like a review session.

Distribution is definitely important, so humor me for a minute.

Distribution is a concept we use when we've got a value that's being multiplied into an expression within parentheses. Have you ever noticed how hard it is to understand math when it's just expressed in terms of words? Yeah, me too. With that in mind, let's look at a concrete example.

Suppose you have $3(x + 2)$. You need to distribute that 3 to both the $x$ and the 2. Once you do, you'll have $3x + 6$.

A couple of distribution pitfalls: if you have a negative coefficient outside the parentheses, you need to distribute the negative sign to all of the terms too.

### Example of that:

$$x - 3(2x + 4)$$

The negative three in front of the parentheses is a little sneaky—you can miss it if you're not careful. Let me show you how to distribute that as -3.

$$x - 6x - 12$$

Then CLT (aka Combine Like Terms)

$$-5x - 12$$

**One other distribution wrinkle you want to keep your eyes on: FOILing.**

You want to FOIL when you have two terms in one set of parentheses times two terms in another set of parentheses. Like so:

$$(x + 4)(2x - 1)$$

We're going to distribute here; we just need to do so a little more carefully and with a little more patience. We've got two terms times two terms, and we need to multiply each pair of them and then combine the like terms of the results. That's where this FOILing idea comes into play—each of the letters stands for a pair of terms to multiply together.

***F, for 'front'***: $x \times 2x$
***O, for 'outside'***: $x \times -1$
***I, for 'inside'***: $4 \times 2x$
***L, for 'last'***: $4 \times -1$

Those four terms will be $2x^2$, $-x$, $8x$, and $-4$. Last thing: add them together and combine like terms.

$$2x^2 + (-x) + 8x + (-4) = 2x^2 + 7x - 4$$

## FACTORING

I paired factoring up with distribution because it's basically the opposite process: instead of multiplying through to get rid of parentheses, we're starting from the end result and trying to put it back into parentheses.

Why? Doing so is going to give us some useful tools when it comes to quadratic equations. Factoring can give us both the x-intercepts and the vertex of a quadratic equation. We want both of those.

### Let's see an example.

The function $f(x) = 3x^2 - 4x + 1$ crosses the x-axis at two points. What are the $x$-coordinates of these two points?

A) $x = \frac{1}{3}, 1$
B) $x = 1, 3$
C) $x = -1, -\frac{1}{3}$
D) $x = -1, -3$

You've got a couple of things going on in this problem. First, you've got to know what it means to cross the x-axis. Whenever you cross the x-axis, the y-value is zero. So you're trying to figure out where a graph crosses the x-axis, plug in y = 0 to find out.

After you set y = 0, you have a couple of ways to solve for $x$. The "brute force" way to solve it would be to try the answer choices. The *potentially* faster and *definitely* more elegant way would be to factor it. Let me show you how.

Because it's a quadratic equation (that's the fancy name for an equation where the highest-powered term is an $x^2$ term), we should try to factor it into two binomial terms. Basically, we want to un-FOIL it.

Start with the first terms, the ones that will multiply to get you to $3x^2$. Those two terms should be $3x$ and $x$. Put them at the front of each set of parentheses.

$$(3x \quad )(x \quad )$$

$$3x \quad x$$

Next, ask yourself what would multiply to get to that last term, the +1 at the end of $3x^2 - 4x + 1$. Two possibilities, either $(1) \times (1)$ or $(-1) \times (-1)$. In this case, since the middle term ($-4x$) is negative, we know we need the negative values.

$$(3x - 1)(x - 1)$$

If you FOIL that out, you'll see that it gets us back to where we started from:

$$3x^2 - 4x + 1$$

Then you could factor it again. Then FOIL it. Then factor again. Then FOIL. Really, you can keep going on for as long as you like.

## Now let's practice.

# Distribution and Factoring

**1**

$$3(4x - 12) - 2(7 + 2x) = 6$$

What value of $x$ satisfies the equation above?

**2**

$$(160y^3 + 4793) - 20(y^3 - 65)$$

The expression above can be written in the form $ay^3 + c$, where $a$ and $c$ are constants. What is the value of $a + c$?

**3**

$$4(3 - 2x) - 2(x^2 - 1) + 3x(x + 1)$$

Which of the following polynomials is equivalent to the expression above?

A) $x^2 - 5x + 14$
B) $x^2 - 5x + 10$
C) $x^2 - 2x + 12$
D) $-2x^2 - 5x + 17$

**4**

$$y = x^4 - 2x^3 - 3x^2 + 8x - 4$$

The polynomial function above can be written as $y = (x^2 - 4)(x - 1)^2$. What are all of the zeros of the function?

A) -2, -1, and 2
B) -2, 1, and 2
C) -1, 1, and 2
D) 1 and 4

**5**

$$6(k - 2) + 3(k + 2) = 2k$$

What value of $k$ is the solution of the equation above?

**6**

$$(x - 1)^2 - 6(x - 1) = -9$$

Which of the following is the solution to the equation above?

A) 1
B) 2
C) 4
D) 8

**7**

$$2(3x + 1)(5x + 2)$$

Which of the following is equivalent to the expression above?

A) $16x^2 + 6$
B) $30x^2 + 4$
C) $30x^2 + 22x + 4$
D) $60x^2 44x + 8$

**8**

$$5xy + 5z - 13 = 17$$

Based on the equation above, what is the value of $xy + z$?

A) 6
B) 12
C) 20
D) 25

**9**

The expression $25x^2 - 4$ can be written in the form $(ax + b)(ax - b)$, where $a$ and $b$ are constants. Which of the following could be the value of $a$?

A) 2
B) 4
C) 5
D) 25

**10**

The expression $(2.2x + 1.3)^2 - (6.5x^2 - 8.2)$ is equivalent to which of the following?

A) $-1.66x^2 + 5.72x - 6.51$
B) $-1.66x^2 + 5.72x + 9.89$
C) $-2.1x^2 - 5.6$
D) $-2.1x^2 + 10.8$

**11**

$$\left(x + \frac{1}{3}\right)(x - 4) = 0$$

What is the sum of the solutions of the equation above?

A) $-\frac{13}{3}$
B) $-\frac{11}{3}$
C) $\frac{11}{3}$
D) $\frac{13}{3}$

**12**

$$x^2 + 8x + 8$$

Which of the following is equivalent to the expression above?

A) $(x + 4)^2 + 8$
B) $(x + 4)^2 - 8$
C) $(x - 4)^2 + 8$
D) $(x - 4)^2 - 8$

**13**

Which of the following is equivalent to $\left(\frac{x}{2} - 4\right)^2$?

A) $\frac{x^2}{2} - 16$
B) $\frac{x^2}{4} - 16$
C) $\frac{x^2}{4} - 2x + 16$
D) $\frac{x^2}{4} - 4x + 16$

**14**

If $4x^2 + y^2 = m$ and $xy = n$, which of the following is equivalent to $4m + 16n$?

A) $(x + 4y)^2$
B) $(2x + 4y)^2$
C) $(4x + 2y)^2$
D) $(4x + 4y)^2$

**15**

$$\frac{3x - 4}{(x - 3)^2} - \frac{3}{x - 3} = \frac{c}{(x - 3)^2}$$

In the equation above, $c$ is a constant and $x \neq 3$. What is the value of $c$?

**16**

$$abc = acd + ab + cd$$

In the equation above, $a$, $b$, $c$, and $d$ are positive integers. Which of the following is equivalent to $a$?

A) $\frac{cd}{bc - cd - b}$
B) $\frac{1}{bc - b}$
C) $\frac{1}{bc + b}$
D) $c - 2cd$

## PROPORTIONS AND CROSS MULTIPLICATION

**Math concepts are like children: you're not supposed to have a favorite but everyone secretly does.**

This one is mine. It's so clean, so useful. And it always works the same way.

You want to use a proportion to solve any question that involves scaling a value up or down. Suppose that a map represents 1 mile as ¼", and a question asks you how many inches would be required to represent 18 miles? Proportion. What if a recipe requires 3 tablespoons of spice mix for every two ears of corn, and you need to know much spice mix is needed for two dozen ears of corn? Proportion.

How does it work? You set up two equal fractions and just put everything in its proper place.

For example, in the map problem proposed above, you would have

$$\frac{\frac{1}{4}\text{ inch}}{1\text{ mile}} = \frac{x\text{ inches}}{18\text{ miles}}$$

Notice that in both fractions, inches are on top and miles are on bottom. That's kind of all that you need to worry about.

Once you have two equal fractions—in fact, *whenever* you have two equal fractions—you then cross multiply to solve.

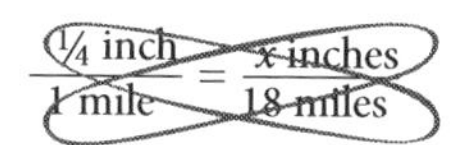

$$\frac{1}{4}\text{ inch} \times 18\text{ miles} = x\text{ inches} \times 1\text{ mile}$$

$$4.5\text{ inches} = x\text{ inches}$$

Do me a favor: every time you see a fraction equal to another one, cross multiply it. Just do it. Your life will be better as a result.

## Proportion/Cross-multiplication

**1**

A certain factory produces screws and safety pins. On Monday, the factory produced 9,000 screws. If the ratio of the number of screws produced to the number of safety pins produced is 1 to 3, how many safety pins did the factory produce on Monday?

A) 3,000
B) 9,000
C) 18,000
D) 27,000

**2**

It takes Erin 2 hours to read 80 pages. If she reads at the same rate, how many pages can she read in 5 hours?

A) 40
B) 100
C) 160
D) 200

**3**

The length of a certain squid, in centimeters, is directly proportional to its age, in years. If an 8-year-old squid is 104 centimeters long, how long is a 5-year-old squid?

**4**

A certain test has 100 questions. Arthur answered $\frac{3}{5}$ of the questions on his test, and Lucy answered $\frac{3}{4}$ of the questions on her test. If they both left the remaining questions blank, how many more questions did Lucy answer on her test than did Arthur answer on his test?

A) 10
B) 15
C) 60
D) 75

**5**

Giant kelp can grow 10 inches in one day. At this rate, how many feet does giant kelp grow in 9 days?

(1 foot = 12 inches)

A) 7.5
B) 90
C) 108
D) 1080

**6**

If $\frac{x}{3y} = \frac{1}{9}$, what is the value of $\frac{4y}{x}$?

A) $\frac{4}{9}$
B) $\frac{4}{3}$
C) 12
D) 36

**Questions 7 and 8 refer to the following information.**

$$p = \frac{A}{96}$$

An interior decorator uses the formula above to estimate the number of cans of paint $p$ needed to paint a wall with area $A$, in square feet.

**7**

Which of the following is closest to the interior decorator's estimate of the number of cans of paint needed for a wall with an area of 36 square meters?

(1 square meter is approximately 10.7 square feet)

A) 0.3 cans
B) 0.4 cans
C) 3.0 cans
D) 4.0 cans

**8**

In a certain house, the area A of the walls in the dining room is 6 times the area of the walls in the kitchen. What is the ratio of the number of cans of paint needed for the dining room to the number of cans of paint needed for the kitchen?

A) 1 to 16
B) 1 to 6
C) 6 to 1
D) 96 to 1

## ABSOLUTE VALUE

Absolute value is math's most aesthetically pleasing function. Who could deny that? Take a look:

$|x|$

Minimal, elegant, symmetrical—it's the must-have symbol for every fashion-conscious mathematician.

Most students think of absolute value on the most practical level: if you have something positive inside the absolute value brackets, it stays positive; if you have something negative in there, it turns positive.

Another way to think of it is as a measure of distance. I know, I know...that sounds irritatingly math-teacher-conceptual, but hear me out—this is actually useful.

When you have the absolute value of ONE term, you're finding the distance between that value and zero. $|5|$ and $|-5|$ are both exactly 5 units away from 0; that's why both of them have an absolute value of 5.

When you have the absolute value of the difference between TWO terms, like this...

$$|-6 - 4|$$

...you are finding the distance between those two terms. Here, you're finding the distance between -6 and 4. Like so:

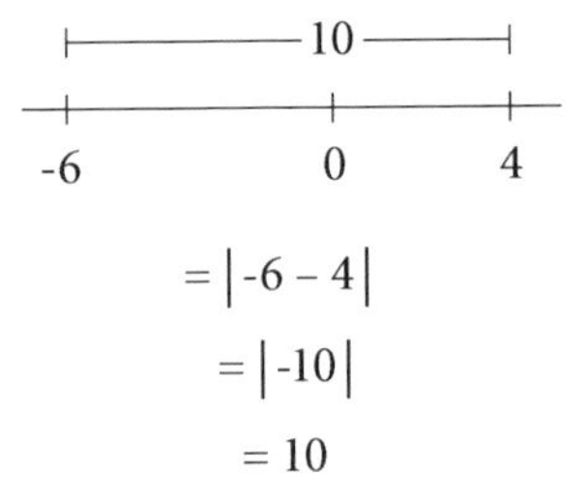


$$= |-6 - 4|$$
$$= |-10|$$
$$= 10$$

This is where absolute value starts to become really useful. Suppose you want to write an inequality expressing that the variable $x$ has a value between 70 and 90. Here's how you'd do that.

$$|x - 80| < 10$$

If you're asking "where on earth did 80 and 10 come from?" Lemme explain to ya. You want $x$ to be between 70 and 90. What's exactly between 70 and 90? 80. What we do here is say, using the absolute value brackets, that $x$ needs to be less than 10 units away from 80. That means it can go as low as 70 and as high as 90.

If you want to know the concept that underlies the most difficult absolute value questions on the SAT... that is it.

# Absolute Value

**1**

For what value of $a$ is $|a - 1| + |a + 1|$ equal to 0?

A) -1

B) 0

C) 1

D) There is no such value of $a$.

**2**

$$|9 - x| = 7$$

The equation above has two solutions. If the value of one of the solutions is 2, what is the value of the other solution?

**3**

Which of the following expressions is greater than 0 for all values of x?

A) $|x + 1| - 1$

B) $|x - 1| - 1$

C) $|1 - x| - 1$

D) $|1 - x| + 1$

**4**

Two different points are plotted on a number line such that each point is 4 units from the point with coordinate -2. Which of the following equations has solutions that give the coordinates of both points?

A) $|x + 2| = 4$

B) $|x - 2| = 4$

C) $|x + 4| = 2$

D) $|x - 4| = 2$

**5**

$$\left|n - \frac{3}{2}\right| = 5$$

What is the least value of $n$ that satisfies the equation above?

A) $\frac{13}{2}$

B) $\frac{7}{2}$

C) $-\frac{7}{2}$

D) $-\frac{13}{2}$

**6**

When graphed in the $xy$-plane, which of the following equations does not intersect the $x$-axis?

A) $y = x + 1$

B) $y = |x - 1|$

C) $y = |x| - 1$

D) $y = |x| + 1$

**7**

Which of the following inequalities describes all of the points on a number line that are within 3 units of the point with coordinate 1?

A) $|x - 3| \geq 1$

B) $|x - 3| \leq 1$

C) $|x - 1| \geq 3$

D) $|x - 1| \leq 3$

**8**

Let $a$ and $b$ be numbers such that $a > |b|$. Which of the following must be true?

I. $a > b$

II. $a > 0$

III. $b > 0$

A) II only

B) I and II only

C) II and III only

D) I, II, and III

## SOLVING SYSTEMS OF EQUATIONS

**Let's back the truck up for a second.**

A "system" of equations is when you have more than one equation, and the solution to a system is/are the point(s) they have in common. If you were to graph the equations, you could see the solutions—they're the points of intersection between the graphs...the points that are solutions within both equations.

You've got a few different ways to solve systems of equations. Knowing all of the ways so you can choose the best one is our goal here.

I know that y'all know and love substitution, so I am not going to put it first for that reason. Let's start with SAT's favorite: combination.

Some people call the combination method "adding." The thing is, you can combine equations by any operation—not just adding. You can subtract equations, you can multiply them, and you can divide them. Let me show you.

$$2x + 2y + z = 11$$
$$x + y + z = 4$$

In the system of equations above, what is the value of $x + y$?

### Hold your horses! Don't substitute yet!

Watch how easily these equations combine to get us a solution.

$$\begin{array}{r} 2x + 2y + z = 11 \\ -\ \ x + y + z = 4 \\ \hline \boxed{x + y = 7} \end{array}$$

That's one way of solving equations. Don't sleep on it—when it's the fastest way, it can really make your life easy.

Next up is, *OK fine you win*, substitution. Substitution means we're going to isolate a variable on one side of the equation, then substitute what that variable equals into the other equation. Math words failing again...let's see substitution in action instead.

$$2x + 3y = -4$$

$$3x - y = 5$$

In the system of equations above, what is the value of $x + y$?

I think the most valuable thing here is to realize that substitution is the best way to solve. How would we see that? Notice that on the example for combination, we were able to get to what we wanted in one simple step. This question does not provide us with that convenience. What it does give us, though, is an equation with a simple y value. In that second equation, it is going to be pretty convenient and easy to get y by itself and then substitute that value into the first equation. Watch and see.

$$2x + 3y = -4$$
$$3x - y = 5$$

$$\begin{aligned} +y \quad +y & \\ 3x &= 5 + y \\ -5 \quad -5 & \\ 3x - 5 &= y \\ 2x + 3(3x - 5) &= -4 \\ 2x + 9x - 15 &= -4 \\ 11x &= 11 \\ x &= 1 \\ 3(1) - y &= 5 \\ -3 \quad -3 & \\ -y &= 2 \\ y &= -2 \\ x + y = 1 + (-2) &= \boxed{-1} \end{aligned}$$

So far, we've seen that combination is sometimes the best way to solve, and at other time, substitution is. One other way to solve a system is to use the calculator's graphing functions. Obviously, you can only do this on the calculator section...which is one more reason why you want to know the two methods we just discussed...but if you are on Section 4 and calculators are allowed, well, let it rip. Here's how to do that on the TI-83+/TI-84 family of calculators:

- ***Set each equation so that y = is on one side.***
- ***On the "y=" screen, enter the equations.***
- ***Press "GRAPH."***
- ***Once the equations are drawn, press "2nd" "TRACE" to get to the "CALC" functions of the graphing app.***
- ***Choose "intersect" from that menu.***
- ***Press "enter" to pick the first function.***
- ***Press "enter" again to pick the second function (if you need to switch between functions, press the up or down arrow)***
- ***When it asks for a "Guess?" just scroll to a point near to the point of intersection and press enter.***

Voila! The calculator is now displaying the point of intersection. If you can use the calculator, I recommend this method highly—the calculator is smart and does not make careless errors. Hooray calculator.

## Systems of Equations

**1**

$$x - 3y = -4$$
$$3x + y = -2$$

Which ordered pair $(x, y)$ satisfies the system of equations above?

A) (-7, -1)
B) (-1, 1)
C) (1, -1)
D) (1, -5)

**2**

$$x + y = -2$$
$$x + 3y = -18$$

According to the system of equations above, what is the value of $x$?

**3**

$$3y + x = -11$$
$$2x - 4y = -42$$

What is the solution $(x, y)$ to the system of equations above?

A) (4, -5)
B) (-6, 7)
C) (-11, 5)
D) (-17, 2)

**4**

$$5x + y = 12.5$$
$$-x - y = 1.5$$

If $(x, y)$ satisfies the system of equations above, what is the value of $x$?

**5**

$$x - 2y = 6$$
$$2x + y = -3$$

For the system of equations above, what is the value of $x + y$?

A) -15
B) -3
C) 5
D) 9

**6**

$$\frac{1}{4}(x + 3y) = \frac{15}{4}$$
$$x = 3y$$

The solution to the system of equations above is $(x, y)$. What is the value of $y$?

**7**

$$5x + 5y = 14$$
$$6x - 5y = 8$$

If $(x, y)$ is a solution to the system of equations above, what is the value of $x - y$?

A) $-\frac{7}{6}$
B) $-\frac{1}{6}$
C) $\frac{6}{5}$
D) $\frac{14}{5}$

**8**

$$y = -x^2 + 7x - 14$$
$$y + 6 = x$$

Which of the following gives all of the solutions $(x, y)$ to the system of equations above?

A) (4, -2)
B) (2, 4) and (2, -4)
C) (2, -4) and (4, -2)
D) There is no solution to this system of equations.

**9**

A fisherman caught 300 fish. Some were flounder and the rest were tuna. All together, the fish he caught weighed 18,116 pounds. He estimates that each flounder weighs 39.4 pounds and each tuna weighs 189.3 pounds. Which of the following systems of equations describes this situation, where $f$ is the number of flounder caught and $t$ is the number of tuna caught?

A) $\begin{cases} f + t = 300 \\ 39.4f + 189.3t = 18{,}116 \end{cases}$

B) $\begin{cases} f + t = 18{,}116 \\ 39.4f + 189.3t = 300 \end{cases}$

C) $\begin{cases} f + t = 300 \\ 150f + 150t = 18{,}116 \end{cases}$

D) $\begin{cases} 39.4f = 150 \\ 189.3t = 150 \end{cases}$

**10**

$$2x - 9 = 3y$$
$$4x = 5 - y$$

According to the system of equations above, what is the value of $x$?

**11**

$$x^2 - y = 7$$
$$2x + y = 8$$

Which value is a $y$-coordinate of a solution to the system of equations above?

A) -3
B) -1
C) 2
D) 5

**12**

$$A = 0.20x + 6.15$$
$$B = 0.45x + 4.90$$

The equations above estimate the stock price, in dollars, for Companies $A$ and $B$ on Thursday $x$ hours after 9am. What was the stock price for Company $A$ when it was equal to the stock price for Company $B$?

A) \$5.00
B) \$7.15
C) \$11.05
D) \$17.00

**13**

A shipping container can hold up to 5,000 pounds. It needs to be loaded with both boxes and crates. Boxes weigh 40 pounds each, and crates weigh 200 pounds each. If $b$ represents the number of boxes and c represents the number of crates, which of the following systems of inequalities models this situation?

A) $\begin{cases} 40b + 200c \geq 5{,}000 \\ b \geq 1 \\ c \geq 1 \end{cases}$

B) $\begin{cases} 40b + 200c \leq 5{,}000 \\ b \geq 1 \\ c \geq 1 \end{cases}$

C) $\begin{cases} 40b + 200c \geq 5{,}000 \\ b + c \leq 1 \end{cases}$

D) $\begin{cases} 40b + 200c \leq 5{,}000 \\ b + c \leq 1 \end{cases}$

**14**

$$6x + 2y = 8$$
$$kx + y = 2$$

In the system of equations above, $k$ is a constant. If the system has no solutions $(x, y)$, what is the value of $k$?

A) -1
B) 1
C) 3
D) 6

**15**

$$y = 3x^2 - 10$$
$$y = 3x + 8$$

One of the solutions to the system of equations above can be expressed as $(a, b)$.
If $a > 0$ and $b > 0$, what is the value of $b$?

**16**

$$\frac{1}{2}x - \frac{1}{4}y = 20$$
$$ax - by = 7$$

In the system of equations above, $a$ and $b$ are constants. If the system of equations has no solutions, what is the value of $\frac{a}{b}$?

## INEQUALITIES

The neglected stepsister of equations, inequalities have been struggling to be recognized as a legitimate partner of equations for centuries.

Here's the guiding wisdom for you when it comes to inequalities: they pretty much behave exactly like equations do. They only do one unusual thing:

**When you divide or multiply by a negative, the inequality sign switches direction.**
If it was pointing right, now it's pointing to the left. If it used to point to the left, guess what? Now it points to the right.

Here's how it goes:

$$14 - 3x < -1$$

$$-14 \qquad -14$$

$$\frac{-3x}{-3} < \frac{-15}{-3}$$

$$\boxed{x > 5}$$

That's it. That's literally all you need to know and worry about when it comes to inequalities.

I want there to be a Cinderella-like fairy tale ending to the story of poor ol' inequalities, but let's face it; inequalities ain't that pretty.

# Inequalities

**1**

$$y \geq 2x + 3$$
$$x + y < 2$$

Which of the following ordered pairs $(x, y)$ satisfies the system of inequalities above?

A) (4, 1)
B) (2, 1)
C) (1, -2)
D) (-3, 2)

**2**

Chester had $30 to spend at the mall. He bought a shirt for $s$ dollars and a tie for $t$ dollars. After these purchases, Chester had at least $12 left to spend. Which of the following inequalities can be used to correctly represent this situation?

A) $12 - s + t \geq 15$
B) $12 - s - t \geq 15$
C) $30 - s + t \geq 12$
D) $30 - s - t \geq 12$

**3**

$$4x + 10y \leq 20$$

Which of the following inequalities is equivalent to the inequality above?

A) $x + y \leq 5$
B) $2x + 5y \leq 10$
C) $5x + 2y \leq 10$
D) $5y - 2x \leq 10$

**4**

$$y < 4x + 3$$
$$4x < 1$$

Which of the following inequalities represents all of the values of $y$ that satisfy the system of inequalities above?

A) $y < 4$
B) $y < \frac{13}{4}$
C) $y < \frac{1}{4}$
D) $y < -2$

**5**

Emilia has $400 to spend on food for a dinner party. She needs to buy at least 5 steaks and at least 3 porkchops. Each steak costs $20, and each porkchop costs $15. If $s$ represents the number of steaks and $p$ represents the number of porkchops, which of the following systems of inequalities represents this situation?

A) $\begin{cases} s + p \leq 400 \\ s \geq 5 \\ p \geq 3 \end{cases}$

B) $\begin{cases} 5s + 3p \leq 400 \\ s \geq 5 \\ p \geq 3 \end{cases}$

C) $\begin{cases} 5s + 3p \leq 400 \\ s \geq 20 \\ p \geq 15 \end{cases}$

D) $\begin{cases} 20s + 15p \leq 400 \\ s \geq 5 \\ p \geq 3 \end{cases}$

**6**

$$y > b - x$$
$$y < x^2 + c$$

In the $xy$-plane, the point (0, 0) satisfies the system of inequalities above. Which of the following relationships between $b$ and $c$ must be true?

A) $b = c$
B) $b = -c$
C) $b < c$
D) $c < b$

**7**

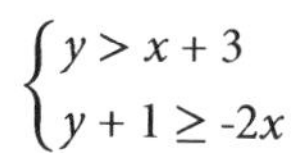


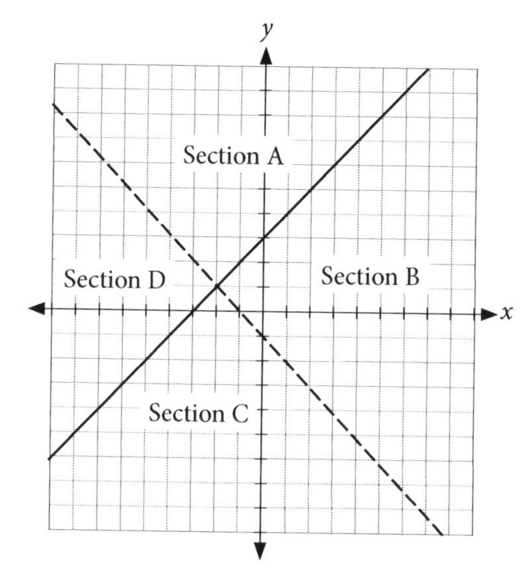


The system of inequalities above is graphed in the $xy$-plane as shown. Which sections of the graph could represent all of the solutions to the system?

A) Section A
B) Section B
C) Sections A and C
D) Sections A, B, and D

**8**

A baker has to make a cake for a party with 100 guests. He estimates that the cake will need to have a volume of at least 2700 cubic inches in order to feed all of the guests. He decides to make a cake with a rectangular base and a height of 4 inches. If he wants the length of the cake to be 3 times its width, which of the following inequalities represents the possible values for the width $w$, in inches, of the cake?

A) $w \geq 1.5$
B) $w \geq 15$
C) $w \geq 168.75$
D) $w \geq 225$

## FUNCTION NOTATION

**Function notation is all about keeping track of two different things: what goes in, and what comes out.**

It looks like this:

$$f(x) = 3x^2 + 2x + 1$$

And here's how you want to think about these things in SAT terms.

> ***There are two values, x and f(x).***
> ***x is what goes in, f(x) is what comes out.***

Here's a typical problem of the easier variety:

$$h(x) = 2x^2 - 2$$

For the function $h$ above, what is the value of $h(5) - h(3)$?

Notice how 5 and 3 have replaced the $x$ in the parentheses? Those are our input values. We're going to use the function twice, once with 5 plugged in for $x$, and once with 3 plugged in for $x$.

$$h(x) = 2x^2 - 2$$

$$h(5) - h(3) = ?$$

$$[2(5)^2 - 2] - [2(3)^2 - 2]$$

$$48 - 16 = \boxed{32}$$

That's it. $h(5) - h(3) = 32$.

When the test makers want to get trickier, they'll give you the output value and ask you to find the input. Like so:

The function of $f$ is defined by $f(x) = (x + 3)(x - 1)(x - 2)^2$.
For how many distinct values of $a$ is $f(a) = 0$?

A) One
B) Two
C) Three
D) Four

### Hold on, where did that "a" come from? I thought we were dealing with *x*?!

That "a" value is just a variable standing in for a value that we don't know yet. What we need to focus on is where the "a" appears in the equation. Because it's in the parentheses, it is an $x$, or input value. The question is asking us for how many different $x$ values will this function output a zero.

Well, how would you figure that out? This function is already factored for us, which is nice. Because of the zero product property—the fancy way of saying that whenever you multiply by zero, the answer is zero—one of our factors must be zero.

$f(x) = (x + 3)(x - 1)(x - 2)^2$

$0 = (x + 3)(x - 1)(x - 2)(x - 2)$

$x + 3 = 0$
$x = -3$

$x - 1 = 0$
$x = 1$

$x - 2 = 0$
$x = 2$

$\boxed{x = -3, 1, 2}$

How many distinct values of *x* (or *a*—same thing) did we find? Three, right? OK, that's the answer.

So function problems boil down to determining whether we know the input or output value, and deciding whether we're being asked to produce an input or output value as the answer.

## Now you try.

## Function Notation

**1**

A rental car company charges a flat fee of \$9.00 and \$0.10 per mile driven. Which of the following functions gives the total cost, in dollars, to rent a car and drive it $m$ miles?

A) $C(m) = 9 + 10m$

B) $C(m) = 9 + 0.1m$

C) $C(m) = 9m + 0.1$

D) $C(m) = 9.1m$

**2**

$$f(x) = \frac{x^2 + 5x - 8}{x - 3}$$

For the function $f$ above, what is $f(-1)$?

A) 7

B) 3

C) -3

D) -7

**3**

If $h(x) = 4x - 1$, what is $f(-2x)$ equal to?

A) $-2x - 1$

B) $-8x - 1$

C) $-8x + 1$

D) $-8x^2 + 2x$

**4**

| $(x)$ | $f(x)$ | $g(x)$ |
|---|---|---|
| -4 | 3 | -1 |
| -2 | 2 | 0 |
| 0 | 1 | -1 |
| 2 | 0 | -4 |

The table above shows some values of the functions $f$ and $g$. For which value of $x$ is $f(x) + g(x) = x$?

A) -4

B) -2

C) 0

D) 2

**5**

$$f(x) = x^2 - x + c$$

In the function $f$ defined above, $c$ is a constant. If the point $(3, 8)$ lies on the graph of $f(x)$ in the $xy$-plane, what is the value of $c$?

**6**

| $(x)$ | $f(x)$ |
|---|---|
| -1 | 3 |
| 0 | 5 |
| 1 | 2 |
| 3 | 0 |

The function $f$ is defined by a polynomial. The table above shows some values of $x$ and $f(x)$. Which of the following must be a factor of $f(x)$?

A) $x - 5$

B) $x - 3$

C) $x - 1$

D) $x + 1$

**7**

A function $g$ satisfies $g(1) = 4$ and $g(2) = 1$. A function $h$ satisfies $h(1) = -2$ and $h(4) = 2$. What is the value of $h(g(1))$?

A) -2

B) -1

C) 2

D) 4

**8**

If $f(x + 2) = 3x - 1$ for all values of $x$, what is the value of $f(-1)$?

A) -4

B) -6

C) -8

D) -10

**9**

$$f(x) = 5 - g(x)$$
$$g(x) = x^2 - 1$$

The functions $f$ and $g$ are defined above. What is the value of $f(0)$?

A) 7
B) 6
C) 5
D) 4

**10**

If $g(x) = 4x^2 + 9$ and $g(x + k) = 4x^2 - 8x + 13$, what is the value of $k$?

A) -8
B) -1
C) 1
D) 8

**11**

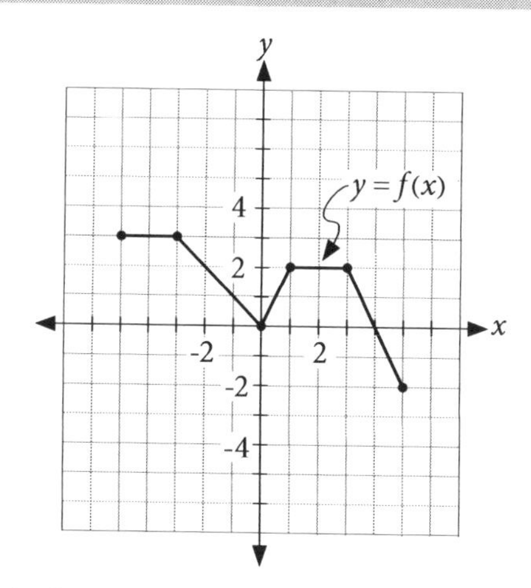


The function $f$ is graphed in the $xy$-plane above. Which of the following are equal to 2?

I. $f(-2)$

II. $f\left(\frac{5}{2}\right)$

III. $f(5)$

A) I only
B) II only
C) I and II only
D) I, II, and III

**12**

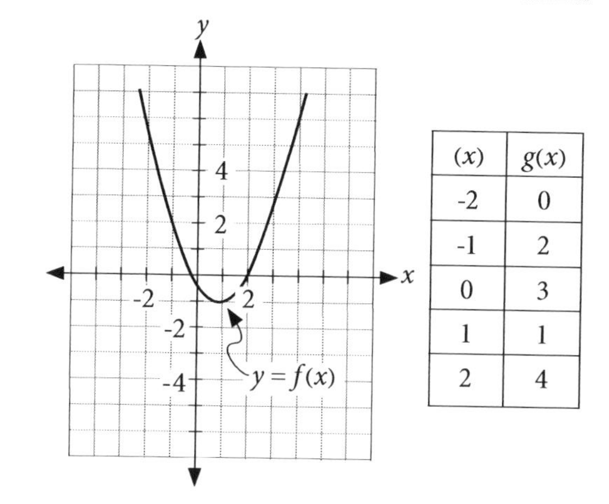


| $(x)$ | $g(x)$ |
|---|---|
| -2 | 0 |
| -1 | 2 |
| 0 | 3 |
| 1 | 1 |
| 2 | 4 |

The graphs of the function $f$ is shown in the $xy$-plane above, and selected values for the function $g$ are shown in the table. For which value of $x$ is $f(x) - g(x) = 0$?

A) -2
B) -1
C) 0
D) 1

**13**

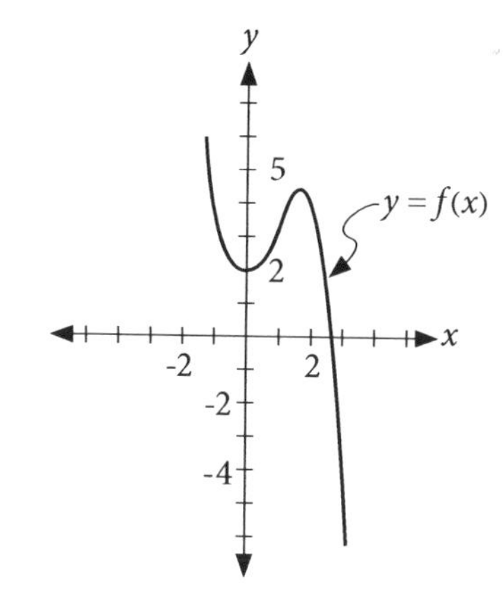

The function $f(x) = -x^3 + 2x^2 + x + 2$ is graphed in the $xy$-plane above. When the function $g(x)$ is graphed in the $xy$-plane, $f(x) = g(x)$ has three real solutions. Which of the following could be the equation of $g(x)$?

A) $g(x) = 4$
B) $g(x) = 1$
C) $g(x) = -1$
D) $g(x) = -4$

**14**

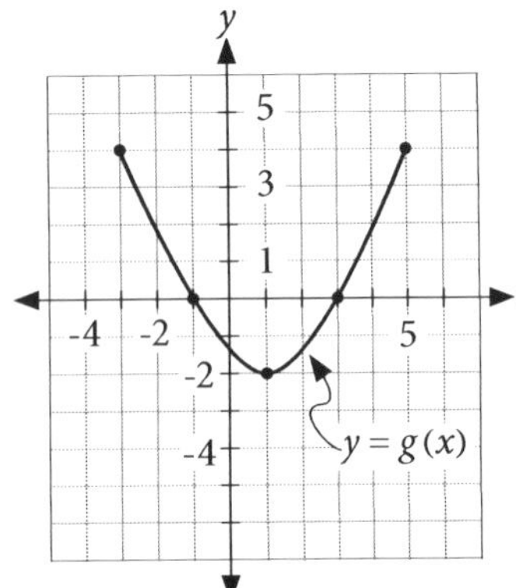


| $(x)$ | $h(x)$ |
|---|---|
| -4 | 5 |
| -3 | 4 |
| -2 | 3 |
| -1 | 2 |
| 0 | 1 |
| 1 | 0 |
| 2 | -1 |

The complete graph of the function $g$ and a table of values for the function $h$ are shown above. The minimum value of $g$ is $a$. What is the value of $h(a)$?

A) 4
B) 3
C) 0
D) -3

**Questions 15 and 16 refer to the following information.**

$$v_t = v_0 - gt \quad \text{(velocity-time)}$$

$$v_t^{\,2} = v_0^{\,2} - 2gh \quad \text{(position-velocity)}$$

$$h = v_0 t - \tfrac{1}{2}gt^2 \quad \text{(position-time)}$$

The equations above describe the motion of a projectile launched directly upward, where $v_0$ is the initial velocity of the projectile in feet per second (ft/s), $v_t$ is the velocity of the projectile at time $t$ seconds after launch, $h$ is the height of the projectile above the ground, and $g$ is a constant representing the acceleration due to gravity (32.2 ft/s²).

**15**

A projectile is launched with an initial velocity of 300 ft/sec. To the nearest foot per second, what is the velocity of the projectile when it attains a height of 1,300 feet?

**16**

If a projectile is launched with an initial velocity of 400 ft/sec, what is maximum height of the projectile to the nearest foot?

## EXPONENT RULES

**Good news! You'll never need to use logs to solve an SAT question.**
You *will* need exponents, though. Here are the three basic properties of exponents that are tested on the SAT.

$$(x^a)(x^b) = x^{a+b}$$

$$\frac{x^a}{x^b} = x^{a-b}$$

$$(x^a)^b = x^{ab}$$

Here's the first strategy for employing these rules:

Notice how each of these properties relies on having the same base, *x*. You will see problems where the bases are different. The important thing: you will often be able to manipulate the equation so that the bases are equal.

### Take, for example, a problem like this one:

$$8^{2x-2} = 2^{4x-4}$$

What is the value of $x$?

A) 0
B) 1
C) 2
D) 3

You *could* use logs to solve this puppy, but you don't need them. Why? Because 8 is a power of 2—it's $2^3$. When we substitute $2^3$ in for 8, we can now use our exponent properties to solve the equation.

$$8^{2x-2} = 2^{4x-4}$$

$$(2^3)^{2x-2} = 2^{4x-4}$$

$$2^{6x-6} = 2^{4x-4}$$

$$6x - 6 = 4x - 4$$

$$-4x + 6 \quad -4x + 6$$

$$2x = 2$$

$$\boxed{x = 1}$$

**More exponent stuff: you've got two more properties of exponents to memorize.**
Negative exponents push the base into the denominator (that's the bottom part) of a fraction.

$$2^{-3} = \frac{1}{2^3} = \frac{1}{8}$$

If a negative exponent is already in the denominator, it gets flipped up to the top.

$$\frac{1}{x^{-4}} = x^4$$

**Fractional exponents** are another way of expressing roots.

$$n^{1/3} = \sqrt[3]{n}$$

If an exponent is a fraction with multiple values besides 1, such as $8^{4/3}$, raise the base to the exponent in the numerator, and take the root at the value of the denominator. With $8^{4/3}$ for example, you want to raise 8 to the $4^{th}$ power, then take the cube root of the result (or you could take the cube root of 8 and raise it to the $4^{th}$ power...you'll get the same answer either way).

$$8^{4/3}$$

And there you have it: *the world's quickest, least-boring review of the entirety of Algebra.*

## Exponent Rules

**1**

Which of the following is equal to $x^{\frac{3}{2}}$, where $x > 0$?

A) $\sqrt{x^3}$
B) $\sqrt[3]{x^2}$
C) $\sqrt[3]{x^{½}}$
D) $\sqrt{x^{½}}$

**2**

If $x^9 = 3$ and $x > 0$, what is the value of $x^{27}$?

A) $\sqrt{27}$
B) 9
C) 27
D) 81

**3**

If $(x^4)^k = (x^6)^6$ and $x > 1$, what is the value of $k$?

A) 3
B) 4
C) 8
D) 9

**4**

Which of the following is equivalent to $8^{\frac{2}{3}}$?

A) $\sqrt[3]{2}$
B) $\sqrt[3]{4}$
C) $2\sqrt[3]{2}$
D) 4

**5**

Which of the following expressions is equivalent to $(64a^6b^5)^{\frac{1}{2}}$, where $a \geq 1$ and $b \geq 1$?

A) $8a^{\frac{3}{2}}b^{\frac{5}{2}}$
B) $8a^3b^{\frac{5}{2}}$
C) $32a^3b^{\frac{5}{2}}$
D) $64a^3b^5$

**6**

$$(x^{a-1})(x^{a+1}) = x^{24}$$

In the equation above, $x > 0$. What is the value of $a$?

A) 5
B) 12
C) 20
D) 24

**7**

The area of a forest increases at an average rate of 1.4 percent per year. In 2004, the forest had an area of 3,000 acres. Which of the following functions represents the area of the forest $A$, in thousands of acres, $t$ years since 2004?

A) $A(t) = 1.014t + 3$
B) $A(t) = 1.14t + 3$
C) $A(t) = 3(1.014)^t$
D) $A(t) = 3(1.4)^t$

**8**

Which of the following is an equivalent form of $\sqrt[3]{a^{-1}b^{9c}}$, where $a > 0$ and $b > 0$?

A) $a^{-\frac{1}{3}}b^{3c}$
B) $a^{-\frac{1}{4}}b^{\frac{1}{6c}}$
C) $a^{-3}b^{\frac{1}{3c}}$
D) $a^{-4}b^{6c}$

**9**

Which of the following expressions is equivalent to $(36y^2)^{\frac{1}{2}}$?

A) $6|y|$
B) $18|y|$
C) $36|y|$
D) $\sqrt{6y}$

**10**

$$x = y^{-2}$$

In the expression above, $y > 0$. What is $y$ in terms of $x$?

A) $\frac{1}{\sqrt{x}}$
B) $\sqrt{x}$
C) $-\sqrt{x}$
D) $-\frac{1}{\sqrt{x}}$

**11**

Which of the following describes an exponential relationship?

A) The population of a small town increases by 200 people per year.
B) The value of a stock increases by $5 per month.
C) The speed of a projectile decreases by 6% per second.
D) The price of a car decreases by 8% for a two-day sale.

**12**

If $2a - 3b = 24$, what is the value of $\frac{4^a}{8^b}$?

A) $2^{24}$
B) $2^{12}$
C) $4^8$
D) The value cannot be determined from the information given.

**13**

$$B = 450(1.03)^d$$

The equation above models the number of bacteria, $B$, in a petri dish $d$ days after the start of an experiment. Which of the following equations models the number of bacteria in the petri dish $w$ weeks after the start of the experiment?

A) $B = 450(1.03)^{\frac{w}{7}}$
B) $B = 450(1.03)^{7w}$
C) $B = 450(1.004)^{7w}$
D) $B = 450(1.23)^{w}$

**14**

$$\frac{x^{\frac{2}{3}}y^{-\frac{1}{2}}}{x^{-1}y^2}$$

In the expression above, $x > 1$ and $y > 1$. Which of the following is an equivalent expression?

A) $\frac{y\sqrt{y}}{\sqrt[3]{x}}$

B) $\frac{\sqrt[3]{x}}{y\sqrt{y}}$

C) $\frac{x(\sqrt[3]{x})}{y\sqrt{y}}$

D) $\frac{x\sqrt[3]{x^2}}{y^2\sqrt{y}}$

**15**

Julie's car loses 20 percent of its value every 5 years. If she purchased the car for $16,000, which of the following expressions represents the value of Julie's car $t$ years from now?

A) $16{,}000(0.2)^{5t}$
B) $16{,}000(0.2)^{\frac{t}{5}}$
C) $16{,}000(0.8)^{5t}$
D) $16{,}000(0.8)^{\frac{t}{5}}$

**16**

A new photo storage company expects the number of photos uploaded to its website to double every 16 months. The company currently has 400 photos stored on its website. Which of the following equations best models the number of photos, $p$, stored on the website $n$ years from now?

A) $p = 400\left(1 + \frac{n}{16}\right)$

B) $p = 400\left(1 + \frac{3n}{4}\right)$

C) $p = 400(2)^{\frac{n}{16}}$

D) $p = 400(2)^{\frac{3n}{4}}$

# Linear Equations

## EVERYTHING YOU CAN DO WITH A LINEAR EQUATION

**On a scale of 1-100, how comfortable are you with the equation of a line?**
If your answer was less than 114, you want to read this chapter.

Aren't lines really easy, though? Yeah, they're not too hard. You just need to know every damn thing about them on the SAT. Like, everything. And then you need to demonstrate that comprehensive knowledge about 15 times on every SAT.

### Let's dig in and learn literally everything about lines.

First off, lines represent a relationship between two different quantities or variables. For example, even though you probably don't pay bills yet (but get excited!), you can probably imagine there is a relationship between how much you pay for your mobile plan and how much data you can use each month. That is likely a linear relationship with a positive rate of change, or slope: as the price goes up, so does the amount of data you can use.

### Oh you have an unlimited plan? Look at you! I'm so happy for you! Why don't you go try to write an equation with infinite data as a variable.

Another linear relationship, this time with a negative slope: mentions of the Kardashian family in the media versus my desire to use the internet. The more often the Kardashians show up in my feed, the less I want to be online. I'm fairly close to moving to a desert island based on this relationship.

We just talked about positive and negative rates of change, or slopes. Slope is the quick, visual way of describing the rate of change. If one quantity goes up (the amount of the bill) as the other goes up (the amount of data you get), the relationship is positive. If one goes up (the introduction of Khloe's new baby perfume) as the other goes down (my desire to be a member of society), then the relationship is negative.

That explains the difference between what positive and negative slopes mean. What about the value of the slope itself? Well, we compute slope as the change in the y-values of two points divided by the change in the x-values of the same two points.

$$m = \frac{y_2 - y_1}{x_2 - x_1}$$

**In terms of understanding the relationship and the value of the slope, I start by thinking about a slope of 1.**
A slope of 1 means that the y- and x-values are changing by the same amount at the same time. If the y-value goes up 4, the x-value goes up 4. On a graph, a slope of 1 will make a 45° angle with the two axes. Once you know that, you can picture what other slopes will look like. A line with a slope greater than 1 will be steeper than that 45° angle and a line with a slope of less than 1, like 1/3, say, will have a

softer slope than 45°. The same is true in reverse for negative slopes—the same rules of steepness and softness apply—they'll just point in the opposite direction.

***Hot Tip:*** Make sure to look at the axes before you is the 45° trick for steepness of a slope. The College Board could include axes with units in different scales. If they do the 45° trick no longer applies.

Here's another common value we use to describe linear equations: the y-intercept. I know you know what that is *mathematically* (I can almost hear you yelling, "it's *b*!"), but what is it in the real world?

### I like to think of the y-intercept as the *starting point.*

Here's another linear relationship. You open a stand at the local farmers market. It costs $10 to have the stand each week, and at the end of the market you also pay 5% of your revenue to the market. If *x* is how much revenue you do in a given week, then you could write a model of your expenses as:

$$e(x) = 10 + 0.05x$$

The y-intercept there, the *b*, is definitely 10. It's the part of the expenses that you pay as a starting point. You want a booth at the farmers market? No problem—you just need $10.

It never changes, either. The flat fee does not care if you make $0 or $1,000,000. The flat fee is $10.

If the y-intercept is the starting point—the thing that isn't changing—then the slope is the thing that IS changing. It shows you how the two quantities are moving together. In the farmers market example, the relationship is positive: as you make more, the farmers market people make more. You sell a $1 carrot? The market makes $0.05. You sell a dozen carrots for $9? The market makes $0.45.

When it comes to real world problems featuring linear equations, think of your y-intercept as your starting place and slope as the representation of how the two variables change relative to each other.

Let's look at some of the technical things you can do with lines and their equations.

### When you know two points, you can find their slope.

$$\begin{matrix}(3, -7)\\(5,\ 1)\end{matrix} \quad m = \frac{y_2 - y_1}{x_2 - x_1}$$

$$\begin{matrix}(3, -7)\\(5,\ 1)\end{matrix} \quad m = \frac{-7 - 1}{3 - 5}$$

$$\begin{matrix}(3, -7)\\(5,\ 1)\end{matrix} \quad \boxed{m = \frac{-8}{-2} = 4}$$

### When you know a point on a line and the line's slope, you can write an equation:

$$y - y_1 = m(x - x_1)$$

$$y - 1 = 4(x - 5)$$

That's called "point-slope form" because you can see a point on the line and its slope within the equation. Also, the store where they sell good names was closed that day.

**If you have an equation in the format $y = mx + b$, you can see the y-intercept and slope.**

$$y - 1 = 4(x - 5)$$

$$y - 1 = 4x - 20$$
$$+1 \qquad +1$$
$$y = 4x - 19$$

m ↗ ↖ b

**An equation in "standard form" gives you an easy way to find the x- and y-intercepts... you just plug in 0 for the other value.**

$$2x + 3y = 6$$
$$2(0) + 3y = 6$$
$$y = 2$$
$$2x + 3(0) = 6$$
$$x = 3$$

That's just about everything you can do with ONE line. Things get really fun (???) when we introduce a second line.

**When you have two or more equations of any kind, you have what's called a *system of equations.* When the equations in a system have a point of intersection, that's called a *solution.***

(I highlighted those two vocabulary terms just because they could show up on as math vocabulary on an SAT problem.)

When the two equations in a system are both lines, there are three different ways that they can have solutions. If they have different slopes, they will intersect one time, and only one time.

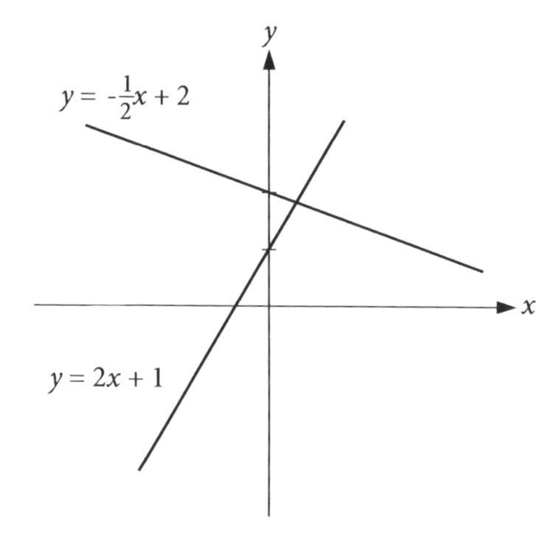


That's it—they have *one solution* at that point, and that's it. See ya later, other line. It was fun getting to know you a little bit.

Non-parallel lines have one solution. What about parallel lines? If two lines are parallel but have different y-intercepts—i.e. if one is above or below the other one—then they will *never* intersect.

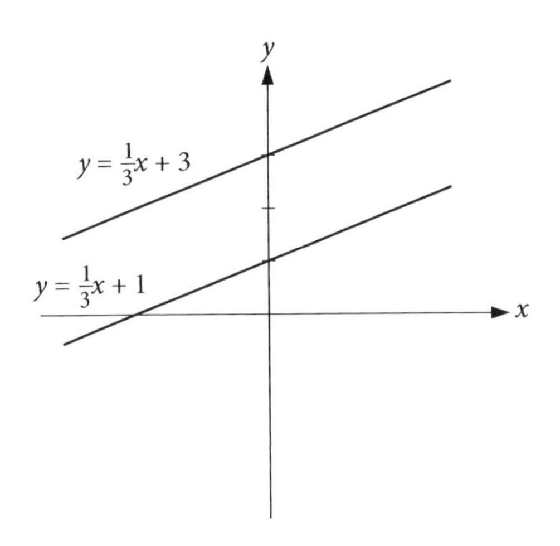


Different parallel lines have zero solutions. The last possibility is that we could have two lines with the same slope and the same y-intercept. Essentially, they are two lines with the same equation.

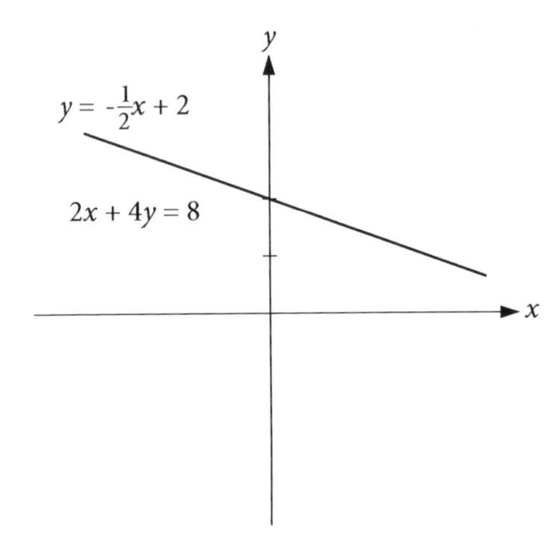


How many times will these two equations—equations that are basically the same as each other—intersect? *At every single point*, so an infinite number of times.

**So a system of equations featuring two lines can have one solution, no solutions, or an infinite number of solutions.**

Here's how we know that lines are parallel: they have the same slope. That makes sense when you visualize the graph of two lines. If they're both going up-and-over at the same rate, they'll keep on doing that—next to each other but never crossing—forever.

Parallel lines have the same slope. What about perpendicular lines? Think of the way that two slopes could be the most different, the most *opposite* from each other. Perpendicular lines have slopes that are negative reciprocals of each other, for example 4 and -1/4. Math books will tell you that "the product of the slopes of two perpendicular lines is -1." That's true, but I think it's easier to think of perpendicular lines as negative reciprocals—flip one slope upside-down, add a negative sign out front, and you've got the slope of a perpendicular line.

I think that's it—everything you can do with a line. Only thing to do now is a barrelful of line problems.

You ready? Let's go.

# Linear Equations

**1**

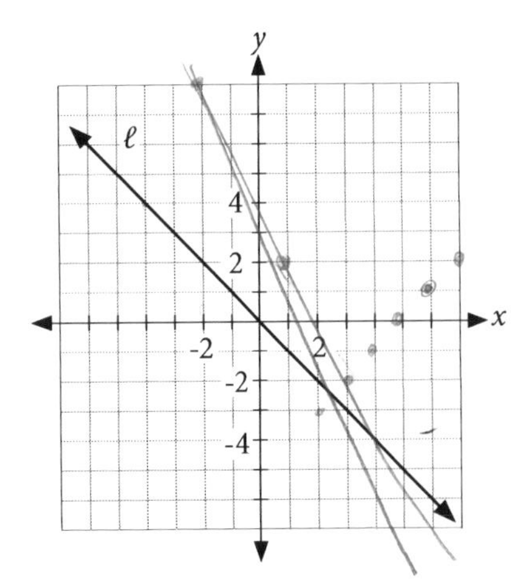


Which of the following is an equation of line $\ell$ in the xy-plane above?

A) $y = -1$
B) $x = -1$
C) $y = x - 1$
D) $y = -x$

**2**

Leo has to peel a basket of potatoes. The number of potatoes he has left to peel can be estimated with the equation $P = 249 - 51h$, where $P$ is the number of potatoes left in the basket and $h$ is the number of hours he has spent peeling. What is the meaning of the value 249 in this equation?

A) Leo will finish peeling all of the potatoes in the basket within 249 hours.
B) The basket contained 249 potatoes before Leo started peeling.
C) Leo peels potatoes at a rate of 249 per day.
D) Leo peels potatoes at a rate of 249 per hour.

**3**

| x | 1 | 2 | 3 | 4 |
|---|---|---|---|---|
| $f(x)$ | 3 | 1 | -1 | -3 |

The table above shows some values of the linear function $f$. Which of the following defines $f$?

A) $f(x) = 4 - x$
B) $f(x) = 5 - 2x$
C) $f(x) = 6 - 3x$
D) $f(x) = 7 - 4x$

**4**

Which of the following is the graph of the equation $y = 3x + 2$ in the $xy$-plane?

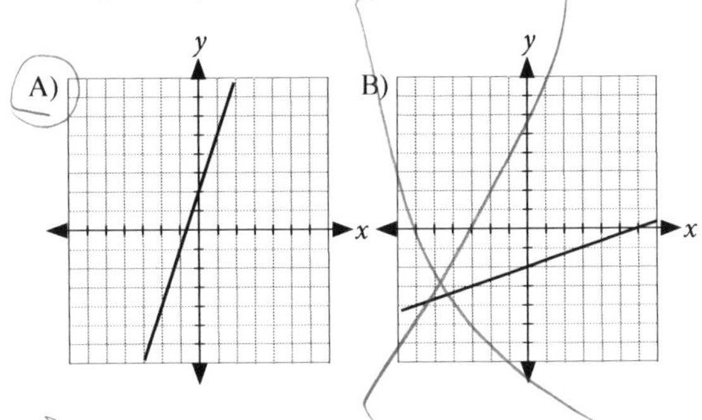


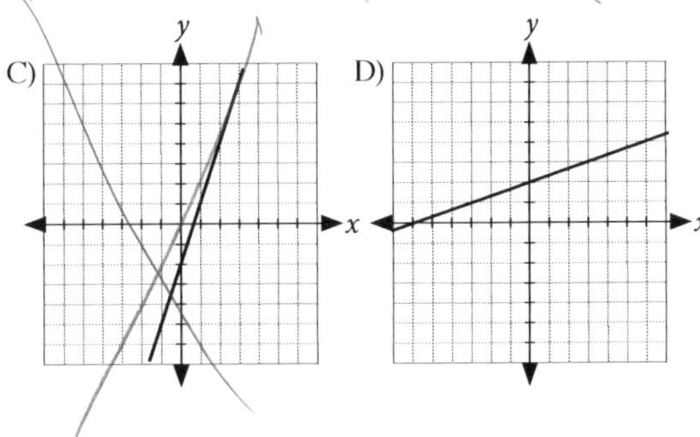

**5**

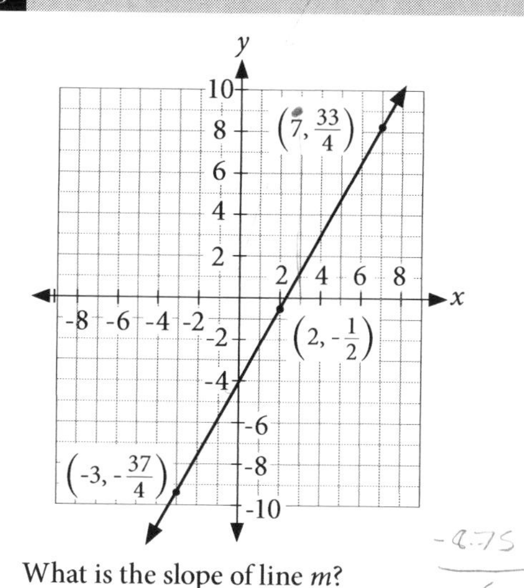


What is the slope of line $m$?

**6**

Which of the following questions represents a line that is parallel to the line with equation $y = 2x - 1$?

A) $3x + 6y = 1$

B) $x - 2y = 7$

C) $-2x - y = 3$

D) $-4x + 2y = 9$

**7**

$$\frac{5}{8}x + \frac{3}{7}y = 2$$

The line with the equation above is graphed in the $xy$-plane. What is the $x$-coordinate of the $x$-intercept of the line?

---

**Questions 8 and 9 refer to the following information.**

$$L = 189 - 3n$$

The formula above can be used to estimate the length $L$, in millimeters, of a pencil based on the number of times $n$ that the pencil has been sharpened.

**8**

What is the significance of the value 3 in the equation?

A) The minimum length of the pencil is 3 millimeters.

B) The length decreases by 3 millimeters each time the pencil is sharpened.

C) The formula provides an estimate of the length of the pencil that is accurate to within 3 millimeters.

D) The pencil can be sharpened a maximum of 3 times.

**9**

Which of the following values represents the number of times the pencil must be sharpened to reduce its length to 42 millimeters?

A) 14

B) 49

C) 63

D) 126

---

**10**

Line $\ell$ in the $xy$-plane contains points from Quadrants I and IV only. Which of the following could be the equation of line $\ell$?

A) $x = 3$

B) $y = 3$

C) $x + y = 3$

D) $x - y = 3$

**11**

Bill can complete $x$ homework questions in $m$ minutes. If $m = x + 3$, how many additional minutes will Bill need to complete each additional homework question?

A) None
B) One
C) Two
D) Three

**12**

$$4x - y = 5$$

Which of the following equations is perpendicular to the equation above when both are graphed in the $xy$-plane?

A) $-2x + 8y = 10$
B) $x + 4y = 5$
C) $3x - 2y = 5$
D) $8x + y = 10$

**13**

The average battery life of a cell phone decreases by 1 hour for every 5 months of use. A new cell phone has an average battery life of 30 hours. Which equation gives the average battery life $b$, in hours, of a cell phone after $m$ months of use?

A) $b = 5m$

B) $b = \frac{m}{5}$

C) $b = 30 - 5m$

D) $b = 30 - \frac{m}{5}$

**14**

The function $w$, defined by $w(t) = at + b$, where $a$ and $b$ are positive constants, models the weight, in kilograms, of a hippopotamus $t$ days after it was born at a local zoo and during a period of time in which the change in its weight is approximately linear. What does $a$ represent?

A) The total increase in the weight of the hippopotamus, in kilograms, during the period.
B) The number of kilograms the hippopotamus grows each day during the period.
C) The weight, in kilograms, of the hippopotamus on the day it was born.
D) The weight, in kilograms, of the hippopotamus at the end of the growth period.

**15**

The line $y = ax - 3$, where $a$ is a constant, is graphed in the $xy$-plane. If the point $(p, q)$, where $p \neq 0$ and $q \neq 0$, lies on the line, what is the slope of the line in terms of $p$ and $q$?

A) $\frac{p+3}{q}$

B) $\frac{p-3}{q}$

C) $\frac{q+3}{p}$

D) $\frac{q-3}{p}$

## 16

The graph of a line in the $xy$-plane has slope 1 and passes through the point (6, 1). The graph of a second line contains the points (1, 2) and (-2, 8). If the two lines intersect at the point $(a, b)$, what is the value of $a - b$?

A) -2
B) 1
C) 3
D) 5

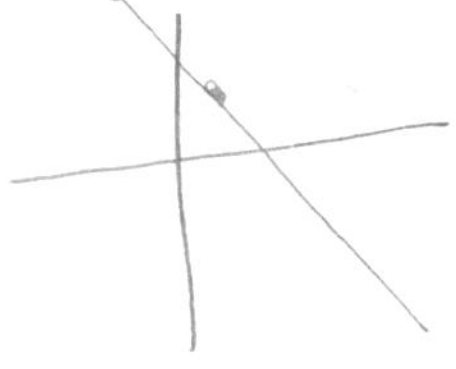

## 17

The graph of line $\ell$ has intercepts at $(0, a)$ and $(b, 0)$ in the $xy$-plane. If $a = b$ and $a \neq 0$, which of the following is true about the slope of the graph of line $\ell$?

A) It is positive.
B) It is negative.
C) It is undefined.
D) It is zero.

## 18

| $x$ | 0 | 3 | 5 |
|---|---|---|---|
| $f(x)$ | 5 | 11 | 15 |

Some values of the linear function $f$ are shown in the table above. What is the value of $f(-1)$?

A) 1
B) 2
C) 3
D) 4

## 19

In the $xy$-plane, line $\ell$ includes points $(3, a)$ and $(a, 27)$ and passes through the origin. Which of the following could be the value of $a$?

A) 0
B) 3
C) 9
D) 18

## 20

$$d(m) = -\frac{1}{38}t + 509$$

During a period of drought, the maximum depth $d$, in meters, of a certain lake can be estimated using the function above, where $t$ is the number of days since the drought began. According to the function, which of the following statements is true?

A) Every 380 days, the maximum depth decreases by 10 meters.
B) Every 38 days, the maximum depth decreases by 0.1 meters.
C) Every 10 days, the maximum depth decreases by 3.8 meters.
D) Every 100 days, the maximum depth decreases by 380 meters.

**Questions 21 and 23 refer to the following information.**

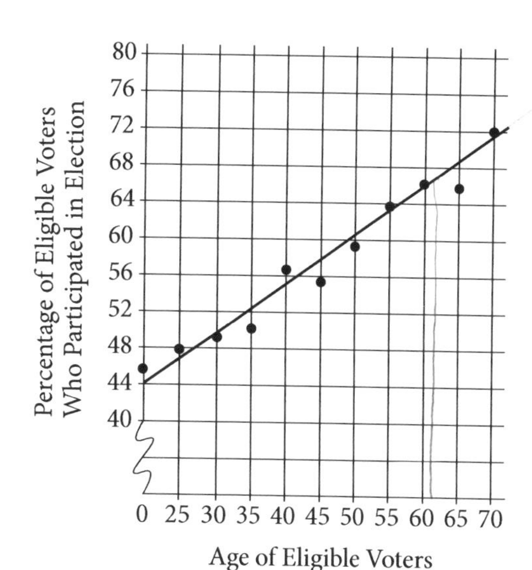


The town of Sunnyview held an election for mayor and recorded the participation percentage for eligible voters of various ages. In the scatterplot below, $x$ represents the age of eligible voters and $y$ represents the percentage of voters at each age who participated in the election. The line of best fit for the data is shown.

21

Based on the line of best fit, what is the approximate percentage of voters aged 62 years who participated in the mayoral election?

A) 44
B) 55
C) 66
D) 77

22

Which of the following is the best interpretation of the line of best fit shown for these data?

A) The actual percentage of eligible voters of each age who participated in the election.
B) The actual number of eligible voters of each age who participated in the election.
C) The predicted percentage of eligible voters of each age who participated in the election.
D) The predicted number of eligible voters of each age who participated in the election.

23

Which of the following is closest to the equation of the line of best fit shown?

A) $y = \frac{3}{4}x$
B) $y = \frac{3}{4}x + 44$
C) $y = \frac{8}{15}x + 44$
D) $y = \frac{8}{15}x + \frac{100}{3}$

24

$$E = \frac{5}{6}(D - 22)$$

An international bank uses the formula above to convert the money in customers' accounts from dollars to euros, using the exchange rate and including a flat transaction fee. If $D$ represents the value of the account in dollars and $E$ represents the value of the account in euros, which of the following statements must be true?

I. An increase in value of 1 dollar is equivalent to an increase in value of $\frac{5}{6}$ euro.
II. An increase in value of 1 euro is equivalent to an increase in value of 1.2 dollars.
III. An increase in value of $\frac{5}{6}$ dollar is equivalent to an increase in value of 1 euro.

A) I only
B) II only
C) I and II only
D) I and III only

# Quadratic Equations

## What's the difference between a quadratic equation and a linear equation?

**That is a sincere question, not the setup to a math teacher joke.**
Do you remember those, math teacher jokes? I literally cannot share them here—my fingers will not allow me to type the words onto these pages.

Earlier in the book, I made the point that Social Studies teachers are the most boring people on planet Earth. Here, I will make the claim that Math teachers are the people most likely to think they are funny when they are in fact not funny.

**Anyway, what is the difference between a quadratic function and a linear equation?**
Well, the quadratic equation is a curve—aka a parabola—when you graph it. It also has less immediate, real-world application than do lines. We use linear equations to model lots off stuff. We basically use parabolas to model projectiles thrown into the air from the top of a building.

Story time. This is not SAT-productive, so skip it if you don't have time for fun right now. I have to tell this since we're talking about projectiles. I, uh, once accidentally threw a bouncy rubber ball off a 12th story rooftop. It was an accident! We were playing catch with it on the rooftop of a building (yes...that was stupid) and I sort of...overthrew my friend, and the ball flew off the rooftop. I was simultaneously thrilled (would it bounce back UP six stories???) and terrified (have I killed a pedestrian, an innocent bystander who *never saw that rubber bouncy ball coming*??) I was so mortified that I couldn't even look. The happy ending is that nobody was killed by a falling rubber ball in downtown LA that day. Worst case scenario avoided!

Seriously, you pretty much only use parabolas to model projectiles. Because they model fewer real-world situations, what we do with them on the SAT ends up being quite a bit more technical and mathematical. We'll stress that stuff in this chapter.

**First, the practical stuff.**
Quadratic equations are ones that have $x^2$ as their highest-powered term. Here are a few ways they can be presented:

Standard form: $y = ax^2 + bx + c$

Vertex form: $y = a(x - h)^2 + k$

Intercept form: $y = a(x - p)(x - q)$

Here's how to interpret each of these in a practical, semi-useful way.

## STANDARD FORM

Standard form: $y = ax^2 + bx + c$

Standard form tells you a couple of things right off the bat. One is hidden in the a value. Notice how all three versions of the quadratic equation have an *a*—in all three cases, a will tell you the same thing: how steeply curved the parabola is, and whether the parabola is facing up or down. Our starter parabola (Baby's First Parabola?) is $y = x^2$, and it has an a value of positive 1. You can play with that a in two ways. When the a value is greater than 1, you'll have a steeper parabola; less than 1 (like 1/3, for example) and it'll be a softer parabola. If the a value is negative, the parabola will flip; it'll point downward instead of upward. That's what a does.

One more thing we can read from the standard parabola equation is the *c* value. Notice that you'll get the c value as your output when $x = 0$. That's useful—*c* is the *y*-intercept of the parabola.

What does a *y*-intercept mean when it comes to quadratics? Just like with lines, the *y*-intercept is your starting place. When I accidentally threw that rubber ball off that 12 story building, 12 would have been the *y*-intercept.

On a technical, mathematical level (which, by the way, is a good level to start to think at when it comes to quadratics), you could think of that as the height of the ball at time $t = 0$. But you can also think of it in a more practical way: it's the starting point, the height at the point of origin.

## VERTEX FORM

Vertex form: $y = a(x - h)^2 + k$

As described above, vertex form gives you that *a* value—the one that tells you about the steepness of the parabola and whether it faces up or down.

In addition, it gives you the vertex, the point $(h, k)$. The vertex is, in my opinion at least, the one interesting point on a parabola. It's the place where the curve changes direction.

***Hot Tip:*** Look carefully at that equation and notice that we are SUBTRACTING *h* and then ADDING *k*. Suppose you have the equation $y = 2(x + 1)^2 + 3$. What are the *h* and *k* values? You want to imagine that there is a minus sign inside the parentheses in order to figure out what your *h* value is. That equation would be the equivalent of $y = 2(x - (-1))^2 + 3$, and your vertex $(h, k)$ would be $(-1, 3)$.

Parabolas are so moody! Half the time they're all positive, and half the time they're, like, the complete opposite.

The vertex can also be thought of as either the minimum (in an upward-facing parabola) or a the maximum (in a downward-facing one) of the parabola.

Also, because parabolas are symmetrical around their vertices, you can essentially think of the vertex as the midpoint of the parabola. More on that later in the chapter.

## INTERCEPT FORM

Intercept form: $y = a(x - p)(x - q)$

Again, the *a* value does what the a value does: tells you how steep the parabola is and whether it points up or down.

The other values in intercept form, *p* and *q*, tell you where the graph crosses the *x*-axis. The reason that they do is our old pal, the Zero Product Property. All of the terms in this form of the equation are being multiplied by each other. If $y = 0$, which is the *y*-value you'll get whenever you cross the *x*-axis, then one of the terms within our sequence of terms that are multiplied by each other must be zero.

**In other words, either $(x - p)$ or $(x - q)$ has to equal zero.**

**Which means that $p$ and $q$ must be the two $x$-intercepts.**

**Hence the name "intercept form."**

Next up: a series of fun facts pertaining to quadratics. Literally, this is *everything I can think of that you can do with a parabola.*

$$x = \frac{-b \pm \sqrt{b^2 - 4ac}}{2a}$$

Quadratics written in standard form provide the *a*, *b*, and *c* values that you need to use the quadratic equation, and the *x*-values that get out of the equation are the *x*-intercepts. The quadratic equation is somewhat awkward, but occasionally using it is the best way to solve an SAT question.

***Hot Tip:*** If you don't have this bad boy memorized, there's an irritating-but-effective mnemonic device you can use to help you out—singing the formula to the tune of "Pop Goes the Weasel." I can't get that stupid song out of my head sometimes, which is the sign of either a great or a terrible mnemonic device.

### *THE QUICK WAY TO FIND THE VERTEX:*

Vertex: $\left(\frac{-b}{2a}, f\left(\frac{-b}{2a}\right)\right)$

That notation looks terrible, but it's not nearly as bad as it looks. The only thing you need to memorize is that lead part, -b/2a. If that feels perfectly random, don't worry, it's not: It's actually the front part of the quadratic equation.

$$\frac{-b \pm \sqrt{b^2 - 4ac}}{2a}$$

That ugly quadratic equation, as it turns out, *is actually kinda helpful.*

So, when you have a quadratic equation in standard form, you can use the b and a values to quickly find the x-coordinate of the vertex. Once you know that, you can plug that x-value into equation one more time to find the y-coordinate of the vertex.

That might sound tedious and/or way-too-technical, but believe me: it really is useful. $-\frac{b}{2a}$ is definitely worth memorizing.

## *PARABOLAS ARE SYMMETRICAL; WHY IS THAT INTERESTING?*

To answer that question...I'm not totally sure. Is it interesting? The migration patterns of the monarch butterfly—that is interesting. The evolution of independent music, from punk, to college radio, to "alternative," to indie rock—*that* is interesting. By that standard, I'm not sure the fact that the symmetrical nature of parabolas is interesting.

By SAT standards, it's g**d*** fascinating, though.

What can you do with that knowledge?

**If you know the two *x*-intercepts, you can use those values to find the *x*-coordinate of the vertex...**

...it'll be dead in-between those values, at the midpoint.

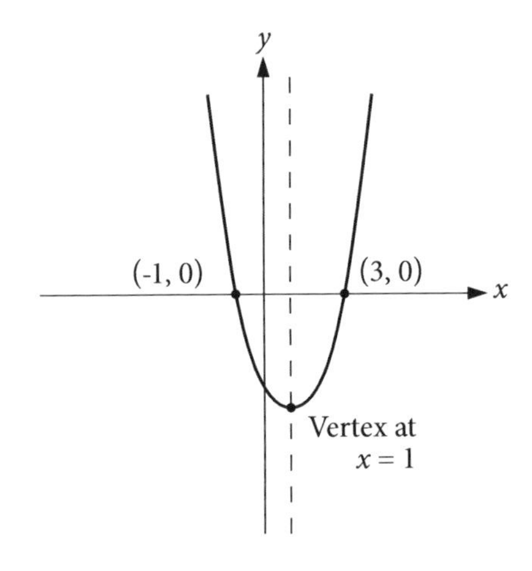


**And if you know the vertex and one of the *x*-intercepts, you can use that info to find the *other* *x*-intercept.**

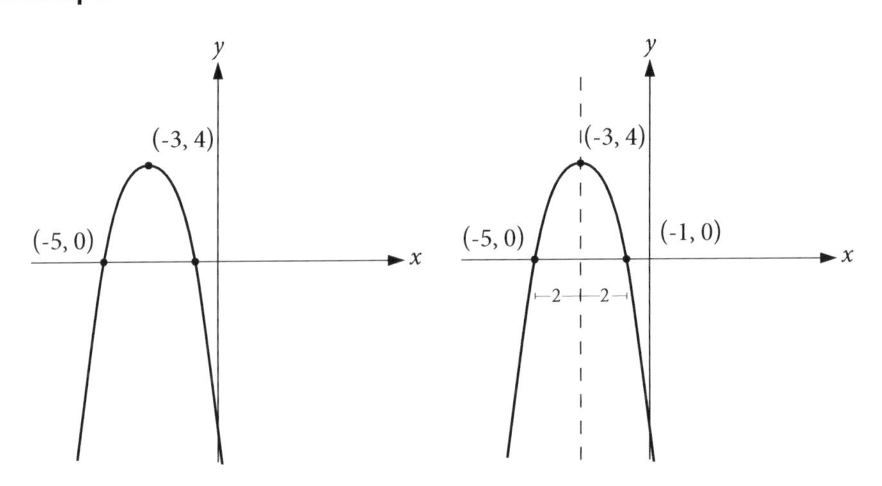

## *ANOTHER USEFUL THING ABOUT QUADRATICS: THE DISCRIMINANT.*

If you thought "discriminant" describes how some white students treated the black students who integrated Little Rock Central High School in 1957, well...you're pretty much off base. Slightly different spelling, completely different usage.

**The discriminant is the name of the term that's under the radical in the quadratic equation.**

The value of it is $b^2 - 4ac$ (and, by the way, this is *yet another reason* why it's a good idea to memorize the quadratic formula...).

**Here's what the discriminant tells us.**

When the value of the discriminant is positive then we know that the parabola has two real roots, aka two separate points of intersection with the x-access. This actually makes sense. When you think about the *x*-coordinate of the vertex as $-\frac{b}{2a}$, aka the "front" side of the quadratic equation, to find the roots from the quadratic equation, you're going to add/subtract the square root of the discriminant. If what you're adding/subtracting is positive, then the two roots will be equally spaced to the left and the right of the vertex.

**Now, imagine that the discriminant is zero.**

Just by coincidence, $b^2 - 4ac = 0$. Well, in that case, when you're trying to find the roots based on the vertex, you'll be adding and subtracting a big, fat zero. The two roots will be in the same spot: on the *x*-axis, at the exact same point as the vertex. Yep: the vertex is on the *x*-axis, and both of the roots (it's actually called a "double root") are in that exact same spot.

Now...let's get *really* crazy for second.

**What if the value of $b^2 - 4ac$ is negative?**

When you plugged it into the quadratic equation...you'd have a negative number under the radical. You can't take the square root of a negative! That would be chaos!

Or not. Think about what the discriminant has told us so far. If it's positive, the parabola has two real roots. If it's zero, the parabola has one "double root" at its vertex. If it's negative...well, the parabola has no real roots. It has imaginary ones! We'll discuss the imaginary number *i* in a later chapter, but for now, know this fun fact: when $b^2 - 4ac < 0$, your parabola has no real roots.

## *COMPLETING THE SQUARE*

As we move into this "quadratic fun fact," I invite you to pull up Spotify and have an ironic listen to the Vanessa Williams song "Save the Best for Last." Because I have yet to meet someone who *likes* completing the square.

Nevertheless, it is useful, especially to manipulate a quadratic equation into vertex form.

Watch and see.

$$y = x^2 - 4x + 5$$

$$-5 \qquad -5$$

$$y - 5 = x^2 - 4x$$

$$+4 \qquad +4$$

$$y - 1 = x^2 - 4x + 4$$

$$y - 1 = (x - 2)^2$$

$$\boxed{y = (x - 2)^2 + 1}$$

The trick, the key step, the thing that gives "Completing the Square" its name, is when you add (in this case) the 4 to both sides. What you're doing there is creating a "perfect square" trinomial. You can then factor that, which then gets you a big step closer to having your quadratic equation in vertex form.

And that is it! If you have tracked and followed the last three units, you have seen the content that makes up literally 75% of the SAT math section. High five! In a piece of earnest advice because I just can't help it, I recommend you do two things:

> ***#1: Make sure you <u>really understand</u> these sections.***
> ***#2: Do the practice problems to demonstrate that understanding.***

**Why? Because once you get this stuff, you'll be cruising to a really good SAT math score.**

# Quadratic Equations

**1**

What are the solutions of the quadratic equation $3x^2 + 6x - 24 = 0$?

A) $x = -2$ and $x = -4$
B) $x = -2$ and $x = 4$
C) $x = 2$ and $x = -4$
D) $x = 2$ and $x = 4$

**2**

Which of the following describes a function whose graph in the *xy*-plane has no *x*-intercepts?

A) A linear function with a positive rate of change.
B) A linear function with a negative rate of change.
C) A quadratic function with no real zeros.
D) A quadratic function with exactly one real zero.

**3**

$$x(x + 3) = 18$$

Which of the following gives all of the solutions to the quadratic equation above?

A) 18 and 15
B) 6 and -3
C) -6 and 3
D) $\sqrt{15}$

**4**

$$f(x) = 4x^2 - bx + 20$$

The function f is defined above. If the point (3, 2) lies on the graph of *f* in the *xy*-plane, what is the value of *b*?

**5**

$$y = x^2 - 2x + 1$$
$$y = 2x + 1$$

The ordered pair (*x*, *y*) satisfies the system of equations above. What is one possible value of *x*?

**6**

$$f(x) = (x + 5)(x + 1)$$

The function *f* is defined above. The graph of *f* in the *xy*-plane is a parabola. Which of the following intervals contains the *x*-coordinate of the vertex of the graph of *f*?

A) $-6 < x < -5$
B) $-5 < x < -1$
C) $-1 < x < 5$
D) $5 < x < 6$

**7**

When the parabola with equation $y = (x - 9)^2$ is graphed in the *xy*-plane, it intersects the line with equation $y = 36$ at points *A* and *B*. What is the length of $\overline{AB}$?

A) 8
B) 10
C) 12
D) 14

**8**

$$x = y - 1$$
$$y = x^2 - 2x - 9$$

Which of the following is the *y*-coordinate of a solution to the system of equations above?

A) 6
B) 2
C) -2
D) -6

**9**

$$y = (x + 3)(x - 5)$$

Which of the following is an equivalent form of the equation above in which the minimum value of $y$ appears as a constant or coefficient?

A) $y = x^2 - 15$
B) $y = x^2 - 2x - 15$
C) $y = (x + 1)^2 - 12$
D) $y = (x - 1)^2 - 16$

**10**

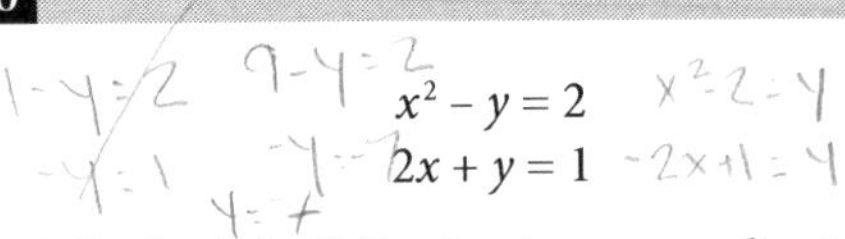

$$x^2 - y = 2$$
$$2x + y = 1$$

Which of the following is a $y$-coordinate of a solution to the system of equations above?

A) 7
B) 1
C) -3
D) -5

**11**

A projectile is launched straight up in the air, and its height $h$, in feet, can be modeled by the function $h(t) = -16t^2 + 60t + 105$, where $t$ represents the number of seconds since the projectile was launched. What does the number 105 represent in the function?

A) The initial height, in feet, of the projectile.
B) The maximum speed, in feet per second, of the projectile.
C) The time, in seconds, before the projectile hits the ground.
D) The speed, in feet per second, of the projectile when it hits the ground.

**12**

When graphed in the $xy$-plane, function $f$ is a parabola. The graph intersects the $x$-axis at (-2, 0) and ($k$, 0). If the vertex of $f$ occurs at (2, -9), what is the value of $k$?

A) 0
B) 2
C) 4
D) 6

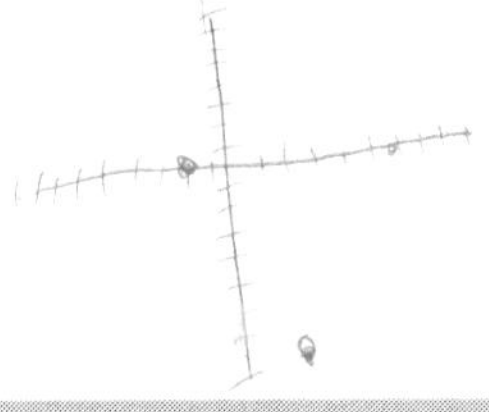

**13**

When the polynomial function $f$ is graphed in the $xy$-plane, it has zeros 2 and -4. If the range of $f$ is all real numbers less than or equal to 3, which of the following could be the graph of $y = f(x)$ in the $xy$-plane?

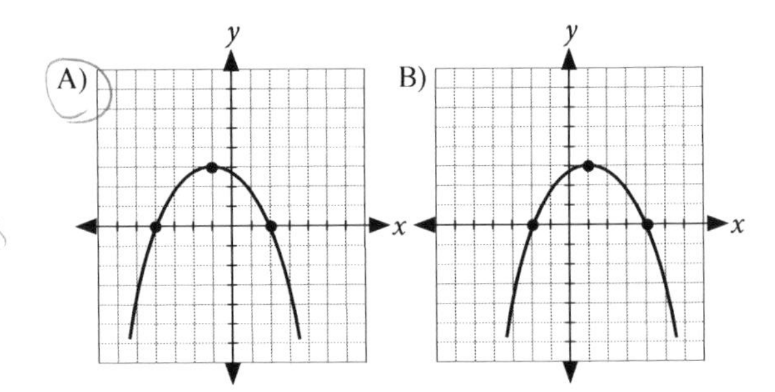


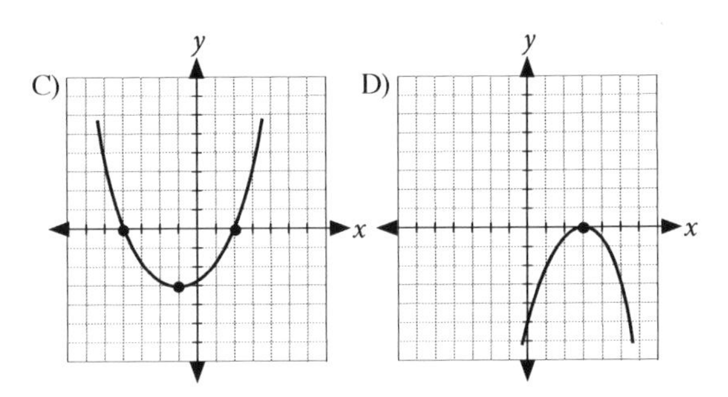

**14**

$$y = k(x - 6)(x + 2)$$

In the quadratic equation above, $k$ is a positive constant. The graph of the equation in the $xy$-plane is a parabola with vertex $(a, b)$. Which of the following is equal to $b$?

A) -16k
B) -12k
C) -8k
D) -4k

**15**

$$0 = 3x^2 - 18x + 6$$

What is the sum of the solutions to the quadratic equation above?

A) 6
B) $2\sqrt{7}$
C) $-2\sqrt{7}$
D) -6

**16**

$$y = ax^2 - b$$
$$y = 2$$

In the system of equations above, $a$ and $b$ are constants. For which of the following values of $a$ and $b$ does the system have exactly two real solutions?

A) $a = -4, b = 2$
B) $a = -2, b = -4$
C) $a = -2, b = -2$
D) $a = 4, b = -3$

# Shape Geometry

**Give me shape geometry over quadratic equations any day of the week.**
You feel me on that? Unfortunately, the SAT does not feel me on that—there is way more algebra than geometry on the SAT.

There is some shape geometry on the test, though, so we do have a reason to study it. Hooray! SAT geometry stuff basically tests your ability to work with triangles, circles, lines and angles. Let's start with the basics of triangles.

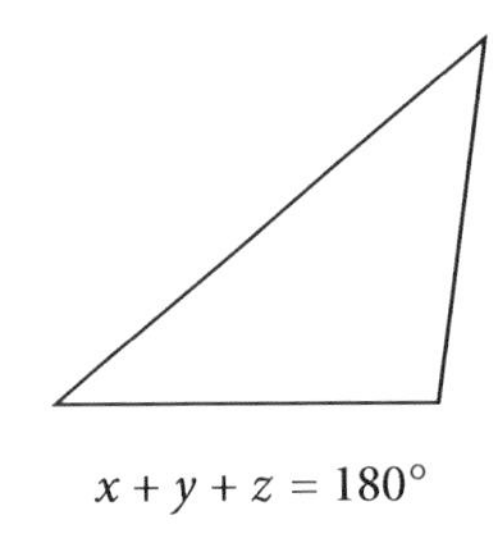

$x + y + z = 180°$

***The total measure of the interior angles of a triangle is 180 degrees.***

If you don't have this one down cold and aren't looking for it on every problem that gives you an angle measure, you might as well be taking the test in ancient Sanskrit while performing a handstand.

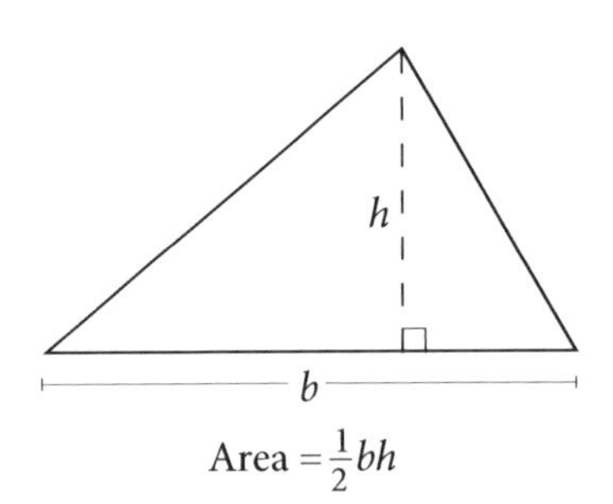


$\text{Area} = \frac{1}{2}bh$

***The area of a triangle is ½bh, where b is the length of the base and h is the height.***

This is pretty basic, right? Finding a triangle's area is as simple as knowing the base and height. The height has to be perpendicular to the base. Perpendicular means "at a right angle." You knew that.

When you have a right triangle, you can use the two legs as the base and height. In an obtuse triangle (one with an angle bigger than 90 degrees), the height may lie outside of the triangle, like so:

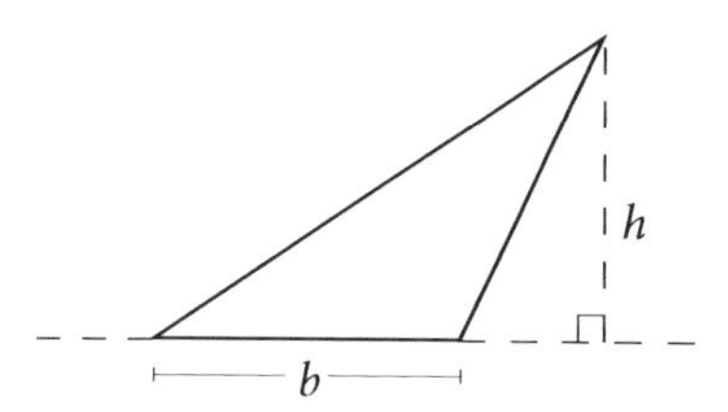


That's as difficult as triangle area will ever be. Next:

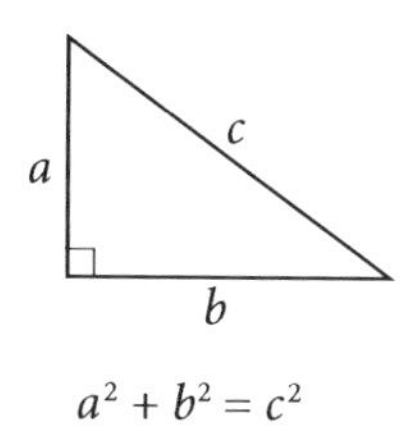


$a^2 + b^2 = c^2$

***The Pythagorean Theorem:* $a^2 + b^2 = c^2$**

That means one little side squared plus the other little side squared equals the big side (hypotenuse) squared. The hypotenuse is always opposite the right angle. Not too hard.

The SAT tends to favor integer answers, so it's not surprising that many of the Pythagorean triangles you will see on the test are "triples," specific sets of integers that happen to make the equation $a^2 + b^2 = c^2$ true. Some of them:

***3-4-5 and its multiples: 6-8-10, 9-12-15, etc.***
***5-12-13***
***8-15-17***
***7-24-25***

One of the best uses for the Pythagorean formula is to find distance. The distance formula is actually just a reconfiguration of Pythagorean. If you have $a^2 + b^2 = c^2$ in your head, you can use it to find distance in many situations—in a triangle, across a rectangle, on the coordinate grid, and even in three dimensions. You'll see examples of that in the practice problems.

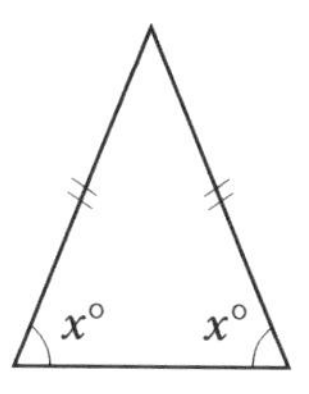


***Isosceles triangles have two equal sides and two equal angles.***

Whenever the test makers tell you that two sides of a triangle are equal, they are really trying to tell you that the angles opposite those two sides are equal. The reverse of that statement is true too.

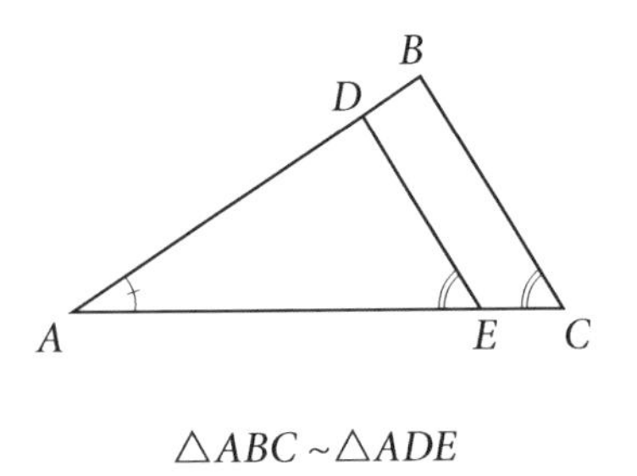


$\triangle ABC \sim \triangle ADE$

***Similar triangles have angle measures that are the same and side lengths that are proportional.***

As soon as you know that two angles of two different triangles are the same, you know you have similar triangles. You can then set up proportions to solve for any missing side lengths.

***Hot Tip:*** Similar triangles is the shape geometry topic we've seen most often on the SAT. It's also one that most students have forgotten. Get ahead of the curve; make sure you know the rules of triangle similarity and look for it whenever you see a shape geometry question.

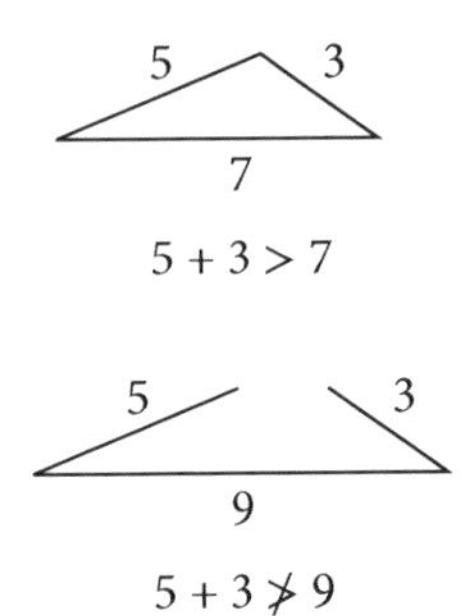


$5 + 3 > 7$

$5 + 3 \not> 9$

***How to make a triangle: the sum of the lengths of any two sides of a triangle has to be greater than the length of the third side.***

Make sense? The little 5 and 3 sides of that 5-3-9 "triangle" aren't long enough to join up and make a triangle above the side of length 9. Whenever the SAT asks a question along the lines of "which of these could be a triangle, this is the rule that they are testing you on.

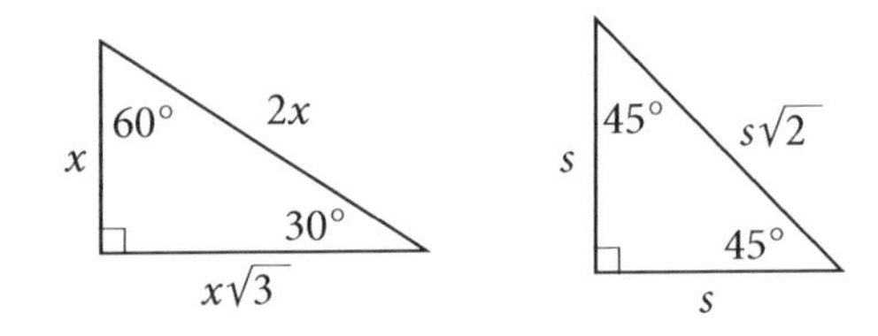


***45-45-90 and 30-60-90 "special" right triangles***

If you know why these triangles are so important to the creators of the SAT, please let me know. My working theory: the SAT folks had some gambling debts, and they were in a lot of trouble, right? So they went to the 30-60-90 and 45-45-90 triangles and were like, "Hey, we're in a lot of trouble." And the triangles said, with a really sinister tone, "Sure, we'll help you out. And then you're gonna help us out." Whatever the case may be, there are a LOT of 30-60-90 and 45-45-90 triangles on the test.

Now, do you remember which leg is which? One of them is like, s, and then another one is 2s and then √3s, right? More good news. You don't have to memorize it. They give it to you on every test, at the beginning of every math section. Awfully nice of them.

Don't believe me? Look at the first page of any SAT math section. Notice that the College Board gives you these two special right triangles on *every single Math section*. Weep tears of joy. Continue to weep. Now let your weeping evolve into maniacal laughter. You know something that other SAT-takers don't, and that feels good.

Laugh like a maniac. Go ahead, you deserve it.

## CIRCLES

### This is a circle.

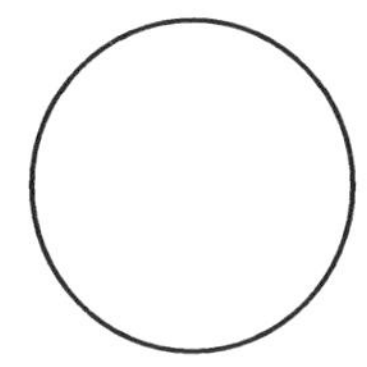

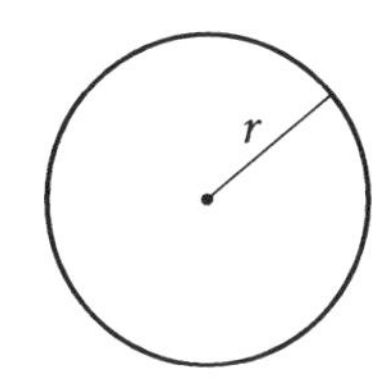


***Radius, r, is the distance from the center of the circle to any point lying on the circle.***

Think "spokes of a bicycle tire."

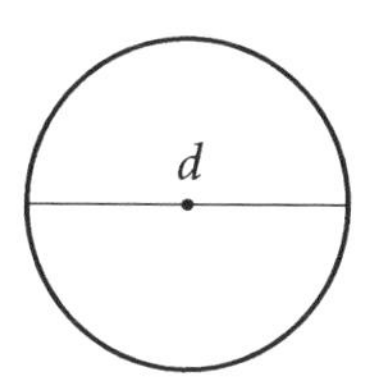


***Diameter, d, is the distance from one point on the circle, passing through the center, to an alternate point on the circle.***

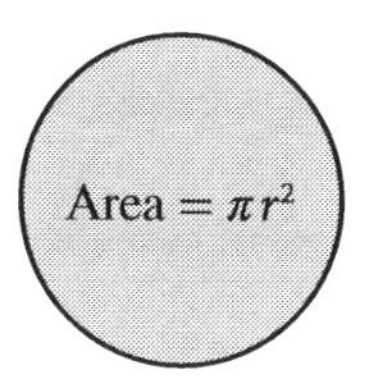


***The area of a circle is the amount of stuff inside the circle.***

We calculate area using this formula:

$$\textit{Area of a circle} = \pi r^2$$

**Just to make sure we're on the same page, which circle has a greater area?**

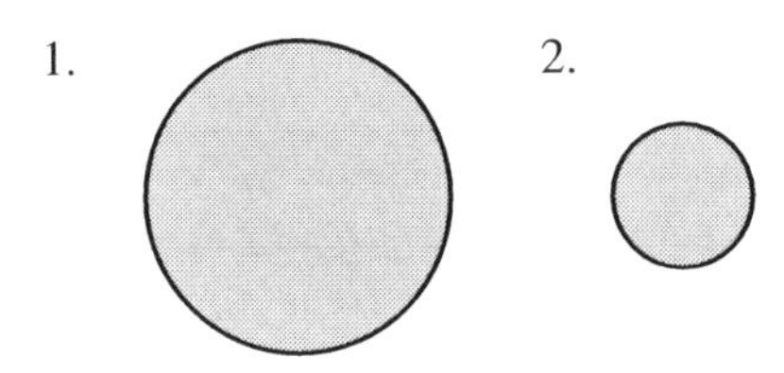


Hint: if you picked #2 it might be time for the ol' "college isn't for everyone" speech.

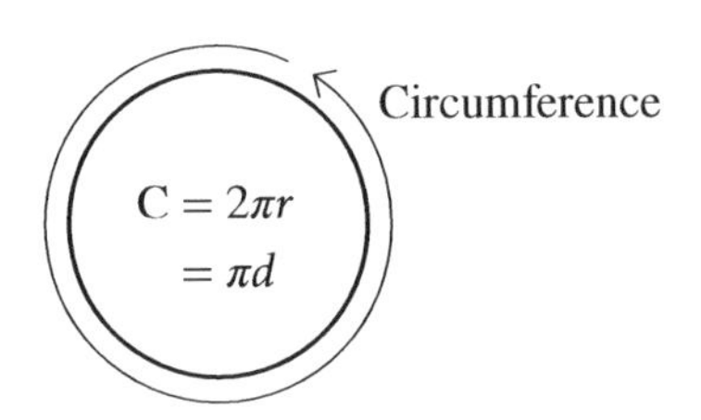


***The circumference or perimeter (circumference and perimeter mean the same thing when it comes to circles) is the distance around the circle.***

Which has a greater circumference: a unicycle wheel or a wheel on your luggage?

If you said "unicycle wheel," you're correct. If you said "luggage wheel," reread the definition of circumference. If you said "it depends on the size of the luggage" then you're a wisecrackin' smartass who's thinking way too much and you should know that your creative thinking will get you nowhere on the SAT.

***Circumference/perimeter is determined using the equation $C=2\pi r$ or $C=\pi d$.***

Two radii of a circle are equal to one diameter. Right? Right.

Here's a key concept: when a wheel spins once, it travels the length of its circumference. Keep that in mind on a problem in which a wheel is turning or a ball is rolling—the distance it travels is the same as its circumference.

Not bad so far, right?

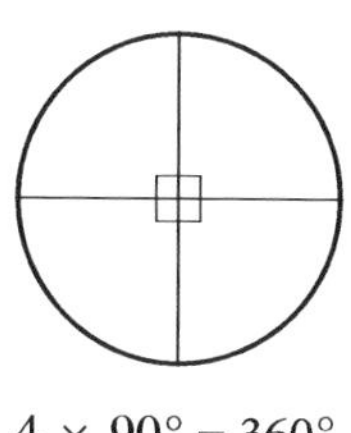

$4 \times 90° = 360°$

***Circles have 360 degrees. Think four right angles.***

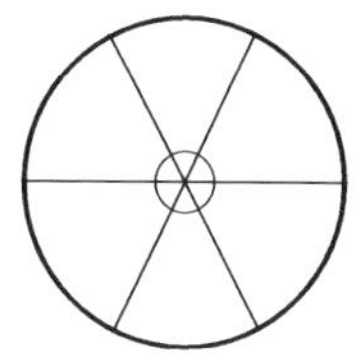

$6 \times 60° = 360°$

Or six 60° angles.

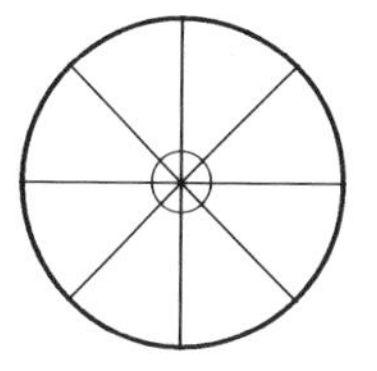

$8 \times 45° = 360°$

Or eight 45° angles.

You get it.

Which brings us to sectors. Sectors are the like slices of pizza, or slices of pie for those of you with a sweet tooth.

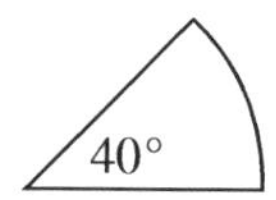


***Like a slice of pizza, a sector is a <u>part</u> of a circle.***

That's the key concept with sectors. We still use the two basic circle formulas—circumference and area—then we use the angle measure of the sector to figure out how much of the circle you have.

This particular sector has a central angle of 40°. How much of a circle is that? A whole circle is 360°, so this is 40°/360° of a circle, or 1/9th. To find the area of this sector, you'd find the area of a whole circle, then take 1/9th of that.

That's it! If you want to express your love for circles, why not lie down on the floor and roll around like you're a circle?

Please do this after I'm gone.

## LINES AND ANGLES

What is up with lines? They're so serious! Just take a look at this guy ----> :|

Take it easy, solemn straight-face guy!

Here are the things you need to know about lines:

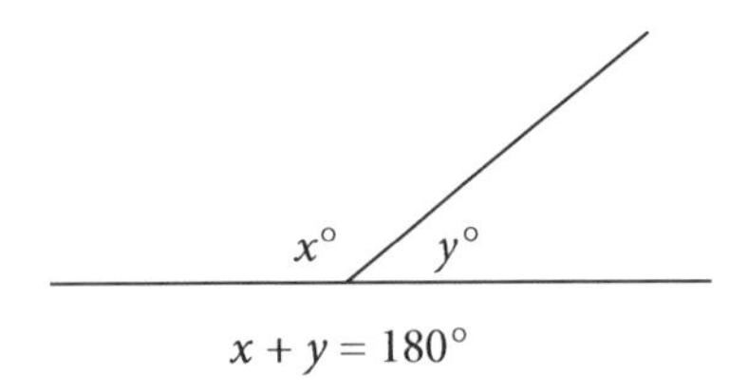


***The sum of the angles on one side of a line is 180°.***

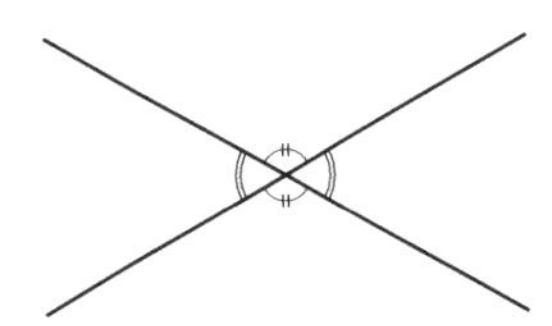

***The angles opposite each other when two lines cross are equal to each other.***

They're called vertical angles. The name is not important but the concept is.

Parallel lines cut by a transversal form a bunch of equal and supplementary angles.

OK, but which ones? When you took Geometry, you had to learn a bunch of names, like "alternate interior angles." We're going to skip the names and use a little shortcut I call number-all-the-angles-around-each-point-in-a-clockwise-fashion. Here's how you do it: you number all the angles around each point in a clockwise fashion.

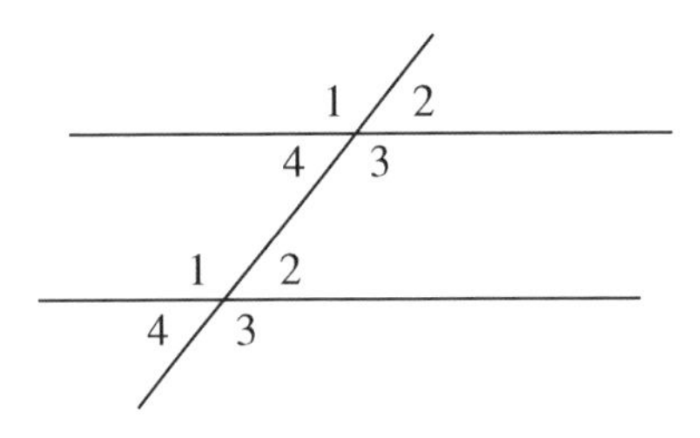

***Hot Tip:*** The key is to start in the same place when you number the angles. I like to start at the top-left angle, number clockwise, then jump to the other point and start at the top-left angle there too.

This will tell you everything you need to know. All the angles marked with odd numbers (1 and 3) are equal to each other. All of the angles with an even number (2 and 4) are equal to each other. Any pair of odd angle and even angles must be supplementary (which means they add up to 180°, in case you forgot).

All that knowledge is enough to put a smile on your face, isn't it, solemn straight-face guy?

:|

Guess not.

## Shape Geometry

**1**

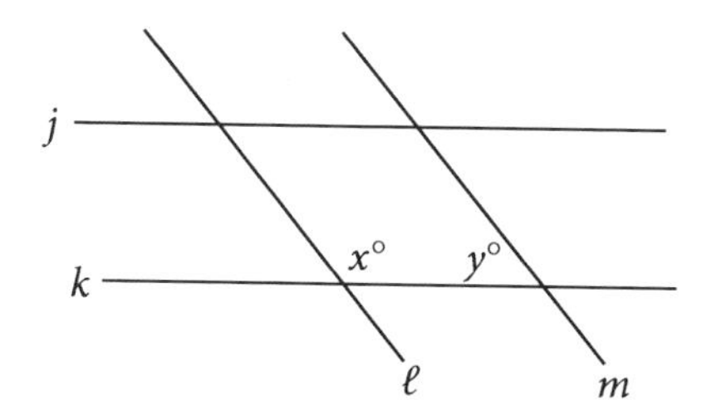


In the figure above, lines $j$ and $k$ are parallel and lines $\ell$ and $m$ are parallel. If the measure of angle $x$ is 128°, what is the measure of angle $y$?

A) 38°

B) 52°

C) 218°

D) 232°

**2**

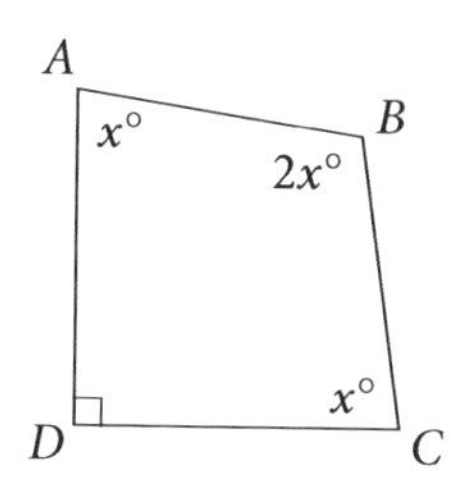


In the figure above, what is the value of $\angle ABC$?

A) 45°

B) 67.5°

C) 120°

D) 135°

**3**

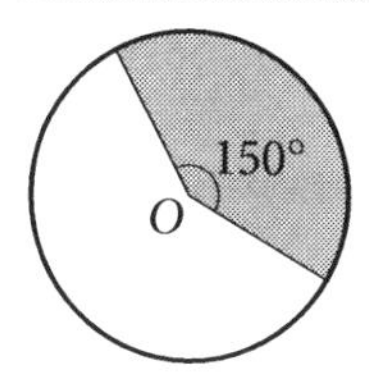


A circle with center $O$ is shown above. The area of the shaded region is what fraction of the area of circle $O$?

**4**

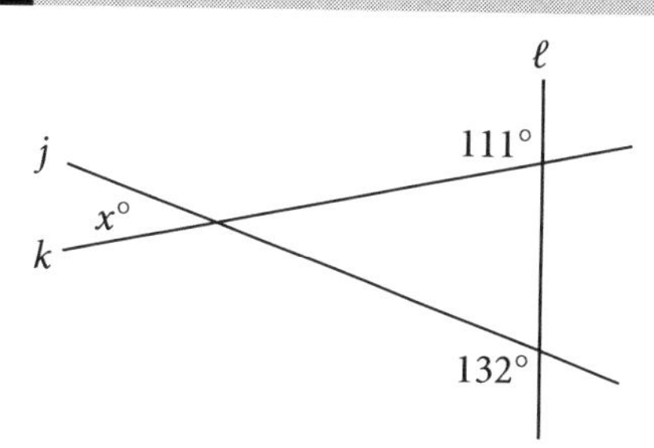


Note: Figure not drawn to scale.

Lines $j$, $k$, and $\ell$ intersect as shown above. What is the value of $x$?

**5**

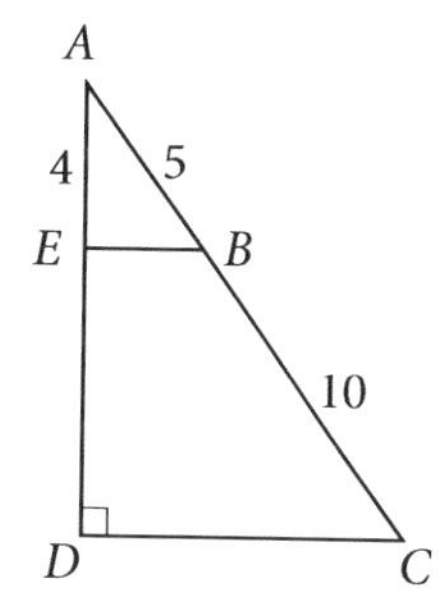


In the figure above, $\overline{EB}$ is parallel to $\overline{DC}$. What is the length of $\overline{DC}$?

**6**

The length of a poster is 4 inches longer than its width. If the width of the poster is $w$ inches, which of the following expresses the perimeter of the poster, in inches?

A) $2w + 4$

B) $4w + 8$

C) $w^2 + 4$

D) $w^2 + 4w$

**7**

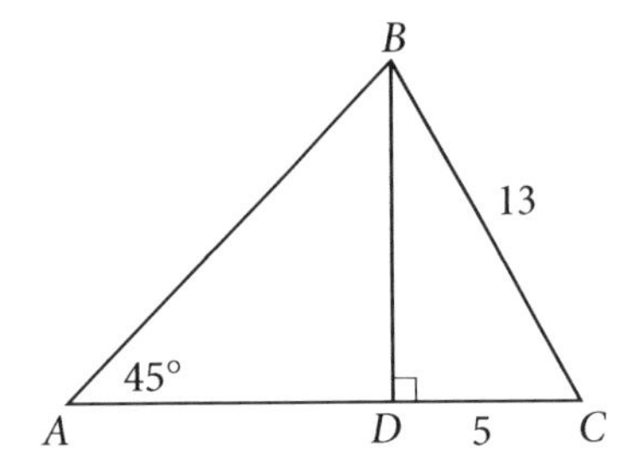


In $\triangle ABC$ above, $\overline{BC} = 13$ and $\overline{DC} = 5$. What is the length of $\overline{AB}$?

A) 8
B) $8\sqrt{2}$
C) 12
D) $12\sqrt{2}$

**8**

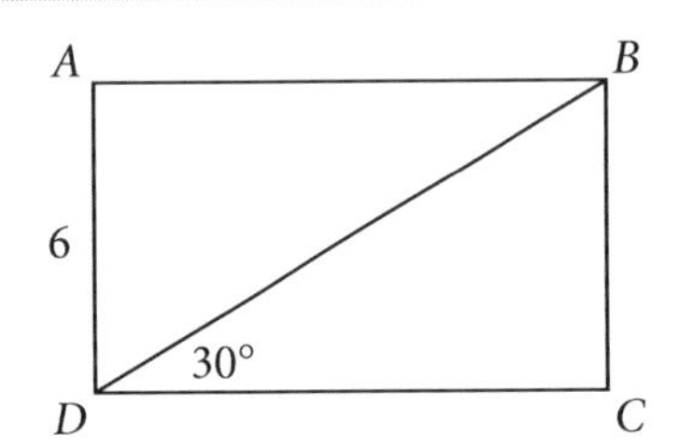


In rectangle $ABCD$ above, what is the length of $\overline{DC}$?

A) 6
B) $6\sqrt{2}$
C) $6\sqrt{3}$
D) 12

**9**

A type of packaging in the shape of a right circular cylinder has a height of 4 inches and a volume of $100\pi$ cubic inches. What is the diameter of the base of the cylinder, in inches?

**10**

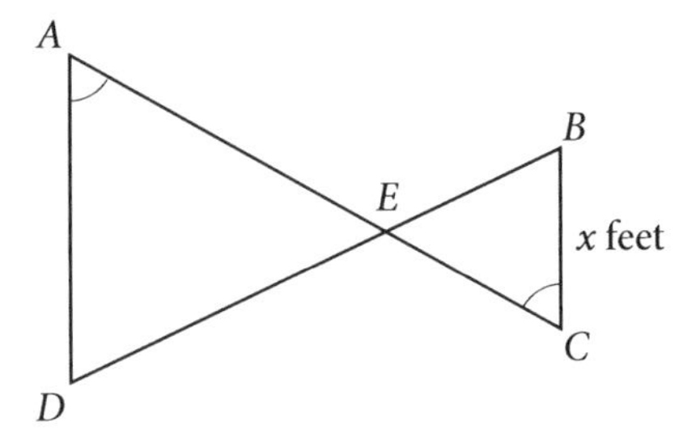


Note: Figure not drawn to scale.

A landscape architect is designing a network of paths between several buildings, which are represented by the points on the diagram above. The lengths of the paths represented by $AD$, $AE$, $EB$, and $EC$ in the diagram will be 200 feet, 160 feet, 40 feet, and 32 feet, respectively. Segments $AC$ and $BD$ intersect at $E$, and $\angle DAE$ and $\angle BCE$ are congruent. What is the value of $x$?

**11**

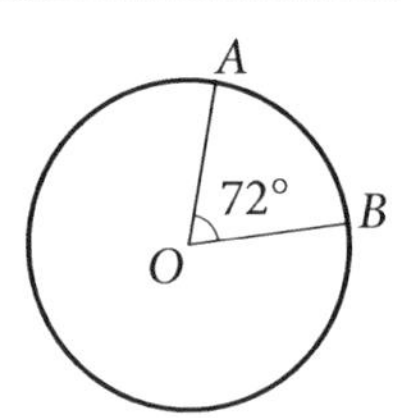


In the figure above, the circle has center $O$ and radius 10. Which of the following is the length of minor arc $AB$?

A) $\pi$
B) $2\pi$
C) $4\pi$
D) $8\pi$

**12**

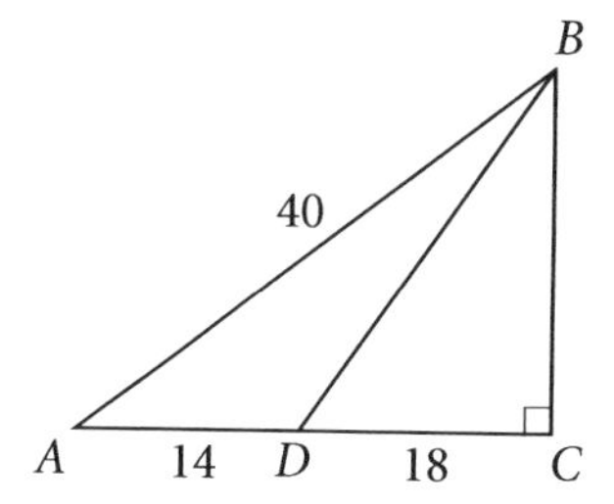


In the figure above, point $D$ lies on $\overline{CD}$. What is the length of $\overline{BD}$?

**13**

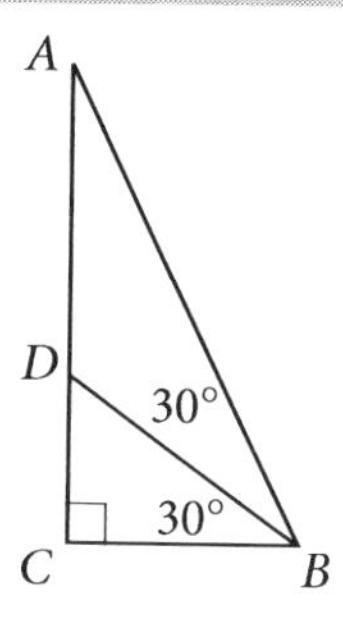


In $\triangle ABC$ above, $\overline{CD} = 2$. What is the length of $\overline{AC}$?

A) 4

B) 6

C) $4\sqrt{3}$

D) 12

**14**

An architect designs a rectangular bedroom with an area of 108 square feet. If the length of the bedroom is 3 feet longer than the width, what is the width of the bedroom?

**15**

The surface area of a cube is $6k^2$, where $k$ is a positive constant. Which of the following expressions represents the perimeter of one face of the cube?

A) $k$

B) $k\sqrt{6}$

C) $4k$

D) $k^2$

**16**

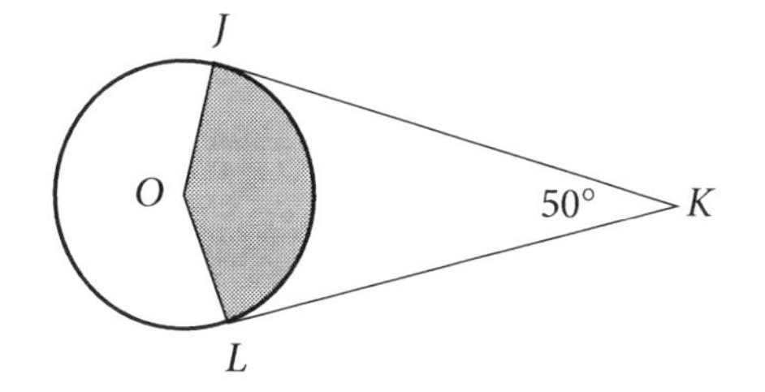


In the figure above, point $O$ is the center of the circle, line segments $JK$ and $KL$ are tangent to the circle at points $J$ and $L$, respectively, and the segments intersect at point $K$ as shown. If the radius of the circle is 6, what is the area of the shaded region?

A) $10\pi$

B) $11\pi$

C) $12\pi$

D) $13\pi$

# Soh-Cah-Toa

**Soh-Cah-Toa. You've heard of it before, and you probably know that it refers to sine, cosine, and tangent.**

You might even know how to use it.

The thing that gets me about Soh-Cah-Toa is the fact that it is an almost perfectly random mnemonic device that everyone—you, your parents, *their* parents—uses to memorize the trig ratios. We just all agree that Soh-Cah-Toa is the best way.

## Huh. Isn't that weird?

Do you ever find yourself in a situation where *you* find something interesting and *no one else does*? I do.

### Here's what Soh-Cah-Toa means.

It's an acronym that helps us remember which trig ratio within a right triangle is which.

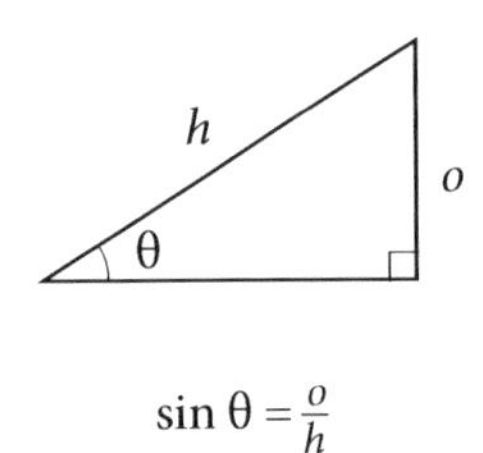


$\sin\theta = \frac{o}{h}$

***Sine is equal to the opposite side over the hypotenuse.***

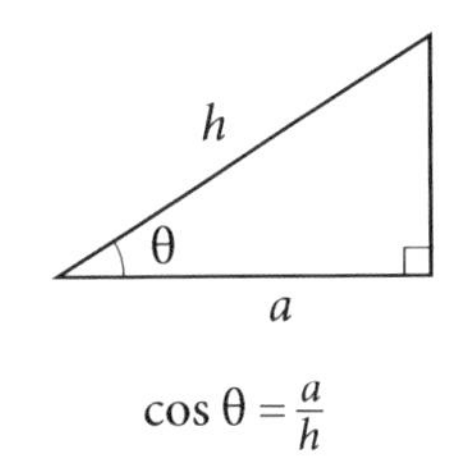


$\cos\theta = \frac{a}{h}$

***Cosine is equal to the adjacent side over the hypotenuse.***

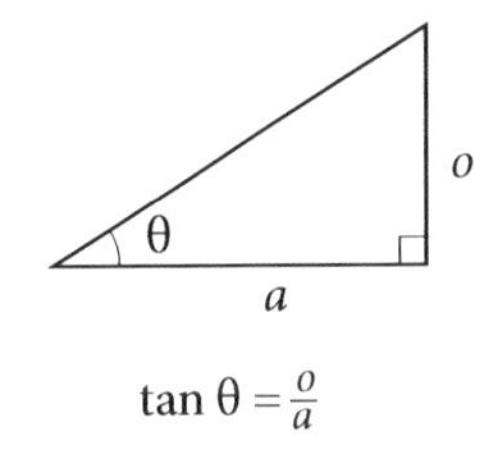


$\tan\theta = \frac{o}{a}$

***Tangent is equal to the opposite side over the adjacent.***

The reason we make mnemonic devices in the first place is to help us memorize stuff. So yeah, you have to memorize this.

### A couple of trig fun facts:

Because the hypotenuse in a right triangle is always going to be the longest side—it has to be, since it's opposite the right angle, aka the largest angle in the triangle—the denominator of both sine and cosine must always be larger than the numerator. That means that cosine and sine both have a maximum value of 1.

> ***Hot Tip***: When you're looking at actual right triangles drawn on the page, you can't get to a sine or cosine of 1, but here's a non-right triangle trig fun fact: the sine of a 90° angle is 1, and the cosine of a 0° is 1.

The tangent value is not restricted like sine and cosine are. In a very, very skinny triangle, you could have a tangent value that's really, really small because the opposite side is many times smaller than the adjacent side.

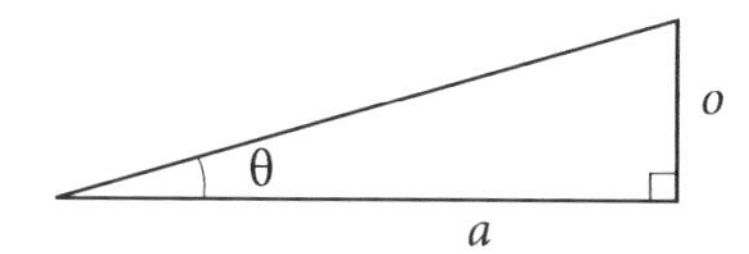


If you look at that same triangle from the perspective of the other acute angle, the tangent value would be really, really BIG since the opposite side is now many times bigger than the adjacent side.

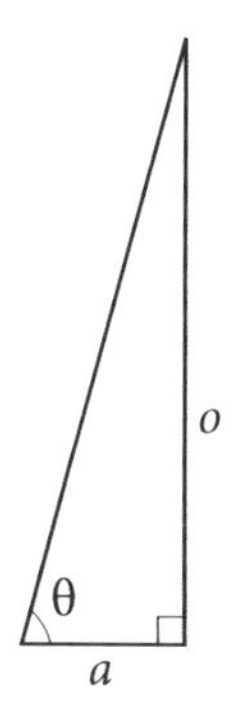


OK, some more trig fun facts you want to bring into the test with you:

$$\tan x = \frac{\sin x}{\cos x}$$

You can see how this is true if you divide the sine ratio (opposite over hypotenuse) by the cosine ratio (adjacent over hypotenuse). When you do the fraction math, hypotenuse cancels out and you're left with opposite over adjacent.

$$\frac{\frac{\text{opposite}}{\text{hypotenuse}}}{\frac{\text{adjacent}}{\text{hypotenuse}}} \qquad \frac{\frac{\text{opposite}}{\cancel{\text{hypotenuse}}}}{\frac{\text{adjacent}}{\cancel{\text{hypotenuse}}}}$$

$$\frac{\text{opposite}}{\text{adjacent}} = \tan$$

**Next, complementary angles.**

$$\sin x^\circ = \cos(90^\circ - x^\circ)$$

$$\cos x^\circ = \sin(90^\circ - x^\circ)$$

This one makes more sense than it first may appear. Start with an angle x, then subtract that angle measure from 90. The new angle would be the complementary angle—aka the *other* acute angle in a right triangle.

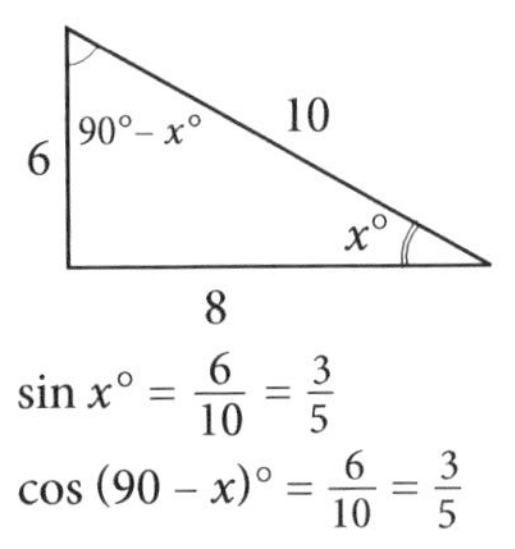


Now, think of what the sine of the angle marked as *x* would be. Opposite over hypotenuse, right? In this triangle, that would be 6/10. What is the cosine of the other acute angle? Adjacent over hypotenuse. That would ALSO be 6/10.

Whenever you have complementary angles, it'll always work like that. That's called a trig identity. There are about 500 trig identities, but the ones you need to know for the SAT are the ones we just learned: tan = sin/cos and sin x = cos (90 – x) and the reverse, cos x = sin (90 – x).

## Trig practice! Get some.

# Soh-Cah-Toa

**1**

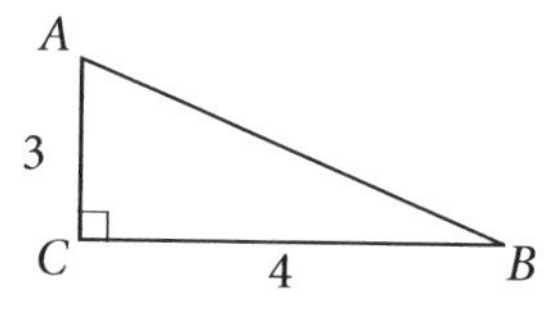


Based on right triangle $ABC$ above, what is the cosine of $\angle A$?

A) $\frac{3}{5}$

B) $\frac{3}{4}$

C) $\frac{4}{5}$

D) $\frac{4}{3}$

**2**

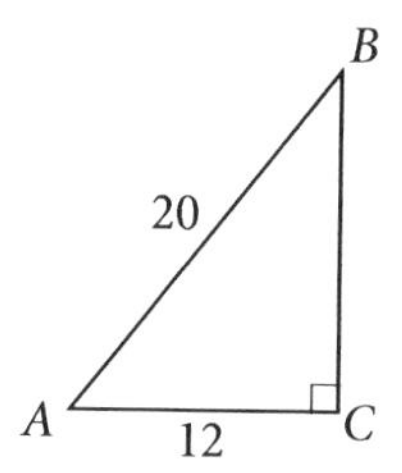


In right triangle $ABC$ above, $\sin A = \frac{4}{5}$. What is the value of $\tan B$?

A) $\frac{3}{5}$

B) $\frac{3}{4}$

C) $\frac{4}{3}$

D) $\frac{5}{3}$

**3**

If $\sin x° = \cos y°$, which of the following possible values of $x$ and $y$ would NOT satisfy the equation?

A) $x = 25$ and $y = 65$

B) $x = 30$ and $y = 70$

C) $x = 40$ and $y = 50$

D) $x = 50$ and $y = 40$

**4**

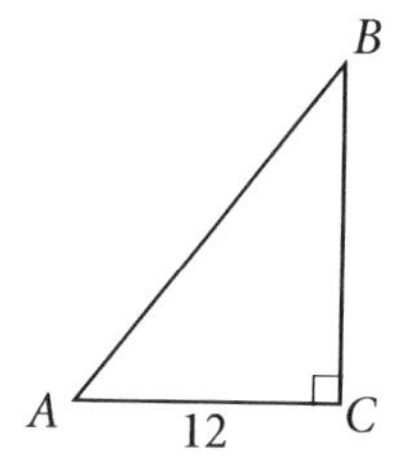


In right triangle $ABC$ above, the cosine of $\angle A$ is 0.6. What is the length of $\overline{BC}$?

A) 7.2

B) 9

C) 16

D) 20

**5**

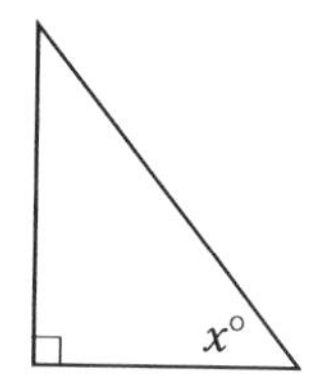


In the right triangle above, $\sin x° = \frac{4}{5}$. What is $\cos(90° - x°)$?

**6**

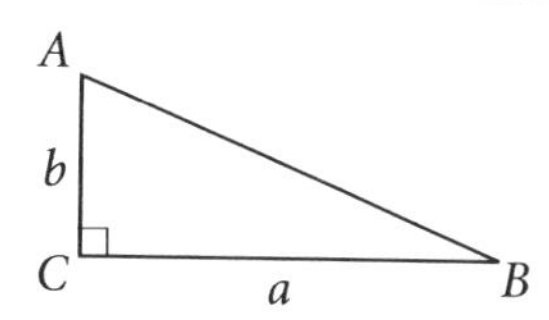


Based on right triangle $ABC$ above, which of the following is equal to $\frac{a}{b}$?

A) $\cos A$

B) $\cos B$

C) $\tan A$

D) $\tan B$

**7**

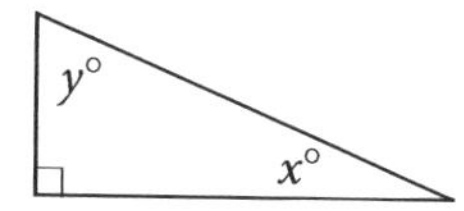


In the triangle above, the cosine of $y°$ is 0.6. What is the sine of $x°$?

**8**

In right triangle $ABC$ above, $a \neq b$. Which of the following is equivalent to $\frac{\cos A}{\sin B}$?

A) 0

B) 1

C) $ab$

D) $\frac{a}{b}$

**9**

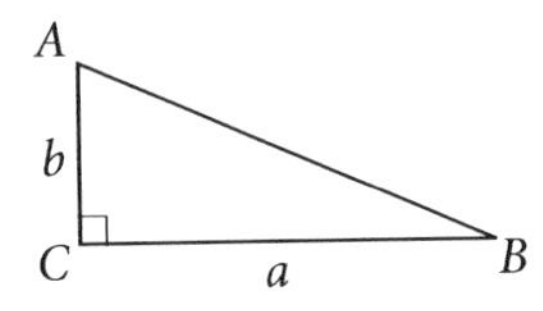


Based on right triangle $ABC$ above, which of the following represents the length of $\overline{AB}$?

A) $a + b$

B) $a\sin A$

C) $\frac{a}{\sin A}$

D) $\frac{b}{\sin A}$

**10**

In triangle $ABC$, $\sin a° = \cos b°$, where $a$ and $b$ are acute angles. If $a = 2x + 10$ and $b = 4x + 14$, what is the value of $x$?

A) 2
B) 4
C) 11
D) 24

**11**

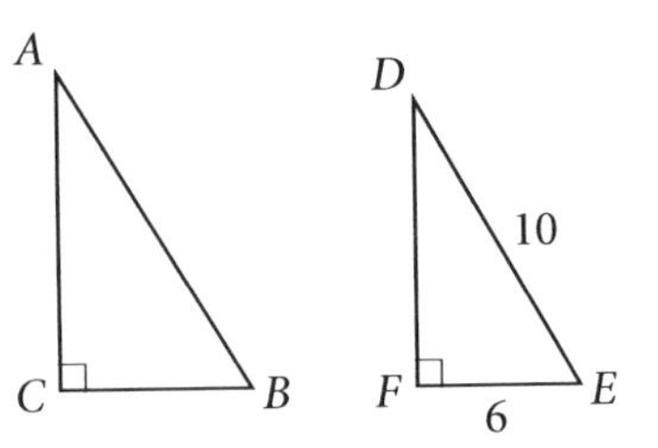


Note: Figure not drawn to scale.

Triangles $ABC$ and $DEF$ are similar, where vertices $A$, $B$, and $C$ correspond to vertices $D$, $E$, and $F$, respectively. If each side of triangle $ABC$ is 4 times the length of the corresponding side of triangle $DEF$, what is the value of $\cos A$?

**12**

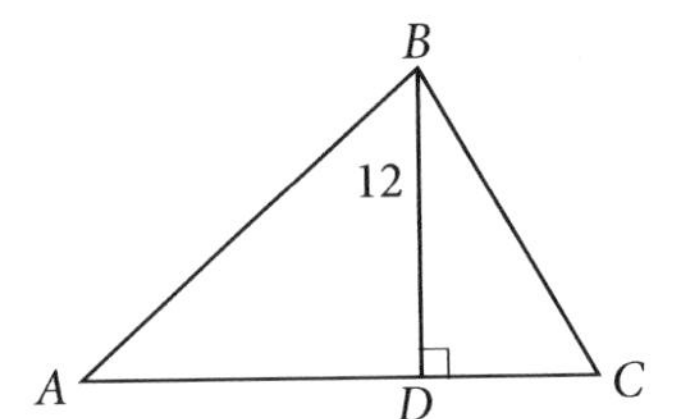


In the figure above, the sine of $\angle A$ is $\frac{3}{5}$ and the sine of $\angle C$ is $\frac{4}{5}$. What is the perimeter of triangle $ABC$?

**13**

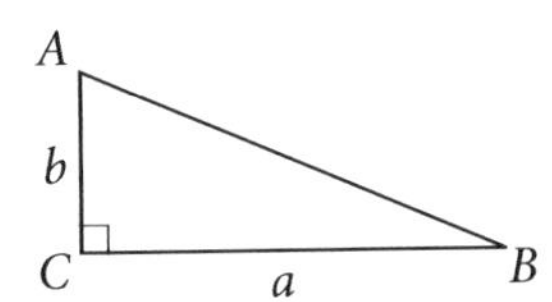


Based on right triangle $ABC$ above, which of the following represents the sine of $\angle B$?

A) $\frac{a}{b}$

B) $\frac{b}{a}$

C) $\frac{a}{\sqrt{a^2 + b^2}}$

D) $\frac{b}{\sqrt{a^2 + b^2}}$

## 14

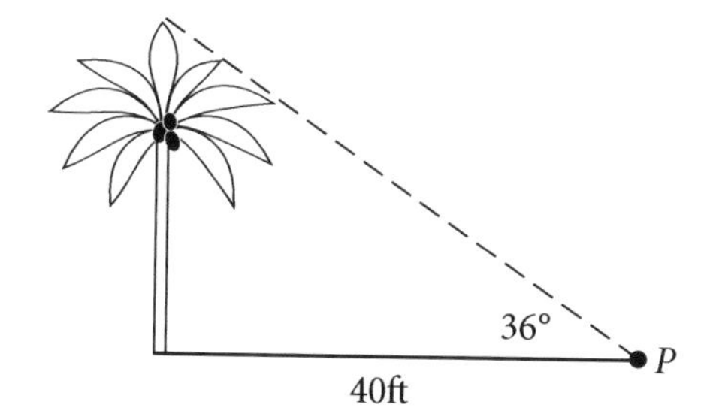


In the figure above, point $P$ marks the end of the shadow of a palm tree. The total length of the shadow is 40 feet, and the angle of elevation from point $P$ to the top of the palm tree is 36°. If the tangent of 36° is approximately 0.73, which of the following is closest to the height of the palm tree?

A) 25 feet
B) 27 feet
C) 29 feet
D) 31 feet

## 15

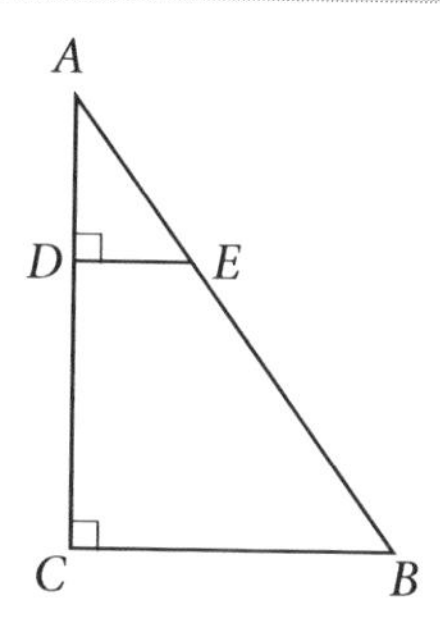


In the figure above, $\overline{CB} = \overline{EB} = 15$. If $\tan B = \frac{4}{3}$, what is the length of $\overline{AD}$?

## 16

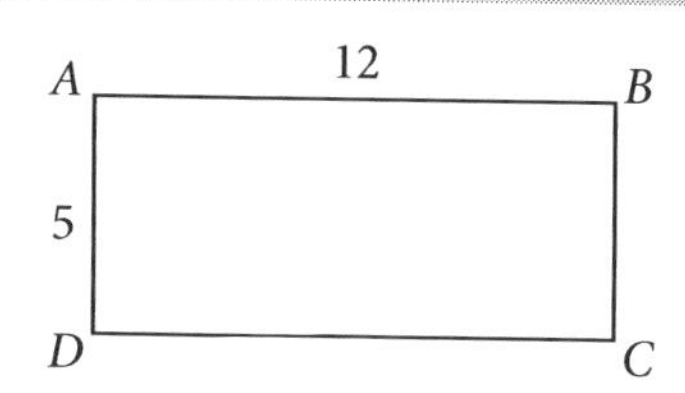


In rectangle $ABCD$ above, point $E$ (not shown) lies on $\overline{DC}$. What is the value of $\sin(\angle ABE) - \cos(\angle EBC)$?

# Charts and Graphs

**If it seems absurd to you that this is *literally the third chapter in this book about charts and graphs*, well, you and I are on the same page.**

If I were not too exhausted by all the chart and graph questions, I would make the "so you thought there was no Science section on the SAT, huh?" joke. Alas.

Let's get straight to the strategies to keep in mind on chart and graph questions on the Math section.

***Pay careful attention to the axes of a graph (or the header of a table/chart).***

What's the easiest place to orient yourself to a graph or chart? In the place where they tell you what information they are providing. You'll find that on the *y*- and *x*-axes, or in the header row of a table. When you know what information is provided, you'll be prepped to find what you need to answer the question.

***Units are your friends.***

In fact, units can give away what you need to find. Suppose a question asks you to find an answer "in miles per hour," and you have miles on the y-axis and time in hours on the *x*-axis. Well, that tells you that you're going to need to divide a *y*-value by an *x*-value to find miles per hour. Let the units tell you what you need to provide.

***Know Your Vocab.***

The language of statistics comes into play on chart and graph questions. Those terms are listed and defined in the statistics chapter. Learn that list! Make sure you know how to find mean, median, mode, and range...and what each of them means too.

***Don't sleep on any text around the chart or graph.***

Here's a great trick the SAT keeps up its sleeve: sometimes, critical information is above or below the chart or graph. Don't sleep on any of the text around the graph, even when it's long and wordy. Which brings us to our final strategy:

***Stay patient.***

These chart and graph questions, though featured in the math section, are almost always careful reading questions. When you get to one, know that the math is going to be easy—but that it might test your patience. Take a deep breath, read all the information around the table, and you'll get these questions right without exception.

## Problem time, yo.

# Charts and Graphs

**1**

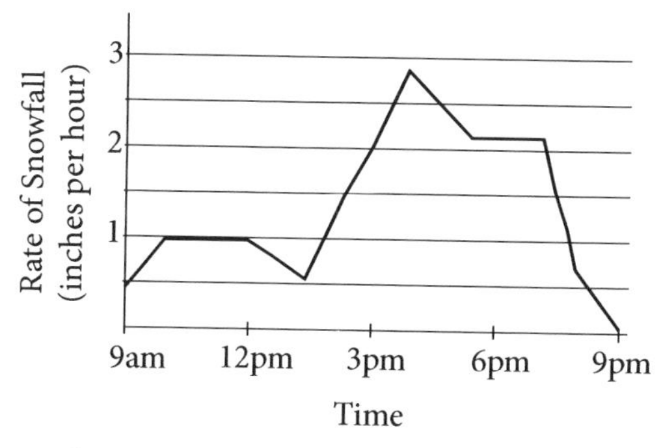


The graph above shows the rate of snowfall at different times during a storm. On which interval is the rate of snowfall strictly decreasing then strictly increasing?

A) Between 9am and 11am
B) Between 12pm and 2pm
C) Between 3pm and 5pm
D) Between 4pm and 6pm

**2**

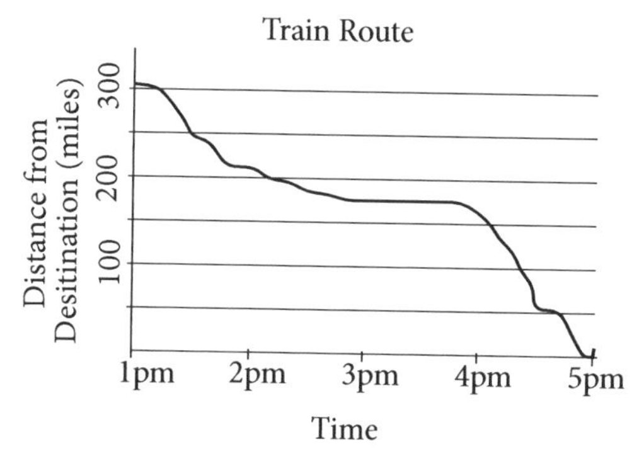


A train leaves a station at 1pm and travels along a route to its destination. The graph above shows the train's remaining distance to its destination at various times during its trip. The train stopped for 1 hour during the trip to repair a mechanical issue. Based on the graph, which of the following is closest to the time the repairs were finished and the train continued along its route?

A) 2:00 P.M.
B) 2:45 P.M.
C) 3:45 P.M.
D) 4:30 P.M.

**3**

The price of a stock during a 5-hour period is graphed below.

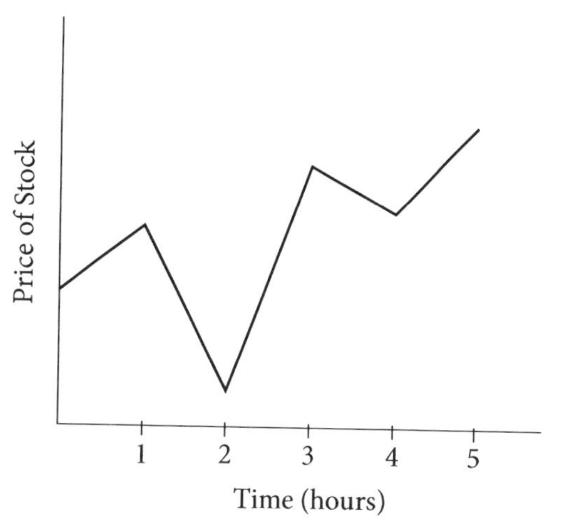


On what interval did the price of the stock increase the fastest?

A) Between 0 and 1 hours
B) Between 1 and 2 hours
C) Between 2 and 3 hours
D) Between 3 and 4 hours

**Questions 4 and 5 refer to the following information**

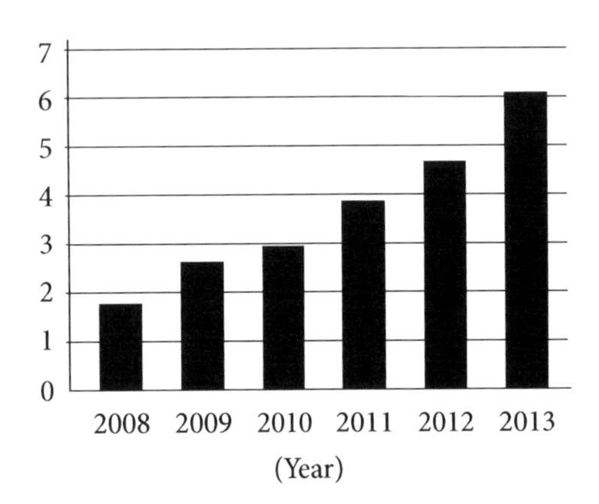


The graph above shows the trend in the number of vinyl records sold in the U.S. each year from 2008 to 2013.

**4**

If the total number of vinyl records sold from 2008 to 2013 was 21,700,000, what is an appropriate label for the vertical axis of the graph?

A) Number of vinyl records sold (in thousands)
B) Number of vinyl records sold (in tens of thousands)
C) Number of vinyl records sold (in hundreds of thousands)
D) Number of vinyl records sold (in millions)

**5**

The number of vinyl records sold in 2009 is approximately what fraction of the number sold in 2013?

A) $\frac{1}{4}$

B) $\frac{1}{3}$

C) $\frac{2}{5}$

D) $\frac{1}{2}$

**Questions 6 and 7 refer to the following information**

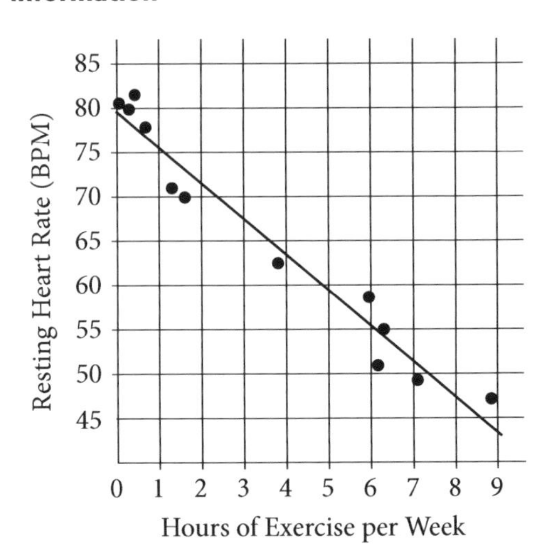


The scatterplot above shows the resting heart rate for 12 members of the same family plotted against the number of hours of exercise they get per week. The line of best fit is also shown.

**6**

For what fraction of the 12 family members does the line of best fit overestimate their resting heart rate?

A) $\frac{5}{12}$

B) $\frac{1}{2}$

C) $\frac{7}{12}$

D) $\frac{3}{4}$

**7**

For the family member whose resting heart rate was 70 beats per minute, the actual amount of exercise the family member got per week was how many minutes less than the amount predicted by the line of best fit?

A) 4
B) 40
C) 80
D) 140

**Questions 8-10 refer to the following information**

A tourism association recorded the number of visitors to a local beach on 10 consecutive days. The graph below plots the number of visitors on each day against the average temperature on that day, in degrees Fahrenheit.

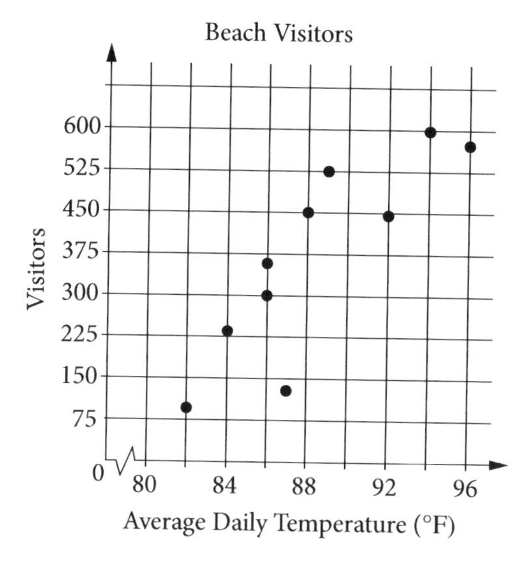


**8**

Which of the following best describes the relationship between the data in the graph?

A) A weak negative association that is linear
B) A strong negative association that is linear
C) A strong positive association that is linear
D) There is no relationship between the data

**9**

On the two days that had the same average temperature, what was the difference in the number of visitors?

A) 4
B) 16
C) 65
D) 525

**10**

$$C = \frac{F - 32}{1.8}$$

The equation above is used to convert degrees Fahrenheit, F, to degrees Celsius, C. According to the graph, what was the temperature, in degrees Celsius, on the day with the most visitors?

A) 20.2 °C
B) 34.4 °C
C) 35.6 °C
D) 201.2 °C

**Questions 11-13 refer to the following information.**

| Material | Friction constant |
|---|---|
| Aluminum | 4.6 |
| Brass | 4.3 |
| Copper | 3.5 |
| Polyethene | 1.9 |
| Ice | 0.3 |
| Wood | 6.1 |

The force, in newtons, required to move an object across a flat steel surface can be found by multiplying the mass, in kilograms, of the object by a friction constant that is specific to the material the object is made of. The table above gives the friction constants for 6 materials.

**11**

According to the information in the table, what is the force required to move a 20-kilogram copper object across a flat steel surface?

A) 8 newtons
B) 38 newtons
C) 70 newtons
D) 86 newtons

**12**

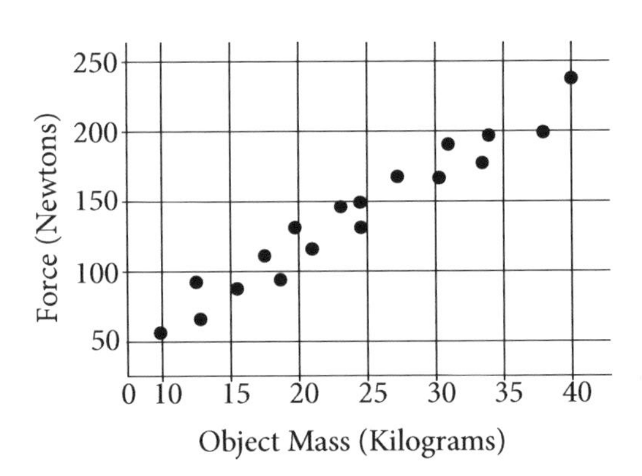


The scatterplot above gives the object mass plotted against the required force to move 20 objects made from the same material across a flat steel surface. The objects were most likely made of which of the following materials?

A) Aluminum
B) Wood
C) Polyethene
D) Ice

**13**

In an experiment, a scientist finds that a piece of aluminum and a piece of brass each require a 200 newton force to move them across a flat steel surface. Which of the following is closest to the difference, in kilograms, between their masses?

A) 0.3 kilograms
B) 3 kilograms
C) 30 kilograms
D) 300 kilograms

**Questions 14-16 refer to the following information.**

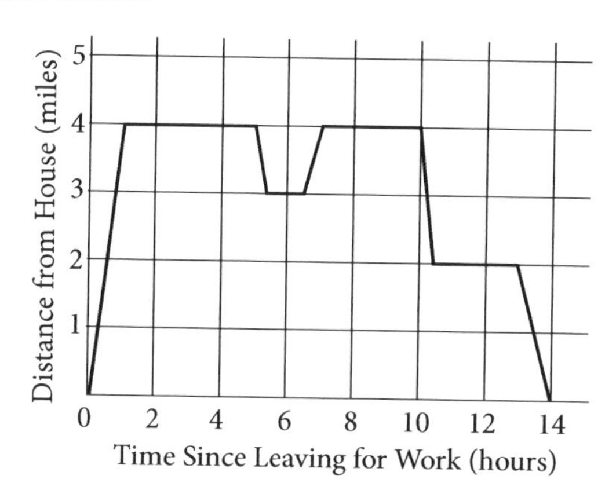


Cassandra rides her bike to work every day. On Tuesday, she had a lunch meeting at another office, and she met some friends for dinner after work before returning home. The graph above shows Cassandra's distance from her house, in miles, from the time she left for work in the morning on Tuesday to the time she returned home at the end of the day.

**14**

According to the graph, how many times was Cassandra exactly 3.5 miles from her house on Tuesday?

A) One

B) Two

C) Three

D) Four

**15**

Based on the graph and the information provided, what was the total distance Cassandra traveled on Tuesday?

A) 4 miles

B) 6 miles

C) 10 miles

D) 14 miles

**16**

If Cassandra left her house at 8 A.M., during which of the following times was she at dinner with her friends?

A) 6 P.M.

B) 8 P.M.

C) 10 P.M.

D) 11 P.M.

# Brief-But-Oddly-Complete Stats

This is the world's shortest yet somehow comprehensive (at least for the SAT) statistics course.

You ready?

## MEASURES OF CENTRAL TENDENCY

What a name, right? Are you as turned off as I am right now?

OK, the name sucks, but the concept is cool. There are three different ways we can describe the middle—the central tendency—of a set of data. Each one has its own specific usefulness.

### *MEAN, OR AVERAGE.*

Those words mean the same thing. Mean is average. Average is mean. They are one and the same.

$$\text{average} = \frac{\text{sum total}}{\text{\# of terms}}$$

> ***Mean/average is equal to the sum of all the terms in a set divided by the number of terms in the set.***

We frequently use mean/average to describe sets of data. Your grade at the end of the semester in school? That's an average. It might be a weighted average (more on that below), but it's an average.

You should definitely know that formula well—just remember, if you know any two of those three things (average, sum total, and number of things), you can use those to find the missing third value.

***Hot Tip:*** Want to find a weighted average? Easy. Just multiply each value/score by its weight, then add them together. For example, suppose your quiz average counts for 30% of your grade, and you've got a 94 as your average quiz score. Tests count for 60%, and you have a 90 as your average test score. Finally, participation counts for 10%, and you've got a 100 there—you're always participating. You'd compute your weighted average as follows:

$$94(0.30) + 90(0.60) + 100(0.10) = 92.2$$

At which point you go beg your teacher to count that as an A, not an A-.

Average is probably the most common measure of central tendency, but there are two more, including...

## MEDIAN

***The median is the middle term in a set that's arranged from least to greatest.***

For example, in the set...

1, 4, 13, 15, 16

...the median is 13 because it's right in the middle. If you have an even number of terms, like so:

7, 12, 13, 20

the median is the average of the two terms in the middle. In this case, those terms are 12 and 13, and their average is 12.5. And that's the median.

Why would you use the median instead of the mean to find the middle of a set of data? The answer has to do with another statistics vocabulary term:

## OUTLIER

***An outlier is a value in a data set that differs significantly from the rest of the values in the set.***

To use the "grades in school" example again, suppose you have one quiz this semester on which you scored a zero. You studied the wrong chapter, or you didn't realize your teacher said the quiz was *this* Tuesday. Anyway, you got a zero on that one. On all the rest, you scored 90 or above. That makes that zero an outlier—it's really different from most of your quiz scores. Now is when you hope that your teacher institutes a "you can drop your lowest quiz score" policy.

### Here's another example.

Real estate prices are almost always reported as a median, as in, "the median home price in Southern California in 2017 was $505,000." Why a median? Well, there are some major outliers in real estate, especially in Southern California. For example, there is a property for sale right now in Southern California for (I am not making this up) $500 million. That is the approximate equivalent of 1,000x the price of the median home. If you *include* that house when you compute the average/mean, you will get an average home price so high that it doesn't give a good indication of what the *typical* house in Southern California is worth.

Our last measure of central tendency is called mode.

## MODE

***Mode is the value in the set that occurs most frequently.***

We don't use it that often, but you might need to know it on the SAT. So here we are.

First off, you find the mode through counting. Whichever term occurs the most often is the mode.

Second, mode is an interesting measure of a set of data when that data breaks out into neat categories. Suppose we took a set of data like the eye color of students in class. If 8 students had brown eyes, 5 had blue, 4 had kinda-greenish eyes, and 1 had titanium alloy visual sensors, then the mode of that set of data would be "brown eyes."

Also, if I were you, I'd keep your eyes on that kid with the titanium sensor eyes. There's something...not quite right about him.

***Hot Tip***: Here's a mnemonic device for keeping mean, median, and mode straight in your head. The median is the divider in the middle of the road, so it's also the middle term in a set of data. The MOde occurs the MOst in the set. And mean is the other one...the average.

## Who's ready for an easy stats term?

[cue the sound of 1,200 students raising their hands at the same time]

### *RANGE*

***Range is equal to the biggest value in a set minus the smallest value.***

It's the *range* of the values in the set. Biggest minus smallest. Isn't that easy? Now you know.

### *QUARTILES*

***The lower quartile is the value at the 25th percentile,***
***and the upper quartile is the value at the 75th percentile.***

Think of the root of this word, "quart." Remind you of "quarter"? Hopefully it does. The quartiles break up a data set into more than just a measure of the middle—it gives us a measure of the data broken up into quarters, or 1/4s. Now we know what happens halfway between the median and the top, and halfway between the median and the bottom.

### *STANDARD DEVIATION*

Standard deviation is a really unappealing name but it's actually an interesting concept, so we're going to learn it.

We're going to learn it qualitatively anyway—the quantitative way of finding standard deviation is so specific and tedious that there is no way the SAT would ever ask you to know it.

***Standard deviation helps measure the spread of a data set.***

If you have a high standard deviation, the set is spread out widely. If you have a lower standard deviation, the set is less spread out.

Once we know it, we can use it to determine how unusual a particular point of data is.
Here are two examples.

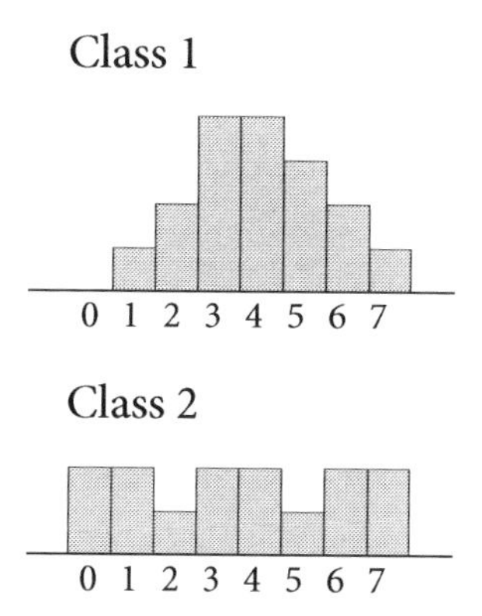


1. The bar graph above shows the number of pull-ups that students in two gym classes were able to complete. Which of the following correctly compares the standard deviation of the number of pull-ups in each of the classes?

   A) The standard deviation of the number of pull-ups in Class 1 is smaller.
   B) The standard deviation of the number of pull-ups in Class 2 is smaller.
   C) The standard deviation of the number of pull-ups in Class 1 and Class 2 is the same.
   D) The relationship cannot be determined from the information given.

The answer here is A because, compared to the data points in Class 2, the data points for Class 1 are less spread out. They're clustered in the middle.

You would never be expected to compute the standard deviation, but you could be expected to make a qualitative assessment like that one.

## *MARGIN OF ERROR*

Next term, margin of error, is one that we use in everyday life both mathematically and figuratively.

> ***Margin of error tells us the difference between the values predicted by a sample and reality.***

For example, suppose a poll said that 47% of voters support a particular candidate ± 3%. That 3% is the margin of error, and what it means is that the surveyors can reliably say that the candidate's support is somewhere between 44% and 50%.

### Why is there a margin of error?

Well, because when polling groups take a survey, they only ask a randomized sample of the population what they think. That's a surprisingly effective way at finding out what the entire population thinks, but it's not perfect—hence the margin of error.

## *CORRELATION*

Correlation is another one that's a fairly sophisticated stats term that you probably won't see on the SAT...but just in case you do need it, let's know it.

> ***Correlation tells you how closely related two statistical variables are.***

Its values range from -1 to 1. A correlation of -1 means perfectly negatively correlated—the more you have of one, the less you have of the other. A correlation of 0 means not at all related. A correlation of 1 means perfectly and directly related, as in, you can't have one without the other.

## Let's take this into the real world.

Suppose your two variables are "school attendance" and "grades in school." You can intuit that there probably IS a relationship between these two variables. If you had a real world data set comparing percent of days in school to GPA, you might get a correlation of 0.6. That's considered a high (or a strong) correlation.

If on the other hand, you compared how often a student wears jeans to school to GPA, you'd probably get a low correlation...say, something like 0.05. That means that there is no strong relationship between students wearing jeans to school and the grades that they get.

If you see a correlation question, it'll almost certainly be qualitative—you might have to identify whether a correlation is strong or not, and whether it's positive or not. Know that a correlation close to zero is weak, and correlations higher than 0.4 (or less than -0.4) are considered strong.

***Hot Tip***: There is a difference between correlation and causation. Correlation means that two factors frequently overlap—that when one happens, the other often does as well. That does not necessarily mean that one causes the other to happen. One example of that: there is a high correlation between students eating breakfast and doing well in school.

Does eating breakfast cause students to do well in school? Not by itself, probably. More likely, student who eat breakfast are well-prepared in general and therefore likely to do well in school as a result of all of that preparation—not just because they had breakfast. Keep correlation and causation separate in that brilliant, flexible mind of yours.

## *SAMPLING*

Sampling is our last topic in this *pretty* concise *but still kinda tedious* stats primer, and this one IS ACTUALLY REALLY IMPORTANT. If you stopped paying attention earlier, start paying attention again now because this one is definitively going to be on your test.

To figure out what the entire population thinks, we usually ask a sample, a subset of the population. The method by which we do that is important.

Like the other more advanced statistical vocabulary terms, on the SAT you'll have to think about sampling in a qualitative way, not a quantitative one. Here are the important factors to keep in mind.

### Were the members of the sample selected at random, or by convenience?

### How to select a sample at random:

- Pick names at random from the phone book.
- Assign members of the population a number, then draw numbers at random using a random number generator or a lottery.
- Survey a large number of people, like 100.

**How NOT to select a sample at random (i.e. how to pick a sample by convenience)**

- Pick people who are in one location, i.e. at a restaurant or at the mall.
- Survey only a small number of people, like 5.

The goal when you're taking a sample is to get a true representation of the whole population. If you sample people at a location like the mall, you're not getting a cross-section of the entire population... you're getting a cross-section of people who like to go shopping. If you only ask 5 people for their opinion, you may not be asking a sample that represents the entire population.

**Basically, the rule of thumb is this: ask enough people, and select them at random.**
You are now ready for the stats problems on the SAT.

## Ready for these practice problems, anyway.

# Statistics

**1**

A movie studio selected 300 people at random from a group of people who said they liked a certain movie titled "Heroman." The 300 people were shown the sequel to "Heroman" and then asked whether they liked or disliked the sequel. Of those 300 people, 80 percent said they liked the sequel. Which of the following inferences can appropriately be drawn from this survey result?

A) Most people who like movies will like this sequel.

B) Most people who like sequels will like this sequel.

C) Most people who like the movie "Heroman" will like this sequel.

D) Most people who like sequels will like the movie "Heroman."

**2**

To determine whether residents of a community would vote in favor of a proposed tax to raise money for the local high school, Christine surveyed 100 adults whose children attend the school. She found that 80 of those surveyed reported that they would vote in favor of the proposed tax. Which of the following statements must be true?

A) The actual vote will show 80 percent of voters support the proposed tax.

B) The sample size of the survey was too small to make any prediction about the actual vote.

C) Flaws in the sampling method may lead to biased results.

D) There are no flaws in the sampling method, and the results are likely to be unbiased.

**3**

Pizza Prices by Number of Toppings

| Number of Toppings | Pizza Price |
|---|---|
| 0 | \$10 |
| 1–2 | \$12 |
| 3–5 | \$14 |

The price of a pizza is based on the number of toppings, as shown in the table above. Todd wants to purchase 10 pizzas for a party.

He will purchase 2 pizzas with 0 toppings.

He will purchase 3 pizzas with 1 topping.

He will purchase 3 pizzas with 2 toppings.

He will purchase 2 pizzas with 4 toppings.

What is the average (arithmetic mean) pizza price, in dollars, for the 10 pizzas?

**4**

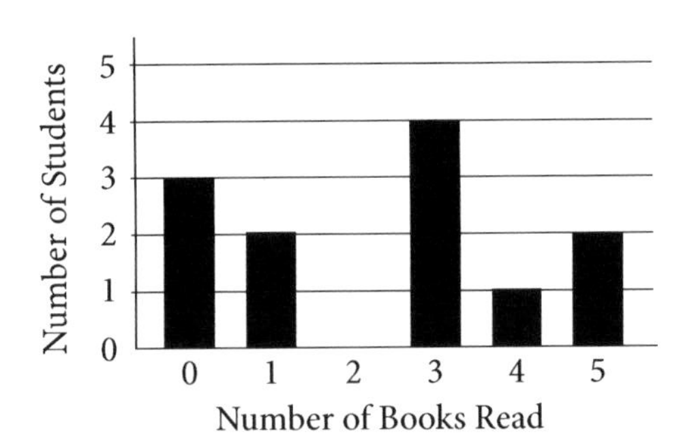


Based on the histogram above, which of the following is closest to the average (arithmetic mean) number of books read per student?

A) 1

B) 2

C) 3

D) 4

**5**

| Weights of Pumpkins (in pounds) | | | | | | |
|---|---|---|---|---|---|---|
| 16 | 17 | 17 | 17 | 18 | 18 | 19 |
| 19 | 20 | 20 | 20 | 20 | 21 | 21 |
| 21 | 22 | 22 | 23 | 23 | 24 | 32 |

The table above lists the weights, to the nearest pound, of the 21 pumpkins in a pumpkin patch. If the pumpkin weighing 32 pounds were removed from the data, which of the following listed values would change the most?

A) Mean
B) Median
C) Mode
D) Range

**6**

A researcher conducted a survey to determine whether people in a certain small town prefer commuting to work by driving or by using public transportation. The researcher asked 96 people who visited a local grocery store on a Tuesday morning, and 5 people refused to answer. Which of the following factors makes it least likely that the researcher can draw a reliable conclusion about the commuting preferences of all people in the town?

A) The number of people who refused to respond
B) Sample size
C) Population size
D) When and where the survey was given

**7**

A teacher found that the median score on a test was 86% and the mean score on the test was 79%. Which of the following best explains the difference between the median and mean scores on the test?

A) Many students scored between 79% and 86%.
B) A few students scored much higher than the rest.
C) A few students scored much lower than the rest.
D) Most of the students received similar scores on the test.

**Questions 8 and 9 refer to the following information.**

A researcher chose 200 families at random from each of two nearby towns and asked how many cars each family had. The results are shown in the table below.

Family Car Survey

| Number of cars | Springfield | Pleasantville |
|---|---|---|
| 0 | 30 | 40 |
| 1 | 70 | 120 |
| 2 | 20 | 20 |
| 3 | 40 | 5 |
| 4 | 40 | 15 |

**8**

What is the median number of cars owned for all the families surveyed?

A) 0
B) 1
C) 2
D) 3

**9**

Which of the following is true about the data shown in the table?

A) The standard deviation of cars owned in Springfield is larger.
B) The standard deviation of cars owned in Pleasantville is larger.
C) The standard deviation of cars in Springfield is the same as that of Pleasantville.
D) The standard deviation of cars in the towns cannot be calculated with the data provided.

---

**10**

Heights of 20 Students

| Height (in inches) | Frequency |
|---|---|
| 59 | 1 |
| 69 | 1 |
| 70 | 1 |
| 71 | 1 |
| 72 | 4 |
| 73 | 5 |
| 74 | 7 |

The table above gives the distribution of heights, in inches, of 20 students in a high school class. Which of the following gives the correct order of the mean, median, and mode of the heights?

A) mean < median < mode
B) mean < mode < median
C) median < mean < mode
D) mode < mean < median

**11**

A polling agency surveyed 1,000 registered voters who were selected at random from a small town and asked, "Will you vote for Harrison in the upcoming election?" Of those surveyed, 64 percent responded that they would vote for Harrison in the upcoming election. Based on the results of the survey, which of the following must be true?

I. Of all registered voters in the town, 64 percent will vote for Harrison in the upcoming election.
II. If another 1,000 registered voters were selected at random and surveyed, 64 percent of them would report that they will vote for Harrison in the upcoming election.
III. If 1,000 registered voters in another town were selected at random and surveyed, 64 percent of them would report that they will vote for Harrison in the upcoming election.

A) None
B) I only
C) II only
D) I and III only

**12**

Number of Players with Bowling Scores of at Least 200

| Bowling Score | Frequency |
|---|---|
| 200 | 4 |
| 201 | 1 |
| 202 | 4 |
| 203 | 1 |
| 204 | 3 |
| 207 | 1 |
| 209 | 2 |
| 214 | 1 |
| 220 | 1 |
| 226 | 1 |
| 240 | 1 |
| 267 | 1 |

Last season 21 players in Karen's bowling league earned scores of 200 or greater, as shown in the table above. Based on the table, what was the median score for these 21 bowlers?

A) 203
B) 204
C) 207
D) 209

**13**

A meteorologist recorded the average daily temperature, in degrees Fahrenheit, for 14 consecutive days and found the mean, median, range, and standard deviation. It was discovered that the day with the highest average temperature was actually 5 degrees hotter than recorded. Which of the following would remain unchanged once the meteorologist recorded the correct average daily temperatures?

A) Mean
B) Median
C) Range
D) Standard deviation

**14**

An American car magazine featured an article about a new car model that would be released in the next year. At the end of the article, readers were encouraged to participate in an online poll that asked, "Would you consider purchasing the car discussed in the article?" In the next month's issue, the magazine reported that 82% responded "Yes," and 18% responded "No." Which of the following provides the best interpretation of the results?

A) The results represent the views of all Americans because the percentages add up to 100%.
B) The results represent the views of all Americans because the magazine gave readers sufficient time to respond to the poll.
C) The results do not represent the views of all Americans because those who responded to the poll were not a random sample of the U.S. population.
D) The results do not represent the views of all Americans because there were not 50% "Yes" responses and 50% "No" responses.

**15**

Anne has a mean score of 78 percent on 6 tests. When her lowest score is removed, the mean score of the remaining 5 tests is 80 percent. What was Anne's lowest score?

A) 12 percent
B) 48 percent
C) 68 percent
D) 72 percent

**16**

If the average (arithmetic mean) of $2x$ and 1 is $a$, the average of $3x$ and 13 is $b$, and the average of $x$ and 10 is $c$, what is the average of $a$, $b$, and $c$ in terms of $x$?

A) $x + 2$
B) $x + 4$
C) $2x + 8$
D) $3x + 12$

# Formulas You Need to Know

This section contains the formulas you should bring into the test with you inside your brain plus witty commentary on each.

## Enjoy.

### PERCENT CHANGE

$$\text{percent change} = \frac{\text{amount of change}}{\text{original amount}}$$

This one is my favorite because it seems so simple...but if you don't know it on the test, you *might not quite be sure what you should be dividing by*. It's a straight-up memorizer, this one—just say it in your head about 15 times and you'll have it down.

### DISTANCE, RATE, AND TIME

$$\text{distance} = \text{rate} \times \text{time}$$

Every time Mary drives her car to the office, or James takes the train from Baltimore, chances are you are going to be using this formula. Distance is how far Mary or James travels, rate is speed, usually measured in miles/hour or kilometers/hour, and time is time.

***Hot Tip:*** Make sure you keep your units consistent when you use this formula. If the rate is given in miles per hour, you have to use hours as your time unit. If you were given minutes instead, convert those minutes to hours before you use them in the formula.

### DIFFERENCE OF SQUARES

$$x^2 - y^2 = (x + y)(x - y)$$

This one's a factoring shortcut that YOU REALLY WANT TO KNOW. Boy, does knowing this one make your life easier. Know it.

### INTEREST

$$A = P(1 + r)^t$$

In that formula, *A* equals the amount money you'll earn after interest, *P* is the principal (or original) amount you invest, *r* is the interest rate expressed as a decimal (so 5% would be 0.05), and *t* is the number of years that the money is invested.

Fun fact: some people say that Einstein called compound interest "the eighth wonder of the world." In fact, Einstein did NOT say that...but pretty much every smart thing that could be said gets attributed to

Einstein, and this is a smart thing! Invest early, kids. Spend less and save more. Money may not grow on trees, but it does when you invest it.

## TRIANGLE FORMULAS

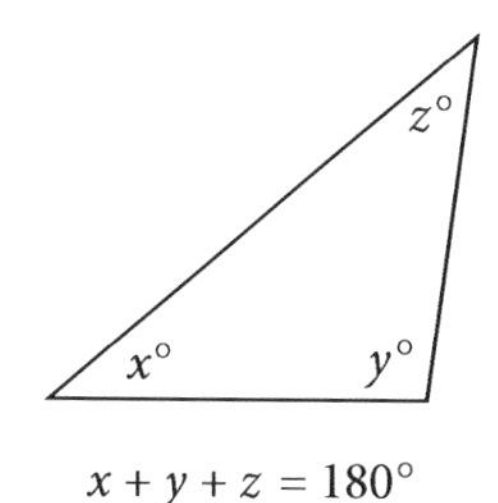


$x + y + z = 180°$

The angles in a triangle measure, in total, 180°.

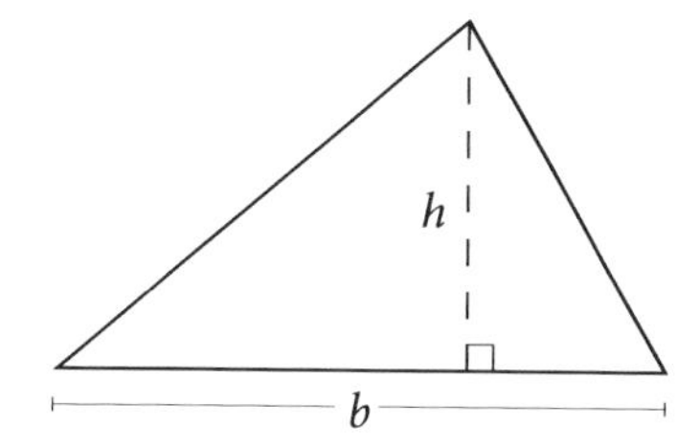


Area of a triangle = 1/2*bh*

## CIRCLE FORMULAS

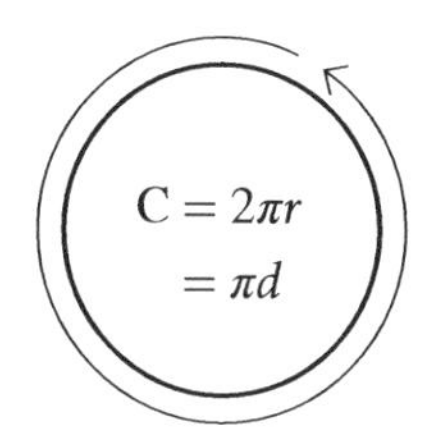


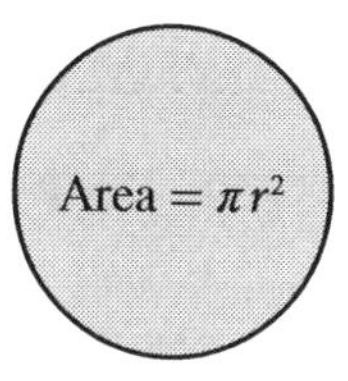


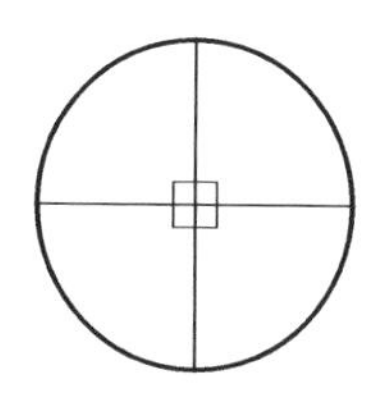

Circumference of a circle $= 2\pi r$ or $\pi d$

Area of a circle $= \pi r^2$

Circles have 360° in total

I explained all of these formulas and shared my witty commentary on them in the shape geometry chapter and I refuse to do it again here. I am not a trained monkey here for your entertainment.

## EQUATION OF A CIRCLE

$$(x - h)^2 + (y - k)^2 = r^2$$

where $r$ is the radius and $(h, k)$ is the center.

The SAT is, like, really into the equation of a circle. Like, weirdly into it.

The h and k values are the coordinates of the center of the circle, $(h, k)$. The $r$ value is the radius. Worst case scenario on these questions? You might have to complete the square to find the center. I bravely volunteer to show you how to do that. OK, let's do this.

## COMPLETING THE SQUARE

$$x^2 + y^2 - 10x - 2y + 22 = 0$$

$$x^2 - 10x + y^2 - 2y = -22$$

$$x^2 - 10x + 25 + y^2 - 2y + 1 = -22 + 25 + 1$$

$$(x - 5)^2 + (y - 1)^2 = 4$$

center: (5, 1)
radius = 2

The key step of completing the square is that you need to create perfect square trinomials. That's why I added 25 to the *x* terms and 1 to the *y* terms. When I did that, I also added the same amount to the right side of the equation to keep the equation balanced. Then I factored and had the pretty version of the circle formula.

## CENTRAL AND INSCRIBED ANGLES

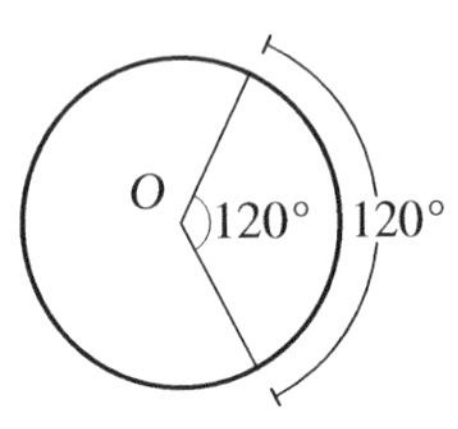


A central angle (one with its vertex at the center of a circle) has the same measure as the number of degrees of arc that it cuts.

Ugly definition, easy concept.

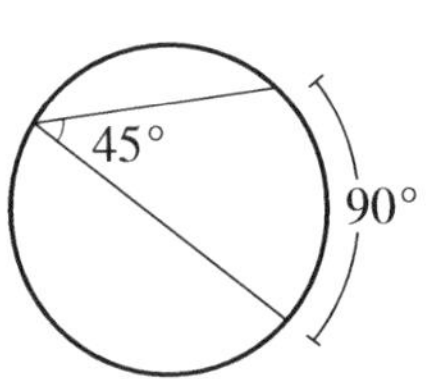


An inscribed angle (one with its vertex on the circle) has a measure that's half as large as the number of degrees of arc that it cuts.

Please see concise, witty comment above.

## STATS FORMULAS

$$\text{average} = \frac{\text{sum total}}{\text{\# of terms}}$$

***Median** = the middle term in a set that's arranged from least to greatest*
***Mode** = the term that occurs most often in a set*
***Range** = the difference between the greatest and the least term in a set*

Please see chapter on statistics terms. Are you not entertained?!

## RADIANS AND DEGREES

$$\pi \text{ radians} = 180 \text{ degrees}$$

OK, world's shortest lecture on radians: radians are just another way to measure angles. You can measure distance in miles, or you can measure it in centimeters. Same deal: you can measure angles in degrees, or you can measure them in radians. The ONE fun fact you have to know is that 180° is *the same thing as π radians*. They are equal. Once you know that, you can use that lil' unit conversion to convert from degrees to radians or the reverse.

## SOH-CAH-TOA

$$\sin x = \frac{\text{opposite}}{\text{hypotenuse}}$$

$$\cos x = \frac{\text{adjacent}}{\text{hypotenuse}}$$

$$\tan x = \frac{\text{opposite}}{\text{adjacent}}$$

hypotenuse
opposite
adjacent
$x°$

Tell me you know what this means. If not, please review the trig chapter to reach a place of deeper understanding.

## PROBABILITY

Also known as Ted's Favorite Math Topic.

$$\text{probability} = \frac{\text{\# of "winners"}}{\text{total outcome}}$$

Probability is a fraction or decimal from 0 (as in impossible, as in "it's never gonna happen") up to 1 (as in, this is GUARANTEED to happen) that tells us how likely it is that something is going to happen.

If you are trying to compute the possibility of multiple things all happening, you take their probabilities and multiply them. If there is a 1/15 probability that the Vikings win the Super Bowl (yes, I know that the Vikings have never won the Super Bowl...it's still POSSIBLE they will...) and a 1/20 chance that the Twins will win the World Series, then there is a $1/15 \times 1/20 = 1/300$ chance that both the Twins and Vikings will win their respective championships this year.

**Dare to dream, Minnesota sports fans. Dare to dream.**

## DIRECT AND INVERSE PROPORTIONS

This is straight-up math vocabulary. If you know the term, you get the question right (and it's easy). If you don't know the term, well, you're screwed.

***Direct Proportion/Direct Variation: $y = kx$, where $k$ is a constant***

This is a really fancy way of saying that to get from any $y$ value to any $x$ value, you've gotta multiply by the same number. Suppose that $k = 2$. That means that every $y$ value is twice as big as any $x$ value.

Another helpful way to think of direct variation is that the graph will always be a line with a $y$-intercept of 0 and a slope of $k$. Think back to the chapter on linear equations to think about why that *always* has to be true.

***Inverse Proportion/ Varies Inversely: $y = k/x$, where $k$ is a constant***

I like remembering this formula alongside the direct proportion formula. In the first one, direct variation, you multiply $k$ by $x$. In the second one, inverse proportion, you divide $k$ by $x$. Simple as that.

Whenever you see either one of these terms on a problem, start by writing the formula down. Using it will make the problem hella easy.

## Formulas You Need to Know

**1**

Results of Baseball Draft

| | Drafted | Was Not Drafted |
|---|---|---|
| Right-handed | 9 | 91 |
| Left-handed | 15 | 85 |

The table above summarizes the results of 200 minor league baseball players who were considered for the major league draft. If one of the players who got drafted is selected at random for an interview, what is the probability that the player chosen is left-handed?

A) $\frac{9}{24}$

B) $\frac{15}{24}$

C) $\frac{24}{200}$

D) $\frac{15}{200}$

**2**

$$4x^2 - a = (bx + 9)(bx - 9)$$

In the equation above, $a$ and $b$ are constants. Which of the following could be the value of $b$?

A) 2

B) 3

C) 16

D) 81

**3**

If $x$ is directly proportional to $y$ such that $x = 6$ when $y = 24$, what is the value of $y$ when $x = 9$?

A) 16

B) 21

C) 27

D) 36

**4**

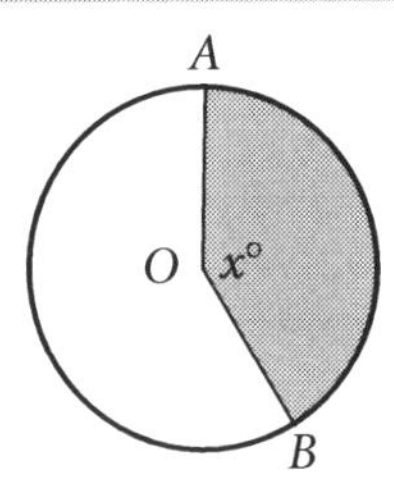


Note: Figure not drawn to scale.

In the figure above, the circle has center $O$ and has radius 6. If the area of the shaded sector is between 37 and 38, what is one possible integer value of $x$?

**5**

Jordan bought a concert ticket online and paid $84.00 after a 5 percent fee was added. What was the price of the concert ticket before the fee was added?

A) $76.50

B) $79.00

C) $80.00

D) $82.50

**6**

In the equation, $a = x + 9$ and $b = x - 9$, $a$ and $b$ are constants. If the product $ab$ can be written in the form $x^2 - k$, where $k$ is a constant, what is the value of $k$?

**7**

James puts $3,000 in a savings account that will earn 5% interest compounded annually. The equation $V = 5{,}000\left(1 + \frac{r}{100}\right)^t$ models the value $V$, in dollars, of the account earning $r$% interest over $t$ years. To the nearest whole dollar, how much more money will James have in the account after 4 years than after 3 years?

## 8

Debbie's Triathlon

| Segment of Triathlon | Distance (kilometers) | Average speed (kilometers per hour) |
|---|---|---|
| Swim | 1.5 | 2.8 |
| Bicycle | 40 | 36.2 |
| Run | 10 | 8.6 |

Debbie is training for a triathlon and the table above gives her average speed over each segment. On race day, Debbie completes the entire triathlon in 2 hours and 48 minutes. To the nearest tenth, what was her average speed, in kilometers per hour, during the race?

A) 14.7
B) 17.2
C) 18.4
D) 20.8

## 9

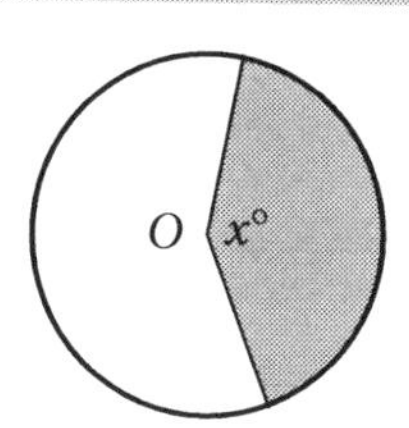


Note: Figure not drawn to scale.

In circle $O$, central angle $x$ has a measure of $\frac{5\pi}{6}$ radians. The area of the shaded sector is what fraction of the area of circle $O$?

## 10

| Type of student | Primary Academic Concentration: Humanities | Primary Academic Concentration: Sciences | Total |
|---|---|---|---|
| Under-graduate | 201 | 157 | 358 |
| Advanced Degree | 25 | 79 | 104 |
| Total | 226 | 236 | 462 |

The table above summarizes the results of a survey in which 462 college students pursuing undergraduate and advanced degrees indicated their primary academic concentration. If one of the students is selected at random, which of the following is closest to the probability that the selected student is pursuing an advanced degree with a primary academic concentration in the Sciences?

A) 0.054
B) 0.171
C) 0.225
D) 0.511

## 11

The price of a certain stock was \$79.16 on Monday. On Tuesday, the price of the stock had increased to \$86.42. To the nearest tenth of a percent, by what percent did the price of the stock increase?

A) 9.2%
B) 8.4%
C) 7.3%
D) 6.8%

**12**

$$a^4 - b^4 = 8$$
$$a^2 + b^2 = 2$$

Based on the equations above, what is the value of $a^2 - b^2$?

A) 4
B) 6
C) 10
D) 16

**13**

$$x^2 + 18x + y^2 - 4y = 15$$

The equation above defines a circle in the $xy$-plane. What are the coordinates of the center of the circle?

A) (18, -4)
B) (9, -2)
C) (-9, 2)
D) (-18, 4)

**14**

An angle with a measure of $\frac{8\pi}{5}$ radians has a measure $d$ degrees, where $0 \leq d < 360$. What is the value of $d$?

**15**

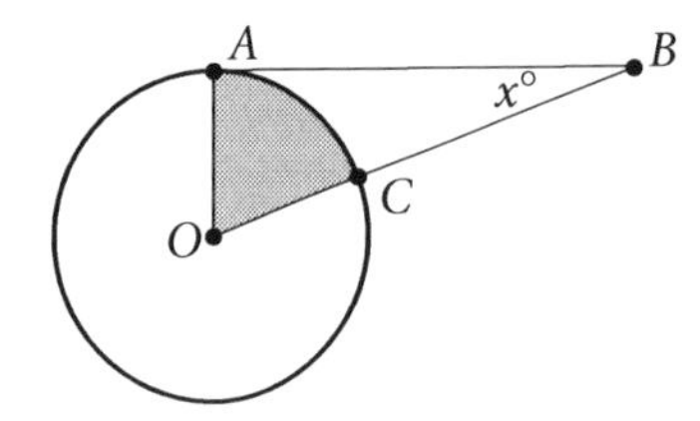


In the figure above, $\overline{AB}$ is tangent to the circle with center $O$ at point $A$, and $\overline{BO}$ intersects circle $O$ at point $C$. If the length of minor arc $AC$ is $\frac{1}{5}$ of the circumference of the circle, what is the value of $x$?

**16**

For an object moving in a straight line, the time that it takes the object to travel a certain distance is inversely proportional to the velocity of the object over the same distance. In an experiment, an object with a velocity of 20 meters per second completes a path in 0.25 seconds. How long will it take the object to complete the same path if it has a velocity of 10 meters per second?

A) 1 second
B) 0.5 seconds
C) 0.125 seconds
D) 0.05 seconds

**17**

The equation $x^2 + y^2 - 2x + 6y = -1$ is a circle when graphed in the $xy$-plane. What is the radius of the circle?

A) 2
B) 3
C) 4
D) 9

**18**

| Sport | Time Zone | | | | |
|---|---|---|---|---|---|
| | Pacific | Mountain | Central | Eastern | Total |
| Baseball | 6 | 2 | 8 | 14 | 30 |
| Football | 5 | 2 | 8 | 17 | 32 |
| Hockey | 5 | 4 | 6 | 16 | 31 |
| Total | 16 | 8 | 22 | 47 | 93 |

The table above gives the home time zone for each of the 93 professional baseball, football, and hockey teams. What proportion of the teams are hockey teams in the central time zone?

A) $\frac{2}{31}$

B) $\frac{6}{31}$

C) $\frac{22}{93}$

D) $\frac{1}{3}$

**Questions 19 and 20 refer to the following information.**

Automobile Sales in the United States

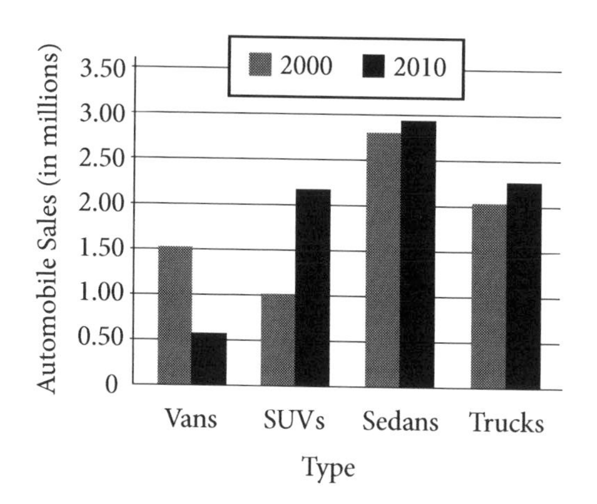


The bar graph above shows the number of automobiles sold, in millions, in the United States, by automobile type, for several types in the years 2000 and 2010.

**19**

Which of the following best approximates the percent increase in sales of trucks in the United States from 2000 to 2010?

A) 6%

B) 13%

C) 24%

D) 30%

**20**

The number of vans sold in 2000 is approximately what percent greater than the number of SUVs sold in 2000?

A) 25%

B) 33%

C) 50%

D) 67%

**21**

A circle in the $xy$-plane has equation $(x + 1)^2 + (y - 4)^2 = 16$. Which of the following points does NOT lie in the interior of the circle?

A) (2, 2)

B) (-2, 5)

C) (0, 1)

D) (3, -1)

**22**

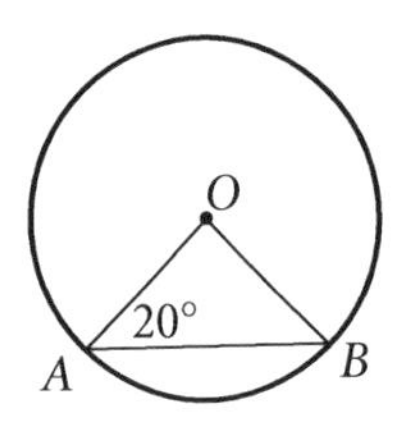


Note: Figure not drawn to scale.

If $O$ is the center of the circle above, which of the following represents the radian measure of angle $AOB$?

A) $\frac{\pi}{9}$

B) $\frac{5\pi}{9}$

C) $\frac{7\pi}{9}$

D) $\frac{11\pi}{9}$

**23**

$$y = ax^2 - 1$$

In the equation above, a is a positive constant and the graph of the equation in the $xy$-plane is a parabola. Which of the following is an equivalent form of the equation?

A) $y = (x\sqrt{a} + 1)(x\sqrt{a} - 1)$

B) $y = (ax + 1)(ax - 1)$

C) $y = \left(\frac{a}{2}x + 1\right)\left(\frac{a}{2}x - 1\right)$

D) $y = (ax + 1)^2$

**24**

Books Read in One Year

| | 1 | 2 to 3 | 4 or more | Total |
|---|---|---|---|---|
| Group A | 11 | 67 | 22 | 100 |
| Group B | 36 | 55 | 9 | 100 |
| Total | 47 | 122 | 31 | 200 |

The data in the table above were produced by a researcher studying the number of books people read in one year. Group A consisted of 100 people who had a library card, and Group B consisted of 100 people who did not have a library card. If a person is chosen at random from those who read at least 2 books, what is the probability that the person belonged to Group A?

A) $\frac{22}{100}$

B) $\frac{89}{100}$

C) $\frac{89}{153}$

D) $\frac{153}{200}$

**25**

Which of the following is an equation of a circle with radius 8 that passes through the origin when graphed in the $xy$-plane?

A) $(x + 4)^2 + (y - 4)^2 = 8$

B) $(x + 4)^2 + (y - 4)^2 = 64$

C) $(x + 8)^2 + (y + 8)^2 = 64$

D) $(x + 4\sqrt{2})^2 + (y - 4\sqrt{2})^2 = 64$

**26**

$$2{,}000\left(1+\frac{r}{400}\right)^4$$

The expression above gives the amount of money, in dollars, generated in a year by a $2,000 deposit in a bank account that pays an annual interest rate of $r$% compounded quarterly. Which of the following expressions shows how much less money is generated at an interest rate of 3% than at an interest rate of 1%?

A) $2{,}000\left(1+\frac{\frac{3}{1}}{400}\right)^4$

B) $2{,}000\left(1+\frac{3-1}{400}\right)^4$

C) $\dfrac{2000\left(1+\frac{3}{400}\right)^4}{2{,}000\left(1+\frac{1}{400}\right)^4}$

D) $2{,}000\left(1+\frac{3}{400}\right)^4 - 2{,}000\left(1+\frac{1}{400}\right)^4$

**27**

$$2x^2 - 2x + 2y^2 + 10y = 19$$

The graph of the equation above is a circle in the $xy$-plane. What is the radius of the circle?

A) 4
B) $\sqrt{6}$
C) $\sqrt{19}$
D) $\sqrt{32}$

**28**

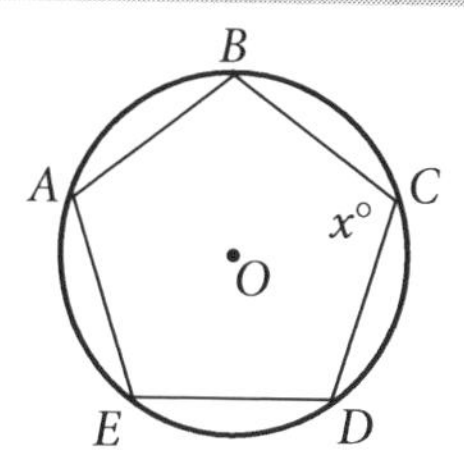


Regular pentagon $ABCDE$ is inscribed in circle $O$ as shown above. What is the value of $x$?

# Advanced Stuff

SAT Math includes a category of topics called "Passport to Advanced Math."

**Regardless of how you feel about that metaphor—I personally would say it falls somewhere on a continuum between *lazy* and *simplistic*—it is fair warning that you're going to run into some more advanced math concepts on this test.**

Here are the ones we've seen so far on the test. I would make absolutely sure you know these. They don't appear on the test as often as lines and quadratics do, but they do appear on there regularly, and they are not too difficult to know and master.

## *THE IMAGINARY NUMBER* ***i***

Some people think of *i* as "the square root of -1." *Technically*, the definition is this:

$$i^2 = -1$$

But you can pretty much get away with thinking of it as the square root of -1.

### Let me show you a couple of problems involving i.

Which of the following complex numbers is equivalent to $\frac{7+i}{4+i}$? (Note: $i = \sqrt{-1}$)

A) $\frac{7}{4} + i$

B) $\frac{11}{4}$

C) $\frac{29}{17} - \frac{3i}{17}$

D) $\frac{29}{17} + \frac{3i}{17}$

$$\frac{7+i}{4+i} \times \frac{(4-i)}{(4-i)} = \frac{28 + 4i - 7i - i^2}{16 + 4i - 4i - i^2}$$

$$= \frac{28 - 3i - (-1)}{16 - (-1)}$$

$$= \frac{29 - 3i}{17}$$

$$\boxed{= \frac{29}{17} - \frac{3}{17}i}$$

$(x + iy)(x - iy)$

Which of the following expressions is equivalent to the expression above?

A) $x^2 - y^2$

B) $x^2 - iy^2$

C) $x^2 + y^2$

D) $x^2 + iy^2$

$$(x + iy)(x - iy) = x^2 + iyx - iyx - i^2y^2$$

$$= x^2 - i^2y^2$$

$$= x^2 - (-1)y^2$$

$$\boxed{= x^2 + y^2}$$

## *POLYNOMIAL DIVISION*

One of the most dreaded topics in algebra is long division of polynomials. If you've done it, you know what I'm talking about. If you love tedium, you will probably dig long division of polynomials. If not, well...

The good news is that polynomial division is not that complex on the SAT. I've only ever seen you have to divide a $2^{nd}$ power polynomial by a $1^{st}$ power binomial. Let's do a really simple one so I can show you what I'm talking about.

If $x > 0$, which of the following is equal to $\frac{10x + 5}{5x + 1}$?

A) $2x + 3$

B) $2x + 5$

C) $2 - \frac{3}{5x + 1}$

D) $2 + \frac{3}{5x + 1}$

$\frac{10x + 5}{5x + 1}$

$$\begin{array}{r|l} & 2 + \frac{3}{5x+1} \\ 5x + 1 & 10x + 5 \\ & -\ 10x + 2 \\ \hline & 3 \end{array}$$

$= 2 + \frac{3}{5x + 1}$

Here's an advanced topic related to polynomial division. This is the headiest thing you'll run into on the SAT math test. It is TOTALLY WORTH LEARNING because, while it might not be intuitive at first, it's really pretty easy and can buy you a free point on a difficult question. It's called Remainder theorem.

## *REMAINDER THEOREM*

***Remainder theorem says that when polynomial f(x) is divided by (x–a), the remainder is f(a).***

Now, *what does that mean*? Here's how I would think about it: if you plug a value, let's say 3, into a function, and you get a value *other than zero* in return, then that number 3 is not a root/factor of the function. AND, if you divided the original function by $(x – 3)$, you would get a remainder exactly equal to what you got when you plugged 3 into the function. Let's see an example.

What is the remainder when $3x^2 - 7x + 2$ is divided by $x - 3$?

A) 0

B) 3

C) 4

D) 8

The long division method:

$$\begin{array}{r|l} & 3x + 2 \\ x - 3 & 3x^2 - 7x + 2 \\ & -\ (3x^2 - 9x) \\ \hline & \quad 2x + 2 \\ & \quad -\ (2x - 6) \\ \hline & \quad\quad \boxed{8} \end{array}$$

The remainder theorem method:

$f(x) = 3x^2 - 7x + 2$

$f(3) = 3(3)^2 - 7(3) + 2$

$f(3) = 27 - 21 + 2$

$f(3) = \boxed{8}$

On the other hand, if the value you plug into the function (let's say it's 2 this time) gives you an output value of 0, then you know that 2 is a root of the function and that $(x – 2)$ is a factor of the function.

What is the remainder when $3x^2 - 7x + 2$ is divided by $x - 2$?

A) 0
B) 1
C) 2
D) 3

The long division method:

$$\begin{array}{r} 3x - 1 \\ x - 2 \,\overline{)\, 3x^2 - 7x + 2} \\ -(3x^2 - 6x) \\ \hline -x + 2 \\ -(-x + 2) \\ \hline \boxed{0} \end{array}$$

The remainder theorem method:

$$f(x) = 3x^2 - 7x + 2$$
$$f(2) = 3(2)^2 - 7(2) + 2$$
$$f(2) = 12 - 14 + 2$$
$$f(2) = \boxed{0}$$

Here's the cool thing: this actually makes sense. If you get a zero when you plug an $x$-value into a function, then clearly that x-value has to be a root of the function. If you *don't* get zero, then you know that particular $x$-value is NOT a root of the function. Then it's just a really nice fun fact that whatever value you got as the output at that particular $x$-value (let's call it $a$) *is also the remainder when you divide the polynomial by $x - a$.*

Let's do one more problem to bring it home.

The expression $\frac{30x^2 - 4x - 2}{x - 1}$ can be written as $30x + 26 + \frac{a}{x - 1}$, where $a$ is a constant and $x \neq 1$. What is the value of $a$?

The long division method:

$$\begin{array}{r} 30x + 26 + \frac{\boxed{24}}{x-1} \\ x - 1 \,\overline{)\, 30x^2 - 4x - 2} \\ -(30x^2 - 30x) \\ \hline 26x - 2 \\ -26x - 26 \\ \hline \boxed{24} \end{array}$$

The remainder theorem method:

$$f(x) = 30x^2 - 4x - 2$$
$$f(1) = 30(1)^2 - 4(1) - 2$$
$$f(1) = 30 - 4 - 2$$
$$f(1) = \boxed{24}$$

## *INVERSE FUNCTIONS, OR $F^{-1}(X)$*

Last topic of the Advanced Stuff chapter is inverse functions. Fancy name, easy concept, these guys. To find an inverse function, follow these three simple steps:

**Step 1)** Replace $f(x)$ with $y$.
**Step 2)** Swap $x$ for $y$ and $y$ for $x$.
**Step 3)** Re-solve the equation for $y$.

You now have the inverse of your previous function.

Want to see an example?

The function $f$ is defined as $f(x)=2x^2+4$. What is $f^{-1}(x)$?

The $f^{-1}(x)$ notation is code for "the inverse function." OK, let's find it—by following those three li'l steps.

**Step 1)** Replace $f(x)$ with $y$.

$$y = 2x^2+4$$

**Step 2)** Swap $x$ for $y$ and $y$ for $x$.

$$x = 2y^2+4$$

**Step 3)** Re-solve the equation for $y$.

$$x = 2y^2+4$$

$$x - 4 = 2y^2$$

$$\frac{(x-4)}{2} = y^2$$

$$\sqrt{\frac{(x-4)}{2}} = y$$

Was that a ton of fun? Not especially. But was it easy? You bet your boots it was.

Is your "Passport to Advanced Math" current? Do you have stamps in it to all of the exotic countries of East Mathematia?

Screw the metaphor... you know what you're doing.

Now go and do it.

# Advanced Topics

**1**

For $i = \sqrt{-1}$, what is the sum $(4 + 6i) + (-3 + 8i)$?

A) $1 - 2i$
B) $1 + 14i$
C) $7 - 2i$
D) $7 + 14i$

**2**

Which of the following is equal to the sum of $(-2 + 11i)$ and $(7 - 4i)$, for $i = \sqrt{-1}$?

A) $9 + 15i$
B) $5 + 7i$
C) $5 - 7i$
D) $9 - 15i$

**3**

$$f(x) = x^2 + 2x - 8$$
$$g(x) = x^3 - 16x$$

Which of the following expressions is equivalent to $\frac{f(x)}{g(x)}$, for $x > 4$?

A) $\frac{1}{x(x+2)}$

B) $\frac{x-2}{x-4}$

C) $\frac{x-2}{x(x-4)}$

D) $\frac{x-2}{x(x+4)}$

**4**

Which of the following complex numbers is equal to $(3 + 11i) - (8i^2 - 5i)$, for $i = \sqrt{-1}$?

A) $11 + 16i$
B) $5 + 6i$
C) $-5 - 6i$
D) $-11 - 16i$

**5**

Which of the following is equal to the product $(5 - 2i)(4 + i)$? (Note: $i = \sqrt{-1}$)

A) $16 - 2i$
B) $18 - 3i$
C) $20 - 2i$
D) $22 - 3i$

**6**

$$\frac{8x-3}{x-1}$$

Which of the following is equivalent to the expression above?

A) $8x + 3$

B) $8 + \frac{3}{x-1}$

C) $8 + \frac{5}{x-1}$

D) $8 - \frac{11}{x-1}$

**7**

$$f(x) = 2^{x+1}$$

The function $f$ is defined by the equation above. Which of the following represents the graph of $y = -f(x)$ in the $xy$-plane?

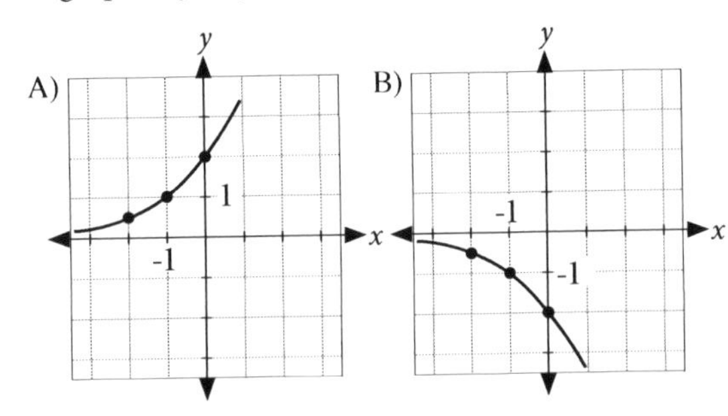


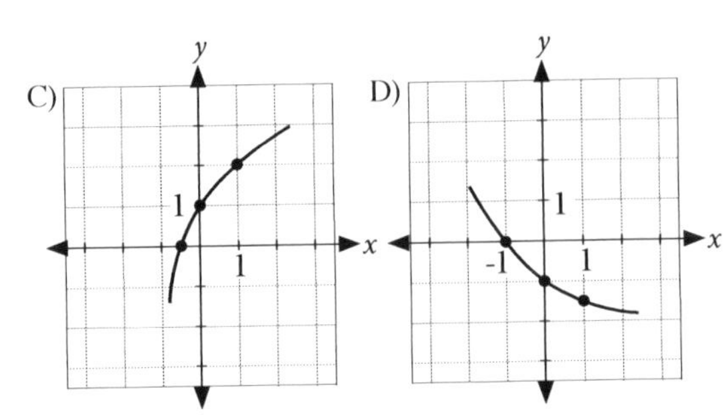

**8**

The expression $\frac{6x-1}{x+2}$ is equivalent to which of the following?

A) $\frac{6-1}{2}$

B) $6-\frac{1}{2}$

C) $6-\frac{1}{x+2}$

D) $6-\frac{13}{x+2}$

**9**

$$x^3(x^2-10) = -9x$$

If $x > 0$, what is one possible solution to the equation above?

**10**

Which of the following expressions is equivalent to $\frac{x^2-4x-3}{x-2}$?

A) $x-2+\frac{1}{x-2}$

B) $x-2-\frac{7}{x-2}$

C) $x-6+\frac{9}{x-2}$

D) $x-6-\frac{15}{x-2}$

**11**

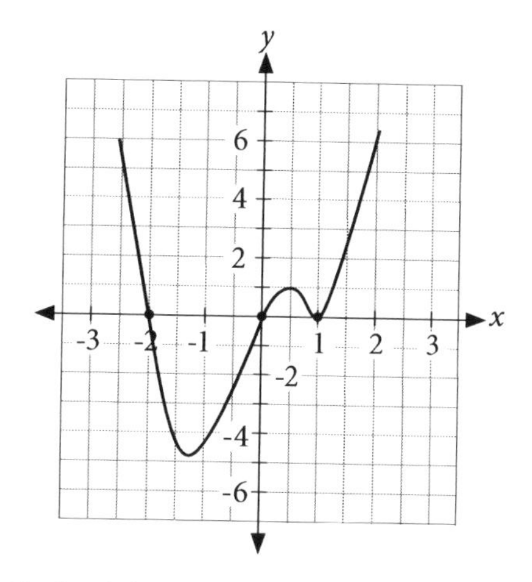


Which of the following could be the equation of the graph above?

A) $y = x(x-2)(x+1)$

B) $y = x(x-2)(x+1)^2$

C) $y = x(x+2)(x-1)$

D) $y = x(x+2)(x-1)^2$

**12**

If the complex number $\frac{2-7i}{4+3i}$ is rewritten in the form $a + bi$, where $a$ and $b$ are real numbers, what is the value of $a$?

(Note: $i = \sqrt{-1}$ )

A) $-\frac{13}{25}$

B) $-\frac{1}{2}$

C) $\frac{1}{2}$

D) $\frac{13}{25}$

**13**

Which of the following is equivalent to $\frac{3x^2 + 12x}{3x + 3}$?

A) $3x$

B) $x + 4$

C) $x + 3 - \frac{9}{3x + 3}$

D) $x + 3 + \frac{9}{3x + 3}$

**14**

$$\frac{14 - 2i}{1 - 3i}$$

If the expression above is rewritten in the form $a + bi$, where $a$ and $b$ are real numbers, what is the value of $b$? (Note: $i = \sqrt{-1}$ )

A) $\frac{2}{3}$

B) 4

C) $\frac{5}{3}$

D) 5

**15**

$$\frac{x^2 + 7x + 15}{x + 6} = x + 1 + \frac{a}{x + 6}$$

In the equation above, $a$ is a constant and $x \neq -6$. What is the value of $a$?

A) 93

B) 9

C) -9

D) -93

**16**

$$\frac{6 + 2i}{3 - i}$$

Which of the following complex numbers is equal to the expression above, for $i = \sqrt{-1}$?

A) $2 - 2i$

B) $2 + 2i$

C) $\frac{8}{5} - \frac{6i}{5}$

D) $\frac{8}{5} + \frac{6i}{5}$

**17**

What is the remainder when $x^2 - 9x + 19$ is divided by $x - 7$?

A) 12

B) 5

C) -5

D) -12

**18**

Which of the following complex numbers is equivalent to $\frac{7 - 4i}{3 + 6i}$? (Note: $i = \sqrt{-1}$)

A) $\frac{7}{3} - \frac{2i}{3}$

B) $\frac{7}{3} + \frac{2i}{3}$

C) $-\frac{1}{15} - \frac{6i}{5}$

D) $-\frac{1}{15} + \frac{6i}{5}$

**19**

$$x^3 - 6x^2 + x - 6 = 0$$

For what real value of $x$ is the equation above true?

**20**

$$\frac{6x^2 + 15x - 22}{x + 3}$$

Which of the following is equivalent to expression above?

A) $6x + 33 + \frac{77}{x + 3}$

B) $6x + 33 - \frac{121}{x + 3}$

C) $6x - 3 - \frac{13}{x + 3}$

D) $6x - 3 - \frac{31}{x + 3}$

**21**

If $f(x)$ is a polynomial such that $f(4)$ is -3, which of the following must be true about $f(x)$?

A) $x - 7$ is a factor of $f(x)$.

B) $x - 3$ is a factor of $f(x)$.

C) $x + 3$ is a factor of $f(x)$.

D) The remainder when $f(x)$ is divided by $x - 4$ is -3.

**22**

$$f(x) = 3x^3 - 6x^2 + 9x$$
$$g(x) = x^2 - 2x + 3$$

The polynomials $f(x)$ and $g(x)$ are defined above. Which of the following polynomial functions is divisible by $3x + 4$?

A) $a(x) = f(x) + g(x)$

B) $b(x) = f(x) + 4g(x)$

C) $c(x) = 3f(x) + 4g(x)$

D) $d(x) = 4f(x) + 3g(x)$

**23**

The equation $\frac{36x^2 + 43x - 19}{kx - 3} = -9x - 4 - \frac{31}{kx - 3}$ is true for all values of $x \neq \frac{3}{k}$, where $k$ is a constant. What is the value of $k$?

A) 27

B) 4

C) -4

D) -27

**24**

The polynomial function $f(x)$ passes through the point with coordinate (3, -2) in the $xy$-plane. Which of the following must be true about $f(x)$?

I. 5 is a zero of $f(x)$.

II. -5 is a zero of $f(x)$.

III. The remainder when $f(x)$ is divided by $x - 3$ is -2.

A) I only

B) II only

C) III only

D) I and III only

# strategies

The best way to solve an SAT math question is not necessarily the way that would earn you full credit on a math quiz in school. This is a weird test designed to test your problem-solving ability, not just your math knowledge. On a lot of problems—probably all of them, really—you need to have some math content knowledge, but the way you approach problems will help you work with efficiency and accuracy. Both of those qualities are critical on SAT Math.

Now that we have that completely unfunny introduction out of the way, let's get to the strategies!

## PLUGGING IN NUMBERS

The first one is called plugging in, and it is the most useful—yet least intuitive—math strategy on the SAT.

**The idea behind plugging in is simple: math is easier when we are working with concrete values. We use plugging in to turn an abstract, theoretical problem into one that we understand on a practical level.**

### When should you plug in numbers?

***#1: When a number is described hypothetically.***

If the problem tells you that *n* is an even integer greater than 4, go ahead and plug in a number for *n*.

***#2: When a story problem contains variables.***

Like if Martha is *m* years old. Or Suzie eats *s* slices of pizza. Or Joe hits *h* home runs. You get the idea.

***#3: When working with percentage.***

If the price of a theoretical shirt goes up 20 percent, go ahead and price that shirt yourself.

***#4: To check your work when you didn't listen to me and used algebra anyways.***

I get it—you love algebra. Just run a number through your formula to make sure that it works.

### But Ted, what if I choose the wrong number?

Great question—I'm so glad you asked. As long as you play by the rules of the question, there are no wrong numbers! If the problem tells you that *n* is an integer, you don't want to plug in 1.78, right? Any integer value that you plug in for *n* will help you solve the problem, though—so pick an integer and go to town.

**Now let's see how this plugging in business works.**

## *PLUGGING IN SITUATION #1: WHEN A NUMBER IS DESCRIBED HYPOTHETICALLY.*

On a problem like this, you pay attention to what they tell you about the number, pick a number that fits the criteria, plug that number into the problem, and see what happens.

> If $x$ is an even integer, which of the following must represent an odd integer?
>
> A) $\frac{x}{2}+1$
> B) $2x+2$
> C) $3x+2$
> D) $4x+1$

So, we're going to plug in for $x$, obviously. What are the defined limitations for $x$? It's got to be even and an integer. Pick an even integer. Now write it down. Draw a box around it so you don't forget what you've picked.

Let's plug in 4. When we do that, we find that answer (A) gives us 3, an odd integer. That must be the answer, right? *Mais non, mon petit choux!* You have to try all of the answer choices because more than one might give you an odd value. On this problem, both (A) and (D) will give you an odd integer when you plug in 4. The next step is to plug another even number into those two remaining answer choices. Let's try 2. Now answer (A) gives us a value of 2, while (D) gives us 9, an odd number. Now we're sure of the answer: it's (D).

See? Pretty easy, right?

## *PLUGGING IN SITUATION #2: WHEN A STORY PROBLEM CONTAINS VARIABLES.*

Tell me, which is easier to visualize, 4 apples and 2 bananas or $x$ apples and $z$ bananas? Or imagine that you're at a restaurant with friends. At the end of the meal, would you rather split the $30 check plus a 20% tip with your 4 friends, or the $d$ dollar check plus an $x$ percent tip with your $n$ friends?

Yup, our brains work a lot better with numbers than they do with variables. So on a problem that describes a real-world situation in terms of variables, we want to replace those variables with plausible values and solve the problem based on those. Here is how:

> The circus is coming to town! It costs $x$ dollars to see the elephants and half of that amount to see the monkeys. If the $n$ people in a group buy tickets to see both attractions, what will the total cost for the group be in terms of $n$ and $x$?
>
> A) $x\left(n+\frac{1}{2}\right)$
> B) $\frac{3n}{2x}$
> C) $\frac{3nx}{2}$
> D) $\frac{nx}{2}$

We have two variables to plug in for on this problem, $x$ and $n$. How much do you think it should cost to see the elephants? I'm going to pick $10. It's an easy number to work with and it's divisible by two, which is handy since it costs half as much to see the monkeys. And how many people do we want in the group? I'm going to go with 4. It's easy to work with but big enough to help differentiate the answer choices.

Write those values down: $x = 10$ and $n = 4$. Now, figure out how much you would expect this group to pay for their circus adventure. It's $10 for the elephants, which means it's $5 for the monkeys. OK great, it's $15 to see both. If 4 people are in the group, the total cost will be 4 X $15 = $60. That's your target value. Circle that number: it's the key to the problem.

Go through your answer choices, plugging in your $x$ and $n$ values. The right answer is the one that gives you the same result as your target value. And the winner is... C.

## *PLUGGING IN SITUATION #3: WHEN WORKING WITH PERCENTAGE.*

Many percent problems on the SAT will tell you about a change in the percent of something without giving you any concrete starting value. The secret on these is to supply your own value. When it comes to percent, the best starting value is 100. If you're not sure why, you'll see in a second.

> An online t-shirt retailer charges full price for a t-shirt the first week that it is on sale. At the end of the first week, the t-shirt is put on sale and its price is reduced by 10 percent. At the end of the second week, the sale price is reduced by 20 percent. The final price is what percent of the full price?
>
> A) 60
> B) 70
> C) 72
> D) 75

Something is very conspicuously missing from this problem: the price of the t-shirt. We are going to plug in our own value for that price. Even though no one should ever pay this much for a t-shirt, let's set the price at $100.

Now solve the problem using that price.

First, you take a 10% discount off of $100:
$100 – 0.10(100) = $90.

Then, you take a 20% discount off of that sale price:
$90 – 0.20(90) = $72.

$72 is what percent of $100? Um, 72%. That's C, the right answer. The advantage of starting at $100 is that the final answer is both a dollar value and a percent of the original.

For those of you whom I have not yet convinced that plugging in is the greatest multiple choice math strategy ever, I present...

## *SITUATION #4: TO CHECK YOUR WORK WHEN YOU DIDN'T LISTEN TO ME AND USED ALGEBRA ANYWAYS.*

If you simply must write your own algebraic expression instead of relying on plugging in numbers, I *strongly suggest that you check your work by plugging in a set of values* to confirm that your answer choice gives you the result that you expect. Accuracy counts on the SAT—take that extra 25-30 seconds to make sure that you're right.

***Hot Tip:*** I told you that there are no wrong numbers when it comes to plugging in. That's true, but there are better numbers—numbers that will get you the right answer more quickly. Here are a few rules for picking high-quality numbers to plug in.

**How to pick the best numbers to plug in.**
Suppose you're going to have to divide the variable by 3. Wouldn't it be a good idea to pick a number that's evenly divisible by 3? Just makes life easier, right?

If $x$ is the measure of an angle in a triangle, pick a value that is easy to work with but that is not the most obvious value. In other words, pick 80° instead of 90°. It's very easy to do arithmetic with 80°, and that value is more likely to get you to the right answer on the first pass.

Don't use the same value twice; pick different numbers. Don't send 4 people to the circus at a ticket price of $4. Choosing different values for each variable will help you to distinguish between answer choices.

It's NOT a good idea to use 1 as a plug-in value on a story problem. Consider the circus problem. Setting $n = 1$ will cause a couple of problems. First, going to the circus by yourself is lonely and a little bit creepy too. Second, you get the same result when you multiply or divide by 1. That could make a couple of different answer choices seem to work.

Finally, don't be a hero. Pick numbers that are easy to work with. Use values like 4, and 10, and 20. There is no penalty for going easy on yourself; you'll earn the same number of points as the jackass who used 37.

# TURN WORD PROBLEMS INTO EQUATIONS

Lots of wordy word problems are systems of linear equations in disguise. *Isn't that fun!*

The good news is that we already know how to solve these things. The bad news is that we have to do it *right now.*

At intermission, the high school theater sells refreshments. Each cup of hot cider costs $3, and each cookie costs $2. If the theater sold a total of 60 refreshments on Friday for a total of $164 in combined sales, how many cookies did the theater sell?

A) 16
B) 20
C) 40
D) 44

Here's how to solve this bad boy by writing a system of equations:

Let's assign a variable to each of our unknowns. The most convenient things we want to find are the number of cookies and the number of cups of cider. Let's call the cookies x and the cider y.

Since the total number of refreshments has to add up to 60, our first equation is this:

$$x + y = 60$$

Now, since each cookie costs \$2 and each cup of cider \$3, let's write an equation for the total revenue:

$$2x + 3y = 164$$

Put 'em together and you have a system!!! That's not exciting...is it? Let me try that again.

Put 'em together and you have a system.

$$x + y = 60$$
$$2x + 3y = 164$$

We talked earlier about the best way to solve a system depending on the situation. Here, I would isolate $y$ in the first equation and then substitute.

$$y = 60 - x$$

$$2x + 3(60 - x) = 164$$
$$2x + 180 - 3x = 164$$
$$-x = -16$$
$$x = 16$$

Then look back to make sure you found the thing you were trying to find. Cookies? **Check.**

So that strategy was to turn a real-world situation into a mathematical one. Here's another strategy we could have used to solve that question...a strategy that's probably a lot faster and easier to use.

## WORK BACKWARDS FROM THE ANSWERS

I know you know this strategy. I know you LOVE this strategy. If anything, I want to warn you *against using this strategy too much*. That said, it sure does come in handy some times!

Let's look back at that last problem again.

> At intermission, the high school theater sells refreshments. Each cup of hot cider costs \$3, and each cookie costs \$2. If the theater sold a total of 60 refreshments on Friday for a total of \$164 in combined sales, how many cookies did the theater sell?
>
> A) 16
> B) 20
> C) 40
> D) 44

The SAT gods have smiled on you and made this a multiple choice question rather than a free-response one. If it's free response, you're screwed—you really need to write the system. But here, we can just jump in and try the answer choices.

I would start in the middle, with 20. All you need to do is play out the scenario as if the theater sold 20 cookies. If they did, then they would have sold 40 ciders (since those two numbers have to add up to 60). That would be a total of $\$2 \times 20 + \$3 \times 40 = \$160$. We know two things: that 20 is not right, and that we're low on money. We need a total bill of $164.

How can we spend more? By buying more of the expensive cups of cider. If we need more cider, we need fewer cookies. Only answer choice A has fewer cookies on order. We should check to make sure it's right, but if we worked carefully in the first step, we kinda know it's going to be. Sure enough, $\$2 \times 16 + \$3 \times 44 = \$164$.

If they give you the answer choices on a system of equations, well, that's a situation when I am perfectly OK with you working backwards from the answers.

## UNLESS THEY SAY OTHERWISE, FIGURES ARE DRAWN TO SCALE.

I really tried to come up with a better name for this strategy. I did. I tried. It didn't happen. You can't force magic.

Let's look at a problem that shows you how this strategy might be really useful to you.

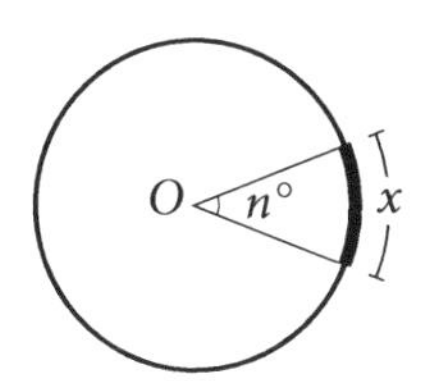


> In the figure above, the circle has center $O$ and radius 15. If the length of the darkened arc measures $10 < x < 11$, what is one possible integer value of $n$?

First off, there is a *real*, mathematical way to solve this question, but humor me for a second. If you had to ballpark an answer to this question just based on the visuals in the diagram, what would you guess? Maybe something around 45 degrees? You'd be close to right. If you guessed 40 degrees, you *would* be right.

So the point here is that, since the figure doesn't say anything about NOT being drawn to scale, then it must BE drawn to scale. And once you know that, you can feel free to draw clues straight from the look of the figure.

OK, fine, I'll do the math too. You want to make a proportion that compares the arc measure to the circumference. Since $C = 2\pi r$, the circumference here is $30\pi$.

We'll set up a proportion with arc measure on top and the measure of the whole circle on bottom. Like so:

$$\frac{\text{arc}}{\text{whole circle}} = \frac{10}{30\pi} = \frac{n^\circ}{360^\circ}$$

$$n = 38.19\ldots\ldots$$

$$\text{or} \quad \frac{11}{30\pi} = \frac{n^\circ}{360^\circ}$$

$$n = 42.016$$

$$38.19 < n < 42.016$$

$$\boxed{n = 39,\ 40,\ 41,\ \text{or}\ 42}$$

## WHAT YOU CAN DO WITH YOUR CALCULATOR

The SAT obviously knows that the calculator is a powerful tool.

**Why would they include a "no calculator" section otherwise?**

When you *can* use a calculator, well, you can pretty much go to town with it. Basically every graphing calculator is allowed on the test—you just can't use one with wireless internet or a stylus. And you're also not allowed to use the calculator on your phone, for obvious reason.

**Besides that, you can use a calculator, and you can do anything with it that a calculator can do. Including...**

### *STORING VALUES*

One fun thing you can do on the Texas Instruments family of graphing calculator is store values.

Excuse me...did you just say that storing values sounds like literally the *least* fun thing in the world to do?

## How dare you.

Fine. Storing values is not necessarily fun, but it does make your life easier by making you mistake-proof when you do some mechanical math. Lemme show you.

Suppose a question gives you a function, like $h(x) = 4x^3 + 2x^2 + x$ and asks you to find $h(-4/3)$. You probably know that you should use your calculator on this question. Try storing values to make it even easier to use that calculator.

In the home screen (the normal ol' calculator screen), type -4/3. Then press the button right above ON, the one that says STO->. That confusing button name means "store as." Then press *x*. Then press enter.

Now *x* is stored as -4/3 in the home screen. Don't worry—this won't mess with the graphing function of your calculator. All the letters on your calculator have a stored value from the moment you pressed the ON button for the first time. Bet you didn't know that. Now you do.

Once -4/3 part is stored as *x*, the rest is easy. Type the function exactly as written, in terms of *x*. Press enter. That is the answer to the question. (In this sample problem referenced above, you should have gotten approximately -7.259.)

## USING PROGRAMS

There are boatloads of potentially useful programs you can download for your calculator—ones that can factor, that can calculate every aspect of a linear equation, or a quadratic...all the stuff that we're learning how to do in this book.

Now, before you get carried away and start thinking that your calculator is going to be your heaven-sent savior on the SAT Math section, a few words of warning:

- ***You will pretty much always have to do some math in addition to using a program.***
- ***You will have to use the programs in advance so you know when to use them and what to do with them.***

In other words, the calculator is not a replacement for knowing math, and you can't just jump in with calculator programs—you need to practice with them too.

OK, enough warnings.

To get programs on your calculator, Google your calculator's model number plus 'programs,' so for example, search for "TI-84+ programs."

Use that search to find a website that hosts program files. For Texas Instruments calculator users, I recommend ticalc.org.

Follow the instructions on how to download and install programs to your calculator.

And enjoy!

# DON'T FORGET THE REFERENCE INFORMATION

Some of these strategies seem like they really don't need a whole lot of explanation. Every math section starts with a page of reference information, including nearly every specific shape geometry formula you would ever need to know. Let me show you how handy this stuff can be.

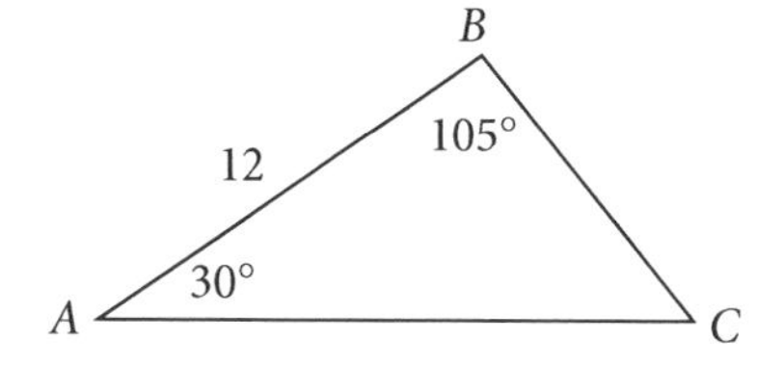


In $\triangle ABC$ above, what is the length of $\overline{AC}$?

A) $6 + 6\sqrt{3}$

B) $6 + 6\sqrt{2}$

C) $6\sqrt{3} + 6\sqrt{2}$

D) $12\sqrt{3}$

What reference information might be handy here? Two clues to help you answer that question: the 30° angle and all the $\sqrt{3}$ and $\sqrt{2}$ stuff in the answers. Give up? This is definitely a special right triangle question.

**But Ted...there IS no right triangle!!!**

Fair enough. Let's make our own.

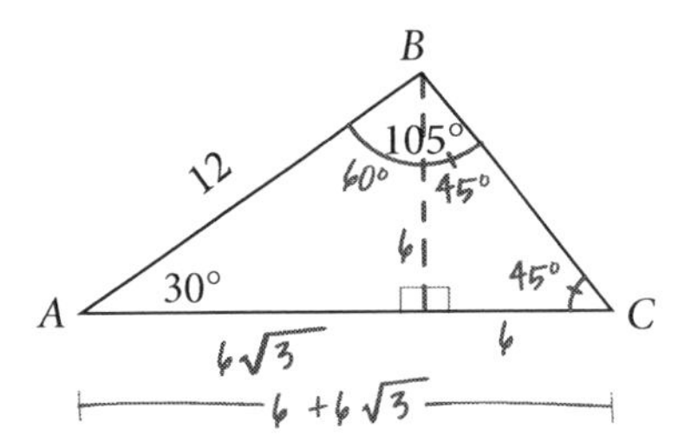


Here's where your reference information will come in REALLY HANDY. Check out the first page of an SAT math section—either a real SAT online or one of the tests from our book. Notice in the lower-right of the page that you are given the 30-60-90 and 45-45-90 triangles. The diagram above might look really smart and complicated, but it's just a dead copy of the information from that page.

So don't sleep on the reference information.

## KEEP YOUR ALGEBRA CLEAN

This might sound counter-intuitive, but sometimes you want to do *less* algebra, not more. Let me show you what I mean.

$$B_t = P - t\left[\frac{P-s}{n}\right]$$

The formula above gives the current value $B_t$ of a piece of equipment, where $P$ represents the original price of the equipment, $s$ represents its current salvage value, $n$ represents the number of years until the equipment is obsolete, and $t$ represents the number of years the equipment has been used so far. Which of the following gives $t$ in terms of $P$, $s$, $n$, and $B_t$?

A) $-\dfrac{B_t - P}{\left[\frac{P-s}{n}\right]}$

B) $\dfrac{B_t + P}{\left[\frac{P-s}{n}\right]}$

C) $\dfrac{B_t}{\left[\frac{P-s}{n}\right]} - P$

D) $\dfrac{B_t}{\left[\frac{P-s}{n}\right]} + P$

Now, if you're like every living human being who has not yet read this strategy, you should see that formula and get moderately nauseous. Amazingly, this is not too hard a problem. The key is to keep your algebra clean. Make the moves that you've known how to make since 7th grade Pre-Algebra and you'll get to an answer quickly.

Watch:

$$B_t = P - t\left[\frac{P-s}{n}\right]$$

$$-P \qquad -P$$

$$\frac{B_t - P}{\left[\frac{P-s}{n}\right]} = \frac{-t\left[\frac{P-s}{n}\right]}{\left[\frac{P-s}{n}\right]}$$

$$-1 \times \frac{B_t - P}{\left[\frac{P-s}{n}\right]} = -t \times -1$$

$$\boxed{-\frac{B_t - P}{\left[\frac{P-s}{n}\right]}} = t$$

The most important move in this simplification process is leaving the $[(P - s)/n]$ term within the brackets alone. Think of that as one big chunk, and move it around as one big chunk. Don't distribute the $t$ within that term, in other words, and you'll have a much, much, much easier path to getting $t$ by itself.

## USE YOUR COMMON SENSE

The SAT clearly wants to draw connections between the math you've learned and the real world. I think a lot of students tend to draw a line between the real world and the math world. See if you can bridge that gap on these questions. When you do, trust your common sense. Let's look at a sample problem.

Typical Human Sleep Cycle
Distribution by Time

| | |
|---|---|
| Stage 1 | 4-5% |
| Stage 2 | 45-55% |
| Stage 3 | 4-6% |
| Stage 4 | 12-15% |
| Stage 5 | 20-25% |

The typical human sleep cycle lasts 90 minutes. If an individual's total sleep is five cycles long, which of the following represents the likely amount $t$, in minutes, that the individual spent in Stage 4?

A) $5 \times 90 \times 0.12 < t < 5 \times 90 \times 0.15$

B) $5 \times 90 \times 0.12 \times 100 < t < 5 \times 90 \times 0.15 \times 100$

C) $5 \times 90 \times 0.12 < 100t < 5 \times 90 \times 0.15$

D) $\frac{5 \times 90 \times 0.12}{100} < t < \frac{5 \times 90 \times 0.15}{100}$

To me, this question is a lot simpler than it looks. I would recommend you solve it for yourself and then find the answer you got, rather than entertaining all the answer choices as possibilities. That's a useful strategy, especially when the answer choices are as dense as this.

So what would you do to find the amount of sleep time spent in Stage 4? Just use your common sense. Each sleep cycle is 90 minutes long, and the person sleeping in this problem had five complete sleep cycles. That's 90 × 5 total minutes of sleep. Now multiply that number by 12% and 15% to get the range of Stage 4 sleep amounts. How do we multiply by a percent? By changing it to a decimal, like 0.12 and 0.15. The finished product would be 5 × 90 × 0.12 for the minimum and 5 × 90 × 0.15 for the maximum. That's answer choice A.

Common sense helps us put that equation together, and it helps us make sure that we're right, too. Try multiplying 5 × 90 × 0.12. You get 54 minutes. Does that sound like about 12 percent of your night's sleep? Now try the left side of answer choice B. You should get 5,400 minutes, or 90 hours. While I'm sure you could use 90 hours of sleep right about now, it's not a strong likelihood that you will sleep for nearly four days straight. That number does not make common sense, so get rid of it!

The SAT does its best job to relate math to the real world. They aren't perfect at it, but when they do, you should feel free to rely on your common sense to solve those questions.

## REVENGE OF THE QUESTION STEM

On the SAT, you've got math on the Reading test, data on the Writing & Language test and... guess what? You've got reading on the Math test. Read carefully, and always make sure you know what's being asked. How? By reading the question stem. Here's a sample question where reading the question stem carefully pays off.

| National Park | Visitors in 2015 | Visitors in 2016 |
|---|---|---|
| Great Smoky Mountains | 10,712,674 | 11,312,786 |
| Grand Canyon | 5,520,736 | 5,969,811 |
| Yosemite | 4,150,217 | 5,028,868 |
| Rocky Mountain | 4,155,916 | 4,517,585 |
| Zion | 3,648,846 | 4,295,128 |

The table above shows the five U.S. National Parks that were visited by the most people in 2016. Based on the information in the table, which park showed the least growth in the number of visitors, measured by percent change from 2015 to 2016?

A) Great Smoky Mountains
B) Grand Canyon
C) Rocky Mountain
D) Zion

This question has a couple of different components to it; for one, it's a chart and graph/data question. That means we're going to have to mind the details. It also has a wordy question stem, which means we need to read carefully to make sure we're answering the right question.

So let's do that. The questions asks for the park that showed the *least* growth as measured by percent change. Do you think the percent change part is going to be important? Yeah, me too.

Let's start calculating percent changes. We can ignore Yosemite since it's not one of the answer choices (but don't ignore Yosemite in real life—it's incredible!). To find percent change, we put the amount of change over the original amount and multiply by 100. Do that carefully for all four parks in the answer choices, and you'll see that, by a narrow margin (8.1% for Grand Canyon, 8.7% for Rocky Mountain), Grand Canyon showed the least amount of growth.

Notice that by AMOUNT of growth, Rocky Mountain had the least growth. But that's not the question you had to answer.

### Boring? Yes. Hard? No.

Just got to read that question stem carefully to make sure that you're answering the question that SAT asked.

## STAY ACCURATE, PONYBOY

Not sure if that cultural reference has ANY relevance for today's high school student or not. Whatever: keep in mind that this not just a test of your brilliance. I would say it's MORE a test of your patience and accuracy than your brilliance, in fact. It doesn't hurt to be brilliant of course, but you don't get to 1600 on brilliance alone. No, you've got to work towards it carefully. Here's how:

On each Math section, after you've finished your first pass on the questions, I recommend you double-check as many questions as you can. By double-check, I do not mean "do the question the same way a second time." The problem with checking your work that way is that if you made a mistake the first time around, there's a pretty good chance that you won't see that mistake when you review.

So instead of doing that, try doing the problem a different way. That could be as simple as plugging your answer back into the original question. Or running a number through an algebraic equation to confirm that you get out of it what you'd expect to get. When you find a *different* way to solve the question and you get to the same result, you *pretty much know you got the question right*. That's the place where we want you to get.

Tutor Ted®

# MATH: ANSWERS

# Answers

## YOUR ALGEBRA TOOLBOX

### Order of Operations

1) C
2) D
3) B
4) D
5) 3.5 or 7/2
6) D
7) 11
8) B

### Combine Like Terms

1) A
2) A
3) B
4) D
5) C
6) B
7) 50
8) C

### Distribution & Factoring

1) 7
2) 6233
3) A
4) B
5) 6/7 or .857
6) C
7) C
8) A
9) C
10) B
11) C
12) B
13) D
14) C
15) 5
16) A

### Proportion / Cross-Multiplication

1) D
2) D
3) 65
4) B
5) A
6) C
7) D
8) C

### Absolute Value

1) D
2) 16
3) D
4) A
5) C
6) D
7) D
8) B

### Systems of Equations

1) B
2) 6
3) D
4) 7/2 or 3.5
5) B
6) 5/2 or 2.5
7) C
8) C
9) A
10) 12/7 or 1.71
11) C
12) B
13) B
14) C
15) 17
16) 2

### Inequalities

1) D
2) D
3) B
4) A
5) D
6) C
7) A
8) B

### Function Notation

1) B
2) B
3) B
4) C
5) 2
6) B
7) C
8) D
9) B
10) B
11) C
12) B
13) A
14) B
15) 79
16) 2484

## YOUR ALGEBRA TOOLBOX

### Exponent Rules

1) A
2) C
3) D
4) D
5) B
6) B
7) C
8) A
9) A
10) A
11) C
12) A
13) B
14) D
15) D
16) D

## LINEAR EQUATIONS

1) D
2) B
3) B
4) A
5) 7/4 or 1.75
6) D
7) 16/5 or 3.2
8) B
9) B
10) A
11) B
12) B
13) D
14) B
15) C
16) D
17) B
18) C
19) C
20) A
21) C
22) C
23) D
24) C

## QUADRATICS

1) C
2) C
3) C
4) 18
5) 0 or 4
6) B
7) C
8) A
9) D
10) A
11) A
12) D
13) A
14) A
15) A
16) B

## SHAPE GEOMETRY

1) B
2) D
3) 5/12 or .416 or .417
4) 63
5) 9
6) B
7) D
8) C
9) 10
10) 40
11) C
12) 30
13) B
14) 9
15) C
16) D

## SOH-CAH-TOA

1) A
2) B
3) B
4) C
5) 4/5 or 0.8
6) C
7) 0.6 or 3/5
8) B
9) C
10) C
11) 4/5 or 0.8
12) 60
13) D
14) C
15) 8
16) 0

## CHARTS AND GRAPHS

1) B
2) C
3) C
4) D
5) C
6) A
7) B
8) C
9) C
10) B
11) C
12) B
13) B
14) D
15) C
16) B

## STATISTICS

1) C
2) C
3) 12
4) B
5) D
6) D
7) C
8) B
9) A
10) A
11) A
12) B
13) B
14) C
15) C
16) B

## FORMULAS YOU NEED TO KNOW

1) B
2) A
3) D
4) 118, 119, or 120
5) C
6) 81
7) 289
8) C
9) 5/12 or .416 or .417
10) B
11) A
12) A
13) C
14) 288
15) 18
16) B
17) B
18) A
19) B
20) C
21) D
22) C
23) A
24) C
25) D
26) D
27) A
28) 108

## ADVANCED TOPICS

1) B
2) B
3) C
4) A
5) D
6) C
7) B
8) D
9) 1 or 3
10) B
11) D
12) A
13) C
14) B
15) B
16) D
17) B
18) C
19) 6
20) C
21) D
22) B
23) C
24) C

# MATH: SOLUTIONS

# Solutions

## Your Algebra Toolbox:

### ORDER OF OPERATIONS

**1) C**
This is a straightforward Algebra question, so just be careful. Start by subtracting 10 from both sides of the equation, then divide both sides by 2 to get $x$ by itself. You should get that $x = 4$. But you're not done! The SAT loves to add in one extra step at the end. They want the value of $x + 15$, so substitute 4 in for $x$ to get 19.

**2) D**
This one is easy, but don't take shortcuts! Students who get this wrong usually do $4m - 2m = 2m$ and pick B. You can prevent that mistake by plugging in 6 for $m$ right away. So $4m = 24$ and $-2m = -12$. The difference between 24 and -12 is written like this: $24 - (-12) = 24 + 12 = 36$.

**3) B**
Start by turning the words into an equation. Be especially careful with the subtraction, since it reads a little backwards from how we'll write it. Your equation should be $6y + 18 = 40 - 16$. We should simplify and subtract 18 from both sides to get that $6y = 6$, and so $y = 1$. Of course, the SAT wants a little more, so substitute 1 in for $y$ to get that $y + 2$ is 3.

**4) D**
We want to solve this equation by getting $d$ by itself. We should multiply both sides by $d$ to cancel out the division. This gets us $400d = 10$. Now divide by 400 to get that $d = 0.025$. It's tempting to take shortcuts and just start multiplying or dividing the 10 and the 400, but if we obey the order of operations, we'll be fine.

**5) 3.5 or $\frac{7}{2}$**
We're going to solve for $x$, but let's take care of the parentheses first. Distribute the 2.4 to get $3x - 6.9 = 2.4x - 4.8$. Subtract $2.4x$ to get all of the $x$'s on one side of the equation, and add 6.9 to both sides. You should get $0.6x=2.1$. Divide to get that $x = \frac{7}{2}$, which can also be written as 3.5.

**6) D**
This question says to solve for $3n$. Follow the order of operations by solving from the outside in. Start by dividing both sides by 4 to get that $\frac{t}{4} = \sqrt{3n}$. You can eliminate the square root by squaring both sides, but remember that everything gets squared: $\left(\frac{t}{4}\right)^2 = (\sqrt{3n})^2$. That means both the numerator and denominator of the fraction get squared, like this: $\frac{t^2}{4^2}$. Since they asked for $3n$, we don't need to go any further. Just square the 4 to get $\frac{t^2}{16} = 3n$.

**7) 11**
Let's convert the words into an equation: $4x - 8 < 40$. Even though it's an inequality, we can still solve for $x$. Add 8 to both sides, then divide by 4. You should get $x < 12$. But we're not quite done. We need the greatest possible integer value of $x$. Since $x$ can't equal 12, the greatest integer it can be is 11. (An integer is a whole number—no fractions or decimals.)

**8) B**
This is a system of equations, so we should try to eliminate one of the variables. The second equation can be solved for $y = 20$ by multiplying both sides by 4. Plug 20 in for $y$ in the first

equation. Now let's solve for $x$. The order of operations says that we should get rid of the fraction first, so multiply both sides by 4 to get $x + 20 = 32$. Subtract 20 to find $x = 12$. The most common error on this question comes from taking Algebra shortcuts. Even though it looks like $\frac{y}{4}$ is in the first equation, it's a bit more complicated, so you can't easily substitute the 5.

---

## COMBINE LIKE TERMS

**1) A**
Combine all the t terms and all the number terms, and this equation should simplify to $4t + 3 = 10 - 3t$. Add $3t$ and subtract 3 from both sides to get $7t = 7$. So $t = 1$.

**2) A**
Just add the similar terms. They're trying to trick you into adding the exponents too, but don't fall for it. You know that $2x^2 + 4x^2 = 6x^2$. Similarly, to add the second terms, we only add the coefficients, like this: $-3x + -x = -4x$.

**3) B**
If Nikita worked b hours a day for 6 days, then she worked $6b$ hours in all. Similarly, Desmond worked $4c$ hours in all. Add them up to find the total. If it helps, make up numbers for $b$ and $c$ so you can understand the math more easily.

**4) D**
We can't combine the two $w$ terms because they have different exponents. Most students who get this wrong mistakenly add the exponents to get $w^3$, but that's not how exponents work when you're adding like terms. ($w^2$ times $w$ would give us $w^3$.) You can add the $z$ terms because they have the same exponent (1). That should get you $w^2 + w - z$.

**5) C**
There are basically two places that students make mistakes on this question. First, you should remember that $y^2$ and $y$ are not like terms, so they can't be combined with each other. Second, make sure you distribute the 5 and -2 to both terms in the parentheses. Distributing correctly should give you $5y^2 + 5y - 2y^2 - 2y$. We can combine terms that have the same exponent, which would give us $3y^2 + 3y$.

**6) B**
In math class in school, you'd probably have to solve this with Algebra. If you do that on the SAT, don't forget to check your answers at the end by plugging them back into the original equation. Radicals can sometimes produce solutions that don't actually work. Our best bet is to guess and check the choices by plugging in the numbers for $x$. Start with -2 and be organized: $\sqrt{3(-2) + 7} + 5 = (-2) + 6$. Simplifying this gives us $\sqrt{1} + 5 = 4$, which is not mathematically true. That eliminates everything but choice B, but let's double check to be safe: $\sqrt{3(3) + 7} + 5 = 2 + 6$. This simplifies to $\sqrt{16} + 5 = 9$, which is a valid solution.

**7) 50**
This looks much worse than it is. The SAT is asking for something very simple in a very confusing way. Trust yourself and just follow the instructions. We can find the sum of the expressions by combining like terms to get $3x^2 + x + 46$. Now line up our expression with the weird one they gave us, and you should see that $a = 3$, $b = 1$, and $c = 46$. The question wants us to add up these numbers too, which gives us 50.

**8) C**
Don't get intimidated by this complicated story. As usual, most of it is unnecessary. Focus on what they're asking for and you'll see that you just need to solve the equation for $C$. Follow the order of operations and you'll be fine. Start by subtracting $pA$ from both sides. Then divide both sides by $q$ to get $C$ alone: $C = \frac{R - pA}{q}$.

---

## DISTRIBUTION AND FACTORING

**1) 7**
This is a classic distribution question. Keep track of the negatives, and distribute to everything in parentheses. You should get $12x - 36 - 14 - 4x = 6$. Combining like terms will

give you $8x - 50 = 6$. Add 50 and divide by 8 to find that $x = 7$.

**2) 6233**

Distribute the -20 to get $160y^3 + 4793 - 20y^3 + 1300$. Combine like terms and you should get $140y^3 + 6093$. The instructions seem complicated, but the SAT just wants you to add the two numbers, so $140 + 6093 = 6233$.

**3) A**

This question is all about distribution, so make sure you distribute to both terms in each of the parentheses and don't lose any negatives. Distributing should give you $12 - 8x - 2x^2 + 2 + 3x^2 + 3x$. Combine like terms to get $x^2 - 5x + 14$.

**4) B**

The zeros are the points where the function crosses the $x$-axis, which is when $y = 0$. We can ignore the original equation and go right to the factored version in the question. But be careful. It's not fully factored just yet. We need to recognize that $(x^2 - 4) = (x - 2)(x + 2)$. That means that both +2 and -2 are zeros of the function. The second term cannot be factored any further. If we want to expand it, we'd see that $(x - 1)^2 = (x - 1)(x - 1)$. This means that 1 is a zero because that's the value where $(x - 1) = 0$. Choice B lists all of the zeros.

**5) $\frac{6}{7}$ or .857**

There's no negative to distribute, so this one is pretty straightforward. Distribute the 6 and the 3 to get $6k - 12 + 3k + 6 = 2k$. Combining like terms should get you $9k - 6 = 2k$. Add 6 and subtract $2k$ to get $7k = 6$. Divide by 7 and you'll get that $k = \frac{6}{7}$.

**6) C**

Let's start by FOILing the first parentheses and distributing the -6 to the second parentheses. You should get $x^2 - 2x + 1 - 6x + 6 = -9$. When we combine like terms, we should keep in mind that this is going to be a quadratic equation because of the $x^2$ term. That means we need to have all the terms on one side and zero on the other, like this: $x^2 - 8x + 16 = 0$. Factor to get the solution: $(x - 4)(x - 4) = 0$. So $x = 4$.

**7) C**

You've got some options here, but it's probably easiest to distribute the 2 first so you don't forget about it later: $(6x + 2)(5x + 2)$. Now you can FOIL and combine like terms to get $30x^2 + 22x + 4$.

**8) A**

You can't solve for the individual variables, so don't bother trying. Instead, focus on the expression the SAT is asking for: $xy + z$. We can try to get that term by itself by first adding 13 to both sides. Next, you can see that there's a 5 in front of both variable terms. Let's factor it out to get $5(xy + z) = 30$. Just divide both sides by 5 and you've found that the answer is 6.

**9) C**

This sounds complicated, but it's testing something very common on the SAT—difference of two squares. We can factor like this: $25x^2 - 4 = (5x + 2)(5x - 2)$. The instructions ask for the value of $a$, which would be 5.

**10) B**

This one is a pain because of all the decimals, but the process is the same. Start by FOILing $(2.2x + 1.3)^2$ to get $4.84x^2 + 5.72x + 1.69$. Don't forget to distribute the negative to both parts in the second parentheses. When all the parentheses are gone, you should have $4.84x^2 + 5.72x + 1.69 - 6.5x^2 + 8.2$. When you combine like terms, you'll get choice B.

**11) C**

To find the solutions, set each set of parentheses equal to 0 and solve. Don't let the fraction scare you. The solutions are 4 and $-\frac{1}{3}$. Now find the sum: $4 + \left(-\frac{1}{3}\right)$. It's a little easier if you change the 4 into thirds so you're subtracting fractions with common denominators: $\frac{12}{3} - \frac{1}{3} = \frac{11}{3}$.

**12) B**

The fastest way to solve this question is to complete the square. If we simultaneously add and subtract 16, we can change the way the expression looks without changing its value. You should get something like this:

$(x^2 + 8x + 16) + 8 - 16$. The parentheses keep everything organized, so that we can easily simplify to get the answer: $(x + 4)^2 - 8$. Completing the square is an advanced factoring technique, but it's tested on almost every SAT so you should get comfortable with it.

**13) D**

The SAT is really hoping you take shortcuts on this question, but be patient and take the time to FOIL correctly. Write it out and go in order (first, outer, inner, last):

$\left(\frac{x}{2} - 4\right)\left(\frac{x}{2} - 4\right) = \frac{x^2}{4} - \frac{4x}{2} - \frac{4x}{2} + 16$. You can reduce the $-\frac{4x}{2}$ terms to $-2x$. Combine them to get choice D.

**14) C**

Oh boy. This one is tough. You should start by substituting the first two equations for $m$ and $n$ in the third: $4(4x^2 + y^2) + 16(xy)$. Distribute and you'll get $16x^2 + 4y^2 + 16xy$. If you're not sure where to go from here, you could always guess an answer choice, FOIL it out, and see if it matches our expression. But the faster way is to factor our expression directly. First, we should rearrange our expression so that it's easier to factor: $16x^2 + 16xy + 4y^2$. Some skillful factoring should get you $(4x + 2y)(4x + 2y)$, which simplifies to C.

**15) 5**

The SAT loves to scare you with Algebra that looks very complicated. Try to focus on one thing at a time. In order to subtract fractions, we need common denominators, so let's work on that first. We can multiply the numerator and denominator of the second term by $(x - 3)$. The parentheses are important because we don't want to forget to distribute later: $\frac{(3x-4)}{(x-3)^2} - \frac{3(x-3)}{(x-3)^2}$. With common denominators, we can now combine the numerators. Make sure you don't lose the minus sign: $\frac{(3x - 4 - 3(x-3))}{(x-3)^2}$. Distribute and combine like terms. The $3x$ terms will cancel out, leaving you with $\frac{5}{(x-3)^2} = \frac{c}{(x-3)^2}$, so $c = 5$.

**16) A**

This one is messy! It's clear that we need to solve for $a$, but the $a$'s are all over the place, which makes it hard to get $a$ by itself. We want to get all the $a$ terms on one side, so subtract $acd$ and $ab$ from both sides to get $abc - acd - ab = cd$. Unfortunately, we can't combine these terms since each of them has other variables besides $a$. The only thing we can do is factor, which means dividing each of the terms by $a$ and putting it outside of some parentheses. Your equation should look like this:
$a(bc - cd - b) = cd$. Notice that if you distribute the $a$, you'd get back to our last step. Now to get $a$ by itself, we divide both sides by the long parentheses term. That will eliminate it on the left and make it the denominator on the right. There's nothing more we can do. Even though the $cd$ term is in both the numerator and denominator, we can't cross it out and reduce. The subtraction means the whole denominator has to stay together as if it's one term. It looks messy, but $a = \frac{cd}{(bc - cd - b)}$.

## PROPORTION / CROSS-MULTIPLICATION

**1) D**

The big numbers make this look harder than it is. The question tells us to create ratios. We're given that the ratio of screws to safety pins is 1 to 3. We can make that a fraction and set it equal to the actual number of screws and safety pins produced on Monday: $\frac{1\ screw}{3\ pins} = \frac{9{,}000\ screws}{x\ pins}$. Cross multiply to find that the factory made 27,000 pins.

**2) D**

You might be able to get this by reducing the rate in your head to 40 pages per hour. But if not, use a proportion to stay organized:

$\frac{80\ pages}{2\ hours} = \frac{x\ pages}{5\ hours}$. Cross multiply to get $2x = 400$. Divide by 2 to find that Erin reads 200 pages in 5 hours.

**3) 65**

You might get thrown off by the phrase "directly proportional" because it sounds like complicated math, but it just means we can set up a proportion to solve: $\frac{8\ yrs}{104\ cm} = \frac{5\ yrs}{x\ cm}$. Cross multiply to get $8x = 520$, and divide to get 65cm.

**4) B**

At first, it seems like you need to get common denominators and subtract the fractions, but it's much easier if you first find the number of questions that each student answered. Arthur answered $\frac{3}{5}$ of his 100 questions, which is 60 questions. Lucy answered $\frac{3}{4}$ of her 100 questions, which is 75. The difference between 75 and 60 is 15.

**5) A**

If you choose to set up a proportion, don't forget that they're asking you to change your units. You can do it in two steps to be safe. First, figure out how many inches the kelp grows in 9 days: $\frac{10\ in}{1\ day} = \frac{x\ in}{9\ days}$. That's 90 inches of kelp! You can simply divide by 12, or you can use another proportion to convert to feet: $\frac{1\ ft}{12\ in} = \frac{x\ ft}{90\ in}$. Either way, you'll get 7.5 feet of kelp.

**6) C**

Even though there are no units or rates here, you should still recognize that the equation looks like a proportion, so we can cross-multiply and get $3y = 9x$. Simplify so you have $y = 3x$. You can plug $3x$ in for $y$ in the second expression: $\frac{4(3x)}{x}$. Multiply and eliminate the $x$'s to get 12. The SAT gives questions like this fairly often, so you should feel comfortable using cross-multiplication even when there isn't a story or unit conversion.

**7) D**

Even though these questions are paired, you can answer them independently—the answer to the first question doesn't help you with the second question. The first thing you should notice here is that meters is underlined. The SAT is trying to trick you into missing the unit conversion. The original formula requires that the area be in square feet, so let's set up a proportion to convert: $\frac{1\ sq\ m}{10.7\ sq\ ft} = \frac{36\ sq\ m}{x\ sq\ ft}$. Cross multiply and you'll get that this wall has an area of 385.2 square feet. Now you can plug that into $A$ in the equation, which gives the value of $p$ as approximately 4.

**8) C**

If you're comfortable with Algebra, you might be able to get this just by looking at the original equation. But it can't hurt to play it safe. Let's pick numbers that let us see what's going on. We can say that the kitchen walls have an area of 96 square feet, which we're choosing because it works out nicely in the equation. Just divide 96 by 96 to find that our hypothetical kitchen needs exactly 1 can of paint. The question tells us that the dining room is 6 times as large as the kitchen, which means its walls have an area of 6 times 96, which is 576 square feet. Plugging that into our formula tells us that it takes 6 cans of paint to cover the dining room. Since the question asks for the ratio of cans for the dining room to the cans for the kitchen, we need to put the dining room first. So 6 to 1 is our ratio.

## ABSOLUTE VALUE

**1) D**

This looks complicated, but the SAT did us a favor here by giving us answer choices. You can plug each of them into the expression to see if they work. Choice A would simplify to $|-2| + |0|$, which is +2. Substituting in 0 and 1 will also give us 2. In fact, there is no value of $a$ that will make this expression equal to 0. That's because both of the absolute value pieces have to be greater than or equal to 0. Since the pieces won't equal 0 at the same time (with the same value of $a$), the equation will always be greater than 0.

**2) 16**

Absolute value equations can yield 2 solutions, which we can find by dropping the absolute value and creating two new equations: $9 - x = 7$ and $9 - x = -7$. The first equation represents the positive absolute value, and the second equation represents the negative absolute value. Since the question has essentially solved the first equation for us, we need to solve the second one. Subtract 9 from both sides to find that $-x = -16$. Divide by -1 to get that $x = 16$.

**3) D**

This question is mostly asking if you know what absolute value is, so there's not really any Algebra. Just think about it. The term in the absolute value won't ever be negative. The least it can be is 0 (when $x$ is 1 or -1, depending on the choice). So the expression in choice D will be greater than 0 for every value of $x$ because we're adding 1 to something that can't be negative. All the other choices could equal -1 when the absolute value part equals 0.

**4) A**

This one is tricky, but it becomes a lot easier if you take the time to draw a number line. Put the point -2 in the middle, then count 4 units in either direction. You should land on the points at +2 and -6. The question is asking which equation has solutions of +2 and -6, so we should substitute those values in for $x$ and see if they fit. The +2 works in Choice A: $|2+2| = 4$. And so does the -6: $|-6 + 2| = |-4| = 4$. There's no need to try the other choices once we've found that A works for both of our points, but if you try the others, you'll get equations that don't make sense, which is how we know they're wrong.

**5) C**

You could guess and check here, but if you want to do the Algebra, you'll need to make two equations to represent the positive and negative absolute values: $n - \frac{3}{2} = 5$ and $n - \frac{3}{2} = -5$. It's easier to work out the math if you convert 5 to $\frac{10}{2}$. Solving the first equation gives us $n = \frac{13}{2}$, and solving the second equation gives us $n = -\frac{7}{2}$. They want the least value of $n$, so C is the answer.

**6) D**

The SAT has found yet another way to ask if you know what absolute value means. In this case, they're adding in stuff about graphs, but think about what they're saying. What do you know about a point on the $x$-axis? The $y$-coordinate of the point will be 0. So we can set all of these choices equal to 0 and see which one does not give us a solution. If we subtract the 1 from both sides of choice D, we'd get $-1 = |x|$. We know that doesn't work because absolute values can't be negative. If you graphed choice D in your calculator, you'd see that it doesn't touch the $x$-axis.

**7) D**

This is an interesting question in terms of picking an approach. You could test values, but you won't be able to eliminate wrong answer choices easily and confidently. For example, choice A is wrong, but both 4 and -2 make it a true statement. The inequality is causing us a problem. We can overcome this difficulty a couple of different ways. One is to try a bunch of values, values that should work and that should NOT work. That method is effective but a little tricky because you need to make sure you know when you want a number to work and when you want it not to work. A more advanced way to solve these guys, and a method I recommend to all my students, is to translate the sentence directly using your knowledge of what absolute value means. When you subtract one number from another number

and take the absolute value of the difference, you are finding the distance between them. In this case, we are interested in the distance between $x$ and 1. The left side, then, should be $|x-1|$. We want the distance to be within 3 units. So we want the one where $|x-1|$ is less than or equal to 3, and that's D. Using that method we can jump straight to the right answer.

**8) B**

These questions can be tough because you have to think about a lot of different situations at once. You can plug in numbers to better visualize the algebra, but we can also use our knowledge of absolute value. We know that absolute values can never be negative, so $|b|$ will always be greater than or equal to 0. If $a$ is greater than $|b|$, then $a$ must be greater than 0, so II is true. But this does not mean that $b$ has to be greater than 0. Here's an example of numbers that prove III wrong: $5 > |-2|$. These numbers also suggest that I is true, but why? Whether $b$ is negative or positive doesn't matter, as long as its absolute value is less than $a$ (so $5 > |-6|$ wouldn't work because $5 > 6$ is not true). If $b$ is positive, then it's like the absolute value isn't even there, so $a$ has to be greater than $b$. We know that I and II are right and III is wrong, so B is our answer.

## SYSTEMS OF EQUATIONS

**1) B**

If you're not confident in your Algebra skills, you can plug each of the answer choices into the equations to see what fits. But remember that you need to check both equations. Choice A works for the first equation, but not for the second, so it is not correct. You could also use combination to eliminate a variable. Multiplying the second equation by 3 will let you eliminate the $y$ term. You should get $10x = -10$, so $x = -1$. Choice B is the only one with that $x$-value.

**2) 6**

Since this isn't a multiple choice question, we have to find an algebraic path to the answer. You can combine the equations or rearrange one of them so you can substitute. If you multiply the second equation by -1, you can eliminate the $x$ terms and get $-2y = 16$, so $y = -8$. Plug that back into one of the equations to find that $x = 6$.

**3) D**

You have the option of guessing and checking the answer choices, but if you choose to combine the equations, make sure you line up the like terms. You can rearrange the first equation to $x + 3y = -11$ so that the $x$ terms are on the left side for both equations. Multiply the first equation by -2 and you'll get $-2x - 6y = 22$, which allows you to eliminate the $x$ terms. Your equations should combine to $-10y = -20$, so $y = 2$, which means D is the answer. Check the point in both equations if you want to be absolutely sure.

**4) $\frac{7}{2}$ or 3.5**

The decimals don't change the process at all. Combine the equations as they are by adding them. That will eliminate the $y$ terms and give you $4x = 14$. Dividing both sides by 4 gives you $x = 3.5$.

**5) B**

By asking for the value of $x + y$, the SAT is essentially eliminating guess and check as an option. Multiplying the second equation by 2 lets you eliminate the $y$ terms. (You could eliminate the $x$ terms instead by multiplying the first equation by -2, but keep in mind how easy it is on the SAT to accidentally lose a negative. If you're careful, it won't matter, but if you are aware of the most common SAT mistakes, then you'll be less likely to make them.) Distributing a 2 to the entire second equation gives us $4x + 2y = -6$, which we can combine with the first equation to get $5x = 0$. Since $x = 0$, we can easily find $y$ using the second equation: $0 + y = -3$.

**6) $\frac{5}{2}$ or 2.5**

Here's a good example of a question where anticipating the most likely algebra mistake could make this easier to solve. Fractions can be confusing, so why not multiply the first equation by 4 to clean the equation up? You would make it $x + 3y = 15$. The second equation makes it very easy to substitute in for $x$: $3y + 3y = 15$. Combine and divide to get that $y = \frac{5}{2}$.

**7) C**

This question is already set up for us to eliminate the $y$ terms. Combine the equations to get

$11x = 22$, so $x = 2$. Plugging that into the first equation, we get $10 + 5y = 14$. Subtract 10 and divide by 5 to find that $y = \frac{4}{5}$. To find the value of $x - y$, convert $x$ into fifths and subtract: $\frac{10}{5} - \frac{4}{5} = \frac{6}{5}$.

**8) C**

If the quadratic equation confuses you, just guess and check the answer choices in each equation. To solve algebraically, start by subtracting 6 from both sides in the second equation to solve for $y$: $y = x - 6$. This lets you set the two equations equal to each other, since we know they're both equal to $y$: $x - 6 = -x^2 + 7x - 14$. To solve quadratic equations, we need to get all of the terms onto one side so the other side equals 0. Moving everything to the left side will make things easier by making the $-x^2$ term positive: $x^2 - 6x + 8 = 0$. Factor this into $(x - 2)(x - 4) = 0$ to get the $x$ values of our solutions: $x = 2$ and $x = 4$. That points to choice C, and we can check those points in each equation to be sure.

**9) A**

This is a common SAT question type. The story will change, but you'll usually need to make two equations that represent the total number of things (fish in this case) and the total value of those things (the weight of all the fish). We know there are 300 fish, so one equation should be $f + t = 300$, which says that the number of flounder plus the number of tuna is 300. The weight of all the flounder is $39.4f$, which is the weight of one flounder times the number of flounder. The tuna will weigh $189.3t$ in all, and we add those terms together to find the total weight of all the fish: $39.4f + 189.3t = 18{,}116$. These equations match with choice A.

**10) $\frac{12}{7}$ or 1.71**

Even though these equations aren't perfectly aligned, you can still combine them because both of the $x$ terms are on the left and both of the $y$ terms are on the right. Multiply the second equation by 3 to get $12x = 15 - 3y$, which lets you eliminate the $y$ terms. Combining gives you $14x - 9 = 15$. Add 9 and divide by 14 to get $x = \frac{24}{14}$, which can be simplified to $x = \frac{12}{7}$.

**11) C**

The $x^2$ term makes this question look a little different from the other systems of equations, but it's really not. You can combine these equations to eliminate the $y$ terms: $x^2 + 2x = 15$. Subtract 15 so you can get this equation equal to 0: $x^2 + 2x - 15 = 0$. Factor into $(x + 5)(x - 3) = 0$ to see that $x = -5$ and $x = 3$. Substitute each of these into one of the equations to find the corresponding $y$ values: $y = 18$ and $y = 2$, respectively.

**12) B**

The story makes this question more confusing than it needs to be. You have two equations, and they want to know about the point where Company A's price is equal to Company B's price. Set these equations equal to each other: $0.20x + 6.15 = 0.45x + 4.90$. Subtract $0.20x$ and 4.90 from both sides to simplify this to $1.25 = 0.25x$. Solving this gives you $x = 5$, but that's not an answer because they don't want the value of $x$. They want the value of A and B at the point where $x$ is 5. Just substitute 5 in for $x$ in the first equation to find that $A = 7.15$.

**13) B**

This question is a lot like #9. We need an equation that captures the value of items (the weights of the boxes and crates). We know that the weight of all the boxes ($40b$) plus the weight of all the crates ($200c$) has to be less than or equal to 5,000 pounds (the maximum for this container). Choices A and C use the wrong inequality sign, so we can eliminate them. The second part of this question is a little harder, but you can use logic to eliminate D. Why would the number of boxes plus the number of crates be less than or equal to 1? We know that there are going to be multiple boxes and crates, so choice D doesn't really make sense. Choice B is correct because the question says the container will have both boxes and crates. We're not sure how many of each, but we know it has to be at least 1.

**14) C**

This is a twist on the typical systems of equations questions. Since these two equations have no solution, they won't intersect and won't have a

point for us to find. Since these are both linear equations, we know the only way they won't have any solutions is if they're parallel. That means they have to have the same slope. You can convert each equation into the $y = mx + b$ format so you can see the slope more easily. Subtract $6x$ and divide by 2 to rearrange the first equation into $y = -3x + 4$. The second equation would be $y = -kx + 2$. These equations need to have the same $m$ in order to be parallel, so $k$ would need to be 3. You could get this without rearranging the equations because the coefficients of the $x$ and $y$ terms are proportional for parallel lines. You could compare the first equation to the second by setting up a proportion like this: $\frac{6}{2} = \frac{k}{1}$. You'd still get that $k = 3$.

**15) 17**

Since both of these equations are equal to $y$, we can set them equal to each other: $3x^2 - 10 = 3x + 8$. Subtract the terms on the right to get it equal to 0: $3x^2 - 3x - 18 = 0$. Divide this equation by 3 to make it easier to factor: $x^2 - x - 6 = 0$. When you factor this, you'll get $(x - 3)(x + 2)=0$, which means $x = 3$ and $x = -2$. Since the question says that $a > 0$, we know we need a positive $x$ value. Plug $x = 3$ into one of the equations to find that $y = 17$, which is our $b$ value in this case.

**16) 2**

This question is similar to #14. Rearranging into $y = mx + b$ form is a little tougher here, so it's easier to set up the proportion. These equations will only have no solutions when they are parallel, so we can compare the coefficients of our x and y terms like this: $\frac{a}{b} = \frac{\frac{1}{2}}{\frac{1}{4}}$. If that confuses you, just convert to decimals: $\frac{a}{b} = \frac{0.5}{0.25} = 2$.

## INEQUALITIES

**1) D**

In order for a point to satisfy the system, it has to be valid in both inequalities. The simplest way to solve this question is by guessing and checking each of the points. When you plug (4, 1) into the first inequality, you'll get $1 \geq 11$, which clearly isn't true. We can eliminate A. In fact, the only point that works in the first inequality is (-3, 2), which yields $2 \geq -3$. We can check the point in the second inequality as well: $-1 < 2$. Since it works in both inequalities, we know it's the right answer.

**2) D**

Even though this question involves inequalities, it's much more about reading carefully and following instructions. If Chester has \$30 and spends $s$ dollars on a shirt, he has $30 - s$ dollars left. Subtract $t$ to take care of the tie: $30 - s - t$. And since he has at least \$12 left, we should make this expression greater than or equal to 12: $30 - s - t \geq 12$.

**3) B**

Look for a common factor. In this case, we can divide each of the terms by 2 and reduce the inequality to $2x + 5y \leq 10$. There's no need to change anything else.

**4) A**

This question looks complicated because of the inequalities, but you can solve it as if these were equations with equals signs instead. If that were the case, you'd have no problem substituting 1 in for $4x$ in the first equation. We can do the same thing here, which means we can rewrite the first inequality as $y < 1+3$, which is the same as choice A.

**5) D**

Since each of our choices starts with an inequality related to the \$400, we should look at the cost first. Essentially, we need an inequality that gives the total cost of the steaks and porkchops. Each steak is \$20, so Emilia will spend $20s$ dollars on steak. In the same way, the total cost of the porkchops will be $15p$ dollars. Our inequality should convey that the total cost of the steaks plus the total cost of the porkchops will be less than or equal to the \$400 Emilia has: $20s + 15p \leq 400$. Only choice D has this inequality. The other two inequalities show that Emilia is going to buy at least 5 steaks and at least 3 porkchops.

**6) C**
This question looks really hard, but it becomes considerably easier once we substitute the point (0,0) in for $x$ and $y$. The first inequality would be $0 > b - 0$, which we can rearrange to $b < 0$. The second inequality would be $0 < 0^2 + c$, which we can rearrange to $c > 0$. If we know that $b < 0$ and $c > 0$, then we also know that $b < c$ because a negative number will always be less than a positive number.

**7) A**
The most important thing for this question is knowing where our solutions lie. The first inequality is for the solid line in the picture. If $y$ is greater than that line, then we want to look for the solutions above the line. In other words, we want to shade the area where the $y$ values are greater than the values on the line (sections A and D). We can rearrange the second inequality if we want to make it look more like a line: $y \geq -2x - 1$. But for this inequality, we also want $y$ values that are greater than the line, so we want to shade the area above the dashed line (sections A and B). The solution for the system is the area where these shaded regions overlap. Since section A is in the solution sets for both of our inequalities, it is the solution to the system.

**8) B**
For this question, we'll need to do a little Geometry. A cake with a rectangular base will end up being a rectangular prism. The volume formula is given in the Reference Chart at the beginning of every math section: $V = lwh$. We know the height (4 inches), and we know that the length is 3 times the width (so $l = 3w$), and we know that the volume will be 2700 cubic inches. Substitute these into the volume formula: $2700 = (3w)(w)(4)$. We can simplify this to $2700 = 12w^2$. Divide by 12 and take the square root to find that $w = 15$. But we should express this as an inequality because the problem says that the volume should be "at least 2700 cubic inches," which means the width could be greater than 15: $w \geq 15$. One thing to note is that the 100 guests don't matter when we're solving. It's rare for an SAT question to give you information that you don't end up using, but it does happen occasionally.

## FUNCTION NOTATION

**1) B**
Technically this question involves advanced math, but only because it uses function notation: $C(m)$. You can see that it doesn't really matter, though. This question is really about lines because it has a flat fee, which acts as a $y$-intercept, and a rate, which acts as a slope. Just like in any $y = mx + b$ equation, the variable is "attached" to, or multiplied by, the slope. In this case, 9 stands alone and is added to $0.1m$, which yields $C(m) = 9 + 0.1m$.

**2) B**
Substitute -1 in for $x$. Use parentheses so you don't lose any negatives: $\frac{(-1)^2 + 5(-1) - 8}{(-1) - 3}$. When you clean everything up, you should get $\frac{(-12)}{(-4)}$, which reduces to 3.

**3) B**
We're used to seeing a number or a variable inside a function's parentheses, but it's unusual to see both at the same time. It shouldn't affect how we solve this, though. Like always, substitute the term in parentheses in for $x$ in the equation: $f(-2x) = 4(-2x) - 1$. Multiply by 4 to find that $f(-2x) = -8x - 1$. It's important to remember that function notation is really just a set of instructions for substitution. The rules don't change just because we're substituting something besides an ordinary number.

**4) C**
Don't get lost in the chart. The instructions for this question say that when we add the 2nd column to the 3rd column, we should get the first column. C is the answer because $f(0) + g(0) = 0$, which looks like this when we substitute: $1 + (-1) = 0$.

**5) 2**
Remember that $f(x) = y$, so we can plug the point into our function like this: $8 = 3^2 - 3 + c$. We can simplify and combine like terms to solve for $c$. First you should get $8 = 9 - 3 + c$, and then $8 = 6 + c$. Subtract 6 from both sides to find that $c = 2$.

**6) B**

This is a very common SAT question, and it doesn't take very long to solve if you know what you're looking for. We know what factors are, but they don't usually involve weird tables. We often see factors when we're working with quadratic equations. Suppose you had an equation like $y = x^2 - 16$. You would factor it to get $y = (x + 4)(x - 4)$, and then $x = \pm 4$, right? Remember why we do this? We want to find the values of $x$ where $y$ equals 0. The same logic applies here. We want to know the values of $x$ that make $y$, or $f(x)$ in this case, equal to 0. That happens when $x$ is equal to 3. And just like when we factor quadratics, the factor is a binomial: $x - 3$.

**7) C**

Focus on the end of the question. This is still function notation, but we need to go in the right order. Work from the inside out. We'll start with $g(1)$, which the question tells us is equal to 4. Now do $h(4)$, which is 2.

**8) D**

Be careful here. It's very tempting to just do $f(-1)$, which would give you -4. The $x + 2$ should tell you that there's more to this question than meets the eye. You need to recognize that the two parts in parentheses should be equal: $f(x + 2) = f(-1)$. In other words, -1 isn't equal to $x$. It's equal to $x + 2$. This means that $x$ is actually equal to -3 because $f(-3 + 2) = f(-1)$. We can substitute -3 into the function now: $3(-3) - 1 = -10$.

**9) B**

Just follow instructions: $f(0) = 5 - g(0)$. We don't know $g(0)$ yet, but we can find it: $g(0) = 0^2 - 1$. Now substitute -1 for $g(0)$ in our first equation: $f(0) = 5 - (-1)$. If you don't lose that extra negative, you should get that $f(0) = 6$.

**10) B**

This is another function with a weird thing inside the parentheses, and it can be difficult to understand what this question is saying. It's very similar to question #3. We're given $g(x)$, which is a function, AKA a set of instructions in the form of an equation. When we put numbers in for $x$, we follow the instructions and get a new number. But we can also put other variables or expressions in for $x$. Doing so doesn't give us new numbers, though. It gives us a new equation. That's our $g(x + k)$. If we take $x + k$ and substitute it in for $x$ in the original $g(x)$ function, we'll actually get to see how the equation changes: $g(x + k) = 4(x + k)^2 + 9$. FOIL the $x + k$ to get $4(x^2 + 2kx + k^2) + 9$. Distribute the 4 to all parts of the parentheses: $4x^2 + 8kx + 4k^2 + 9$. Why does this look so much different from the $g(x + k)$ equation that we were given? Because we haven't yet found $k$, a mystery number that will make everything line up perfectly. Compare the two equations: $4x^2 - 8x + 13 = 4x^2 + 8kx + 4k^2 + 9$. Notice that you can also compare specific terms. For example, both of the single $x$ terms look very similar: $-8x = 8kx$. If $k$ were -1, these terms would be exactly the same. We can test that theory with the non-$x$ terms: $13 = 4k^2 + 9$. Again, if $k$ were -1, these terms would be exactly the same. That's how we know that B is the answer.

**11) C**

Function notation can be translated into more understandable language. Essentially, numeral I is asking, "When $x$ is -2, does the function equal 2?" If we go to -2 on our $x$-axis, we can see that yes, the line's $y$-value is 2, so numeral I is true. Numeral II is also true because when $x$ equals $\frac{5}{2}$, our function is flat and the $y$-value is 2. Numeral III is not true because when $x$ is equal to 5, our function is below the $x$-axis and $y$ is actually equal to -2. So C is the answer.

**12) B**

This problem takes two ways of looking at functions and combines them into one question. If it helps, you can rearrange the equation in the question by adding $g(x)$ to both sides: $f(x) = g(x)$. Now it's clear that we're looking for a point where the $y$-value on our graph is equal to the second column in our table. The answer is -1 because the point (-1, 2) lies on the graph, and the same point is also in the table. In other words, $f(-1) - g(-1) = 0$.

**13) A**

Don't worry about the equation for $f(x)$. This is much more about the picture. All of the equations for $g(x)$ in the choices are straight horizontal lines. We want the line that is going to intersect $f(x)$ three times (has three real solutions). A line where $y$ is 4 will intersect three times.

**14) B**

Let's find $a$ first. The minimum value of our graph is at the point $(1, -2)$. In mathematical terms, we would say that the minimum occurs when $x = 1$, but that the actual minimum is -2, so $a = -2$. Now we can use the chart on the right to find $h(-2)$, which is 3.

**15) 79**

To figure out which equation to use, think about the variables we'll need to work with. The question gives us an initial velocity ($v_0$) and a height ($h$), and it wants a velocity at a different time ($v_t$). We should use the second equation (position-velocity) to solve, and we can start by plugging in the numbers we know: $v_t^2 = 300^2 - 2(32.2)(1300)$. We got the value of $g$ from the general information about the question. Squaring and multiplying gets us: $v_t^2 = 90{,}000 - 83{,}720$. You should get that $v_t^2 = 6{,}280$, and you can take the square root of both sides to get that $v_t = 79.25$, which rounds to 79 feet per second.

**16) 2484**

There are two ways of solving this, depending on how well you know physics. The easiest way requires that you know that when a projectile reaches its maximum height, its velocity will be 0. Think about a ball that you throw into the air. At some point, it's going to stop going up and start coming back down. For a split second at the top, that ball has a velocity of 0. We can use the second equation to solve for the maximum height: $0^2 = 400^2 - 2(32.2)(h)$. Squaring and multiplying gets you $0 = 160{,}000 - 64.4h$. You can move the $h$ term to the other side of the equals by adding: $64.4h = 160{,}000$. Divide by 64.4 to find $h = 2484.47205$, which rounds to 2484.

You can also solve this using the third equation, which is in the form of a quadratic. The maximum or minimum of a parabola can be found using the axis of symmetry equation: $x = \frac{-b}{2a}$. First, plug the numbers we know into the equation: $h = 400t - \frac{1}{2}(32.2)t^2$. The axis of symmetry will tell us the time when the projectile reaches its maximum height: $t = \frac{-400}{2(-16.1)}$. You should get that $t = 12.422$ seconds. Don't round too much because we now need to plug that number in for t to find the height at that time: $h = 400(12.422) - 16.1(12.422)^2$. This will simplify to 2484 feet.

## EXPONENT RULES

**1) A**

You can think of fractional exponents as two exponents in one. The denominator (bottom number) gives the root. For example, a denominator of 2 is a square root, and a denominator of 3 is a cube root. The numerator (top number) gives the exponent of whatever is under the root. In this case, the 2 tells us we're taking the square root, and the 3 tells us there's an $x^3$ under the radical: $x^{\frac{3}{2}} = \sqrt{x^3}$.

**2) C**

What would you have to do to $x^9$ to make it $x^{27}$? If you know your exponent rules, you know that raising an exponent to another exponent means you multiply the exponents. In this case, $(x^9)^3 = x^{27}$. So you would raise 3 to the third as well: $3^3 = 27$.

**3) D**

When you raise an exponent to an exponent, you multiply the exponents. So you can rewrite this equation as $x^{4k} = x^{36}$. Since these terms have the same base ($x$), you can set the exponents equal to each other: $4k = 36$. Dividing by 4 gets you $k = 9$.

**4) D**

Refer back to question #1 for rules about fractional exponents. We can rewrite this as $\sqrt[3]{8^2}$, which we can simplify a few different ways. The simplest is $\sqrt[3]{64}$, but you might not know the cube root of 64 off the top of your head. You might be better off simplifying the 8 into 2's: $\sqrt[3]{(2^3)^2}$, or $\sqrt[3]{2^6}$. The cube root of $2^6$ is $2^2$, which you know is 4.

**5) B**
You can distribute this exponent to each part of the term by multiplying the exponents by each other: $64^{\frac{1}{2}}a^3b^{\frac{5}{2}}$. You can simplify further by knowing $64^{\frac{1}{2}} = \sqrt{64} = 8$. So the simplified expression is $8a^3b^{\frac{5}{2}}$.

**6) B**
When you multiply exponential terms that have the same base, you add the exponents. So $(x^{a-1})(x^{a+1})$ can be rewritten as $x^{a-1+a+1}$. Combine like terms in the exponent and your new equation is $x^{2a} = x^{24}$. Since the bases are the same, you can set the exponents equal to each other: $2a = 24$. Divide by 2 to find that $a = 12$.

**7) C**
Since the area of the forest is increasing by 1.4 percent each year, we know we're looking for an exponential equation, which eliminates choices A and B (they're linear). An increase of 1.4 percent means that the term inside the parentheses should be $(1 + 0.014)$ because we need to convert our percentage into a decimal by moving the decimal point two places to the left. Add those numbers and multiply by the starting value to find the correct equation: $A(t) = 3(1.014)^t$.

**8) A**
Start by converting the cube root into an exponent: $(a^{-1}b^{9c})^{\frac{1}{3}}$. Now multiply the exponents for each term: $a^{-\frac{1}{3}}b^{\frac{9c}{3}}$. Simplify the exponent on the $b$ to get the answer: $a^{-\frac{1}{3}}b^{3c}$.

**9) A**
The $\frac{1}{2}$ as an exponent means we should take the square root: $\sqrt{36y^2}$. That gives us $6y$, which isn't exactly a choice. You'd probably guess choice A at this point anyway since it's the most similar. The reason we need the absolute value is that our expression should never be negative, even if our value for $y$ is. In the original expression, the $y^2$ means that we always have a positive number, so the absolute value lets us stay positive after we simplify.

**10) A**
In school, you might eliminate exponents by using logarithms, but you never need to use logs on the SAT. Instead, raise both sides of the equation by the reciprocal of the $y$ exponent: $x^{-\frac{1}{2}} = (y^{-2})^{-\frac{1}{2}}$. Since we're multiplying the exponents, the right side simplifies to $y^1$. The negative exponent means the left side can be rewritten as $\frac{1}{x^{\frac{1}{2}}}$, which is the same as $\frac{1}{\sqrt{x}}$.

**11) C**
Linear relationships increase or decrease by a constant amount. So choices A and B are linear because the amount of the increase does not change (always 200 people or \$5). Choices C and D involve percentages, which usually means an exponential relationship, but obviously they can't both be correct. Choice D is a one-time decrease of 8%, so it's not exponential. Choice C is exponential because the speed continues to decrease by 6% of its value each second.

**12) A**
Whenever you're dealing with exponents, you need to have the same base before you can combine terms. Both 4 and 8 can be converted into bases of 2: $4 = 2^2$ and $8 = 2^3$. Your new expression should look like this: $\frac{2^{2a}}{2^{3a}}$. When you divide exponential numbers, you subtract the exponents: $2^{2a-3b}$. Luckily, the question tells us that $2a - 3b = 24$, so $2^{2a-3b} = 2^{24}$. The SAT frequently sets up these convenient substitutions. Keep that in mind whenever you need to manipulate expressions. You might be surprised to find that the answer is closer than you think!

**13) B**
First off, cross off choices C and D. The term in parentheses should be a decimal representing the percent increase $(1 + 0.03)$. To decide between A and B, plug in for the number of days and weeks. If you wanted to know how many bacteria there were after 1 week, you could use the original equation and just plug in 7 for the number of days: $B = 450(1.03)^7$. Converting to weeks should give us the same equation when we plug in 1 for the number of weeks, which only happens with

choice B: $B = 450(1.03)^{7(1)}$.

**14) D**

Remember that dividing exponential numbers means you have to subtract the exponents. For the $x$ terms, you'd simplify like this: $\frac{x^{\frac{2}{3}}}{x^{-1}} = x^{\frac{2}{3}-(-1)} = x^{\frac{5}{3}}$. The $y$ terms are a little easier: $\frac{y^{-\frac{1}{2}}}{y^2} = y^{-\frac{1}{2}-2} = y^{-\frac{5}{2}}$. You can eliminate the negative exponent on the y by making it into the denominator of the fraction: $x^{\frac{5}{3}}y^{-\frac{5}{2}} = \frac{x^{\frac{5}{3}}}{y^{\frac{5}{2}}}$. Now convert the fractional exponents into roots: $\frac{\sqrt[3]{x^5}}{\sqrt{y^5}}$. You can simplify further by breaking apart the terms under the radicals and pulling out whatever you can take the root of, leaving the remainder under the radical: $\frac{x\sqrt[3]{x^2}}{y^2\sqrt{y}}$.

**15) D**

First of all, be careful with percent decrease. We still need to turn our percentages into decimals for the term in parentheses, but decreasing by 20% will look like this: $(1 - 0.20)$, which is 0.8. That gets rid of A and B. To figure out the exponent, we can plug in easy numbers. If it loses 20% of its value every 5 years, then we want our exponent to equal 1 when $t = 5$. We need to divide $t$ by 5, which means D is our answer.

**16) D**

This question is not that different from #15. First, you can eliminate choices A and B because those are not exponential equations (they're linear). To figure out what our exponent should be, we should plug in numbers. There are currently 400 photos on the site, and in 16 months there will be 800 photos. But since $n$ is the number of years, we'll have to convert using a proportion $\frac{12\,months}{1\,year} = \frac{16\,months}{n\,years}$. If you cross-multiply and divide, you should get that $n = \frac{4}{3}$. If you plug that into choice D, you get the exponent equal to 1, which gives us 800 photos—exactly what we wanted.

# Linear Equations

**1) D**

Almost every question about lines on the SAT will involve the basic line formula $y = mx + b$ in some way. Easier questions like this one will be fairly transparent about it. Remember that $m$ gives us the slope of the line and $b$ gives us the $y$-intercept. This graph has a $y$-intercept of 0 because it passes through the origin, so there won't be a $b$ in our equation. The slope is -1, which means that D is the answer.

**2) B**

Here's an example of a line question that tries to disguise the line formula. But if we rearrange the potato equation a bit, we can see that it matches nicely with our standard line equation: $P = -51h + 249$. Looking at it this way, it's clear that 249 is our $y$-intercept, or our $y$-value when $h$ is 0. In less mathematical terms, it's our starting point. Choice B basically says that there were 249 potatoes to start.

**3) B**

Instead of trying to come up with the line equation from the points, it's easier to pick a point and plug it into all the answer choices. Just keep in mind that the SAT absolutely loves to make the first point fit into multiple equations. In this case, the point (1, 3) lies on literally every one of these lines. But when we check the second point (2, 1), we can get down to one answer: $f(2) = 5 - 2(2) = 5 - 4 = 1$.

**4) A**

This is the reverse of question #1. We're given the equation and need to find the correct graph. It's easiest to start with the $y$-intercept, which is 2. That eliminates choices B and C, which show $y$-intercepts of -2. Next, we need to look at the slope. The equation has a slope of 3, which means that for every 3 units we go up, we move 1 unit to the right. Choice A is correct. Choice D shows a slope of $\frac{1}{3}$.

**5) $\frac{7}{4}$ or 1.75**

To solve this, we'll need to use slope formula,

which is one of the most important formulas for the SAT. You MUST memorize it! There are many ways to remember it:

"slope" $= \frac{rise}{run} = \frac{\Delta y}{\Delta x} = \frac{y_1 - y_2}{x_1 - x_2}$. We can take any two of the points on the graph and plug them into the equation. Let's choose the bottom point and the top point so our fractions have the same denominator: $\frac{\frac{33}{4} - (-\frac{37}{4})}{7 - (-3)}$. As long as you don't lose any negatives, you should get $\frac{\frac{70}{4}}{10}$, which simplifies to $\frac{7}{4}$. If you want to check, find some points that have easy coordinates and count the boxes. The $y$-intercept of the line is $(0, -4)$, and going up 7 units and to the right 4 units seems to land us exactly on $(3, 4)$, as we would expect.

**6) D**

Parallel lines have the same slope, so we're looking for an answer choice that has a slope of 2. Unfortunately, these choices aren't in our standard linear form. To be safe, we should manipulate these equations so they're in $y = mx + b$ form. For choice A, subtract $3x$ and then divide both sides by 6. You should get $y = -\frac{1}{2}x + \frac{1}{6}$, which has a slope of $-\frac{1}{2}$. Since that's not right, we have to check choice B. Subtract $x$ and divide by -2 to get $y = \frac{1}{2}x - \frac{7}{2}$. Still not right, so we'll try choice C, which will become $y = -2x - 3$. D is probably the answer, but you should check to be sure. Adding $4x$ and dividing by 2 gets you $y = 2x + \frac{9}{2}$, which has a slope of 2.

**7) $\frac{16}{5}$ or 3.2**

The $x$-intercept is the point where the line crosses the $x$-axis, so the $y$-coordinate is 0. Substitute 0 in for $y$, and the second term in the equation disappears, leaving us with $\frac{5}{8}x = 2$. You can eliminate the fraction by multiplying both sides by $\frac{8}{5}$ to get that $x = \frac{16}{5}$.

**8) B**

Once again, the SAT is using a story to distract us from the fact that this is just a question about lines. Match this equation up with $y = mx + b$, and you'll see that the 3 is functioning as the $m$, or slope. In SAT story questions about lines, the slope is usually a rate of some kind, telling us how something changes. In this case, it tells us the number of millimeters that the pencil shrinks with each sharpening, which is essentially choice B.

**9) B**

Lines are just a collection of points, and this question is asking us to find one of them. It says that the length of the pencil is 42 millimeters, so we should plug that into $L$ in our equation: $42 = 189 - 3n$. Subtract 189 from both sides: $-147 = -3n$. Divide by -3 to find that $n = 49$. If you accidentally plug 42 into the wrong variable, you'll get choice C, so always be careful on these!

**10) A**

Occasionally you'll need to know the locations of the four quadrants in the xy-plane. Quadrant I is in the top right; Quadrant II is in the top left; Quadrant III is the bottom left; and Quadrant IV is the bottom right. This line only goes through Quadrants I and IV, so it only goes up and down. The line $x = 3$ is completely vertical and passes through every point with an $x$-coordinate of 3.

**11) B**

For some reason, people tend to have trouble with questions like this. As always, match the parts up with our standard $y = mx + b$ format. The question is asking for a rate—how many additional minutes per question?—so we should look for the slope. When there's no number in front of our $x$, then the slope is 1, which is the answer. But if you're unsure, it's easy to plug in numbers. If there were 5 questions ($x = 5$), then it would take Bill 8 minutes to complete them($m = 5 + 3$). If there were one additional homework question ($x = 6$), then it would take

Bill 9 minutes to complete his assignment ($m = 6 + 3$). Now we have proof that each additional question requires 1 additional minute.

**12) B**

Parallel lines have the same slope, but perpendicular lines (which form 90 degree angles) have negative reciprocal slopes. We should rearrange the original equation into $y = mx + b$ form by subtracting $4x$ and dividing by -1 to get $y = 4x - 5$. Our slope is 4, so we're looking for an equation with a slope of $-\frac{1}{4}$. We get the negative reciprocal by flipping the fraction and multiplying it by -1. Let's rearrange choice A by adding $2x$ and dividing by 8 to get $y = \frac{1}{4}x + \frac{5}{4}$. Close, but not correct. Rearrange choice B by subtracting $x$ and dividing by 4 to get $y = -\frac{1}{4}x + \frac{5}{4}$. That's what we wanted, so there's no need to check the others.

**13) D**

You could try to answer this by coming up with the correct equation directly, but you can also plug in numbers to make sure you don't do something careless. First, we know that our starting point is 30 hours of battery life, which corresponds to the $y$-intercept of the line. Choices A and B can be eliminated because they have $y$-intercepts of 0. To find the correct slope, we should pick a point that we know lies on the line. According to the question, it takes 5 months for the battery to lose 1 hour of life, so we should expect that the point (5, 29) lies on the line. If we plug that point into choice C, we get $29 = 30 - 5(5)$, which isn't true. However, choice D gives us what we want: $29 = 30 - \frac{5}{5}$.

**14) B**

Even though the story is very confusing, we can still see that they are asking about the slope of the line because a is where our $m$ would be in the standard line equation ($y = mx + b$). Choices A and D do not correspond to any part of the standard line equation. Choice C is the $y$-intercept because it's the starting point. Choice B is the correct answer because it describes a rate of growth.

**15) C**

Even though most of the line questions on the SAT test slopes and $y$-intercepts, there's another part of the line equation that is often overlooked. In $y = mx + b$, $x$ and $y$ represent the coordinates of points on the line. If you're stuck on a line question, see if you can plug a point into $x$ and $y$. In this case, we can substitute $p$ in for $x$ and $q$ in for $y$ to get $q = ap - 3$. The question wants us to find the slope, which means we need to solve for $a$. Add 3 to both sides and divide by $p$ to get $\frac{q+3}{p}$.

**16) D**

This question takes a long time, but it's a good one to be able to solve because it tests almost everything you need to know about lines. Our first line has a slope of 1 and includes the point (6, 1), so we should plug those numbers into $y = mx + b$ and see what we get: $1 = (1)(6) + b$. We can solve for $b$ by subtracting 6 from both sides to get $b = -5$. Now we know that the equation of the first line is $y = x - 5$. The second equation gives us two points, so we should use the slope formula: $\frac{8-2}{-2-1} = \frac{6}{-3}$. This reduces to a slope of -2, which we can plug into $y = mx + b$, along with one of the points, to solve for $b$: $2 = (-2)(1) + b$. Add 2 to both sides to get that $b = 4$ and that our second line has an equation of $y = -2x + 4$. Now that we have our two equations, we can set them equal to each other to find the point of intersection: $x - 5 = -2x + 4$. Add $2x$ and 5 to both sides to get

$3x = 9$, so $x = 3$. We can find $y$ by plugging 3 into either of our equations: $y = 3 - 5$. Our point of intersection is (3, -2), which the question labels as $(a, b)$. The last step is to solve for $a - b$: $3 - (-2) = 5$.

**17) B**
Plug in numbers to turn this algebra into something you can actually see. If $a = 2$, then the line includes points (0, 2) and (2, 0). Plot those points on an $xy$-plane, and you'll see that the resulting line has a negative slope.

**18) C**
Since this is a linear function, we know that it has a constant slope. The chart gives us the $y$-intercept (0, 5), so we can use $y = mx + b$ to find the equation of the line. Pick another point and substitute the values for $x$ and $y$: $11 = m(3) + 5$. Subtract 5 and divide by 3 to find that $m = 2$. So the equation of the line is $y = 2x + 5$. To find $f(-1)$, plug -1 in for $x$: $2(-1) + 5 = 3$.

**19) C**
Lines have a constant slope, and we can create an equation based on that fact. This question actually gives us three points to work with: $(3, a)$, $(a, 27)$, and (0, 0), which is the origin. Use $\frac{\Delta y}{\Delta x}$ to set the slopes equal to each other: $\frac{a-0}{3-0} = \frac{27-0}{a-0}$. Simplifying gets you a proportion: $\frac{a}{3} = \frac{27}{a}$. Cross-multiply to get $a^2 = 81$, and take the square root to find that $a = 9$.

**20) A**
Each of these answer choices is essentially giving you a point, which you can test in the equation to see if it lies on the line. We know that the starting point, or $y$-intercept, is (0, 509) because of the equation. Choice A tells us that (380, 499) should lie on the line because it represents a decrease of 10 meters from the starting point (509 – 10) after 380 days. Substitute the point into the equation to test it: $499 = -\frac{1}{38}(380) + 509$. Multiplying the fraction by 380 simplifies the equation to $499 = -10 + 509$, which checks out. So A is the answer.

**21) C**
Most scatterplot questions on the SAT will involve lines. This first question wants us to find a point that lies on the line. The age is 62, so we should find that value on the $x$-axis. Go up to the line to find the corresponding $y$-value, which is approximately 66.

**22) C**
If you look at the choices, there are only two sets of words that change, so we should focus on those differences. First, we need to decide between "actual" and "predicted". Since they're asking about the line of best fit, we know that we're looking at predicted values. Basically, the dots represent the actual data, and the line is an estimation of the trend. This eliminates choices A and B. Next, we need to decide between the "percentage" and "number" of eligible voters. We should just look at the $y$-axis, which is labeled to tell us the answer: "percentage of eligible voters who participated in election." The distinction between percentages and actual numbers is commonly tested on the SAT, but they almost always tell you explicitly in the question when you're working with percentages.

**23) D**
This question is very tricky, so don't rush to judgment. Many students pick choice B because it seems to match with the graph. First, be careful finding the slope. If you just count the boxes, you'll get $\frac{3}{4}$, but the scales on the $x$ and $y$-axes are different, so we have to actually calculate the slope using the formula. The line of best fit seems to pass through (35, 52) and (50, 60), so set up your slope equation: $\frac{60-52}{50-35}$. This simplifies to $\frac{8}{15}$, which means we can eliminate choices A and B. If you pick different points to use, you might get a different value, but it should still be a lot closer to $\frac{8}{15}$ than it is to $\frac{3}{4}$. We also need to be careful

of the $y$-intercept. Even though it looks like the intercept is 44, it's actually not even close. Again, the scale of the axis is throwing us off. The line of best fit hits the axis at (20, 44), but the $y$-intercept is supposed to be where $x = 0$. You can pick D at this point because you know that choice C is wrong, but you can figure out the $y$-intercept using $y = mx + b$, plugging in a point that we know: $60 = \frac{8}{15}(50) + b$. When we multiply the fraction by 50, we get $\frac{80}{3}$. Subtract that from 60 to find that the y-intercept is $\frac{100}{3}$.

**24) C**

This can be tough to visualize, so it's helpful if you can plug in sensible points to test each option. First, when $D = 22$, we know that $E = 0$. We'll use the point (22, 0) as a baseline. To test numeral I, we should increase our $x$ by 1, so $D = 23$. Plugging in that value, we'll see that $E = \frac{5}{6}(23 - 22)$, which means that $E = \frac{5}{6}$. Since that's the increase we were expecting, we know that numeral I is true. To test numeral II, we should plug in 1 for $E$ and solve for $D$: $1 = \frac{5}{6}(D - 22)$. Multiply both sides by $\frac{6}{5}$, then add 22 to both sides. You should get that $D = 23.2$, which is an increase of 1.2, as expected. Since we know that both numeral I and numeral II work, we now know the answer must be C. We don't need to check numeral III, but you could using the same method. Plug in $22\frac{5}{6}$ for $D$: $E = \frac{5}{6}\left(22\frac{5}{6} - 22\right)$. The parentheses will simplify so you have $E = \frac{5}{6}\left(\frac{5}{6}\right)$, which means $E$ will increase by $\frac{25}{36}$ instead of 1.

# Quadratics

**1) C**

It's much easier to factor quadratics when the $x^2$ coefficient is equal to 1, so divide by 3 to simplify the equation to $x^2 + 2x - 8 = 0$. Factor into $(x - 2)(x + 4) = 0$. Remember that the solutions need to make each term equal to 0, so $x$ can be 2 and -4.

**2) C**

The vocabulary in this question makes it a little tricky, but the SAT is still talking about the same properties of lines and quadratics that they always do. The rate of change of a line is its slope. Regardless of whether the slope is positive or negative, a line will always cross the $x$-axis at some point. (The only exception is when the slope is 0.) The zeros of a quadratic are—by definition—the $x$-intercepts, so a quadratic with no real zeros has no $x$-intercepts.

**3) C**

It's very tempting to set each term equal to 18, but that's not quite how factoring works. You can only do that when you're setting the terms equal to 0, so we need to rearrange the equation. Start by distributing the $x$ to both parts of the parentheses: $x^2 + 3x = 18$. Subtract 18 from both sides: $x^2 + 3x - 18 = 0$. Now you can factor: $(x + 6)(x - 3) = 0$. The solutions would be -6 and 3.

**4) 18**

With everything else that you need to know about quadratics, it's easy to forget that they are just a series of points. When you have a point, plug it into the equation: $2 = 4(3)^2 - b(3) + 20$. This simplifies to $2 = 56 - 3b$. Subtract 56 and divide by -3 to find that $b = 18$.

**5) 0 or 4**

Since both equations are equal to $y$, we can set them equal to each other: $x^2 - 2x + 1 = 2x + 1$. Subtract $2x$ and 1 to get this equation equal to 0: $x^2 - 4x = 0$. Factor out an $x$: $x(x - 4) = 0$. The solutions are 0 and 4.

**6) B**

You don't actually need to know the vertex for this question. The vertex will always be between the two $x$-intercepts, so just find the zeros of $f$, which are -5 and -1.

**7) C**

This is a fancy way of asking for the solutions for a system of equations. Set the first equation equal to 36: $(x - 9)^2 = 36$.
FOIL: $x^2 - 18x + 81 = 36$. Subtract 36 to get the equation equal to 0: $x^2 - 18x + 45 = 0$. You can factor into $(x - 15)(x - 3) = 0$, which means that the intersection points are at 15 and 3. The length of line $AB$ is the distance between these two points, which you can get by subtracting: $15 - 3 = 12$.

**8) A**

Because of the way these equations are set up, you can substitute for either $x$ or $y$. It's probably easier to substitute the second equation in for $y$ in the first equation so that you don't need to worry about FOILing: $x = x^2 - 2x - 9 - 1$. Combine like terms and subtract $x$ to get $0 = x^2 - 3x - 10$. Factor into $0 = (x - 5)(x + 2)$ to find that the solutions occur when $x$ is 5 and -2. But be careful. The question is asking for the $y$-coordinate of the solutions, so you need to plug these values back into one of the original equations. The first equation is the simplest: $5 = y - 1$ and $-2 = y - 1$. The two $y$-coordinates are 6 and -1, so A is the answer.

**9) D**

Start by FOILing the equation: $y = x^2 - 2x - 15$. The minimum occurs at the vertex, so we'll need to complete the square. To do that, take half of the $b$ term and square it, then simultaneously add and subtract that number (to keep the equation balanced). An organized equation will look like this: $y = (x^2 - 2x + 1) - 15 - 1$. Factoring the term in parentheses and combining the -15 and -1 gets you the vertex form of the quadratic: $y = (x - 1)^2 - 16$. The vertex of this quadratic would be $(1 - 16)$.

**10) A**

This system is best solved by combining the two equations, which conveniently eliminates the $y$ terms: $x^2 + 2x = 3$. Subtract 3 from both sides: $x^2 + 2x - 3 = 0$. Factor into $(x + 3)(x - 1) = 0$ to find that the $x$-coordinates of the solutions are -3 and 1. But again, the SAT wants the $y$-coordinates, so you need to plug the $x$ values back into one of the equations: $2(-3) + y = 1$ and $2(1) + y = 1$. Solve to find that $y$ could be 7 or -1, making A the answer.

**11) A**

The SAT usually asks questions like this about lines, but occasionally you'll see a quadratic. Just like with lines, the term without an $x$ (referred to as the $c$ term for quadratics) gives us the $y$-intercept. In this case, 105 is the $y$-intercept. Again thinking back to lines, we know that the $y$-intercept usually means the starting point when the question involves a story. Choice A describes a starting point.

**12) D**

You can solve this question by drawing a simple graph. In question #6, we said that the vertex is between the two $x$-intercepts. Since parabolas are symmetrical, we also know that the vertex is exactly halfway between the two $x$-intercepts. In this case, the $x$-distance from (-2, 0) to (2, -9) is 4 units because $2 - (-2) = 4$. The point $(k, 0)$ should also lie 4 $x$-units away from the vertex, but in the other direction, which would be where $x$ is equal to 6.

**13) A**

Start by crossing out any graph that does not have zeros at 2 and -4, which means eliminating B and D. The second sentence of this question sounds complicated, but it really just means that the $y$ values are always less than or equal to 3. Choice C can't be right because there are clearly points on the parabola that are higher than $y = 3$. Choice A is the answer because the maximum of the parabola occurs where $y = 3$, so all of the other points on the parabola are less than 3.

**14) A**

You could try to solve this by distributing the $k$ and carrying it through the entire process, but that makes the question unnecessarily complicated and increases the chances that you'll make a mistake. Instead, pick a number for $k$. Since the question says it just needs to be a positive constant, we should say that $k = 1$ so it's like it's not even there. Now you can FOIL the equation: $y = x^2 - 4x - 12$. To find the vertex, complete the square: $y = (x^2 - 4x + 4) - 12 - 4$. This simplifies to $y = (x + 2)^2 - 16$. The question wants the $y$-coordinate of the vertex, which would be -16. Since we said $k = 1$, it's obvious that A is the answer.

**15) A**

As always, this quadratic will be easier to work with if $x^2$ is by itself, so divide the entire equation by 3: $0 = x^2 - 6x + 2$. Unfortunately, this isn't factorable. To find the solutions, we'll need to use the quadratic formula, which you need to memorize if you're reaching for those top math scores: $x = \frac{-b \pm \sqrt{b^2 - 4ac}}{2a}$. Substitute in the correct values: $x = \frac{-(-6) \pm \sqrt{(-6)^2 - 4(1)(2)}}{2(1)}$, which simplifies to $x = \frac{6 \pm \sqrt{28}}{2}$. Before you spend time simplifying the radical, it's worthwhile to take a look at what this means in terms of our solutions. Another way to put it is that our solutions will be $3 + \frac{\sqrt{28}}{2}$ and $3 - \frac{\sqrt{28}}{2}$. The question wants the sum of those solutions, which means the radical terms will cancel each other out, so there's no real need to simplify them. The sum is just $3 + 3 = 6$. Notice that answer choice B is the right answer...if the question had been asking you to find the difference between the two solutions. It's the right answer to the wrong question, in other words. Read carefully, my homies.

**16) B**

There are many ways of solving this question. The easiest is probably to graph the two equations, substituting each of the answer choices in for $a$ and $b$. If there are two intersection points, then you've found your answer. Another strategy is to set the equations equal to each other and solve for $x$. You would get an equation that looks like this: $x = \sqrt{\frac{2 + b}{a}}$. For this system to have two solutions, the number under the radical would need to be greater than 0. Plugging in choice A gives you $x = \sqrt{\frac{2 + 2}{-4}}$, which can't be right because you can't take the square root of a negative number. Choice B gives you $x = \sqrt{\frac{2 - 4}{-2}}$, which reduces to $x = \sqrt{1}$. Choice B is our answer because there are two possible values of $x$: 1 and -1.

## Shape Geometry

**1) B**

Pairs of parallel lines form a lot of congruent angles when a third line intersects them. In this case, the angle on the bottom right of the point where lines $k$ and $\ell$ intersect is also equal to $y$ because both are alternate interior angles (knowing the vocabulary is much less important than knowing the rule). The angles $x$ and $y$ are supplementary, which means they add to 180°. Subtract 128° from 180° and you'll get that $y$ is equal to 52°. Since there's no note, we can assume that this picture is drawn to scale, so there's no way that C or D could be the answer because they're greater than 180.

**2) D**

This is a quadrilateral (a 4-sided figure), which means that all of its interior angles add to 360°. You can represent this with an equation: $x + 2x + x + 90 = 360$. Combine like terms: $4x + 90 = 360$. Subtract 90 and divide by 4 to find that $x = 67.5°$. But this question is asking about angle $ABC$, so $2x = 135°$.

**3) $\frac{5}{12}$ or 0.416 or 0.417**

We can find the fraction of the area by looking at the fraction of the degrees because different aspects of a circle are in proportion. In other words, the fraction of the area that is shaded is the same as the fraction of the degrees that make up the shaded area: $\frac{150}{360}$. This can be reduced to $\frac{5}{12}$.

**4) 63**
We can use angle constants to label more of the angles on the diagram. Angles that lie on a straight line are supplementary and add to 180. This means that the angle just below $111°$ is $69°$, and the angle just above $132°$ is $48°$. Next we can use the fact that there are always $180°$ in a triangle to get the angle opposite $x$: $180 - 69 - 48 = 63$. Angle $x$ is also $63°$ because vertical angles are congruent.

**5) 9**
Since the lines are parallel, we know that triangle $ABE$ is also a right triangle. We can use Pythagorean Theorem to find the length of EB: $EB^2 + 4^2 = 5^2$. Square the terms: $EB^2 + 16 = 25$. Subtract to get $EB^2 = 9$, so $EB = 3$. You should try to remember that 3–4–5 triangles are common on the SAT. You won't need to use Pythagorean Theorem if you can quickly recognize these triangles and their multiples (6–8–10, 9–12–15, etc.). These are similar triangles, so we can compare the side lengths by setting up a proportion: $\frac{EB}{DC} = \frac{AB}{AC}$. Plug in the values you know: $\frac{3}{DC} = \frac{5}{15}$. Cross-multiply and divide to find that $DC = 9$.

**6) B**
Instead of solving this algebraically, you can pick numbers for the length and width. If the width were equal to 1, then the length would be 5 because the question says it's 4 inches longer. The perimeter is the sum of all the sides, which means two lengths and two widths: $p = 2l + 2w$. In our case that's $p = 2(5) + 2(1) = 12$. Now plug in 1 for $w$ in our choices. You'll see that only choice B also gives us a perimeter of 12.

**7) D**
When you have two sides of a right triangle, use Pythagorean Theorem to find the third: $5^2 + BD^2 = 13^2$. Square and subtract to find that $BD^2 = 144$, so $BD = 12$. When you have only one side of a triangle, you're probably working with one of the special right triangles that are described in the SAT reference chart at the beginning of the section. $ABD$ is a 45-45-90 right triangle, which means the sides are always in the proportion listed in the chart. If $BD$ is 12, then $AB$ is $12\sqrt{2}$.

**8) C**
Since this is a rectangle, all of the big angles are $90°$. Since $BDC$ is $30°$, we know that $DBC$ is $60°$, making triangle $BCD$ a 30-60-90 right triangle. The proportions of the side lengths are given in the SAT reference chart. The short leg ($BC$) is equal to 6, so the long leg ($DC$) is equal to $6\sqrt{3}$.

**9) 10**
The formula for the volume of a cylinder is given in the SAT reference chart: $V = \pi r^2 h$. Plug in the values that you're given: $100\pi = \pi r^2(4)$. Divide by $4\pi$ to get that $r^2 = 25$ and $r = 5$. But be careful! the question is asking for the diameter. Double the radius to find that the diameter is 10 inches.

**10) 40**
On most SAT geometry questions, the information will already be placed on the diagram for you. This question is purposely leaving it off to make the question harder. Be organized and label the line segments as follows: $AD = 200$, $AE = 160$, $EB = 40$, and $EC = 32$. These are similar triangles because they have all the same angle measures ($AED$ and $BEC$ are congruent vertical angles). We're going to need to set up a proportion, but make sure you're comparing the right sides: $\frac{BC}{AD} = \frac{EC}{AE}$. We do not need $EB$ at all. We have to compare $EC$ and $AE$ because they are both next to the congruent angles. Substitute in the numbers you know: $\frac{x}{200} = \frac{32}{160}$. Cross-multiply to get $160x = 6400$. Divide to get that $x = 40$.

**11) C**
Just like in #3, we are working with a part of a circle. This time we'll set up a proportion that compares the angle of the part to the

whole 360° and the length of $AB$ to the whole circumference. First, the reference chart tells us the circumference formula: $C = 2\pi r$. The circumference of this circle is $20\pi$. Our proportion is $\frac{72}{360} = \frac{AB}{20\pi}$. Cross-multiply and divide to find that $AB = 4\pi$.

**12) 30**
Notice that we have two sides of the big triangle $ABC$, so we can use Pythagorean Theorem to find $BC$: $32^2 + BC^2 = 40^2$. Use your calculator to help you square and solve: $BC = 24$. Now we have two sides of the smaller triangle $BCD$, so we can use Pythagorean Theorem a second time: $18^2 + 24^2 = BD^2$. Square and solve to find that $BD = 30$.

**13) B**
$CD$ is the short leg of a 30-60-90 right triangle. Use the reference chart to find that $CB = 2\sqrt{3}$. The big triangle $ABC$ is also a 30-60-90, and now $CB$ is the short leg. If $CB = 2\sqrt{3}$ is our $x$ value and $AC = x\sqrt{3}$, then $AC$ would be $(2\sqrt{3})(\sqrt{3})$, which is $2 \times 3 = 6$.

**14) 9**
You can figure this out using Algebra. The area of a rectangle is length times width, and the question tells us that $l = w + 3$. Substitute this expression in for $l$ in our area equation: $108 = (w + 3)(w)$. Distribute: $108 = w^2 + 3w$. Subtract 108 so we can factor: $0 = w^2 + 3w - 108$. No one would blame you for not knowing the factors of 108, but you can use a calculator to guess and check your way to $0 = (w + 12)(w - 9)$, which means that $w = -12$ and $w = 9$. Since you can't have a negative length, our width must be 9.

**15) C**
One of the few formulas that is not included in the reference chart is the surface area of a cube: $6(side)^2$. Match that up with the expression they give us, and we find that $k$ represents the side length (the sides, or edges, of a cube are all equal). The perimeter of a square is 4 times the side length, so the perimeter of a face of this cube would be $4k$.

**16) D**
Most of the first sentence simply describes what is obvious from the figure. However, there's one very important piece of information: "$JK$ and $KL$ are tangent to the circle." A line that is tangent to a circle will form a 90° angle with the circle's radius. In other words, $OJ$ is perpendicular to $JK$. The entire shape $JKLO$ is a quadrilateral, which means that its angles add up to 360°. We can create an equation: $360 = 90 + 50 + 90 + \angle JOL$. Solve to find that $\angle JOL = 130°$. Before we can set up a proportion to compare the different parts of the circle, we need to find the area of the entire circle. Use the area formula from the reference chart ($A = \pi r^2$) to find that the total area is $36\pi$. The proportion should be $\frac{130}{360} = \frac{x}{36\pi}$, where $x$ is the shaded area. You can probably see that $x = 13\pi$.

## Soh-Cah-Toa

**1) A**
Trigonometry confuses a lot of people because there are so many rules and formulas and identities... It's overwhelming. But luckily, the SAT only tests two trigonometry ideas. Memorize them and you'll be in great shape for the one trigonometry question you're likely to see. The most important thing to memorize is soh-cah-toa, which tells you the ratios for the trigonometry functions. This question wants the cosine of $A$, so we'll use the "cah" portion of soh-cah-toa. "Cah" reminds us that cosine is equal to the adjacent side over the hypotenuse. Since we're looking at angle $A$, the adjacent side is 3. You can find the hypotenuse ($AB$) by using Pythagorean Theorem, but it will be very helpful to remember that 3-4-5 right triangles are common on the SAT. Either way, the hypotenuse is 5, so the cosine of $A$ is equal to $\frac{3}{5}$.

**2) B**

This question gives us the sine of $A$, so we'll focus on the "soh" portion of soh-cah-toa, which reminds us that the sine of an angle is equal to the opposite side over the hypotenuse. We can create an equation using the information in the question and the lengths on the diagram: $\frac{4}{5} = \frac{\overline{BC}}{20}$. Cross-multiply and divide to find that $BC$ is 16. Now we need the "toa" portion of soh-cah-toa to find the tangent of angle $B$. "Toa" reminds us that the tangent of $B$ will be equal to the opposite side ($AC$) divided by the adjacent side ($BC$), which is $\frac{12}{16}$. This reduces to $\frac{3}{4}$.

**3) B**

This question tests the other trigonometry idea that you need to memorize: $\sin(x) = \cos(90 - x)$. Comparing this rule with the equation in the question, we can see that $y = 90 - x$. If we add the $x$ to the other side, we can more clearly see what we're looking for: $x + y = 90$. The only choice where this is not true is choice B.

**4) C**

Most SAT trigonometry problems won't require the use of a calculator. This one feels like it does, but only because the cosine is given as a decimal. We're used to seeing these values as fractions, so it's probably a good idea to convert 0.6 into its equivalent fraction, which is $\frac{3}{5}$. If $\cos A = \frac{3}{5}$, then $\frac{3}{5} = \frac{12}{AB}$ because cosine is the adjacent side divided by the hypotenuse. Cross-multiply and divide to find that the hypotenuse is 20. This question wants the length of $BC$, so we should use Pythagorean Theorem: $12^2 + BC^2 = 20^2$. When you finish the arithmetic, you'll find that $BC$ is 16. You could have also seen that this is yet another 3-4-5 right triangle.

**5) 4/5 or 0.8**

This question is hinting pretty hard that we're going to use the $\sin(x) = \cos(90 - x)$ rule. If $\sin(x) = \frac{4}{5}$, then $\cos(90 - x)$ also equals $\frac{4}{5}$.

**6) C**

This question is all about soh-cah-toa. Go choice by choice until you find one that gives you $\frac{a}{b}$. For choice A, the cosine of $A$ is $\frac{b}{AB}$. We don't know the value of the hypotenuse, but it probably won't matter, so don't worry about it for now. Choice A is not looking like $\frac{a}{b}$ even without knowing the hypotenuse. Choice B is $\frac{a}{AB}$, which is also not quite right. Choice C is $\frac{a}{b}$, which is what we want. You can check D is you want, but it gives us $\frac{b}{a}$.

**7) 0.6 or $\frac{3}{5}$**

There are two ways to solve this, depending on which of the two trigonometry ideas you feel more comfortable with. If you want to use soh-cah-toa, convert 0.6 into $\frac{3}{5}$. This tells us that the side adjacent to $y$ is 3 and the hypotenuse is 5. The sine of $x$ will be the opposite side over the hypotenuse, which uses the exact values we just labeled. The sine of $x$ is also $\frac{3}{5}$. If you used the $\sin(x) = \cos(90 - x)$ idea, you would know that $y = 90 - x$ because that's how it is in every right triangle. So $\cos y = \sin x$.

**8) B**

Use soh-cah-toa to find equivalent ways to express the fraction. To make our lives easier, let's label $AB$ (the hypotenuse) side $c$ for now. The "cah" tells us that $\cos A = \frac{b}{c}$, and the "soh" tells us that $\cos B = \frac{b}{c}$. Put those fractions back together and you get: $\frac{\cos A}{\sin B} = \frac{\frac{b}{c}}{\frac{b}{c}}$.
This reduces to 1.

**9) C**

This one looks tricky, but the answer choices are giving us a hint about what to do. They all involve sine, so we should think about the "soh" part of soh-cah-toa. We can make an equation: $\sin A = \frac{a}{AB}$. This helps a lot because now we can solve for $AB$. Multiply both sides by $AB$ to get $\overline{AB} \sin A = a$. Divide by $\sin A$ to get that $\overline{AB} = \frac{a}{\sin A}$.

**10) C**

The equation where sine equals cosine should make us think of the $\sin(x) = \cos(90 - x)$ rule. To put it in terms of $a$ and $b$: $\sin(a) = \cos(90 - a)$. This does not mean that $a = b$, but it does mean that $b = 90 - a$ because $\cos b = \cos(90 - a)$. We can substitute the other two equations for $a$ and $b$: $4x + 14 = 90 - (2x + 10)$. Distribute the negative: $4x + 14 = 90 - 2x - 10$. Combine like terms: $4x + 14 = 80 - 2x$. Now add $2x$ and subtract 14 to get $6x = 66$. Divide to find that $x = 11$.

**11) $\frac{4}{5}$ or 0.8**

This question has a lot of text, but the very end of the question tells us that it's about trigonometry. We also know that the sides of $ABC$ are 4 times the corresponding sides of $DEF$, so $AB$ is 40 and $CB$ is 24. In order to find the cosine of $A$, we'll need the length of $AC$. We can use Pythagorean Theorem or recognize that this is yet another 3-4-5 right triangle. Either way, the length of $AC$ is 32. The cosine of $A$ is $\frac{32}{40}$, which can be reduced to $\frac{4}{5}$.

**12) 60**

Yet again, we're working with 3-4-5 right triangles and soh-cah-toa. If sine of $A$ is $\frac{3}{5}$, then we can set up the proportion $\frac{3}{5} = \frac{12}{AB}$ to find that $AB$ is 20. If sine of $C$ is $\frac{4}{5}$, then we can set up the proportion $\frac{4}{5} = \frac{12}{BC}$ to find that $BC$ is 15. There are a lot of ways to get the remaining side of $ABC$. You can see that triangle $BCD$ is a 3-4-5 triangle in the proportion 9-12-15 (so $DC$ is 9) and that triangle $ABD$ is a 3-4-5 triangle in the proportion 12-16-20 (so $AD$ is 16), so the total length of $AC$ would be 25. Or you could have recognized that triangle $ABC$ is itself a 3-4-5 triangle in the proportion 15-20-25, so $AC$ is 25. Regardless, the perimeter of $ABC$ is the sum of its sides: $20 + 15 + 25 = 60$.

**13) D**

If you're not confident with trigonometry, you might be intimidated by the answer choices, but you can still use basic knowledge of soh-cah-toa to intelligently eliminate choices that don't make sense. Let's temporarily label side $AB$ as $c$ so that we have a convenient placeholder. The question wants the sine of $B$, which would be $\frac{b}{c}$. Just looking at the answers, we know that choices A and C probably won't be correct because we need a $b$ on the top of the fraction. You can also eliminate choice B because the bottom of the fraction won't be only $a$ because the hypotenuse of a right triangle cannot equal one of its legs. That leaves D, which happens to be the answer. The reason is that we could figure out the value of c in terms of $a$ and b using Pythagorean Theorem: $a^2 + b^2 = c^2$. Taking the square root would give us that $c = \sqrt{a^2 + b^2}$. If we plugged that expression in for $c$ in our sine of $B$ equation, we'd still get choice D.

**14) C**

The question tells us that $\tan 36° = 0.73$. We also know that the tangent of an angle is the opposite side over the adjacent side, which means that the tangent of $36°$ is also equal to the height of the palm tree divided by 40. We can combine these two equations: $0.73 = \frac{\text{height}}{40}$. Find the height by multiplying 0.73 and 40. Unfortunately, this is not a calculator question, so you need to multiply by hand. You should get that the height is 29.2, which is approximately 29 feet.

**15) 8**

Notice that the tangent involves a 4 and a 3, so we're probably looking at 3-4-5 right triangles again. The tangent of angle $B$ is equal to $\frac{AC}{CB}$. We are given the value of $CB$, so we can set up this proportion: $\frac{4}{3} = \frac{AC}{15}$. Cross-multiply and divide to find that $AC$ is equal to 20. We can now find the full length of AB using 3-4-5 triangles or Pythagorean Theorem. Either way, $AB$ is equal to 25. Since $EB$ is 15, $AE$ must be 10. The small triangle $AED$ is similar to the big triangle $ABC$ because they both have right angles and they share angle $A$. That means that $AED$ is also a 3-4-5 triangle, but in the proportion 6-8-10 (because $AE$ is the hypotenuse). $AD$ is 8 because it corresponds to side $AC$ in the big triangle, which was also the "4" side of the big 3-4-5 triangle.

**16) 0**
It's smart to draw point $E$ somewhere on $DC$. The answer you get for the question won't change regardless of where you put $E$, but there are easier places to locate it to get to the answer quickly. My favorite is to put it at the same point as $C$. Now angle $ABE$ is a right angle, and $\sin 90° = 1$, and $EBC$ is an angle of zero degrees, and $\cos 0° = 1$, so $\sin ABE - \cos EBC = 1 - 1 = 0$.

## Charts and Graphs

**1) B**
Many chart and graph questions on the SAT are really just about reading the question. There's almost no math involved! This question directs us to the $y$-axis (rate of snowfall), so we need to look for an interval where the graph is going down then going up. That happens between 12pm and 2pm, so B is the answer. Choice C is the exact opposite, so make sure you read carefully!

**2) C**
In the story, the train stops for an hour, which means that its distance won't change. We're looking for a long, flat line. It looks like the train was stopped from 2:45pm to 3:45pm. Since the question wants to know when the train restarts, the answer is C.

**3) C**
Remember from line questions that the rate of change is usually represented by the slope. Since this question wants the fastest rate of increase, you are looking for the steepest slope in the positive direction, which is between 2 and 3 hours.

**4) D**
All the bars should add up to 21,700,000, so we'll need the units on the $y$-axis to be pretty large. Even at hundreds of thousands, 2013 would only be 600,000 records sold—way too little to get us to 21,700,000. The answer is D, and you could estimate the heights of the bars and add them up to double check.

**5) C**
The number of records sold in 2009 is approximately 2.5 million, and the number of records sold in 2013 is approximately 6 million. You can ignore the millions and just make a fraction from the numbers: $\frac{2.5}{6}$. Enter it in your calculator, and you'll get 0.41666, which is very close to 0.4, or $\frac{2}{5}$. (The actual value for 2009 is 2.4 million, which would give you 0.4 exactly.)

**6) A**
Remember that a line of best fit is an estimation based on the actual values, which are the plotted points. If a point is above the line of best fit, then it means the actual value was greater than we'd expect. This question wants the opposite—when the actual value is less than the line of best fit. In other words, the line of best fit overestimated the actual value. Just count the points below the line! There are 5 points out of 12 total.

**7) B**
The point that lies on the $y$-value 70 is a little greater than 1.5 hours of exercise per week. The line of best fit crosses the $y$-value of 70 at a little less than 2.5 hours of exercise per week. The question wants the difference, which would be a little less than an hour. Since the question wants the answer in minutes, the only value that is

slightly less than 60 minutes is B.

**8) C**
This question involves some important math vocabulary. First, a weak association is one where the points are very spread out. These points are fairly close together. We could draw a line of best fit pretty easily based on the points, so this would be a strong association. It's also a positive association because our line of best fit would go from the bottom left to the top right. Basically, as the $x$-values increase, the $y$-values also increase. If there were no relationship, then we would not be able to draw a line of best fit.

**9) C**
Two days with the same temperature will be above and below each other at the same $x$-value. This happens when the temperature is 86 degrees. The difference between the points is slightly less than one box on the graph, so we want an answer that is slightly less than 75 visitors. Choice C is the only one that works.

**10) B**
The day with the most visitors is the point with the greatest $y$-value. That point is (94, 600), so the temperature is 94 degrees Fahrenheit. We need to plug 94 in for F in the equation and solve. First subtract 32 and you'll get 62. Divide by 1.8 to get 34.4 degrees Celsius.

**11) C**
On the SAT, charts and graphs frequently contain information you don't end up using. However, the instructions that accompany the charts and graphs rarely have extra information, so make sure you read carefully. This set of questions requires that you understand the story and create the right equation. The story tells us that "the force... can be found by multiplying the mass... by a friction constant." Turn this into an equation: $F = mc$. Having the equation makes this question much easier because we can plug our values into the right variables. The mass is 20, and the constant for copper is 3.5, so our equation should be $F = (20)(3.5)$. Multiply to find that the force is 70 newtons.

**12) B**
Return to the equation at the heart of this story: $F = mc$. This is actually the equation of a line, and we can see that the scatterplot is roughly in the shape of a line. The mass is our $x$, and the force is our $y$. That makes the friction constant the slope of the line. You can solve for it by plugging in a point that would come close to the line of best fit. The point (15, 100) is in the middle of the pack. Plugging those values into our equation gives $100 = 15c$. Dividing by 15 should give you that $c$ is approximately 6.7. Even though none of the materials has that exact constant, there is only one that is close—wood.

**13) B**
We're given the force and the material, so we need to plug those values into the equation to find the mass. Since we're dealing with two different materials, we'll have to do this twice. First for aluminum: $200 = m(4.6)$. Divide by 4.6 to find that m is approximately 43.5 kilograms. For brass: $200 = m(4.3)$. Divide by 4.3 to find that m is approximately 46.5. The difference between them is approximately 3 kilograms.

**14) D**
Another way to phrase this question is "how many times does $y = 3.5$?" Go up the $y$-axis to 3.5 and go across. You'll intersect the graph 4 times.

**15) C**
Cassandra's office is 4 miles from her house, but she travels 8 miles because she has to ride her bicycle to work in the morning and back home at night. She also travels an extra 2 miles during the middle of the day to get to and return from her lunch meeting. Cassandra's dinner appears to be along her route home, so the total is just 10 miles.

**16) B**
This is confusing because the units on the $x$-axis aren't labeled with the actual time. That's up to us. Label $x = 0$ as 8am. Continuing along, $x = 4$ is 12pm and $x = 10$ is 6pm. She's does not leave her office till a little bit after 6pm, so that can't be the answer. Two hours later, at $x = 12$, or 8pm, Cassandra is at dinner because her distance is shown as a flat line (i.e. she isn't moving).

# statistics

**1) C**
Most SAT statistics questions are more about logic than math. You need to sort through the long text and draw the appropriate conclusion. For this question, you can't infer more than the survey allows. Since the survey is restricted to 300 people who liked "Heroman", we can't assume anything about people who like movies or sequels in general. The survey asked a large enough number of people that we can conlude that most people who like "Heroman" will probably like the sequel, which is choice C.

**2) C**
Go choice by choice and eliminate the ones that are too strong. Choice A is not necessarily true because Christine only surveyed 100 people. Her survey is an estimate of the actual vote, but the final tally could be different. Choice B is too strong in the other direction. Christine's survey is an estimate, so we can't say that it is a definitive prediction of what will actually happen, but it still lets us make some prediction. Choice C is correct because Christine's sampling method is flawed. She only asked adults whose children go to the school, so she probably over-represented people who support the proposed tax. For surveys to be reliable, they need to represent a random sample of the general population. Choice D is incorrect because, as we just said, there are indeed flaws in the sampling method.

**3) 12**
To find the average, take the sum of the set of numbers and divide by the number of numbers in the set. In this case, add up the cost of all the pizzas: 2 with 0 toppings is $20; 3 with 1 topping is $36; 3 with 2 toppings is $36; and 2 with 4 toppings is $28. The total should be $120. Divide that by 10 (the number of pizzas) to get that the average price per pizza is $12.

**4) B**
A histogram is just a graphical way of displaying the frequency of numbers in a set. It's almost exactly like the chart in #10, but the frequency is the $y$-axis and the values are the $x$-axis. In other words, three students read 0 books, two students read one book each, zero students read two books, etc. The average will be the total books read by all the students (28) divided by number of students (12), which is 2.333, or approximately 2.

**5) D**
You could take the time to calculate each of these values, but you can also use logic. The 32 pound pumpkin is a clear outlier, weighing much more than any of the others. If it were removed, the mean wouldn't change that much because all of the other pumpkins weigh about the same. The median and mode wouldn't change at all. The range would change considerably because we're removing the highest value, and it's much greater than any of the others. In fact, the range goes from 16 pounds to 8 pounds.

**6) D**
This is a tough question. There are two answers that we can quickly eliminate. Choice A won't affect the results because it's a fairly low number of people who didn't respond. The population size also won't affect the results since that's the population of the town, so we can eliminate Choice B. It seems like the sample size is too small to get an accurate result because 96 isn't really that many people. However, the bigger issue is where the survey was given. The researcher wants to know how people commute to work, but she's asking people who are at a grocery store on a Tuesday morning. Will you get an accurate prediction of the preferences of people who work when you take a sample on a Tuesday morning? Probably not, because a lot of the people who work will be at work at that time rather than at the grocery store. The researcher is getting an unreliable result because she is not getting a random sample of the working population. So even though larger sample sizes usually make the results more accurate, asking 1000 people at the grocery store on Tuesday morning will still give you an inaccurate result.

**7) C**
To answer this question, it helps to think of the median as the middle number of a set, and the mean/average as a measurement of the medium value of the set. In this case, the middle test score is 86%, but the value of the test scores is only 79%. Why would the value be lower? Because a

few students scored lower than the others, which would bring down the average.

**8) B**
It might be easier to add the two towns together so that you don't miscalculate. You can cross out values from the top and bottom until you've reached the middle. You can also add up all the families (400), add 1 (401) and divide by 2 to find which number in the set is the median. Since our answer is 200.5, we need to find the 200th and 201st numbers and average them to get the median. Whichever direction you count from, you'll find that both the 200th and 201st numbers are families that have 1 car, so 1 is the median.

**9) A**
Standard deviation is a measurement of how spread out the data is. You NEVER need to calculate the standard deviation on the SAT, but you should know that you could calculate it if you have the list of values, so Choice D is not correct. A larger standard deviation would mean that the numbers deviate, or vary, more from the average. In other words, if all the numbers are bunched around one number, you have a low standard deviation, but if they're more spread out along all the numbers, you have a high standard deviation. In this case, the families in Springfield seem to have a wide variety of numbers of cars, but the families in Pleasantville mostly have 1 car per family. For that reason, Springfield has a larger standard deviation.

**10) A**
Calculate each value. The mode is the most common number, which is clearly 74. The median will be the average of the 10th and 11th numbers in the set, which is 73. The mean will require use of a calculator, but you should be dividing 1,440 by 20, which is a mean of 72. So the mean is the smallest, then the median, then the mode.

**11) A**
The key to this question is "must be true." Let's go through the options. Numeral I is not necessarily true because a survey predicts results, but it does not guarantee them. For example, Harrison could win 65% of the vote in the election. Numeral II is not necessarily true because another 1,000 voters might be slightly different from this set of voters. Again, 65% of the next 1,000 voters might say they'll vote for Harrison. Numeral III is also not necessarily true because different towns have different voters, and we have no idea how this other town might feel about Harrison. As with most SAT survey questions, we don't want to see certainty in any of the results, so Choice A is the answer.

**12) B**
Since there are 21 scores in this list, you can find the median by finding the 11th score. Either way you count, you'll land on 204.

**13) B**
It might be helpful to think back to question #5 to help you visualize what's happening here. If the hottest day were actually hotter than previously recorded, the range would definitely change. The range is just the highest temperature minus the lowest, so changing the highest will change the range. The mean will also change because one hotter day will make the average of all the days hotter. (Think about how one good grade affects your average in a class.) Since the standard deviation is based on the mean, it will also change. The median will not change because it's always the middle number. If the hottest day is slightly hotter than we thought, it wouldn't affect the middle temperature.

**14) C**
Look at the choices and eliminate those that draw a conclusion that seems too strong. Both Choices A and B say that this poll is representative of all Americans, but that can't possibly be true. The only participants would be people who read this particular magazine, so the poll is not a random sample of the general population of Americans. Choice D is half right, but it doesn't really matter that the responses weren't 50/50. Americans aren't perfectly divided on every issue. Choice C is correct because, as we said, the poll does not represent a random sample.

**15) C**
To solve this question, we'll need to use the average formula twice. We know the average and the number of tests, so we're using the formula to calculate the sum of Anne's scores. For the 6 tests, she scored a total of 468 points (78 times 6). After removing the lowest score, Anne scored a total of 400 points (80 times 5). Subtract these

two numbers to find the value that was removed ($468 - 400 = 68$).

**16) B**

You could solve this question with only Algebra, but it's very easy to make careless mistakes. You are much better off plugging in numbers. Let's say that $x=1$. In that case $a$ is the average of 2 and 1, which is 1.5; $b$ is the average of 3 and 13, which is 8; and $c$ is the average of 1 and 10, which is 5.5. Now take the average of those three numbers: $\frac{(1.5 + 8 + 5.5)}{3} = \frac{15}{3} = 5$. Now just look for an answer that gives you 5 when you plug in 1 for $x$. Only Choice B works.

## Formulas You Need to Know

**1) B**

Probability on the SAT is much easier than the probability you have to learn in school. (No permutations or combinations. Hooray!) In almost every case, your goal is to read carefully and find the numerator and denominator of a fraction. The denominator is the group that you are choosing from. Sometimes it's the whole chart, but this question tells us to only consider the players who got drafted, which is a total of 24 (9 + 15). Out of those 24 drafted players, we need the number who are left-handed, which is 15. So the probability that a randomly selected drafted player is left-handed is $\frac{15}{24}$.

**2) A**

This is a complicated way of testing you on the difference of two squares rule, which is really just a special case of factoring and FOILing. In this question, we need the value of $b$. Our two $b$-terms multiply to 4, so $b$ must be 2.

**3) D**

When variables are directly proportional, they both increase or decrease by the same relative amount. Basically, directly proportional means you should just set up a proportion: $\frac{6}{24} = \frac{9}{y}$. Cross-multiply to get that $6y = 216$. Divide by 6 to get that $y = 36$. Notice what happened: as we increased the value of $x$, the value of $y$ also increased by the same factor. Directly proportional terms will always equal a constant fraction: $\frac{6}{24} = \frac{9}{36} = \frac{1}{4}$.

**4) 118, 119, or 120**

We know that angle $x$ is the same fraction of the circle as the shaded sector. Use the reference chart to help you find the area of the whole circle: $A = \pi(6)^2 = 36\pi$. We can use a proportion to find the value of $x$, but first we need to decide on a value for the shaded area. Let's say it's 37 for now, just so we can get an estimate of $x$: $\frac{x}{360} = \frac{37}{36\pi}$. You can cross-multiply and divide, and you'll have to actually multiply out pi, which is rare on the SAT. You should get that $x$ is approximately 117.77 degrees. Since $x$ MUST be an integer (a non-decimal, non-fraction), we have to round up to 118 degrees. We can double check that it works with another proportion: $\frac{118}{360} = \frac{\text{sector}}{36\pi}$. You'll find that the area of the sector is approximately 37.07, which falls within the range the question gives us. Both 119 and 120 degrees are acceptable, but 121 degrees is slightly too big (38.01).

**5) C**

Percentages can lead to careless mistakes if you aren't paying attention. In this case, the safest thing is to guess and check by multiplying each of the answer choices by 1.05, which represents a 5% increase, until you get \$84.00. But it's also helpful to know the percent change formula for harder questions:

percent change $= \frac{\text{new} - \text{old}}{\text{old}} \times 100$. We don't know the old value, so we'll have to use $x$ for now: $5 = \frac{84 - x}{x} \times 100$. Divide by 100 first: $0.05 = \frac{84 - x}{x}$. Multiply by $x$ to eliminate the fraction: $0.05x = 84 - x$. Add $x$ to both sides: $1.05x = 84$. And divide by 1.05 to find the old value: $x = 80$.

**6) 81**

This is difference of two squares. You can FOIL the two terms if you want: $ab = (x + 9)(x - 9)$. But it's helpful to remember that the middle $x$-term (the $b$-term) will drop out, leaving you with $x^2 - 81$. Difference of two squares comes up a lot on the SAT, so it's good to be comfortable with it.

**7) 289**

This sounds complicated, but we just need to follow instructions. The value of $r$ is 5. Plug in 4 for $t$: $V = 5{,}000\left(1 + \frac{5}{100}\right)^4$. You should get that the account is worth approximately \$6,077.53 after 4 years. Now do the same thing, but with 3 for $t$: $V = 5{,}000\left(1 + \frac{5}{100}\right)^3$. You should get that the account is worth approximately \$5,788.13 after 3 years. Find the difference: $6{,}077.53 - 5{,}788.13 = 289.40$. And round to the nearest dollar: \$289.

**8) C**

One of the few formulas that the SAT expects you to know is that speed is distance divided by time: speed $= \frac{\text{distance}}{\text{time}}$. We can calculate Debbie's average speed because we have the total distance and the total time. But be careful—those speeds in the chart are a distraction! The total distance can be found using the chart: $1.5 + 40 + 10 = 51.5$. The total time is given in the question, but we need to convert 2 hours and 48 minutes into hours. Use a ratio to turn the minutes into a decimal number of hours: $\frac{48}{60} = 0.8$. So our total time is 2.8 hours. Now plug the distance and time into our speed equation: speed $= \frac{51.5}{2.8}$. You should get that Debbie's average speed is approximately 18.39 kilometers per hour, which rounds to 18.4.

**9) $\frac{5}{12}$ or .416 or .417**

Use the formula $\pi$ radians = 180 degrees. Multiply your radian value by $\frac{180}{\pi}$ to convert it to degrees. Solve that and you'll find that the angle measures 150°. Since there are 360 degrees in a circle, we can find the fraction of the shaded area: $\frac{150}{360} = \frac{5}{12} = 0.416666$.

**10) B**

Once again, probability is all about finding the numerator and denominator of a fraction. The question is telling us to select one of the students at random, so the denominator is all of the students in the chart, which is 462. Our numerator is the number who are pursuing advanced degrees in the sciences, which is 79. So the probability is $\frac{79}{462}$, which reduces to approximately 0.171 as a decimal.

**11) A**

This question is perfect for the percent change formula: percent change $= \frac{\text{new} - \text{old}}{\text{old}} \times 100$. Plug in the new and old values: $\frac{86.42 - 79.16}{79.16} \times 100$. Doing the arithmetic gets you a percent increase of approximately 9.2%.

**12) A**
This looks hard, but it's just another version of the difference of two squares: $a^4 - b^4 = (a^2 + b^2)(a^2 - b^2)$. Notice that all three of those terms are in this question. We can substitute the values we know: $8 = 2(a^2 - b^2)$. Divide by 2 to find the value of the expression: $(a^2 - b^2) = 4$. It's common that difference of two squares questions involve less math than it seems at first.

**13) C**
In order to find the center, we'll need to complete the square twice. It's helpful to group the terms as we do it: $(x^2 + 18x + 81) + (y^2 - 4y + 4) = 15 + 81 + 4$. Remember that completing the square requires taking half of the $b$-term and squaring it. Whatever we add on the left also needs to be added on the right for balance. Simplify the equation to find our circle equation: $(x + 9)^2 + (y - 2)^2 = 100$. The general circle equation is $(x - h)^2 + (y - k)^2 = r^2$, where $(h, k)$ is the center and r is the radius. In this case, the center would be (-9, 2).

**14) 288**
Use the $\frac{\text{radians}}{\text{degrees}}$ conversion unit conversion:
$\frac{8\pi}{5} \times \frac{180}{\pi} = 288°$.

**15) 18**
If arc $AC$ is $\frac{1}{5}$ of the circle, then angle $AOC$ is also $\frac{1}{5}$ of the circle: $\frac{x}{360} = \frac{1}{5}$. Angle $AOC$ is 72°. If $AB$ is tangent to the circle at $A$, then angle $OAC$ is 90° because tangent lines form right angles with the radius. Now we have 2 angles of triangle ABO, so we can find the third angle (angle $x$) by remembering that there are always 180° in a triangle: $180 = 90 + 72 + x$. You should get that $x$ is 18°.

**16) B**
When terms are inversely proportional, one will increase as the other decreases. It's basically the opposite of directly proportional. We can use our speed formula to better understand what's happening here. Speed and velocity mean the same thing, so velocity $= \frac{\text{distance}}{\text{time}}$. Let's rewrite the formula like this: $V_t = d$. This experiment involves two sets of velocities and times, but the distance is constant. And that's how inversely proportional terms work—the numbers multiply to a constant. We can better express the relationship like this: $V_1t_1 = V_2t_2$. Let's plug in what we know: $(20)(0.25) = (10)(t_2)$. Solve for the variable to find that $t_2 = 0.5$, which makes sense. When our velocity went down, our time went up.

**17) B**
We need to complete the square to get this circle equation into standard form:
$(x^2 - 2x + 1) + (y^2 + 6y + 9) = -1 + 1 + 9$.
Simplify into $(x - 1)^2 + (y + 3)^2 = 9$. The radius of this circle is 3.

**18) A**
They ask for a proportion, but they mean probability. Once again, set up a fraction. Our denominator is all of the teams, which is 93. The numerator is only the hockey teams in the central time zone, which is 6. The proportion is $\frac{6}{93}$, which reduces to $\frac{2}{31}$.

**19) B**
Let's use the percent change formula:
percent change $= \frac{\text{new} - \text{old}}{\text{old}} \times 100$. Plug in our numbers: $\frac{2.25 - 2}{2} \times 100$. You should get that the percent increase was 12.5%, which rounds to 13%.

**20) C**
This is still percent change, but it's harder to figure out which value is the old and which is the new. Since the vans are a certain percentage greater than the SUVs, we want the SUVs to be the old value. Basically, we're looking at the vans in terms of the SUVs, so we want the SUVs to be our base amount: $\frac{1.5 - 1}{1} \times 100$. The number of vans sold is 50% greater than the number of SUVs sold.

**21) D**

We can plug each of these points into our equation, but we're not looking for them to equal 16. We want them to be less than or equal to 16. Let's try Choice A: $(2 + 1)^2 + (2 - 4)^2 \leq 16$. This simplifies to $9 + 4 \leq 16$, which is true, so this point does lie inside the circle. You may end up trying all the points, but only one will produce an invalid result: $(3 + 1)^2 + (-1 - 4)^2 \leq 16$. Choice D simplifies to $16 + 25 \leq 16$, which is not true, so $(3, -1)$ lies outside the circle.

**22) C**

First we need to find the degree measure of angle $AOB$. This is an isosceles triangle because both of the sides ($AO$ and $BO$) are radii of the circle, and thus have the same length. That means angle $ABO$ is also 20°, leaving us 140° for angle $AOB$. Now use the $\frac{\text{radians}}{\text{degrees}}$ formula to convert: $\frac{140°\pi}{180} = \frac{7\pi}{9}$.

**23) A**

This is another difference of two squares question, but the a makes it confusing. To avoid making a careless mistake, let's pretend that $a$ is 9: $y = 9x^2 - 1$. According to the difference of two squares rule, we can also rewrite this equation as $y = (3x + 1)(3x - 1)$. Matching this with our choices, it's clear that $3 = \sqrt{9} = \sqrt{a}$, so choice A is the answer.

**24) C**

We still need to make a fraction, but this time our denominator is more complicated. The question says that we are only choosing randomly from "those who read at least 2 books." That means we have to cross out the "1" column and ignore it. The total number of people who read at least 2 books is 153 (because $122 + 31 = 153$).

From that selection, we want to know the number who belonged to Group A, which is 89 (because $67 + 22 = 89$). So our fraction is $\frac{89}{153}$. As you can see from the other choices, this question is all about choosing the correct rows and columns.

**25) D**

Unlike #23, this question is only asking about points that lie on the circle, so we can just plug (0, 0) into each of the choices and see if we get a valid equation. Choice A gives us: $(0 + 4)^2 + (0 - 4)^2 = 8$. Simplifying this gives us $16 + 16 = 8$, which is not true. All of the "easy" choices give us invalid equations. Choice B simplifies to $16 + 16 = 64$, and Choice C simplifies to $64 + 64 = 64$. Choice D is all that's left, but it's helpful to know why it works: $(4\sqrt{2})^2 = 4^2(\sqrt{2})^2 = (16)(2) = 32$. So our simplified equation for Choice D is $32 + 32 = 64$, which is proof that (0, 0) lies on that circle.

**26) D**

This question is asking us to find the difference between two numbers: (account value at 3%) – (account value at 1%). Even though it looks complicated, choice D is exactly what we just described. We can't take any shortcuts, like in Choice B. In fact, Choice B is the value of an account at 2% interest. Choice A is the value at 3%, since $\frac{3}{1}$ is just 3. Choice C is nothing. We want a difference, so why would we divide? If you wanted, you could take the time to actually calculate all of these values, and only Choice D will give you the difference in value, which is approximately $40.60.

**27) A**

We'll need to complete the square, but it's not easy to do when there's a coefficient in front of the $x^2$ and $y^2$ terms. We should divide by 2: $x^2 - x + y^2 + 5y = \frac{19}{2}$. To complete the square, we need to take half of the $b$-terms and square them. For the $x$'s, half of -1 is $-\frac{1}{2}$, which becomes $\frac{1}{4}$ after we square it. For the $y$'s, half of 5 is $\frac{5}{2}$, which becomes $\frac{25}{4}$ after we square it. We need to add those values to the other side of the equation, too. Our equation should be: $\left(x^2 - x + \frac{1}{4}\right) + \left(y^2 + 5y + \frac{25}{4}\right) = \frac{19}{2} + \frac{1}{4} + \frac{25}{4}$. What a mess! Start cleaning things up, especially the fractions, which are easier to combine if all the denominators are 4: $\left(x - \frac{1}{2}\right)^2 + \left(y + \frac{5}{2}\right)^2 = \frac{38}{4} + \frac{1}{4} + \frac{25}{4}$. The radius side of the equation combines to $\frac{64}{4}$, which reduces to 16. So the radius is 4.

**28) 108**

Do you know this formula, that the sum of the interior angles of any shape is equal to $180(n - 2)$? If you do, cool. If you don't, don't sweat it. Starting from one vertex, break this shape up into triangles. You should have three triangles. Since each triangle has 180 degrees, the pentagon has $3 \times 180 = 540$ degrees. And since a regular shape has angles that are all the same, each angle will measure $\frac{540}{5} = 108$ degrees.

## Advanced Topics

**1) B**
There are two kinds of imaginary numbers questions—really easy ones and really hard ones. This is one of the easy ones. In fact, the imaginary numbers don't even matter. Just treat them like any other variable. Drop the parentheses and combine like terms: $1 + 14i$

**2) B**
Just like the last question, the $i$'s don't matter. Just add the two expressions: $-2 + 11i + 7 - 4i$. Combine like terms: $5 + 7i$.

**3) C**
The answer choices hint that we'll need to factor these expressions. The first function can be factored into $f(x) = (x + 4)(x - 2)$. The second equation has a common factor that we need to divide out of each term: $g(x) = x(x^2 - 16)$. We can also use difference of two squares to further factor the term in parentheses: $g(x) = x(x + 4)(x - 4)$. Now let's divide them as instructed: $\frac{f(x)}{g(x)} = \frac{(x + 4)(x - 2)}{x(x + 4)(x - 4)}$. We can eliminate the $(x + 4)$ because it's on both the top and bottom, but that's all we can do. Our final expression is $\frac{(x - 2)}{x(x - 4)}$.

**4) A**
As usual, we can drop the parentheses, but this time we need to distribute the negative to the second term: $3 + 11i - 8i^2 + 5i$. Also, we finally have to use the imaginary number rules. As the question says, $i = \sqrt{-1}$, which means that $i^2 = -1$. We need to substitute that into our equation, which flips the sign of the -8 term: $3 + 11i + 8 + 5i$. Combine like terms: $11 + 16i$.

**5) D**
Start by treating the imaginary numbers as if they were regular variables. Just FOIL like you always would: $20 + 5i - 8i - 2i^2$. Replace any $i^2$ terms with -1: $20 + 5i - 8i + 2$. Combine like terms: $22 - 3i$.

**6) C**
Polynomial division is a pain, but the SAT loves it for some reason. If you're comfortable using either long division or synthetic division, you'll be fine with these questions. But let me try to sell you on a faster way to do these—a much faster way. You see the fraction at the end of the answer choices? That's the remainder after we've divided $(x - 1)$ into $(8x - 3)$. Remainder theorem says that, when you run the solution/root of the thing you're dividing by (that's $x = 1$ in this case since we're dividing by $x - 1$), you'll get the remainder when you run that value through the thing you are dividing into, in this case $8x - 3$. To put it simply, run $x = 1$ into $8x - 3$ and you'll know what the remainder should be. $8(1) - 3 = 5$. Only one answer choice has $+5$ as the numerator of that remainder fraction, and sure enough, that is the right answer.

**7) B**
Once again, plugging in numbers will help us understand what's going on. Let's say $x$ is 0. That means our original equation is $f(0) = 2^{0+1}$, which is just 2. The question wants us to find the graph of $y = -f(x)$. If $f(0) = 2$, then $-f(0) = -2$. That's it. Now we just need to find a graph that includes the point (0, -2), and the only one is Choice B. Notice that plugging in numbers can help on a lot of different kinds of hard algebra questions. It's a good strategy that can help you on the SAT, even if you're not 100% confident with algebra.

**8) D**
Again, you could do this the long division or synthetic division way, but you could also use the remainder theory method we proposed in the solution to #6, which is to run the value $x = -2$ through the numerator to find out what the remainder should be. When you do that here, you get a remainder value of -13. Notice how answer D is the only one with a -13 as its remainder? That's because it is the right answer.

**9) 1 or 3**
You may not know where this question is going, but you do know how to start it. Distribute: $x^5 - 10x^3 = -9x$. Assuming that we'll probably need to factor, it's best to add $9x$ to both sides so that this equation is equal to 0: $x^5 - 10x^3 + 9 = 0$. We have a common factor, so we should divide out an $x$ from each term: $x(x^4 - 10x^2 + 9) = 0$. Even though we still have large exponents, we can factor the term in parentheses as if it were a normal quadratic: $x(x^2 - 9)(x^2 - 1) = 0$. Both of these new terms can be factored again using difference of two squares: $x(x + 3)(x - 3)(x + 1)(x - 1) = 0$. There are five solutions to this equation, but the question only wants the ones that are greater than 0, which are 1 and 3.

**10) B**
Divide algebraically if you want, or use the solution mentioned in questions 6 and 8, which is to use the remainder method. Run $x = 2$ into the numerator to find out what the remainder should be. In this case, you'll get -7, which is the numerator of the right answer, B.

**11) D**
We need an equation that has zeros at -2, 0, and 1. Choices A and B have the opposite zeros, so we can cross them out. Between Choices C and D, we need to look at what happens at each of the zeros. The graph passes through -2 and 0, but it bounces at 1. Graphs bounce when they have the same zero twice (or an even number of times), which is what happens in Choice D because the $x - 1$ term is squared.

**12) A**
This is one of the really hard imaginary number questions. First of all, you can't just divide 2 by 4 and get $\frac{1}{2}$. Choices B and C are trying to trick you, so don't fall for it. To actually find the answer, we need to rationalize the denominator by multiplying by the conjugate. The conjugate is the "opposite" version of the denominator, which would be $4 - 3i$ in this case. We need to multiply both the numerator and denominator by that term: $\frac{2 - 7i}{4 + 3i} \times \frac{4 - 3i}{4 - 3i}$. You'll need to FOIL the top two terms: $(2 - 7i)(4 - 3i) = 8 - 6i - 28i + 21i^2$. And remember to replace any $i^2$ with -1: $8 - 6i - 28i - 21$. Combining like terms gives us the numerator: $-13 - 34i$. The bottom is a little easier because this is a difference of two squares: $(4 + 3i)(4 - 3i) = 16 - 9i^2$. Again, replace that $i^2$: $16 + 9 = 25$. The full expression should be $\frac{-13 - 34i}{25}$, so the $a$ term is $-\frac{13}{25}$.

**13) C**
Plugging in will help, but we'll skip to $x = 1$ since $x = 0$ makes the expression 0 and will probably give us multiple choices that work. Our expression becomes $\frac{3(1)^2 + 12(1)}{3(1) + 3}$, which simplifies to $\frac{3 + 12}{3 + 3} = \frac{15}{6}$. Choices A and B are obviously wrong. Choice C gives us $1 + 3 - \frac{9}{6}$, which is $\frac{15}{6}$. Choice D would give us $\frac{33}{6}$, so it also doesn't work, leaving us with just Choice C.

MATH_SOLUTIONS

**14) B**

Multiply by the conjugate: $\frac{14 - 2i}{1 - 3i} \times \frac{1 + 3i}{1 + 3i}$. You should get $\frac{14 + 42i - 2i - 6i^2}{1 - 9i^2}$. Replace the $i^2$ terms with -1 and combine like terms to get $\frac{20 + 40i}{10}$. The $b$-term will be $4i$, so B is the answer.

**15) B**

If you've been dividing using Algebra, this is just the SAT's way of asking for the remainder. If you're plugging in, this doesn't really change things. Set $x$ equal to 0: $\frac{0^2 + 7(0) + 15}{0 + 6} = 0 + 1 + \frac{a}{0 + 6}$. This all simplifies to $\frac{15}{6} = 1 + \frac{a}{6}$. The value of $a$ would have to be 9.

**16) D**

Multiply by the conjugate: $\frac{(6 + 2i)}{(3 - i)} \times \frac{(3 + i)}{(3 + i)}$. You should get $\frac{18 + 6i + 6i + 2i^2}{9 - i^2}$. Replace the $i^2$ terms with -1 and combine like terms to get $\frac{16 + 12i}{10}$. You can reduce the fractions to $\frac{8}{5} + \frac{6i}{5}$.

**17) B**

Plugging in 0 for $x$ still helps. The question becomes, "What is the remainder when 19 is divided by -7?" The negative complicates things, but think about what you'd multiply -7 by to get close to 19. You could multiply -7 by -2 to get +14, which is 5 short of 19. In other words, when you divide 19 by -7, you get -2 with a remainder of 5.

**18) C**

Another hard imaginary numbers question.

Multiply by the conjugate: $\frac{(7 - 4i)}{(3 + 6i)} \times \frac{(3 - 6i)}{(3 - 6i)}$.

You should get: $\frac{(21 - 42i - 12i + 24i^2)}{(9 - 36i^2)}$. Replace the $i^2$ terms with -1 and combine like terms to get $\frac{(-3 - 54i)}{45}$, which simplifies to $-\frac{1}{15} - \frac{6i}{5}$.

**19) 6**

This is another hard algebra questions where you just have to trust that something will work out. Moving the negative terms to the other side helps: $x^3 + x = 6x^2 + 6$. You can factor an $x$ out of the left side and a 6 out of the right side: $x(x^2 + 1) = 6(x^2 + 1)$. You can divide both sides by $x^2 + 1$ to get that $x = 6$.

**20) C**

Plug in 0 for $x$ and you'll get $\frac{(6(0)^2 + 15(0) - 22)}{(0 + 3)}$, which simplifies to $-\frac{22}{3}$, or $-7\frac{1}{3}$. Choice A will be positive, so we can eliminate it. Choices B and C both give us $-7\frac{1}{3}$, but we can at least eliminate Choice D. Let's try $x = 1$, which makes our original expression $\frac{(6(1)^2 + 15(1) - 22)}{(1 + 3)}$, which is $-\frac{1}{4}$. Choice B gives you $8\frac{3}{4}$, but Choice C is also $-\frac{1}{4}$, so that's our answer.

**21) D**

This question is testing remainder theorem, which states that a polynomial (like $f(x)$) that is divided by a linear function in the form $x - a$ (like $x - 4$) will have a remainder that is equal to $f(a)$ (or $f(4)$ in our case). The question tells us that $f(4) = -3$, which means that the remainder when $f(x)$ is divided by $x - 4$ will be -3. This is a very confusing idea, but luckily it's almost never tested. Here's a little tip that might help you out: you can pretend that $f(x)$ is the most basic polynomial we can think of. In this case, let's say that $f(x) = 0x^2 + 0x - 3$. Technically, this is a polynomial, even though the $x$ terms wouldn't matter. And it follows the only rule that the question gives us because $f(4) = -3$. Let's test our choices against this ridiculous polynomial. Choices A, B, and C are all wrong because we can't divide $f(x)$ by $x - 7$, $x - 3$, or $x + 3$ evenly. But if we divide $f(x)$ by $x - 4$, the remainder is actually -3. The expression $x - 4$ goes into $f(x)$ zero times with -3 left over. It's a weird way to get to the answer, but whatever works!

**22) B**

Another complicated algebra problem—the SAT wants to make this one hurt. Take a look at the method I used in my calculator here. If $3x + 4$ is a factor of the new polynomial, then $3x + 4 = 0$ is a root and $x = -\frac{4}{3}$ must give us a zero when we run it through the new function. Notice how I typed this one into my calculator—first I stored $x$

as $-\frac{4}{3}$. Then I wrote out the two polynomials $f(x)$ and $g(x)$. Most helpful thing here: I included a 1 as a coefficient in front of each. That way, I could just scroll up in the calculator screen, grab the previous step, press enter, change the coefficients to try a new answer, press enter again and get the result. That saved a lot of time. SAT thought this problem would take a long time, but as soon as I saw that answer B gave me 0, I knew I had the right answer.

```
NORMAL FLOAT AUTO REAL DEGREE MP
-4/3→X
                      -1.333333333
1(3X³-6X²+9X)+1(X²-2X+3)
                      -22.33333333
1(3X³-6X²+9X)+4(X²-2X+3)
                                 0
3(3X³-6X²+9X)+4(X²-2X+3)
                      -59.55555556
```

**23) C**

For this seemingly tricky and ugly division question, we don't really need to do that much algebra to find our answer. Look at the first step of the polynomial division, $\frac{36x^2}{kx} = -9x$, and think about what value of $k$ would make this true. This would only work if $k = -4$.

**24) C**

This is a more complicated version of the remainder theorem rule. We can convert the coordinate into function notation: $f(3) = -2$. According to remainder theorem, if the polynomial function is divided by $x - a$, the remainder will be $f(a)$. In this case, dividing this mystery function by $x - 3$ leaves a remainder of -2, so numeral III is true. The others could be true, but they don't have to be, so Choice C is the answer.

APPEAL TO:

Reason

Ethics

Emotion

HOW LONG?

50

MINUTES

# ESSAY The Breakdown

## Should you write it?

Technically, the SAT Essay is optional. Since you might need it, and because you can only write it after taking the SAT, yes—you should write it.

## WHAT YOU NEED TO DO:

analyze the techniques of a persuasive essay.

**DO** ARRIVE AT THE TEST WITH PLENTY OF RHETORICAL DEVICES READY TO DEPLOY.

**DON'T** AGREE—OR DISAGREE—WITH THE AUTHOR . YOUR JOB IS TO PRESENT AN ANALYSIS, NOT AN OPINION.

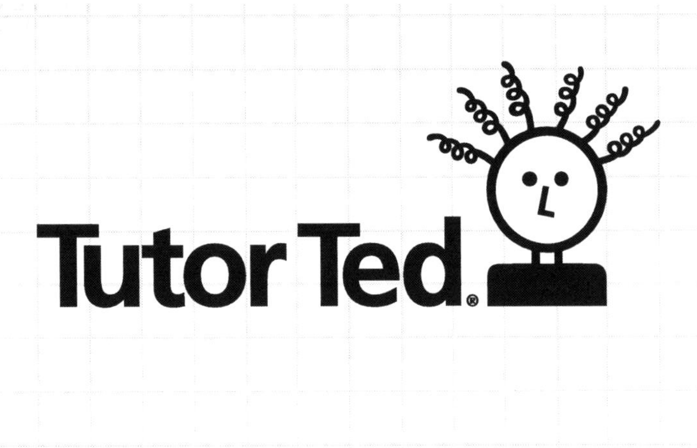
Tutor Ted

Yes, the 50 minute essay at the end of the SAT is optional—but like everything in the college admissions process that's described as optional, it's really mandatory.

**"But whyyyy?" you might ask.**

## Three reasons:

- Even though most schools do not require the essay, it's required at many of the top schools: most Ivy Leagues and the University of California system require students to submit an essay score. Unless you have your list of schools chiseled into stone and know for a fact that none of them have required or ever will require the essay, you should take the safe approach and write it.
- Speaking of the safe approach, you can ONLY write the essay after you've taken the rest of the SAT. If you skip the essay the first time around then find out later that a school on your list requires the essay, you would have to take the whole SAT again just to write the essay. You'll definitely wish you had gutted it out for the essay the first time around.
- The fun reason to write the essay is that it gives you a chance to show off a little bit. Think of the essay as an opportunity for you to differentiate yourself as an excellent writer. If you don't think you're an excellent writer now, well, stick around—we're about to give you the tools you'll need to become one.

# The Details

**The Essay on the SAT is *crazy predictable.***
I can tell you right now what kind of prompt you can expect and what kind of essay down to the tone and the paragraph structure you should write in response.

Which leads us to the first, most important strategy on the essay: know what to expect so that can have your plan of attack ready.

## Let's jump right in and spoil the surprise.

The prompt is a persuasive essay (or speech). It'll be contemporary (written sometime between 1930 and the present), and the reading level will be around 10th or 11th grade level—they want you to be able to understand the passage.

Your job is to write an analytical essay that identifies the persuasive elements in the essay and explains how they help to advance the author's position.

**Your essay will be graded in three categories: Reading, Analysis, and Writing.**
"Reading" is about whether you understood the passage or not. In my opinion, this is the easiest domain for scoring highly. You just need to show that you understood the main points of the piece.

"Analysis" entails the specific persuasive tools you are able to identify within the prompt. This is the one we're going to work on the most in this section. You want to have a small library of rhetorical devices you know and love and are ready to identify.

"Writing" covers how you share your thoughts. You want to communicate clearly and demonstrate some sophistication at the same time—by varying your sentence structure and using precise diction.

So: what's the plan of attack?

# Plan of Attack

## *STEP #1: READ THE ESSAY—CAREFULLY.*

You've got loads of time to write this essay. The best piece of advice I can give you is not to rush the planning process.

This is the research part of the planning process: you're going on a hunt for rhetorical devices (and, by the way, you're also reading to understand the author's point of view...but that seems to me like a secondary priority...if you're able to identify rhetorical devices, my guess is that you also understand whatever point they are being used to make).

Read carefully and slowly. Use your pencil to underline noteworthy moments. Every time you see a rhetorical device, jot it down in the margin.

If you do this part right, your essay booklet should look like the aftermath of a Civil War battle if the Civil War had been fought between pencils. I'm not sure that metaphor makes any sense. Use your pencil a lot.

## *STEP #2: TALLY UP THE SCORE.*

Look back at the rhetorical devices you identified—set a goal of finding at least five per passage. Find the ones that were used more than once, or that were used throughout. If certain devices are prevalent, you want to write about those.

You also want to identify any particularly interesting or unusual devices. Did the author make an ad hominem attack that you are just dying to point out? Highlight that one too.

(For those of you who are thinking, "OK, but can you tell us what these rhetorical devices are now? Please?" the answer is "not now...but soon, I promise.")

Once you have a "top three" or a "top four," you're ready to move onto the next step.

## *STEP #3: OUTLINE.*

Some students LOVE writing outlines. Love it. Could outline all day long.

Other students do not love writing outlines.

Don't panic if you are in the second group—we are going to make this stage as simple and manageable as possible.

All you need to do is put your favorite three or four rhetorical devices in order, and follow each of them up with two pieces of evidence you can cite to prove their existence.

In other words, no system of roman numerals followed by letters and numbers is required. Just put your devices in order from most prevalent/persuasive to least prevalent (but hopefully still persuasive).

## *STEP #4: WRITE, FOLLOWING* ***THIS STRUCTURE.***

Have you heard of "paint-by-numbers?" It was a real thing that eventually became a cliché. Basically, you get a canvas that's outlined and tells you what color to put where. When you're done, guess what? You get the exact painting that you were expecting to get.

The cliché describes anything that is as predictable—and uncreative—as that.

Whether you like paint-by-numbers or not, it's the right strategy to use on the SAT essay. Creativity is a delightful human trait that just does not have a place on the SAT.

In the first paragraph, you want to write one or two sentences giving an overview of the author's main point ("In advocating for a free college education for all students...") followed by a preview of the three or four rhetorical devices you found (...Keith Ellison employs an implicit appeal to ethics, an appeal to reason through statistics, and a call to a sense of patriotic responsibility to persuasively argue his case.")

In the second paragraph, you want to explore your first rhetorical device in this sequence of sentences:

- ***Restate the rhetorical device.***
- ***Cite one piece of textual evidence.***
- ***Write 2-3 sentences exploring the significance of that device in making the author's case.***
- ***Cite your second piece of evidence.***
- ***Write 2-3 sentences again exploring the significance of the device in this example.***

In paragraphs three, four, and five, use the same structure as in paragraph two, but using your other rhetorical devices.

In the last paragraph, draw a close to your essay, showing again your clear understanding of what points the author made throughout the prompt.

uh...that's it. That's all you need to do. Sound easy?

Maybe it is.

# Beat the Grading Rubric

Grading essays on a standardized test must be difficult. How do I know? Because SAT has done such a sh***y job at it over the years.

The grading system for the SAT essay is really pretty simple: on each of the three grading domains (Reading, Analysis, and Writing), you get a score from 1-4 from two different graders. Those scores get added up, and you wind up with a score from 2-8 on each of the three domains.

## Here's the weird thing:

Almost everyone gets 2s and 3s. As in, over 85% of the scores given are either 2s or 3s. When you add up the scores from the two graders, that means everybody is getting a 4, 5, or 6 overall. Everybody.

How can we break free of that grading purgatory? By doing what the students a step up on the grading curve are doing. In the next section, we're going to look at the standards for a 4 (the highest grade) across each of the three domains and talk about what that means—and how you can get there.

## READING

Here's what the official SAT scoring rubric says about an essay that should get a 4 for its Reading score:

> ***Demonstrates thorough comprehension of the source text.***
>
> ***Shows an understanding of the text's central idea(s) and of most important details and how they interrelate, demonstrating a comprehensive understanding of the text.***
>
> ***Is free of errors of fact or interpretation with regard to the text.***
>
> ***Makes skillful use of textual evidence (quotations, paraphrases, or both), demonstrating a complete understanding of the source text.***

### *HERE'S WHAT WE THINK IS IMPORTANT.*

**"Thorough"**
Make sure you examine or identify all the points the author is making in his/her essay. When in doubt, make another point about what the author is trying to relay to his/her audience.

**"Interrelation"**
It's important to point out all of the central ideas within the prompt, but what distinguishes a "meh" essay from a "great!" essay is one that shows how the ideas work together to make one central point. The essays you'll read as the essay prompts are all really well written and will include multiple ideas that serve the same core point.

### "Free of errors"

The "free of errors" thing is actually NOT a hot topic for me. Basically it's just a warning that you actually need to understand the essay. That's pretty obvious.

### "Evidence"

It's back! What, do you think they called this test "evidence-based" by accident? The point I want to make here is that I would do your best to quote your textual evidence directly rather than paraphrase it. Your essay will read as more sophisticated and mature if you do.

## ANALYSIS

Here's SAT's official breakdown of what a "4" essay should do to demonstrate mastery on the analysis task.

> ***Offers an insightful analysis of the source text and demonstrates a sophisticated understanding of the analytical task.***
>
> ***Offers a thorough, well-considered evaluation of the author's use of evidence, reasoning, and/or stylistic and persuasive elements, and/or feature(s) of the student's own choosing.***
>
> ***Contains relevant, sufficient, and strategically chosen support for claim(s) or point(s) made.***
>
> ***Focuses consistently on those features of the text that are most relevant to addressing the task.***

### *AND HERE'S WHAT WE THINK YOU SHOULD FOCUS ON.*

### "Insightful analysis" and "a sophisticated understanding."

They want you to sound smart. They want you to BE smart, actually, because what you have to do to meet this particular requirement is dissect the prompt essay. This is where our rhetorical devices (not there yet...but we're getting close!) will be useful.

To ring the bell of this particular requirement, you don't necessarily want to cite the most obvious rhetorical devices. We'll talk about this in the advanced strategies too, but to spoil the surprise here, you want to imagine what everyone else in the classroom is writing about...and then write about something different and better. By better, I mean smarter and more sophisticated.

### "Thorough" and "well-considered."

You know what this means? It means you should write a lot.

### "Relevant, sufficient, strategically chosen support."

More evidence, homies. Always Be Citing. Again, if you can find interesting evidence that not everyone else in that classroom is citing, you are climbing out of that pit of essays that get a 2-3.

## WRITING

Here's the fun one. What College Board says:

> ***Is cohesive and demonstrates a highly effective use and command of language.***
>
> ***Includes a precise central claim.***
>
> ***Includes a skillful introduction and conclusion. The response demonstrates a deliberate and highly effective progression of ideas both within paragraphs and throughout the essay.***
>
> ***Has a wide variety in sentence structures. The response demonstrates a consistent use of precise word choice. The response maintains a formal style and objective tone.***
>
> ***Shows a strong command of the conventions of standard written English and is free or virtually free of errors.***

### *AGAIN, THE IMPORTANT PARTS:*

**"A highly effective use and command of language."**
This part conveys two important ideas: one, that your use of language needs to prove your freaking point ("effective") and two, that it should show that you are a bad-ass when it comes to writing ("command").

That's a fun and challenging balancing act: to make your point through compelling use of the language.

**"Includes a precise central claim."**
Well, duh!!!

**"A skillful introduction and conclusion."**
I actually kinda disagree with this part. Even College Board's sample high-scoring essays have paint-by-numbers intros and conclusions. The whole point of paint-by-numbers is that it involves next-to-no-skill. If you have a strong structure ready to use to write your intro and conclusion, you'll hit the mark here.

**"Progression of ideas."**
Now we're talking. You want to *progress* through your argument. You don't want your essay to come off as simply a list of rhetorical devices. If you want full marks, write about how those rhetorical devices work together. Make transitions between your body paragraphs to show that continuity and flow. Build your case.

**"Variety in sentence structures."**
My favorite thing to include in my own writing and to teach to my students. It could not be easier to incorporate—you just have to set your mind to doing so. How do you vary your sentences? Include a short one. Include a rhetorical question. Flex your newfound punctuation knowledge and incorporate a semicolon; better yet, use my absolute favorite punctuation mark—the elegant, dramatic, and almost impossible-to-eff-up em-dash.

**"Free of errors."**
Yeah, uh-huh.

# A Plethora of Rhetorical Devices

**Finally: the list of rhetorical devices.**
I'm going to define each device for you, give an example of how you might use it in an essay, and then let you know how useful I think the device is on the SAT. One word of advice: just because a device is not one of my favorites doesn't mean that it's not legitimate and useful.

And here's how you should use this list: find your favorite 6-8 devices. Then, look for those on every essay you read. If you have that many devices at the ready, you'll always be able to find three or four of them within any persuasive essay.

| | | | |
|---|---|---|---|
| **Abstract** | (adj) existing as an idea, not in the physical world | "The author frequently references abstract notions like 'responsibility' in making her argument." | Is the author living in the "real world" or chilling in the realm of the abstract? If it's the latter, point that out! |
| **Aesthetic** | (adj) concerned with beauty or the appreciation of beauty | "By describing the colors of the forest floor in detail, the author shows a clear preference for aesthetic harmony." | Whenever an author uses a lot of visual imagery, use this word! |
| **Allegory** | (noun) a story that can be interpreted as having a hidden meaning | "The author's story about the three little pigs is a clear allegory of the 1992 presidential election." | The most famous allegory of the last 100 years is George Orwell's "Animal Farm." It's not really about animals...it's about people! |
| **Allusion** | (noun) A reference to a person, event, or place in history, religious texts, or literature. For example "The Garden of Eden" is an allusion to the place in Genesis and often symbolizes perfection. It is used to connect ideas to literary or historical ideas, often to emphasize the validity of the idea | "Smith makes frequent allusions to ancient history to illustrate her point." | Hottest allusions: biblical allusions, historical allusions, literary allusions. |

| | | | |
|---|---|---|---|
| **Ambiguity** | (noun) uncertainty or inexactness in language | "The ambiguity of the pronoun 'they' appears to be intentional; the author invites his reader to imagine who 'they' represents." | Ambiguity can be unintentional (which is bad writing) or intentional (which can be really good writing). |
| **Analogy** | (noun) a comparison between two things | "When the author draws an analogy between the current political campaign and Hitler's rise to power, the intention is clearly to evoke dread and even terror in the reader." | Analogies are back on the SAT! Hooray! Analogies are to the SAT what beer commercials are to football games—you simply can't have one without the other. |
| **Anaphora** | (noun) The repetition of the first few words in a series of sentences. | "Martin Luther King's most famous speech, 'I Have a Dream,' uses anaphora to draw in the listener." | Anaphora is especially useful in the context of a speech. Returning to the same phrase is almost like having a familiar chorus in a song. |
| **Anecdote** | (noun) a short story | "The author relies on anecdotes from his own experience rather than empirical evidence to make his point." | Anecdotes don't have to be funny. They don't have to be long, either. As soon as someone writes, "A friend of mine told me the other day that...," they are sharing an anecdote. |
| **Antithesis** | (noun) a pairing of opposite ideas | "Jackson makes clear use of antithesis when he intones, 'they died so that we might live.'" | Any pairing of opposites can be described as antithesis, so fire away with this one! |
| **Aphorism** | (noun) a concise or pithy statement meant to express a common truth | "The author expresses his central point through the aphorism, 'if it ain't broke, don't fix it.'" | Aphorisms are not hallmarks of great writing—they're a little bit "easy"—but they are definitely common. |
| **Appeal To Emotion (or Pathos)** | (noun) an attempt to persuade by manipulating the reader's feelings | "'Won't you please think of these poor, starving children?' pleads the author in a clear appeal to emotion." | Keep an eye out for this one whenever you see a political ad. |
| **Appeal to Ethics (or Ethos)** | (noun) an attempt to convince the reader by establishing the credibility of the author. | "When the author mentions her years of experience volunteering with Doctors Without Borders, she makes a clear appeal to ethics." | You can find this one on most essays on the SAT. People are always trying to convince you that they are credible and/or qualified to have an opinion. |

| | | | |
|---|---|---|---|
| **Appeal To Reason (or Logos)** | (noun) an attempt to persuade the reader through logic | "The author makes an appeal to reason when he asserts that, because innovations in medicine have cured deadly diseases and extended human lifespans, we should continue to invest in medical technology." | I don't know about you, but this is the one that persuades me the most easily. |
| **Argumentum Ad Hominem** | (noun) an attack directed at an individual | "His ad hominem attack questioned his rival's personal integrity rather than the substance of his argument." | Basically, instead of taking on the argument, you take on the person making the argument instead. The elevated version of the "yeah, well you're stupid" playground taunt. |
| **Argumentum Ad Ignorantiam** | (noun) an assertion that something is true because it hasn't been proven false | "The Flat Earth Society relies on the ad ignorantium notion that, when standing on the ground, the earth certainly seems flat." | Isn't this one a fun logical fallacy? Basically, you just pretend like something is true just because you don't know any better. |
| **Argumentum Ad Populum** | (noun) an assertion that something is true simply because many people believe it | "When the author cites the growing number of 9/11 'truthers' as evidence of a conspiracy, she makes a clear argumentum ad populum." | The classic "everyone else is doing it so I should too" mistake... |
| **Begging The Question** | (noun or verb) assuming the conclusion to an argument; a circular argument | "The author begs the question when he states, 'Free trade is good for the country because when commerce is allowed to move freely across borders, all the citizens reap the rewards.'" | "Begging the question" is the most misused rhetorical term of all-time, possibly. It does NOT mean, "raising a question," or "raising a potential issue." Now that you know it really means, listen for how often people use it incorrectly. |
| **Causation** | (noun) the relationship between an event that caused another event | "The author suggests that there is clear causation between the emissions from the plant and the increase in respiratory illness in the community." | I would use this one in a situation where the cause-and-effect is surprising or particularly interesting. If an author says that if you drop a rock, it will fall, that is not a very interesting piece of causation. |

| | | | |
|---|---|---|---|
| **Claim** | (noun) an argument or point within an argument | "The author's primary claim is that, without a sustained effort across all classes of society, affordable drinking water will become a thing of the past." | This one you WILL find on every single SAT Essay since every essay prompt is meant to be persuasive. One "pro" of using this is that it helps establish your comprehension of the passage, which will hopefully boost your Reading score. |
| **Colloquial** | (adj) informal, often regarding word choice/diction | "When the author uses colloquial language to assess the situation, she does so in a clear attempt to embrace a wide variety of readers." | What's the advantage of speaking (or writing) colloquially? You might be able to speak directly to more people, or you might come off more as an "everyman" than a "fancypants." |
| **Compare/ Contrast** | (verb) you know what these mean | "To make his point, the author compares and contrasts the contemporary situation to that of pre-revolutionary France." | To be honest, I would use these two terms/rhetorical devices only if you can't think up something better. They're useful... they're just a little too simple, a little too easy. |
| **Connotation** | (noun) the feeling that a word or term provokes beyond its dictionary definition | "The author draws attention to the connotation of the word 'industrial,' suggesting that what used to be perceived positively is now largely considered a blight." | This is a more specific term, obviously, which means that it might be a little less useful across the board on the essay. Still, it's a fun one; if you like it, keep it in your bag of tricks. |
| **Contradiction** | (noun) a statement in opposition to another statement | "The author points out a clear contradiction between what people say they want and how they actually behave." | You probably knew this term already. It's perfectly fine—functional and fairly common—but if you can find more interesting devices the author used, I would use those instead. |
| **Convention** | (noun) a way in which something is typically done within a culture | "The author argues that an approach based on convention is likely to fail, predictably, based on past results." | Here's a fun one. Whenever the author refers to something that sounds like the common sense of the culture, call it convention. |

| | | | |
|---|---|---|---|
| **Correlation** | (noun) a mutual relationship between two things | "The author highlights a correlation between the lack of available mental health resources and an increase in the number of homeless citizens." | This is a strong term, and if you're planning to study the social sciences in college, get ready because you are going to hear this term a LOT. |
| **Counterpoint** | (noun) an argument used to contrast with the author's main point | "By highlighting a valid counterpoint, the author makes clear that the situation is not a simple one to resolve." | Raising a counterpoint, to me, is code for "I'm a good, thoughtful writer." Pointing out that an issue is complex is pretty much always a smart move. |
| **Critique** | (noun) a detailed, incisive analysis | "Throughout the essay, the author presents a rational critique of both the public and charter school systems." | Kind of a blanket term, critique is a pretty resilient term with broad application. Don't hesitate to use it. |
| **Deductive Reasoning** | (noun) logical analysis, i.e. the process of reasoning from a number of statements to reach a logical conclusion | "When the author points out that inexperienced drivers have an increased risk of accidents, and that teenagers are inherently inexperienced drivers because of their age, he is relying on deductive reasoning to make his point." | In persuasion, this is a "logical" reasoning process that starts with general claims and then moves to specific instances to prove those claims. For example: Drag racing is harmful; last week a police officer was killed by drag racers. (See inductive reasoning.) This is used to argue logically. |
| **Diction** | (noun) word choice | "By using formal diction, the author creates a tone of authority that is effectively persuasive." | Often paired with an adjective, i.e. "formal diction" or "colloquial diction." |
| **Didactic** | (adj) intended to instruct | "The essay's didactic tone establishes the author as an expert—someone who can be trusted to offer a thoughtful solution." | Calling something didactic is often an insult—it means "intended to instruct," but in a kind of heavy-handed way. Nevertheless, if you see it, cite it. |
| **Example** | (noun) something characteristic of a kind or illustrating a general rule | "By citing several real-world examples, the author thoroughly establishes the value of cultural literacy programs." | I'm going to bet the house that you know what an example is. Super common but not the most interesting rhetorical device to cite either. Use in case of emergency. |

| Extended Metaphor | (noun) a metaphorical comparison that extends through a series of sentences or paragraphs | "When she compares the planning process to a game of chess, the author employs an extended metaphor in order to make the situation more accessible to a non-technically minded audience." | When you see the author draw out a comparison, call it an extended metaphor... and then imagine your grader's eyes lighting up with joy. |
|---|---|---|---|
| **Figurative Language** | (noun) a general term describing the use of metaphors, symbolism, or poetic language | "The author makes use of figurative language, such as when he draws the metaphorical comparison between his childhood oak tree and the condition of the modern National Park system." | This is a nice term that allows you to cite a lot of textual examples. Make sure you label those subterms, like metaphors, symbolism, etc. for maximum effect. |
| **Hyperbole** | (noun) extreme exaggeration | "The author employs hyperbole when he draws attention to potentially absurd consequences of the water supply issue, including the complete collapse of the art and culture movement." | Hyperbole—you'll know it when you see it. I don't think you'll see it a lot on the SAT, but good to have it in your back pocket just in case. |
| **Idealism** | (noun) the representation of things in an ideal (i.e. unrealistic) form | "The author draws on a sense of idealism when he proposes that if all citizens voted, they would get the government they deserve." | My favorite fun fact about idealism is that its antonym is 'pragmatism.' An idealist believes that we should accomplish our goals through the best means possible. A pragmatist thinks that we should get there by any means necessary." |
| **Imagery** | (noun) descriptive language that appeals to humans' five senses | "Describing the views, sounds, and smells of the natural landscape, the author uses imagery to effectively engage the reader." | Lots of "bang for your buck" with imagery—we use this term all of the time when we write. Makes you sound smart, so do not hesitate to use this one. |
| **Inductive Reasoning** | (noun) a logical process through which general conclusions are reached through the observance of specific instances | "The author uses inductive reasoning as she traces a series of personal stories and observations to formulate her opinion." | I learned this one in Geometry class. Basically, instead of drawing a logical conclusion through a conscious and clear argument, you observe reality, tell stories, and then draw conclusions from what you noticed. |

| | | | |
|---|---|---|---|
| **Inference** | (noun) a conclusion based on evidence and reasoning | "The inference drawn by the author is that if politicians worried less about getting elected, they would be more effective at the job of governing." | Inferences are like implications: they're not directly stated but they're clearly implied. Kind of a fun one to use if you see it. |
| **Irony** | (noun) a state of affairs that appears to directly contradict expectations | "The author wisely points out the irony in wasting paper on a mailing campaign to promote conservation." | Everyone's favorite, frequently-misused term. Irony, when it's really there, means that there is a direct reversal between what you expect and what turns out to be the case. If the author uses this one, cite it! |
| **Juxtapose** | (verb) placing two things or ideas side by side to establish contrast | "The author illustrates a meaningful difference when she juxtaposes the typical living conditions in New York with those in Lagos, Nigeria." | More common than irony, juxtaposition is simply looking at two ideas or situations side-by-side. It's a cool word that makes you sound smart, so don't hesitate to use. |
| **Metaphor** | (noun) a non-literal comparison of one thing to another | "The author crafts a clever metaphor when she compares the increase in human population to the growth of crystal structures in a petri dish." | Mixed feelings on metaphor from me. On the one hand, it's so common that you could comfortably rely on using on. On the other hand, everyone else could be using it too, so it might not help you differentiate your essay as better. Use with caution. |
| **Mood** | (noun) the emotional feeling a passage produces in the reader | "The passage is written in a sober mood that reflects the seriousness of the situation." | I love tone/mood/attitude. Definitely recommend saving your use of it for when it is more strongly present. Some essays are written in an academic tone; if that's the case, I would not bother citing the mood—the mood is boring. But if there is some drama present, or some melancholy, or reflection, fire away with mood. |

| | | | |
|---|---|---|---|
| **Motif** | (noun) an element that is repeated throughout a passage | "The author returns to the motif of the delicate-yet-resilient monarch butterfly in the final paragraph." | This is a fun one if you see it. One handy thing is that, as a motif, it has to be in the passage more than once. That means you get to cite it more than once, which will beef up your essay. |
| **Paradox** | (noun) a statement that contradicts itself but still seems true somehow | "The author draws attention to the paradox that the American people frequently vote against their own best interest." | I'm not sure how often you'll see a true paradox on the SAT, but this is still a fun word to know. Keep it in your back pocket just in case. |
| **Parallelism** | (noun) the use of words or structures that are consistent in grammar, sound, meaning, or meter | "The author's parallelism in repeatedly using the phrase, 'ain't I a woman?' unifies her argument." | This one is common enough AND sounds smart enough that it's worth learning. Look for parallelism both big and small: it can happen as a result of sentence patterns aligning with each other or structurally as the result of two stories that have elements in common. When you see it, use it. |
| **Parody** | (noun) a comic imitation of a person or situation | "The author employs parody to poke fun at the pretensions of overtly snobby art aficionados, seemingly quoting them in impossibly complex and nonsensical language." | Another very specific one. Here's how to know if parody is present: does the passage include something that would be appropriate on Saturday Night Live? If so, that's parody. Knowing how un-funny the SAT is, don't count on seeing this one too often. |
| **Point Of View** | (noun) the angle from which an author frames his/her perspective, i.e. first person (I, we), second person (you), or third person (he/she/they) | "By employing the collective first person ('we') point of view, the author creates a feeling of joint responsibility with the reader." | For me, this one is a winner... when it's interesting. If the author uses 'we,' in particular, I would cite it 100% of the time. That's a strong choice by the author and will earn you points from your reader. |

| | | | |
|---|---|---|---|
| **Pragmatism** | (noun) a practical approach to solving a problem | "The author is no idealist; instead, he recommends pragmatism—getting the job done by any means necessary." | Here we are at the antonym of idealism. If any author says that we "just need to get the job done" (or something to that effect), cite their pragmatic approach. |
| **Realism** | (noun) the representation of things in a descriptive and accurate manner | "An effective technique the author uses to promote his environmentalist message is the use of realism, representing the earth as it is, rather than as an exaggerated and bleak future vision." | Interesting device from the author—rather than use drama, you use reality. That way you build credibility for your point-of-view. Very clever, passage author... very clever. |
| **Repetition** | (noun) the act of repeating something | "The repetition of the word 'genocide' makes clear how strongly the author feels about the treatment of Native Americans during the 19th century." | Pretty easy one to spot and not a terrible fallback option. Is it the MOST interesting rhetorical device? It is not. Use in case of emergency. |
| **Rhetoric** | (noun) the persuasive use of language | "The author uses informal rhetoric as a way of making her ideas as accessible as possible." | This one is so general that you could literally cite it on every essay. Advice: make sure you add in some more descriptive language (like 'informal' in the sample sentence) to make this one richer and more interesting when you use it. |
| **Rhetorical Question** | (noun) a question that is asked to create emphasis and not to be answered | "The repeated use of rhetorical questions like 'When will we take action?' invites thoughtful speculation from the reader." | This one's pretty fun, isn't it? It's easy to spot and sounds kinda cool and smart too. I would challenge you to identify WHY the author is asking rhetorical questions if you want to earn full marks on using this one. |
| **Satire** | (noun) the use of humor to expose and mock corruption or foolishness | "In a clear satire of reality television, the author imagines a TV show designed to reward the most short-sighted of human behavior." | Like parody, satire is based in the world of comedy. With the lack of humor on the SAT in general, I would not count on earning your stripes using this term. |

| | | | |
|---|---|---|---|
| **Simile** | (noun) a figure of speech that compares two things using the words "like" or "as" | "The author makes use of simile when he writes that cinema of the 1960s was 'like a young child, still idealistic, still enraptured by heroes and villains.'" | See note on metaphor. This one is useful but also potentially being used by a million other students around the country too. If you're shooting for the highest score possible, I would probably avoid simile unless it's a surprising and/or genuinely interesting use. |
| **Slippery Slope** | (noun) a claim that something will inevitably happen as a result of something else | "The author describes a slippery slope, claiming that if any National Monuments are allowed to close, beloved National Parks will soon follow." | Very fun argument technique to cite. This sometimes refers to a logical fallacy, a claim that can't be supported. It can also be used to describe a cascade/avalanche of events that really might transpire too, so don't restrict your usage. |
| **Straw Man** | (noun) the act of arguing against a distorted or misrepresented version of an opposing view | "The author points out that her opponent is arguing against a straw man—that no one wants to increase the level of unemployment." | A straw man is like a fake fight: the author sets up an opposing position that he/she can easily knock down. If you see it, cite it. I'm not sure how often you will see it, because it's kind of a cheap trick, and SAT tends to include strong persuasive passages rather than half-assed ones. |
| **Structure** | (noun) the framework of a passage | "By employing a traditional five paragraph structure, the author helps make clear the simplicity and rigor of his argument." | Not a bad one to cite since EVERY essay has a structure. I would use this one when you can identify WHY the structure serves the argument of the passage. |
| **Style** | (noun) the way an author's word choice, sentence structure, and figurative language work together to establish mood and meaning | "The use of a more formal style helps to establish the author's status as an academic and an expert." | Style matters. Use descriptive adjectives to cite the author's style and why it serves their message and I do believe your grader will eat it up. |

| | | | |
|---|---|---|---|
| **Symbolism** | (noun) a figure of speech in which an object, person, or thing has another meaning in addition to its literal meaning | "The author makes frequent use of symbolism, such as when she uses the 'sturdy maple tree' to represent Puritan pilgrims." | Maybe a half-step better than metaphor and simile? I am not so opposed to this one as I am to the other two, but again, I would use this one with caution, and if you see other, better rhetorical devices, cite those instead. |
| **Syntax** | (noun) how words are arranged to form a sentence | "The terse syntax of the very brief sentences at the conclusion helps create a sense of urgency." | Fun one if it's interesting. You have to be descriptive with this one as well (see 'terse' in the sample sentence). Use freely if the syntax is noticeable and/or interesting. |
| **Thesis** | (noun) a statement or claim that an author intends to prove is true | "The author's central thesis is that investment in education will provide a return both financially and culturally." | Everyone has a thesis. Right? This one kills when you're trying to boost your Reading score. Not so strong on the Analysis front, but worth throwing in there so long as you have another 3-4 rhetorical devices to cite as well. |
| **Tone** | (noun) a literary element which shows the author's attitude towards his subject and toward the audience | "The author's warm and inviting tone invites a friendly response from the reader." | See 'Mood.' I'm a fan. Take in tone when you read—it'll cause you to read at a different, higher, more analytical level. And when the tone is interesting, cite it. |
| **Voice** | (noun) the individual writing style of an author as established by tone, diction, and syntax | "The author's voice is strong and persuasive without ever coming across as forceful." | A pretty easy one to see and cite. General though it is (every author has a voice), this one feels strong to me. Just be descriptive and specific, identifying why the author's voice supports his/her argument. |

# Advanced Strategies

**This chapter is all about the subtle things you can do to pump up your essay score. Do not underestimate their power! Work to include them in your essay—they are score-changers.**

The cool thing is that these aren't just SAT tricks—they're actually tools to make you a better writer anyhow. You can start incorporating them into your own writing... well, *now* if you feel like it.

## *GO BEYOND AGREEMENT OR DISAGREEMENT.*

This is the #1 trap to avoid on the SAT. Sorry to say, but no one really cares if you agree or disagree with the author. Giving the author either a "thumbs up" or a "thumbs down" also does not really show much critical thinking.

**Make it a point *never* to write "I agree" or "I disagree" in your SAT essay.**
Your essay will be much more interesting if you delve into the details of how the author makes his/her point(s). You'll have a lot more to say too... which leads conveniently into our next advanced strategy.

## *WRITE A LOT.*

The grading rubric uses the word "thorough" twice—one in Reading and once in Analysis. Implied in that word is the notion that they want you *to write as much as you possibly can.*

You want to make every point you can about the author's position and rhetorical techniques. I said that you should write about three or four rhetorical strategies. Have time to include a fifth? Do it. Showing depth in your analysis can only boost your score.

From a more cynical point of view, the graders are reading your essay really quickly. You want to include all the hallmarks of a high-scoring essay. One of those is length and depth. If they see that you've incorporated a ton of different rhetorical devices and that your essay stretches a full four pages, they are going to mentally put your essay in the top scoring category.

## *SHOW A LITTLE STYLE.*

The "Writing" category of the grading rubric might have more impact on the score as a whole than you'd expect. Imagine that a student wrote a beautiful essay, full of clever and poignant word choices, but the essay did a really poor job of responding to the prompt.

Would the graders give that an essay a 4 for Writing and 1s for both Analysis and Reading?

I'll bet that not a single SAT essay has ever gotten that score. The reason is that, if you're doing it right, your *writing style* and *what you are writing about* should be entwined.

Another way of saying it is that the *quality of your writing* and *quality of what you're saying* are inseparable. So: if we improve the quality of how you write, *it will reflect positively on what you have to say.*

Here are some of our favorite ways to bump up the style in your writing.

**1. Vary your sentences**

Reading sentences with the same structure over and over again is boring. Make a conscious effort to change up your sentence patterns frequently.

Here's one sentence, written in typical, boring-essay style.

> "The author uses personification when he compares the trees to people in order to make the trees more relatable."

Yeah. It's fine. And about as exciting as a glass of ice water.

Here are a couple of possible revisions:

> "By drawing a parallel between trees in the forest and people in the town, the author creates a sense of connectedness to appeal to readers."
>
> "Personification—the relation, in this case, of trees to the characteristics of people—effectively draws the reader deeper into the argument."

You've got a couple of tools at your disposal: punctuation and syntax.

**2. Punctuation**

One easy way to vary your sentences is to make use of less often-used punctuation marks. My favorite—the em dash—can be used the way you'd use parentheses. The semi-colon is another beloved option; it separates two closely related ideas. Then, of course, there is the question mark. Who doesn't know how to use a question mark?

**3. Syntax**

Syntax is "the arrangement of words and phrases to create well-formed sentences." I couldn't define that in a fun way, so I quoted the dictionary. That's how I handle boring stuff.

So syntax is how you put a sentence together.

You can mess with it by playing with length. Include a short sentence. Four words will do.

By bringing a prepositional phrase to the front of the sentence, you play with the reader's focus in an engaging way.

Keep your syntax active; it is not advisable to fall into the trap that the current part of this sentence is currently falling into, which is to say that it is lacking an active subject.

More than anything, keep up the variety of structures. This is a powerful tool that implicitly tells your grader that *someone really smart is writing this essay.*

## *USE PRECISE WORDS.*

Deep beneath the realm of ordinary words, there exists a set of essay words—words that can be used effortlessly AND that make you sound smart. Here's a list of the words you can use over and over again...on every single SAT Essay.

You'll notice that these aren't necessarily the fanciest words in English. "Fancy" does not mean "good" when you're writing. Saying precisely what you're trying to say—that's what good writing does!

### Great verbs to use

| Verb | Definition | Sample sentence |
|---|---|---|
| advocate | speak in favor of | "The author advocates for a more thoughtful approach to construction noise." |
| articulate | express an idea clearly | "In her essay, the author articulates two primary ideas: ..." |
| assert | state an idea confidently | "When the author asserts that wildlife preservation is essential, she also..." |
| bolster | support | "The author bolsters that claim with a key piece of evidence..." |
| build | establish, develop | "Throughout the essay, the author builds the case that..." |
| call into question | cause doubt about something | "The author calls into question the idea that representative democracy truly represents the people." |
| corroborate | confirm a claim with evidence | "The data from the recent census corroborates the author's notion that..." |
| counterargument | an argument that opposes another argument | "The author raises and refutes the obvious counterargument: that students who don't have breakfast before school..." |
| craft | build with skill | "Throughout the essay, the author crafts a logical argument that..." |
| delineate | describe precisely | "By delineating the distinctions between ethical and moral behavior, the author..." |
| demonstrate | show | "The essay demonstrates in several ways the value of a practical approach..." |
| elucidate | make something clear | "The author wisely elucidates the intricate interactions within the cell." |
| employ | make use of | "Within the essay, the author employs several interesting techniques, including..." |
| establish | set up | "The author establishes two key principles: that..." |

| illuminate | help to clarify | "The brief story the author includes illuminates the idea that..." |
|---|---|---|
| **Verb** | **Definition** | **Sample sentence** |
| illustrate | explain through examples | "The author illustrates this point with a well-chosen anecdote." |
| maintain | state strongly | "The author maintains throughout that the idea of a political middle is an illusion." |
| outline | give a summary | "At the outset, the author outlines three important claims: ..." |
| raise | bring up for consideration | "Here, the author raises a new question: ..." |
| reason | conclude by the use of reason | "If that idea is true, the author reasons, then the second idea must also be true." |
| substantiate | provide evidence | "The author employs hard data to substantiate the claim that..." |

### Adjectives

| Adjective | Definition | Sample sentence |
|---|---|---|
| candid | straightforward, frank | "The author makes a candid assessment that the Eastern Gorilla simply cannot survive without immediate help." |
| cogent | logical, convincing | "In laying out her argument, the author makes a cogent case for..." |
| compelling | powerful, irresistible | "Throughout the essay, the author makes a compelling case that..." |
| didactic | intended to instruct | "The author adopts a didactic tone when she explains the specific process of..." |
| idealistic | aimed at high, noble principles | "In claiming that all men are moral, the author clearly adopts an idealistic position." |
| pragmatic | practical, sensible | "The author makes the pragmatic point that if people see an opportunity, they will take advantage." |

| salient | prominent, noticeable | "One salient example is that of the young woman who..." |
|---|---|---|

**Nouns**

| Noun | Definition | Sample sentence |
|---|---|---|
| anecdote | a brief story | "By relating an anecdote, the author makes his case in a more personal manner." |
| argument | a set of persuasive reasons | "In laying out this argument, the author makes use of..." |
| claim | an assertion of truth | "The author makes one especially persuasive claim regarding..." |
| concession | a point yielded | "The author does include a concession: not all bird species will respond in the same way." |
| consensus | agreement | "The author draws on what appears to be universal consensus when he says that dogs are loving and sweet animals." |
| counterargument | an argument put forth to oppose another idea | "The author raises the potential counterargument that not enough research has been conducted to date." |
| credibility | the quality of being trusted | "By including her academic credentials, the author establishes her own credibility." |
| rebuttal | a refutation | "The author anticipates and responds to a possible rebuttal when he..." |

## *INCLUDE TRANSITIONS.*

The Reading grade asks you to identify the central ideas of the prompt and how those ideas interrelate. The simplest way to show that you see the connections between the ideas in the essay is to include transition words and phrases. Here are a few of the words and phrases I recommend you use within your essay.

Note: This is a list of the transition words and phrases that will help differentiate your essay from the pack. In other words, I decided not to recommend the really obviously useful words. Just because "for example" is not included on this list does not mean that it is not a very useful transition phrase for you to include in your essay.

| Transition Word | Definition | Sample sentence |
|---|---|---|
| Above all | more so than anything else | "The author asserts that recycling is ethical. Above all, the author makes the claim that..." |
| Accordingly | therefore | "...the approach is unlikely to be implemented and accordingly is impractical." |
| By contrast | conversely, on the other hand | "The author makes the point that stricter laws have failed. By contrast, a public relations campaign might actually change behavior." |
| Consequently | as a result | "Restrictions on freedom of speech have had a chilling effect; consequently, investments in journalism have decreased." |
| For instance | as an example | "The author makes the point that anti-poverty measures have sometimes had the opposite effect. For instance, California spends the most public money fighting poverty yet has the highest percent of poor people in the U.S." |
| Furthermore | in addition | "Saltwater is readily available; furthermore, desalination technology has improved significantly." |
| However | on the other hand; nevertheless | "The cost of doing business there is low. However, any new business faces challenges." |
| Importantly | significantly | "Importantly, the author notes that any changes will be slow to take hold." |
| In light of | drawing something into consideration | "In light of the compelling evidence the author provided, he makes a clear case for a free market economic policy." |
| In order to | as a means to | "In order to justify this claim, the author points to recent statistical evidence that..." |

| | | |
|---|---|---|
| Moreover | as a further matter | "Airports were intended to accommodate fewer passengers; moreover, modern planes are larger than those available when the airports were built." |
| Paradoxically | in a seemingly contradictory way | "California spends the most to fight poverty, but, paradoxically, has the highest rate of poverty to show for it." |
| That is to say | to put it another way | "The path from authoritarian regime to democracy is not smooth; that is to say, the current government's failures may be an understandable part of the process." |
| That said | even so | "Data so far has been promising. That said, the author cautions that we should not think of the problem as fixed." |
| With this in mind | taking this into account | "Sixty percent of students agreed. With this in mind, the author claims that implementation would be smooth." |
| Yet | still; even | "The challenges are many, yet the author maintains that, with a positive, productive outlook, they may be overcome." |

## *BE SMARTER THAN THE PERSON NEXT TO YOU.*

This feels like a really heartless thing to say, but it reflects reality. Getting into college is a competitive sport. Comparing you to others is the whole point of the SAT. It's literally the reason that the SAT exists.

The reason I bring up this cynical-but-true *kind-of*-fun fact is that you want to let it guide your test prep and your approach to the test. Learn those fancy words in the list in this chapter and use them in your essay. Use a fancy name for a rhetorical device. Write more. Do the little things that will make your essay stand out from the rest.

So, if competition motivates you, keep that in mind while you're writing your SAT essay. If you are not as competitive as I am—which is totally fine, and probably healthier too—then just make yourself into the most precise writer you can be. You'll stand out in a good way if you do.

## EXERCISE #1: See How They're Scored

**Instructions:** This next section includes an essay prompt followed by sample responses that range in score and quality from best to, um, worst. I hate to use a word like "worst," but wait until you read the essay that got a score of 1/1/1.

Read the prompt and write your own essay within the 50-minute time allotment. Then compare your essay to the ones we included to get a sense of your own essay score.

As you read the passage below, consider how James Gilligan uses

- evidence, such as facts or examples, to support claims.
- reasoning to develop ideas and to connect claims and evidence.
- stylistic or persuasive elements, such as word choice or appeals to emotion, to add power to the ideas expressed.

**Adapted from James Gilligan, "Punishment Fails. Rehabilitation Works." © 2012, The New York Times.**

1 If any other institutions in America were as unsuccessful in achieving their ostensible purpose as our prisons are, we would shut them down tomorrow. Two-thirds of prisoners reoffend within three years of leaving prison, often with a more serious and violent offense. More than 90 percent of prisoners return to the community within a few years (otherwise our prisons would be even more overcrowded than they already are). That is why it is vitally important how we treat them while they are incarcerated.

2 How could we change our prison system to make it both more effective and less expensive?

3 The only rational purpose for a prison is to restrain those who are violent, while we help them to change their behavior and return to the community.

4 We would need to begin by recognizing the difference between punishment and restraint. When people are dangerous to themselves or others, we restrain them—whether they are children or adults. But that is altogether different from gratuitously inflicting pain on them for the sake of revenge or to "teach them a lesson"—for the only lesson learned is to inflict pain on others. People learn by example: Generations of research has shown that the more severely children are punished, the more violent they become, as children and as adults. The same is true of adults, especially those in prison. So the only rational purpose for a prison is to restrain those who are violent from inflicting harm on themselves or others, while we help them to change their behavior from that pattern to one that is nonviolent and even constructive, so that they can return to the community.

5 It would be beneficial to every man, woman and child in America, and harmful to no one, if we were to demolish every prison in this country and replace them with locked, safe and secure home-like residential communities – what we might call an anti-prison. Such a community would be devoted to providing every form of therapy its residents

needed (substance abuse treatment, psychotherapy, medical and dental care) and every form of education for which the residents were motivated and capable (from elementary school to college and graduate school). Getting a college degree while in prison is the only program that has ever been shown to be 100 percent effective for years or decades at a time in preventing recidivism. Prisoners should be treated with exactly the same degree of respect and kindness as we would hope they would show to others after they return to the community. As I said, people learn by example.

6 My colleague Bandy Lee and I have shown that an intensive re-educational program with violent male offenders in the San Francisco jails reduced the level of violence in the jail to zero for a year at a time. Even more important, participation in this program for as little as four months reduced the frequency of violent reoffending after leaving the jail by 83 percent, compared with a matched control group in a conventional jail. In addition to enhancing public safety, this program saved the taxpayers $4 for every $1 spent on it, since the lower reincarceration rate saved roughly $30,000 a year per person. The only mystery is: Why is this program not being adopted by every jail and prison in the country? Why are taxpayers not demanding that this be done?

Write an essay in which you explain how James Gilligan builds an argument to persuade his audience that the prison system should be reformed. In your essay, analyze how Gilligan uses one or more of the features listed in the box above (or features of your own choice) to strengthen the logic and persuasiveness of his argument. Be sure that your analysis focuses on the most relevant features of the passage.

Your essay should not explain whether you agree with Gilligan's claims, but rather explain how Gilligan builds an argument to persuade his audience.

## SAMPLE ESSAY #1

In his essay, "Punishment Fails. Rehabilitation Works," James Gilligan raises a problem—the failure of the American prison system to accomplish its supposed objective—and proposes a solution: an "intensive re-education program," the success of which he has documented personally. In making his case, Gilligan invokes statistics, a hypothetical example, the pragmatic value of a solution, and a sense of responsibility to act.

Statistics play a key role in Gilligan's essay from the outset. In fact, the essay's second sentence points out that "two-thirds of prisoners reoffend within three years of leaving prison," and the next sentence states that "More than 90 percent of prisoners return to the community within a few years." The value of these two numbers, side-by-side and at the beginning of the essay, is two-fold: first, the statistics convey a sense of certainty. We know, based on the numbers, that the situation is not good: prisoners are being released and will likely re-offend, potentially with a worse crime than they committed the first time around. Second, the stats relate a sense of urgency. If we don't act now, we can expect the negative results that the numbers predict. Taken together, these statistics justify Gilligan's claim that "it is vitally important how we treat [prisoners] while they are incarcerated."

Gilligan promotes the idea of an "anti-prison," an alternative to prisons. In this hypothetical example, criminals would still be locked up for crimes, but instead of living in the traditional prison model, they would live in "home-like residential communities." In a way (and construction costs aside), this solution is really a cosmetic change, since prisoners would still be incarcerated. The benefits would be the way that the prisoners were treated. Contemporary prisons are not home-like; they are prison-like—designed to punish, not to rehabilitate. In the "anti-prison," inmates would receive medical care, therapy, and education in order to return to society and participate effectively as citizens. This hypothetical example certainly is appealing, especially if, as Gilligan states, "it would be beneficial to every man, woman and child in America, and harmful to no one." Certainly, the reader's acceptance of the author's claims hinges on this assumption.

Gilligan wisely does not rely solely on hypotheticals and assumptions, however: he draws on pragmatic reasons to appeal to readers who are yet-unconvinced. He mentions specifically a prison program for violent male offenders, a program with which he personally experienced outstanding results. The program "not only reduced the level of violence in the jail to zero for a year," it also "saved the taxpayers $4 for every $1 spent on it." These benefits are significant—almost too good to be believed—but so long as they are true, they should appeal to all but the most hardened reader.

Finally, Gilligan appeals to a sense of shared responsibility for making a change. From using the collective pronoun "we" to asking the hypothetical question, "Why is this program not being adopted by every jail and prison in the country?," Gilligan draws on the power of the collective. These appeals are sweeping, drawing on both a collective moral and pragmatic sensibility. The pitch for prison reform for Gilligan is simple: the problem is clear, the solution is viable, and the only thing holding us back is a lack of collective action.

In drawing on statistics, a hypothetical example, pragmatism, and an appeal to a mutual, collective sense of responsibility, James Gilligan makes an effective case in favor of reforming the American prison system.

## Here are the grades on this essay:

***Reading: 4 out of 4***

***Analysis: 4 out of 4***

***Writing: 4 out of 4***

## And here's why this essay got those scores.

I think the writer (of this essay...when I say "writer," you can assume I mean the person writing an essay to be graded by the SAT) was clear in pointing out what Gilligan was trying to say about the flaws in the prison system and how they could be resolved. That's the Reading grade. The writer really gets to that score in a sort of indirect way—the point of Gilligan's essay is revealed through the analysis of the devices. The writer does mention Gilligan's purpose clearly in the first sentence, so overall, I feel confident that s/he nailed it on the Reading score.

Analysis is the toughest one, and in a way the most important: if you nail the analysis, you probably nailed the other two categories as well. My favorite thing the author did here was to write about FOUR devices that Gilligan used. The fourth, the one about collective responsibility, did a nice job of tying together both the other devices and Gilligan's argument on the whole. Part of your job on the essay is to write a lot and point out a lot of effectively used rhetorical devices. Job well done.

The Writing grade is about the delivery, and I feel most confident giving this essay a 4 on that count. Here's one sentence that does a nice job of establishing the writer's proficiency: "Gilligan wisely does not rely solely on hypotheticals and assumptions, however: he draws on pragmatic reasons to appeal to readers who are yet-unconvinced." The sentence has an interesting structure and effectively ties the paragraph that follows to the preceding one. In doing that, the writer creates a sense of connection within Gilligan's argument as well. That's effective. Overall, the essay is clear but not boring (well, not boring as far as SAT essays go) and employs a variety of sentence structures, with lots of interesting and effective punctuation throughout.

Is it the most entertaining essay ever written? Nope, but it does not need to be—it just needs to hit the marks of a good SAT essay.

## SAMPLE ESSAY #2

James Gilligan writes about prison and the purpose behind it. To make his point that prisons should be reformed, he uses devices such as research and statistics, appeal to reason, and a personal anecdote.

Gilligan cites many statistics while making his case, including the fact that "two-thirds of prisoners reoffend within three years," and that participants in his program "reduced the frequency of violent offending after leaving the jail by 83 percent." These statistics make a compelling case for why prison reform is needed so badly. In addition, Gilligan cites research, such as when he writes that, "research has shown that the more severely children are punished, the more violent they become." By citing research and statistics, Gilligan helps create credibility for his solution.

Gilligan counts on the reader to realize that we all benefit from reformed criminals. He writes that "the only rational purpose for a prison is to restrain those who are violent." Not every American citizen would agree. In fact, many would probably disagree, saying that prisoners also need to pay for their crimes. When Gilligan adds that if "we help them to change their behavior...to one that is nonviolent...they can return to their community," he makes his appeal to reason in a stronger and more believable way, that we will all benefit from reformed prisoners.

Gilligan uses a personal anecdote when he discusses his experience in San Francisco. His re-educational program "reduced the level of violence in the jail to zero" and "saved the taxpayers $4 for every $1 spent on it." This example is easy to believe since the author had direct and personal experience with it. If the results are as good as advertised, then Gilligan makes a good claim for the need for prison reform.

Overall, Gilligan makes a good case for prison reform based on research and statistics, an appeal to reason, and a personal anecdote.

## Here are the grades on this essay:

***Reading: 3 out of 4***

***Analysis: 3 out of 4***

***Writing: 3 out of 4***

## And here's why this essay got those scores.

One of the most useful things I think you can do to understand how the essay grading works is to draw a comparison between essays at the different score marks. Ask the question, Why did this essay fall a point short of the previous one? The Reading grade reflects a slightly simpler understanding of Gilligan's argument. It's still accurate—that prison needs to be reformed—but the discussion about it does not get into as much nuance or detail—hence the 3 out of 4.

The Analysis score, always the bellwether, is a point lower too. The devices are solid and present. The writer's understanding of how and why they work is not especially convincing or interesting, though, so s/he falls a little bit short there. And there are only three devices here instead of four, so there's that superficial reason too.

Finally, Writing. In a way, this score feels like the giveaway. You can tell based on, oh, a half-sentence how well an essay is written. This one is pretty "meh" in the writing. Sentences are clear but simple. It's definitely not bad, but it's not great either. The insight of an essay and its writing style often walk side-by-side. Here, they're holding hands on the "meh" side of the road.

## SAMPLE ESSAY #3

In "Punishment Fails. Rehabilitation Works.," James Gilligan makes a strong case for a thorough reform of the prison system.

The author, Gilligan, begins by outlining the problem: most prisoners are released within a few years, and a supermajority of those people "reoffend within three years" of their release. Clearly this is a problem that needs to be addressed, and the author suggests that the remedy lies in how we treat prisoners while they are incarcerated.

The author then turns his argument to the purposes behind prison, differentiating between "punishment" and "restraint." Punishment entails retribution, which the author claims will simply lead to more bad behavior. Restraint is a more practical goal of prison—that if someone is likely to be violent, they should be kept back from the rest of society to protect the public.

From this distinction, Gilligan jumps to another, higher goal of prison: rehabilitation. Many people do not think of rehabilitation as a specific goal of the American prison system, but Gilligan makes the point that, if we did prioritize it—giving prisoners drug treatment, therapy, and dental care—that it would directly lead to a less violent society because prisoners would have a different mindsest as a result of being "treated with exactly the same degree of respect and kindness," as we would expect from them.

Gilligan concludes his argument by citing his own experience working in the prisons. Together with his colleague Bandy Lee, he has shown that "an intensive re-educational program with violent male offenders" was able to reduce the level of violence within the prison by 100% and reduce the level of reoffending by 83%. Plus, his program saved taxpayers $4 for every $1 that they invested. These results are hard to argue with and make a compelling case for why both the public and the government should listen hard to the case that Gilligan makes.

## Here are the grades on this essay:

***Reading: 4 out of 4***

***Analysis: 1 out of 4***

***Writing: 4 out of 4***

## And here's why this essay got those scores.

Curveball! The objective here was to write an essay that sounded really good and made a ton of sense but *completely bailed* on the analysis task. Here's how the writer did it.

The Reading score is a solid 4 out of 4. As good as that score is, it's actually the beginning of the trouble with this piece because the writer *only* focuses on what Gilligan has to say rather than how he says it.

Analysis is the dog here, simply because the writer does not point out any technique at all. Imagine watching a sporting event on television, and all the commentator did was describe *exactly* what was happening. "The quarterback, #9, threw the ball quite far, and then the receiver, #81, was able to catch it and then continue running..." Even if the commentator did a PERFECT job at that task, it would drive you nuts to listen because the commentator is not adding to your understanding of the game through insight. That's what's happening here: we are reading someone who clearly knows what Gilligan is saying but who never takes the time to take Gilligan's essay apart or point to the tools he uses. This significant problem points out two basic SAT essay lessons: 1) don't just summarize the passage, and 2) keep in mind how valuable the rhetorical devices are and make sure you include them.

The Writing score is a 4 out of 4 too. It's written well! That's a plus! Good job, writer. It almost feels like an afterthought when the analysis is dreadful and/or absent, but hey, you take what you can get.

## SAMPLE ESSAY #4

In this essay, James Gilligan makes the point that prisons do not do as good a job as they could. He cites a difference between punishment and restraint. This difference is about the purpose of prison. If the purpose is to punish, then job well done. Same thing if the purpose is restraint. But if the purpose is to make people more ready to be in society, then we're doing the complete opposite because people who are exposed to violence are just more likely to be violent.

The author cites research to make his point. When he says that "Generations of research has shown that the more severely children are punished, the more violent they become," he is making the point that punishment is not a solution and in fact might make the problem worse. Using this idea he makes the point that restraint is the only purpose for prison that makes sense.

The author also cites his own personal experience as offering a solution. When he and his colleague offered educational programs to inmates, they were way less likely to commit more crimes and showed less violent behavior. The research is so clear and so persuasive that he is able to ask the question, "Why are taxpayers not demanding that this be done?"

### Here are the grades on this essay:

***Reading: 2 out of 4***

***Analysis: 2 out of 4***

***Writing: 2 out of 4***

### And here's why this essay got those scores.

I think the most interesting clue to look at here to figure out why this essay scored 2s across the board is this: length. You might be surprised, even shocked, to learn how closely *length* and *score* travel together. Does that mean that if you write a long essay, you'll score higher? Not necessarily, but if you have more to say and you get all of it down on the page, then the graders are going to recognize that with a better score. This essay is short, and the graders recognized that as well, and rewarded it with 2s in every category.

In terms of how the writer got those specific marks, in each category I would say that the writer did an OK-but-definitely-not-great job. There is basic comprehension of the Gilligan's point. The author cites "research" and "personal experience," so there is some analysis. And the writing is not great but not a train wreck either. So, tip of the cap, 2/2/2 essay writer—you wrote an essay that was not-the-worst.

## SAMPLE ESSAY #5

This essay is about prison, which is where people (adults) go if they do something wrong. Should a prison be allowed to punish people, really punish them? Maybe, I'm not sure. If they do, then we ought to know what's going on so we can do something about it...the prisons, that is.

One things for sure, there are violent people out there. Their violent as kids and their violent as adults and you don't want to have anything to do with them! Kepp them in prison is what I would say.

If your violent you should go to prison, and if your not then you should stay home. End of story.

## Here are the grades on this essay:

***Reading: 1 out of 4***

***Analysis: 1 out of 4***

***Writing: 1 out of 4***

## And here's why this essay got those scores.

I live to write the essays that get 1s across the board—it's what gets me out of bed in the morning. And yes, confession time, I write all these essays. Do you know how hard it is to get anyone else to write an SAT essay? I bet you do—you're prepping for the SAT.

Anyway, why is this essay terrible? It's short. It uses the words "prison" and "violent" but otherwise shows no comprehension of the Gilligan article. It has zero analysis, focusing instead on the writer's half-baked opinions... which the test makers do not care about anyways, even if your opinions are brilliant. And the writing is crap: full of misspelled words ("your," "their," and "kepp," in particular) and unnecessary flourishes, like "End of story." Just a total stinker, and that's all there is to say about it.

## EXERCISE #2: Write One Yourself

**Instructions**: Here are some essay prompts for you to use in practice. I recommend you write your essay within the given time restrictions (50 minutes for most students) to get the best sense of how it feels to write the SAT essay. And, as always, you want to demonstrate your understanding of the given passage (Reading), point out the devices/techniques the author used to make his/her point (Analysis), and employ a writing style that accomplishes those two tasks in a readable and interesting way (Writing). Go get 'em.

### Prompt #1

As you read the passage below, consider how Kaya Dorey uses

- evidence, such as facts or examples, to support claims.
- reasoning to develop ideas and to connect claims and evidence.
- stylistic or persuasive elements, such as word choice or appeals to emotion, to add power to the ideas expressed.

**Adapted from Kaya Dorey, "Why Fast Fashion Needs to Slow Down." © 2018, FoodTank.com.**

1 Have you ever thought about what your clothes are made of? About who makes your clothes, or what happens after you donate them or throw them away? The truth about the fashion industry is actually pretty ugly.

2 A recent study by the Ellen McArthur Foundation found that the equivalent of one garbage truck of textiles is wasted every second. And the Copenhagen Fashion Summit reported that fashion is responsible for 92 million tons of solid waste dumped in landfills each year.

3 The fashion industry is also the second biggest consumer of water, producing 20 percent of wastewater while also generating more greenhouse gas emissions than all international flights and maritime shipping combined.

4 Ahead of World Environment Day on June 5, themed "Beat Plastic Pollution," it's worth remembering that synthetic microfiber pollution is washing up in our oceans at alarming rates. Around 100,000 marine animals are killed each year by plastic waste, including microfibers.

5 We need to rethink our fast-fashion habit—we can't continue to make clothes that do not consider our environment.

6 First, it's up to apparel brands to take responsibility for the waste they're creating. Brands need to address head-on the chemicals, use of textiles waste and synthetic fabrics that don't break down, and unfair working environments in the clothing industry.

7 The no-waste economy must be applied to fashion, just as it is in the food industry. We need action at each stage of the supply chain, starting with sustainable sourcing of fabrics, through to design, exploration of possible alternatives to distribution, and recovery and recycling of clothing.

8 Big brands are starting to take notice: Nike, H&M, Burberry, and Gap have all recently signed up to the Make Fashion Circular initiative. It aims to improve the industry's record on sustainability and reduce global waste from fashion by recycling raw materials and products.

9 While recycling is certainly one solution, it is by no means the only solution. In fact, we should be asking a different question: How can we eliminate the need for recycling altogether? How can we design with the end in mind?

10 I'm developing a take-back program for my sustainable apparel brand, NOVEL SUPPLY CO., where we accept back our apparel at the end of its life and find alternative ways to use, recycle, and compost it. But as a global community, we also need to shift the way we consume fashion.

11 I currently source my fabrics from a Fair Ware mill in China, but this is not ideal. In general, richer countries are consuming fashion that is made and produced in poorer countries. But all countries are involved in the value chain.

12 In countries with emerging economies, there are an estimated 2 billion new consumers waiting to buy the latest trends. We are racing against the clock to include poorer countries in more sustainable manufacturing models so they can produce clothing locally and more sustainably.

13 To shift typically linear take-make-waste fashion toward a circular model with no waste, we all need to be part of the movement to innovate and redesign our fashion industry. We can start by buying clothes with the circular economy in mind.

14 It's up to us as consumers to trigger change by voting with our wallets. The average number of clothing collections in Europe more than doubled between 2000 and 2011: We are buying more clothes and wearing them less.

15 Our fast-fashion habit is expensive. More than US$500 billion in value is lost every year due to under-utilized clothes and lack of recycling. We as consumers need to educate ourselves about circular fashion. We need to buy less clothing, and when we do we need to make sure that is more sustainable and higher quality. We also need to demand transparent sourcing.

16 It will take time for the fast-fashion industry to slow down. The trends already set in motion by the Make Fashion Circular initiative and others are starting to gather steam. But to stop stretching our planet, we all need to play our part.

17 Consume consciously and responsibly by reading the labels before you purchase. Be sure to look for natural and organic fibers, non-toxic dyes, take-back programs, and ethical production. We need you.

> Write an essay in which you explain how Kaya Dorey builds an argument to persuade her audience that consumers should re-think fast-fashion. In your essay, analyze how Dorey uses one or more of the features listed in the box above (or features of your own choice) to strengthen the logic and persuasiveness of her argument. Be sure that your analysis focuses on the most relevant features of the passage.
>
> Your essay should not explain whether you agree with Dorey's claims, but rather explain how Dorey builds an argument to persuade her audience.

## Prompt #2

As you read the passage below, consider how Barack Obama uses

- evidence, such as facts or examples, to support claims.
- reasoning to develop ideas and to connect claims and evidence.
- stylistic or persuasive elements, such as word choice or appeals to emotion, to add power to the ideas expressed.

**Excerpted from former U.S. President Barack Obama, "A More Perfect Union." Speech delivered in 2008 while then-Senator Obama was a candidate for President.**

1 This is where we are right now. It's a racial stalemate we've been stuck in for years. Contrary to the claims of some of my critics, black and white, I have never been so naïve as to believe that we can get beyond our racial divisions in a single election cycle, or with a single candidacy—particularly a candidacy as imperfect as my own.

2 But I have asserted a firm conviction—a conviction rooted in my faith in God and my faith in the American people—that, working together, we can move beyond some of our old racial wounds, and that in fact we have no choice if we are to continue on the path of a more perfect union.

3 For the African-American community, that path means embracing the burdens of our past without becoming victims of our past. It means continuing to insist on a full measure of justice in every aspect of American life. But it also means binding our particular grievances—for better health care and better schools and better jobs—to the larger aspirations of all Americans: the white woman struggling to break the glass ceiling, the white man who has been laid off, the immigrant trying to feed his family.

4 And it means taking full responsibility for our own lives—by demanding more from our fathers, and spending more time with our children, and reading to them, and teaching them that while they may face challenges and discrimination in their own lives, they must never succumb to despair or cynicism; they must always believe that they can write their own destiny.

5 Ironically, this quintessentially American—and yes, conservative—notion of self-help found frequent expression in Reverend Wright's sermons[1]. But what my former pastor too often failed to understand is that embarking on a program of self-help also requires a belief that society can change.

6 The profound mistake of Reverend Wright's sermons is not that he spoke about racism in our society. It's that he spoke as if our society was static; as if no progress had been made; as if this country—a country that has made it possible for one of his own members to run for the highest office in the land and build a coalition of white and black, Latino and Asian, rich and poor, young and old—is still irrevocably bound to a tragic past. But what we know—what we have seen—is that America can change. That is the true genius of this nation. What we have already achieved gives us hope—the audacity to hope—for what we can and must achieve tomorrow.

7 In the white community, the path to a more perfect union means acknowledging that what ails the African-American community does not just exist in the minds of black

people; that the legacy of discrimination—and current incidents of discrimination, while less overt than in the past—are real and must be addressed, not just with words, but with deeds, by investing in our schools and our communities; by enforcing our civil rights laws and ensuring fairness in our criminal justice system; by providing this generation with ladders of opportunity that were unavailable for previous generations. It requires all Americans to realize that your dreams do not have to come at the expense of my dreams; that investing in the health, welfare and education of black and brown and white children will ultimately help all of America prosper.

*8* In the end, then, what is called for is nothing more and nothing less than what all the world's great religions demand—that we do unto others as we would have them do unto us. Let us be our brother's keeper, scripture tells us. Let us be our sister's keeper. Let us find that common stake we all have in one another, and let our politics reflect that spirit as well.

[1] Reverend Wright was pastor at the Obama family's church in Chicago, Illinois. Wright made inflammatory comments about race that prompted Obama's speech.

Write an essay in which you explain how President Barack Obama builds an argument to persuade his audience that America can continue to heal its racial divide. In your essay, analyze how Obama uses one or more of the features listed in the box above (or features of your own choice) to strengthen the logic and persuasiveness of his argument. Be sure that your analysis focuses on the most relevant features of the passage.

Your essay should not explain whether you agree with Obama's claims, but rather explain how Obama builds an argument to persuade his audience.

## Prompt #3

As you read the passage below, consider how John F. Kennedy uses

- evidence, such as facts or examples, to support claims.
- reasoning to develop ideas and to connect claims and evidence.
- stylistic or persuasive elements, such as word choice or appeals to emotion, to add power to the ideas expressed.

**Excerpted from former U.S. President John F. Kennedy, "Address on the Space Effort." Speech delivered in 1962. During this speech, President Kennedy made a public appeal to put a man on the moon.**

1 Despite the striking fact that most of the scientists that the world has ever known are alive and working today, despite the fact that this Nation's own scientific manpower is doubling every 12 years in a rate of growth more than three times that of our population as a whole, despite that, the vast stretches of the unknown and the unanswered and the unfinished still far outstrip our collective comprehension.

2 No man can fully grasp how far and how fast we have come, but condense, if you will, the 50,000 years of man's recorded history in a time span of but a half-century. Stated in these terms, we know very little about the first 40 years, except at the end of them advanced man had learned to use the skins of animals to cover them. Then about 10 years ago, under this standard, man emerged from his caves to construct other kinds of shelter. Only 5 years ago man learned to write and use a cart with wheels. Christianity began less than 2 years ago. The printing press came this year, and then less than 2 months ago, during this whole 50-year span of human history, the steam engine provided a new source of power.

3 Newton explored the meaning of gravity. Last month electric lights and telephones and automobiles and airplanes became available. Only last week did we develop penicillin and television and nuclear power, and now if America's new spacecraft succeeds in reaching Venus, we will have literally reached the stars before midnight tonight.

4 This is a breathtaking pace, and such a pace cannot help but create new ills as it dispels old, new ignorance, new problems, new dangers. Surely the opening vistas of space promise high costs and hardships, as well as high reward.

5 So it is not surprising that some would have us stay where we are a little longer to rest, to wait. But this city of Houston[1], this State of Texas, this country of the United States was not built by those who waited and rested and wished to look behind them. This country was conquered by those who moved forward—and so will space.

6 William Bradford, speaking in 1630 of the founding of the Plymouth Bay Colony, said that all great and honorable actions are accompanied with great difficulties, and both must be enterprised and overcome with answerable courage.

7 If this capsule history of our progress teaches us anything, it is that man, in his quest for knowledge and progress, is determined and cannot be deterred. The exploration of space will go ahead, whether we join in it or not, and it is one of the great adventures of

all time, and no nation which expects to be the leader of other nations can expect to stay behind in this race for space.

*8* Those who came before us made certain that this country rode the first waves of the industrial revolutions, the first waves of modern invention, and the first wave of nuclear power, and this generation does not intend to founder in the backwash of the coming age of space. We mean to be a part of it—we mean to lead it. For the eyes of the world now look into space, to the moon and to the planets beyond, and we have vowed that we shall not see it governed by a hostile flag of conquest, but by a banner of freedom and peace. We have vowed that we shall not see space filled with weapons of mass destruction, but with instruments of knowledge and understanding.

*9* Yet the vows of this Nation can only be fulfilled if we in this Nation are first, and, therefore, we intend to be first. In short, our leadership in science and in industry, our hopes for peace and security, our obligations to ourselves as well as others, all require us to make this effort, to solve these mysteries, to solve them for the good of all men, and to become the world's leading space-faring nation.

[1] Kennedy delivered this speech near the National Aeronautics and Space Administration headquarters in Houston, Texas.

Write an essay in which you explain how President John F. Kennedy builds an argument to persuade his audience that America should be a leader in space exploration. In your essay, analyze how Kennedy uses one or more of the features listed in the box above (or features of your own choice) to strengthen the logic and persuasiveness of his argument. Be sure that your analysis focuses on the most relevant features of the passage.

Your essay should not explain whether you agree with Kennedy's claims, but rather explain how Kennedy builds an argument to persuade his audience.

## Prompt #4

As you read the passage below, consider how Rev. Jesse Jackson uses

- evidence, such as facts or examples, to support claims.
- reasoning to develop ideas and to connect claims and evidence.
- stylistic or persuasive elements, such as word choice or appeals to emotion, to add power to the ideas expressed.

**Excerpted from Rev. Jesse Jackson, "Keynote Address at the 1984 Democratic National Convention."**

*1* As I leave you now, we vote in this convention and get ready to go back across this nation in a couple of days, in this campaign I tried to be faithful to my promise. I lived in old barrios, ghettos and in reservations and housing projects.

*2* I have a message for our youth. I challenge them to put hope in their brains and not dope in their veins. I told them that like Jesus, I, too, was born in the slum, and just because you're born in a slum does not mean the slum is born in you and you can rise above it if your mind is made up. I told them in every slum there are two sides. When I see a broken window that's the slummy side. Train some youth to become a glazier[1]; that is the sunny side. When I see a missing brick, that is the slummy side. Let that child in a union and become a brick mason and build; that is the sunny side. When I see a missing door, that is the slummy side. Train some youth to become a carpenter, that is the sunny side. When I see the vulgar words and hieroglyphics of destitution on the walls, that is the slummy side. Train some youth to be a painter and artist, that is the sunny side.

*3* We leave this place looking for the sunny side because there's a brighter side somewhere. I am more convinced than ever that we can win. We will vault up the rough side of the mountain. We can win. I just want young America to do me one favor, just one favor.

*4* Exercise the right to dream. You must face reality, that which is. But then dream of a reality that ought to be, that must be. Live beyond the pain of reality with the dream of a bright tomorrow. Use hope and imagination as weapons of survival and progress. Use love to motivate you and obligate you to serve the human family.

*5* Young America, dream. Choose the human race over the nuclear race. Bury the weapons and don't burn the people. Dream—dream of a new value system. Teachers who teach for life and not just for a living teach because they can't help it. Dream of lawyers more concerned about justice than a judgeship. Dream of doctors more concerned about public health than personal wealth. Dream of preachers and priests who will prophesy and not just profiteer. Preach and dream! Our time has come. Our time has come.

*6* Suffering breeds character. Character breeds faith, and in the faith will not disappoint. Our time has come. Our faith, hope and dreams have prevailed. Our time has come. Weeping has endured for nights but that joy cometh in the morning.

7 Our time has come. No grave can hold our body down. Our time has come. No lie can live forever. Our time has come. We must leave the racial battleground and come to the economic common ground and moral higher ground. America, our time has come.

[1] A glazier is a person who makes and repairs glass.

Write an essay in which you explain how Rev. Jesse Jackson builds an argument to persuade his audience that America has an opportunity in this moment to better itself. In your essay, analyze how Jackson uses one or more of the features listed in the box above (or features of your own choice) to strengthen the logic and persuasiveness of his argument. Be sure that your analysis focuses on the most relevant features of the passage.

Your essay should not explain whether you agree with Jackson's claims, but rather explain how Jackson builds an argument to persuade his audience.

Tutor Ted®

TED TALKS

# A Note from Ted

**The SAT—not as complicated or difficult as it first appears, huh?**
Hey, do a couple of things before you take the actual test:

1. Take a practice test.

   If you really want to perform well, you should go into the test knowing what it feels like to sit for the full, three-hour-and-fifty-minute exam. You can find practice tests for free at

   **https://collegereadiness.collegeboard.org/sat/practice/full-length-practice-tests**
   (Man that's a long link.)

   I recommend printing your test and completing it on paper rather than on screen!

   If you need more tests, check out our companion book, "Tutor Ted's SAT Practice Tests." We worked really hard to make our tests as realistic as the official ones as possible—so taking those tests will help you improve!

2. If you like the way I teach, check out our online courses.

   It's just me teaching lessons directly to you. That's fun, right? Our online courses are at learn.tutorted.com.

   **How about half off on those courses?** Since you're already a Tutor Ted student, I made a 50% off coupon code you can use when you sign up. Just type the coupon code **BOOKHALFOFF** at checkout and you'll pay half the price. :)

Stay in touch with us! We love to hear from our students. You can find us in all of the usual places on the Internet, or you can email us at sayhello@tutorted.com.

**I would say, "good luck," but you're not going to need luck.**

TED

Made in the USA
San Bernardino, CA
18 July 2018